DISSONANCE

Also by David Detzer

Donnybrook: The Battle of Bull Run, 1861

Allegiance: Fort Sumter, Charleston,
and the Beginning of the Civil War

An Asian Tragedy: America and Vietnam

Brink: Story of the Cuban Missile Crisis

Thunder of the Captains: The Short Summer in 1950

DISSONANCE

The Turbulent Days Between Fort Sumter and Bull Run

David Detzer

HARCOURT, INC.

Orlando   Austin   New York   San Diego   Toronto   London www.HarcourtBooks.com

Library of Congress Cataloging-in-Publication Data
Detzer, David.
Dissonance: the turbulent days between Fort Sumter and Bull Run/
David Detzer. — 1st ed.
p.   cm.
Includes bibliographical references and index.
1. United States — History — Civil War, 1861–1865.   2. Washington (D.C.) —
History — Civil War, 1861–1865.   3. Maryland — History — Civil War, 1861–1865.
4. Virginia — History — Civil War, 1861–1865.   I. Title.
E472.1.D47   2006
973.7'31 — dc22   2005020991
ISBN-13: 978-0-15-101158-2   ISBN-10: 0-15-101158-3

Text set in Cochin
Designed by Kaelin Chappell Broaddus

Printed in the United States of America

First edition
A C E G I K J H F D B

For old friends...

especially Jack Shea,
Sister Mary Anne Powers,
Sergeant Ed Abdella,
and Wayne Spodnick, Esq.

Contents

Preface

Writers sometimes glorify battlefields, cheerily describing colorful incidents and gritty or gallant individuals.

Other observers have opted not to emphasize war's "romance." Consider the Duke of Wellington. Allegedly, when asked the essence of military wisdom, he replied, "Piss when you can." William Tecumseh Sherman was equally crisp. In 1879, General Sherman, almost sixty years old and roly-poly, spoke to the graduating class of the Michigan Military Academy. "I am tired and sick of war," he said. "Its glory is all moonshine. It is only those who have neither fired a shot nor heard the shrieks and groans of the wounded who cry aloud for blood, more vengeance, more desolation. War is hell." A year later Sherman addressed a gathering of Civil War comrades. Many veterans had brought their families to hear their one-time commander. The sky was leaden. Sherman rose, and spoke extemporaneously. He peered through the raindrops at these men who had marched thousands of miles with him — through Tennessee, through Georgia, into South Carolina. "It delights my soul to look on you," he said, "and see so many of the good old boys left yet." Then he added, "The war is away back in the past and you can tell what books cannot." He stared a moment at the crowd, and thought about the futures of the youngsters he saw there, the children of his veterans. Many of these small boys, he thought, probably made the common mistake of thinking that war meant glory. He decided to take this opportunity to speak about combat: "It is all hell," he said.

Strategic analysts of war often strive to remain cerebral, suppressing any emotions they might feel about battle. Henry Kissinger has reminded us that the goal of military strategy, whether a government goes to war or merely threatens to do so, is to alter the will of its enemy. Similarly, Karl von Clausewitz has said that to defeat one's foe, one must eliminate his will to fight. Clausewitz noted that war is "an act of violence intended to compel our opponent to fulfill our will." Perhaps his best line is: "War is nothing else than the continuation of state policy by a different means." To put this concept another way, war is one method to accomplish a goal. To Clausewitz, once a government has decided what it wants, it might try diplomacy or threats or cash payments. It might use trickery or friendliness. Or it might go to war. The essence of Clausewitz's analysis is simple, and true: War and politics are intertwined.

Nations are not inert things. To an outsider, a country may appear quaintly tranquil or dull, unchanging and placid. But beneath its surface, every nation struggles with internal conflicts. Subtle hostilities can exist between neighboring clans or tribes or races, between social classes or regions, between religious factions or language groups. Societies develop mechanisms to mute such rage: compromises, intermarriages, economic ties — but such techniques do not eliminate disputes; they only mask them, so when civil wars break out, participants are often astonished by the intensity of the emotions.

Abraham Lincoln and Jefferson Davis understood this point. Both men recognized that success or failure would depend on political factors: Could they hold on to their respective galaxy of states, or, better yet, add to them? Could they lure the support from other countries — or, at the very least, keep their opponents from receiving such support?

One of the most critical moments of the Civil War occurred during its first weeks, between the fall of Fort Sumter
and the battle of Bull Run. For a while, the District of Columbia was cut off from the rest of the North. If Lincoln's capital
had then fallen to the Confederacy, the reputation of his em-
bryonic administration would have almost certainly been mor-
tally wounded. Great Britain and France, among others, might
have recognized the Confederacy — and perhaps formed an alliance with her. This moment of extraordinary noise, of dissonance, is the subject of this book.

A decade ago I began an analysis of the opening weeks of the
Civil War, the period between Fort Sumter and Bull Run.
Along the way I wrote *Allegiance* (a book about Charleston and
Fort Sumter and a remarkable man named Robert Anderson).
I then examined Bull Run, the first great battle of the war, and
wrote the book *Donnybrook*. Between those two events lay a
critical time, when America's two sections stumbled noisily
into war. This book covers that intermediate period. These
three volumes constitute my trilogy on the first hundred days
of the Civil War.

Authors are asked why he or she happened to chose a particular topic. The first time a radio interviewer queried me about
my motives, I was startled. The question seemed so existential.
Each person's simplest activity, I thought — going bowling on
Tuesday night, for example, or eating pizza — is the result of a
hundred knowable and unrecognized motivations. How could
I possible explain — or even understand — why I had embraced
this large assignment, this literary topic? I recall mumbling a
few unsatisfactory phrases in response. Afterward, however,
my mind kept returning to the query: why, indeed, had I devoted so much of my life to this subject? A partial answer
eventually came to me.

  I am the youngest child of a family permanently altered by
the events of December 7, 1941. My father, a naval officer,

commanded a ship docked that day at Pearl Harbor. He and my mother lived not far from the base. They survived the attack and the ensuing war. But the events of that infamous December day and the weeks to come changed my parents' lives forever. As a boy, listening to their conversations about that period, I grew up sensitized, more than most, to that time, and therefore to all such critical moments when a nation's history changes in a flash. Many of the essays I wrote in school involved similar incidents. I have been particularly fascinated by observing how decisions — sometimes wise, often blundering — made by those at the top affect average folks. I have studied the interrelationships of three things: the decision-making of political leaders, the plans of military men, and the effects these decisions and plans have on common people who get drawn into great events.

Introduction

Elizabeth Lindsay Lomax, fifty-seven, lived in Washington, D.C. Early in 1861 the world she represented was about to disappear — "gone with the wind," as it were.

Born in Norfolk, Virginia, she was the daughter of a wealthy plantation owner, one of George Washington's friends. At sixteen she married a dashing thirty-three-year-old army lieutenant. They begot seven children — six girls and a boy. When her husband died in 1842, Mrs. Lomax was not exactly penniless, because she did receive a monthly pension; but she felt the need to supplement her income to maintain her large brood. She offered piano and harp lessons, and occasionally accepted work as a government scrivener, carefully writing out official documents in her fine hand. A respected member of Washington's society, she was like a minor character from *War and Peace*, one of those bright-eyed, mentally nimble ladies not central to the story but intriguing withal — attractive, well informed about political intrigue and government, and au courant about the latest delicious gossip.

She also kept a journal, whose seventeen volumes allow us a fascinating glimpse into her life. Its entries generally spoke of simple, homey things. The weather played an important part of her daily musings. So did her son's budding pre-war military career, first as a West Point cadet, then as a youthful lieutenant, serving in the West under Jeb Stuart. Eventually, he was among the officers escorting the carriage of Abraham Lincoln to the White House on his inauguration day.

In her journals we find Mrs. Lomax raising her children with love and care, stirring quince jam, cutting roses in her garden, reading novels or the popular histories written by Washington Irving. On occasion we see her, when necessary, tying on her best bonnet to visit some government official — including whoever happened to be the latest resident in the White House — about pension matters or writing assignments. Her parlor echoed with the flirtations and giggles of her daughters with young men as disparate as Fitz Lee and young Bob Lincoln, sons of famous Civil War leaders. Important now mostly forgotten gentlemen came to chat gaily with her, as did men whose names would soon resonate: Jeb Stuart and Robert E. Lee, George B. McClellan and David Farragut.

Mrs. Lomax was especially proud of the new house she had built on the corner of G and Nineteenth Streets, three blocks from the White House. She delighted in her home's fine modern gaslights. And when she finally was able to pipe running water to it, she was thrilled by this marvelous luxury. Elizabeth Lomax was quite aware her life was special. "God is very good," she whispered to herself, "when he permits us to lead a full life — and realize it. Mine still goes on in memories of the past, happiness in the present and hopes for the future."

But clouds began to form. She did not care for slavery. Though she accepted the existence of this institution, her journals provide no trace of crude racial bigotry. Her attitudes stemmed more from class and, perhaps, religious prejudices than skin color. For servants, she much preferred African Americans to those with Irish heritage, because black menials, she believed, when properly trained, were "efficient, faithful and cheerful."

In the autumn of 1859 she was disturbed to hear about John Brown's raid on nearby Harpers Ferry. Brown's tiny band, she reflected, were men of violence; the "goodness of God" had foiled their plans. But when Brown was sentenced to be hanged, she felt a humane pang, and on the day of his execution she prayed God would have mercy on his soul.

Few Americans felt more rooted to the nation's history, or loved it more, than Elizabeth Lomax. As the election of 1860 neared, she confided to her diary how much she hated "the *appalling* war cloud growing darker and darker each day." On November 9 she jotted into her journal these few words: "Great excitement — Mr. Lincoln elected President of the United States. The papers speak of the dissolution of the Union as an accomplished fact — *God spare us from such a disaster.*"

When South Carolina seceded in December, she muttered to her diary, "God defend us from civil war." By January 1861, as Deep South senators departed the Federal capital after their states cut ties with the Union, she remarked that "the Southern Senators" were leaving — a revealing phrase, suggesting that, in her heart she was a Virginian, not a Southerner. To her, Virginia was the Mother of America. Its leaders — Washington, Jefferson, James Madison, Patrick Henry, and all the others — had created her country, had stitched together the core of the American Constitution out of their own notions about representative democracy. Virginians had arguably been America's best presidents. The country's most famous Chief Justice, John Marshall, another Virginian, had insisted on the preeminent standing of the federal government compared to the states. To Elizabeth Lomax, Virginia and America were virtually the same thing. During February 1861 she was glad to learn that unionists remained in control of her native state.

On March 4 Mr. Lincoln took his oath on the steps of the Capitol. That night, reading the *Evening Star,* she pored with great care over the words of his inaugural address. She was pleased at its moderation. "I thought," she told her diary, "there was no doubt of its sanity and its excellence."

But things continued to slide downhill. "Papers very warlike," she said with concern, "trouble brewing!" Three days later she wrote only five words, and underlined them: "*Great anxiety about Fort Sumter.*" Two days afterward, on Saturday,

April 13: "Fort Sumter was attacked yesterday—greatest excitement everywhere. The news from the South makes me wretched—God help us!" On Sunday afternoon, when some of her friends dropped in for tea, everyone carefully avoided talking about secession "and other dangerous topics of the day."

A few days later her fears were realized: "Virginia has seceded!! Heaven help us!"

Things grew worse. An ugly riot broke out in Baltimore, and many people were killed. Her beloved son told her he was resigning from the United States military to join a force forming across the Potomac, in Virginia. Northern troops began arriving in the capital. She could hear their nettlesome boots marching past her doorway. Her favorite daughter's suitor joined the Union army; the young woman refused to speak to him again.

Relatives in Virginia urged Mrs. Lomax to depart Washington because the capital itself might well become the site of a great battle; they invited her to come stay at their place in Charlottesville. In mid-May—mostly for the sake of her daughters—she reluctantly agreed. She packed her family's belongings and left the cherished home that she had scrimped to purchase and improve during so many years. She turned off the gas and locked the door. "Perhaps forever," she sighed.

She and her daughters crossed the Potomac and headed westward toward Charlottesville. Along the way, they passed some Virginia volunteers, "all eager for a fight, all ardent for their rights. Poor fellows," she thought to herself, "they little know what is before them."

In her journal she wept: "I feel *desolate*."[1]

This book is a history of those weeks, of the time when Elizabeth Lomax's world, when antebellum America, exploded.

Timeline

April 12, 1861, Friday

Charleston (South Carolina) Harbor

— Fort Sumter attacked by Confederate cannon.

Montgomery, Alabama

— CSA Secretary of War Leroy Walker announces the news to a large audience, adding that Washington will be taken over by the Confederacy within three months.

Washington

— President Lincoln hears of the attack on Fort Sumter.
— Secretary of the Navy Gideon Welles, uneasy about the status of the Gosport Navy Yard in Virginia, prepares orders to send assistance there.

Harrisburg, Pennsylvania

— The state legislature is in session when it learns of the attack. It immediately passes a bill to organize and arm the state's militiamen. (Similar actions take place in other Northern states during the next few days.)

April 13, 1861, Saturday

Charleston

— Major Robert Anderson surrenders Fort Sumter to the CSA.

Washington

— Lincoln hears the news sometime in the evening.

Richmond, Virginia

— Tension in the city as rumors swirl. Word arrives about Anderson's surrender. A pro-South victory celebration ensues. Governor John Letcher expresses his lack of enthusiasm.

Border states

— The news causes a stir and confusion. In Baltimore emotions run high.

North

— In countless towns people gather to hear and discuss the news about Fort Sumter. Many men volunteer to defend the Union.

April 14, 1861, Sunday

Charleston

— Major Anderson and his garrison board a ship that starts toward New York.

Washington

— *Morning:* Governor Alex Ramsey of Minnesota happens to be in the capital. He offers the services of his militia to Lincoln — the first governor to do so officially.
— *Late morning:* Lincoln meets with his cabinet to discuss the options. They agree he should announce a proclamation that will ask for 75,000 three-month volunteers, whose tasks will be to "suppress" the rebels and to repossess all Federal properties recently taken over by Southerners. Also, the proclamation will announce that Congress will meet on July 4th.
— *Evening:* Lincoln meets with the Democratic leader Stephen Douglas, who agrees to support the coming war.

April 15, 1861, Monday

— Lincoln's proclamation is published in hundreds of newspapers, North and South.

Richmond

— Ex-governor Henry Wise wires John Daniel Imboden to come to Richmond quickly.

Baltimore

— City newspapers print provocative, emotional stories about the growing crisis, as well as Lincoln's proclamation. Governor Thomas Holliday Hicks arrives in town from Annapolis, the state capital.

April 16, 1861, Tuesday

Washington

— Gideon Welles writes a note to the commander of Gosport, Commodore Charles S. McCauley, urging him to remain vigilant.

Richmond

— Morning newspapers announce that Lincoln is asking Virginia to contribute 2,340 volunteers to suppress the rebellion. Letcher officially refuses.
— Imboden arrives. He and others, meeting in Wise's hotel room, plot to capture the Federal arsenal at Harpers Ferry, Virginia.
— Wise wires contacts in Norfolk to stop Federal ships from leaving Gosport. (Three hulks are dropped in the channel there.)
— Wise promises his co-conspirators that he will see to it Virginia secedes in the morning.

Boston

— Ben Butler arrives early at Governor John Andrew's office and wants to lead the state's first volunteers. Andrew puts him in charge of four regiments, but two are sidetracked, ordered to go by sea to Fort Monroe, Virginia.

April 17, 1861, Wednesday

Richmond

— Henry Wise rises at the convention and demands a secession vote. The resolution passes, eighty-eight to fifty-five. (Some of the fifty-five leave the city and return to their homes in western Virginia, a section they will eventually establish as the state of West Virginia.)
— Letcher calls up the militia. Throughout the state, military companies gather. Some, like Imboden's in the Shenandoah Valley, head toward Harpers Ferry.

Boston

— One of Butler's two remaining regiments, the Sixth Massachusetts, assembles quickly, boards a train, and heads toward Washington.

Gosport

— McCauley, after learning about the sunken hulks, hears that Virginia soldiers are gathering outside the Yard.

April 18, 1861, Thursday

Harpers Ferry

— Turner Ashby arrives and announces he intends to take the arsenal.
— Lieutenant Roger Jones, at the arsenal, prepares to destroy what he can.
— Hundreds of militiamen assemble not far from town. As soon as they receive Letcher's official orders, they start toward Harpers Ferry.
— Jones sets fires and leads his garrison across Maryland to Pennsylvania.
— The militiamen save some important equipment and several thousand muskets.

New York City

— Major Anderson and the Fort Sumter garrison arrive and are greeted as heroes.
— The Sixth Massachusetts, passing through the city, are also cheered.

Baltimore

— Five unarmed companies of Pennsylvania militiamen, on their way to Washington by train, march from one depot to another. They are set on by an angry mob.

Washington

— Word spreads that Virginia seceded the day before.
— The soldiers of General Winfield Scott prepare to defend the city—especially the White House.
— Robert E. Lee arrives. He speaks to Francis Blair, Sr., then later, Scott. It is possible he was offered some high-ranking military post.
— The battered Pennsylvanians stagger that evening into the national capital, the first arriving volunteers. They describe their tribulations in Baltimore.

April 19, 1861, Friday

Baltimore

— A huge and vocal anti-Lincoln rally takes place in Monument Square.
— After learning that a train is on its way, carrying thousands of Yankee volunteers, George Proctor Kane, in charge of the city's police force, heads with some policemen to Camden Street Station; he hopes to maintain order. He is joined by Mayor George W. Brown.
— The Sixth arrives at a different station. (On their train are also two other Pennsylvania units.) As the Massachusetts men cross through Baltimore, an angry mob attacks. Many on both sides are killed and

wounded, but the Sixth makes it out of town, and
will arrive in Washington, much bloodied. The
Pennsylvanians on the train find it impossible to get
through Baltimore and flee northward.
— Baltimore is now in an uproar. Governor Hicks and Mayor
Brown wire Lincoln to send no more troops this way.
— Kane, Brown, and Hicks agree that railroad bridges
north of the city must be destroyed to prevent more
volunteers from coming.

Washington

— Lincoln learns that Harpers Ferry has fallen. Since it is
only two hours away, the Federal capital seems in danger.
Rumors fly that more Virginia volunteers are even closer.
— Welles and Scott agree that Gosport ought to be reinforced.
The *Pawnee* steams off with some marines on board. The
ship has orders to take on several hundred Massachusetts
volunteers at Fort Monroe, then proceed to the navy yard.

Richmond

— Letcher and his advisers discuss men they might choose
to lead the state's military. They consider Joseph E.
Johnston and Robert E. Lee. Though both men are still
in the United States Army, they are now in the
Washington area, not far away.

Montgomery

— Jefferson Davis sends Vice President Aleck Stephens to
Richmond to persuade Virginia to join the Confederacy.

New York City

— The Seventh New York leaves for Washington.

April 20, 1861, Saturday

Baltimore

— Bridges north of town are burned.
— Violence and turmoil inside the city. At Fort McHenry,
just outside town, the Federal garrison prepares for an
assault.

— Telegraph lines going north are cut. (The national capital is now virtually cut off.)

Gosport

— During the afternoon, McCauley orders most of the unmanned ships at the Yard scuttled—to keep them out of the hands of the rebels.
— The *Pawnee* arrives, too late to save the ships. A decision is made to abandon the Yard, after destroying as much as possible.

Arlington

— Lee decides to resign his commission in the army. He learns that a representative of Governor Letcher wants to speak to him.

Washington

— Lincoln orders raids on all important telegraph offices, to seize and read every telegram written during the past year, looking for treason.

Philadelphia

— Word spreads here that Baltimore will now be impossible to get through.
— The Seventh arrives, then departs aboard a rented steamer. They hope to go directly to Washington, but if not, to stop at Annapolis, from where they will march to the capital.
— Ben Butler and the Eighth Massachusetts (the only regiment Butler has left) also starts out of Philadelphia, but by a different route, heading toward Annapolis.

April 21, 1861, Sunday

Washington

— Word arrives that Gosport has fallen. (Among other things, this means that the Potomac River may now be unsafe.)
— Mayor Brown and others from Baltimore speak to Lincoln, asking him not to bring more troops through

their volatile city. He agrees. A few minutes later, when he hears that some Pennsylvania volunteers are just north of Baltimore, he orders them to go back.

April 22, 1861, Monday

Washington

— Scott's morning report to Lincoln says that Virginians may attack momentarily. Throughout the capital there is panic. Scott prepares for a long siege.

Richmond

— Lee arrives; Letcher offers him the leadership of Virginia's military.

Annapolis

— Coming via different routes, both the Seventh New York and the Eighth Massachusetts arrive — just in time, apparently, to save the Naval Academy from rebels.

April 23, 1861, Tuesday

Richmond

— General Lee wires the state's main military leaders to act cautiously — at least for the moment.

Annapolis

— The Union volunteers here learn that Washington is in grave danger. They prepare to leave by train, rather than march.

April 24, 1861, Wednesday

Richmond

— Aleck Stephens, representing the Confederacy, and a committee of the convention agree that henceforth Virginia is a member of the CSA. (This agreement will not become official until May 23, when Virginia will hold a popular referendum on secession.)

Annapolis

— The Seventh and Eighth start out, repairing the tracks as they go. They move slowly, watched balefully by rebels in the distance.

April 25, 1861, Thursday

Washington

— Scott's morning message to Lincoln states that an attack "may be expected at any moment."
— The Seventh arrives by train in the capital. Jubilation!

May 23, 1861, Thursday

Virginia

— The referendum about secession occurs as scheduled. The resolution passes. Virginia has officially seceded.

Washington

— Over ten thousand of Lincoln's volunteers secretly prepare to cross into Virginia—that is, the Confederacy—during the night.

Fort Monroe

— A slave named Luke asks for asylum.

DISSONANCE

CHAPTER ONE

City of Magnificent Intentions

The Ball has opened.
—*HARTFORD COURANT,* APRIL 13, 1861

When Charles Dickens visited Washington, D.C., during the 1840s, he was unimpressed. "It is sometimes called the City of Magnificent Distances," he said, "but it might with greater propriety be termed the City of Magnificent Intentions." He considered it characterized by "spacious avenues, that begin in nothing, and lead nowhere; streets, mile-long, that only want houses, roads, and inhabitants; public buildings that need but a public to be complete; and ornaments of great thoroughfares, which only lack great thoroughfares to ornament."

A few years after Dickens wrote these caustic lines, America, puffed up with pride, in light of her successful war with Mexico and expansion to the Pacific, happily threw tax dollars into federal construction. Workmen began building an obelisk to honor George Washington, Father of His Country. According to its design, it would, when completed, soar to a height of 600 feet — making it the tallest man-made structure in the world. The Treasury Building underwent major expansion. Also, two massive wings were added to the Capitol, and the new galleries looking down on the House and Senate could each seat over a thousand observers. And someday, when the cast-iron dome of the Rotunda was finished, topped by a statue of Victory spreading her arms above it to embrace the city and the nation beyond, its roof, 400 feet above the ground, would approximate the height of St. Paul's Cathedral in London and St. Peter's in Rome. Not far away, over at the Patent Office, slack-jawed visitors ogled hundreds of the latest national inventions.

It was easy in those days to wander through such federal buildings. A guidebook proudly said of Washington's public edifices: "No armed sentinels morosely oppose the entrance of the humblest; patience seems to be the universal characteristic of the employees." Even the White House was often open to the public, and its grounds served as a kind of city park, with gravel walkways and pleasant trees and a fountain. When weather permitted, on Wednesday evenings the Marine Band gave concerts on the lawn of the Executive Mansion.

The District offered convenient and inexpensive public transport. For a nickel, travelers went by omnibus from the Capitol to Georgetown, or from Columbia College to the Potomac, or from Seventh Street to the navy yard.

For those who were hungry, Washington City offered scores of eateries; if one wished to tipple, it had hundreds of watering holes. The city was home to four relatively swank hotels—including the largest, the National, in whose saloons politicians often came to chat and drowse; and Willard's (near the White House). Pennsylvania Avenue was cobblestoned for part of its length and handsome trees lined its sides. During each spring, pink peach blossoms tumbled delicately to the ground and the air grew redolent with the scent of magnolias. The flora of the capital magically reflected its position between North and South, having a smattering of plants from both sections—orchids and black walnut, hackberry and sassafras.[2]

According to the 1860 census, the population of the District was 75,080. This figure included 8,733 who lived in Georgetown, a good-sized town both older and quite separate in those days from what was called Washington City. The District's population also included 5,225 people who resided in neither Georgetown nor Washington City, who were described by the census as living in the "rural" sector. Here, farmers worked the tired land above the Capitol. When Abraham Lincoln wished for a little quiet time, he often rode out along the dusty country paths that meandered through that agrarian northern part of the District.

Washington City had its problems. Discreet locals did not usually mention this fact, but the place had numerous prostitutes and gambling establishments. Crime was rampant in parts of Washington City. The District's entire police force numbered only sixteen during daylight hours and fifty at night. Many private homes were squalid, and except for a few impressive shops on Pennsylvania Avenue, most stores were small, dirty, unpainted, shabby. The majority of the city's population consisted of hotel maids and Irish laborers, of hackmen and faro dealers, of clerks and washerwomen. About 20 percent of the population was African American, including 11,131 free blacks and 3,185 slaves.

When the District was first created during the 1790s from land donated by Virginia and Maryland, the federal government did not bother to write special slave laws; it merely adopted the regulations the two states had been using. During ensuing years, both Virginia and Maryland moderated their slave codes, but the District did not, retaining the much harsher colonial regulations. Until halfway into the Civil War, according to District statutes, if a black person struck a white, the miscreant could legally be cropped (that is, have part of his or her ears cut off). For the crime of "false witness," an African American could be punished by a court with thirty-nine lashes, and have his or her ears nailed to a pillory before cropping. Among the punishments judges meted out to District blacks were beheading and quartering. All African Americans were required to carry a document showing their status—free or slave. Visiting blacks were often not aware of this regulation. Cases occurred of free Northern African Americans snatched from the District's streets and thrown into prison for lack of the necessary documentation, then sold into slavery to cover "jail fees." (It was 1862 before Congress finally voted to outlaw slavery in the District. When Lincoln signed the bill into law, he declared himself "gratified" that it provided for payment to the owners, and also that money was being set aside to colonize the freed blacks somewhere else, far outside the United States.)[3]

Georgetown, serving as the District's chief port, was situated at the fall line of the Potomac. Ships jammed its docks; old photographs show a tangle of masts of assorted vessels tied at the wharves. In early 1861 Georgetown was still a bustling commercial town, home to about fifty flour mills that ground grain brought from the interior of Virginia or Maryland. Georgetown was also the center of America's largest shad and herring market.

Some visitors arriving in the national capital were surprised that so much of it was still a wilderness. Deer, otter, skunks, and opossums seemed everywhere. So were nine different types of turtles, nine species of frogs, and toads — to say nothing of countless snakes and salamanders and water lizards. The District was home to eighteen different bivalves and thirty-two univalves. It was also a stopping place for birds migrating north in the spring and south in the autumn. During April, lovers picnicking near Rock Creek might have noticed warblers, small flycatchers, and thrushes. By summertime a person could espy ducks of great variety, sandpipers and cardinal grosbeaks, rails and black-throated buntings. Locals fished the nearby Potomac for eel, pike, sturgeon, perch, or sunfish.

Some things in the District were less bucolic. Inside federal buildings, all the staircases and other public spaces seemed dank and fetid with spittle from tobacco chewers. The carpets of the White House and Congress were equally bespattered. An open canal slicing through the District's center carried raw sewage from the hotels and public buildings. The canal's noxious ooze drifted slowly and pungently past the White House until it floated onto the mud flats next to the Potomac. The remains of dead domestic animals rotted here, along with the occasional body of an unwanted baby. Cattle wandered loose in the city; so did chickens and pigs. There was a city ordinance requiring that pigs be penned, but most owners ignored it, and stray hogs waddled about searching for grub. When the authorities tried to round up the porkers, the animals' shouting owners often fought the policemen, while gleeful crowds gathered to watch. In 1861 a young visitor from Massachusetts wrote home: "Washington is the most filthy city that it has ever been my chance to see." He compared it unfavorably to Boston and Lowell. "When at home, we are not accustomed to see hogs running at large in the principle streets of the city, or the carcasses of dead dogs and goats left to decay by the side of the street, in the heart of the city, as is the case here, much to the disgust of our nasal organs."[4]

Washington, in other words, was not an easy place to categorize. It was a contradictory town. John F. Kennedy's famous description of it as combining Northern charm with Southern efficiency would have been just as apt a century earlier. But his witticism would hardly have amused the populace of 1861 because of their parlous position between those two regions.

One person, more than any other American, was giving deep thought to the prospect of an attack on Washington: Winfield Scott.

Scott was an excellent soldier, and respected. Born in Virginia in 1786 to a middle-class family, he attended William and Mary College, where he studied law. He was then a fine-looking young man, bright and curious. Unlike many of his Virginia peers who thrilled to the hunt, Scott preferred to read. When President Jefferson offered him a commission in the army, the lad did not assume that manly courage alone could guarantee a successful career, and immediately began to study the arcane world of the military, and would eventually, after traveling Europe to observe its armies, write America's first important textbook on tactics. Early in his career he won great fame for winning an important victory during the War of 1812, then later, for successes in several Indian wars. In his middle years he rose to the leadership of the army. During the Mexican War he performed dazzlingly well and was primarily responsible for a relatively painless and quick victory.

Not everything in his life was rosy. He married an extremely wealthy Virginia belle, Maria Mayo, and they produced seven children. She was quick witted and strong willed. They clashed. Lately she had been residing in Europe, using the excuse of fragile health.

In personality, Winfield Scott was a genial, rather ebullient fellow who enjoyed socializing at tables groaning beneath fine foods and wines. More than most military men, he had a sense of the power of the press, and he often entertained reporters in his quarters, expatiating at length on this or that topic. But, oddly, for a man with such a good mind who strived for the White House several times and was actually nominated by the Whigs in 1852, he never truly grasped politics. Though hardly naïve, the nuances and backstabbing of the political world escaped him. Devious politicians like William Seward easily manipulated him.

By 1860 Scott's enemies—and during his long and disputatious career he acquired many—snidely loved to point out his weaknesses. They called him pompous (though he was seldom really that), and politically ambitious (even when he was far past such daydreams). They also said he was old. Here, they were both right and wrong.

When Scott had been a lad he was exceedingly tall and lean. By the time of the Mexican War, fine dining had filled out his healthy and robust six feet four-and-a-quarter inches (and he insisted on that quarter inch). By 1861 time had eroded much of his vigor, if not his pride. He had once enjoyed emphasizing his imposing height by sporting high-heeled boots, but gout and battle injuries had caused him to lay those vanities aside. Now seventy-four and corpulent, with the intestinal discomforts of an old campaigner, he suffered bouts of dropsy and assorted aches that caused debilitating pains to radiate through his legs and feet, and he often chatted with visitors from a supine position. He would be seventy-five on June

13—almost antiquated for a general still in harness, especially one about to face the greatest crisis in his nation's history.

But his mind was clear and his will indomitable. He had commanded his country's army for two generations. He had served more than half the nation's presidents, many unfit to shine his epaulettes. He was certainly the best general America had ever produced—including the sainted George Washington. He was still widely admired, though mostly in a cool and distant way. Americans of that era prided themselves on their disdain for professionalism—which was one reason so many voters had liked Andrew Jackson, considering Old Hickory a "man-of-the-people," ignoring the fact that he was an extraordinarily wealthy planter. (Similarly, many folks—at least in the North—were drawn to "Honest Abe, the Rail Splitter," ignoring the reality that Lincoln had pocketed wads of money as a shrewd and successful lawyer, acting on behalf of powerful business interests.) Given such national prejudices against refinement, it was not surprising that during the Mexican War, most Americans felt more simpatico with "Old Rough and Ready" Zachary Taylor (another rich, Southern slaveowner, but one who made no pretense at having West Point polish) than the far more professional soldier, nicknamed Fuss and Feathers, Winfield Scott. (In reference to that pejorative label, it might be noted that General Scott was no more fastidious about his appearance than George S. Patton, Jr., and that Winfield Scott was arguably a far better soldier, and man, than Patton.)

Scott's primary weakness, such as it was, involved pride. He grew balky and prickly when either his professionalism or expertise was challenged. Inevitably, his relationship with a long string of secretaries of war—including Jefferson Davis in the mid-1850s—tended to be rocky, so lately he had maintained his headquarters in New York and avoided the nation's capital. But in the autumn of 1860 the secession crisis had disturbed him deeply. He recognized, better than anyone, the weaknesses in the American army, which was small, ill-armed, and almost entirely stationed far out on the western side of the

Mississippi. Of equal concern was the fact that a large percentage of its officers were Southerners. He knew the kinds of
pressures they would face from their home states. His experiences in Washington made him distrust the wisdom or toughness of most politicians, and this crisis, he knew, would require
both attributes. He was almost totally unacquainted with this
man Abraham Lincoln, but was fairly intimate with the senator from New York, William Seward, whom Lincoln had just
appointed secretary of state, and who, reputedly, would really
be running things when the new administration took office in
March 1861. Throughout the winter of 1860–1861 General
Scott stayed in close contact with Seward. The two agreed that
a soft approach with the South would be best, particularly
with Virginia. Yet neither Scott nor Seward wanted the federal government to appear weak. This balance would require
a delicate hand.

Until Lincoln's administration took office in March 1861,
much would depend on the abilities of President James Buchanan and his cabinet. This had worried Scott considerably.
He thought Buchanan irresolute and the cabinet divided. Scott
was especially uneasy about Buchanan's secretary of war, John
B. Floyd. If nothing else, Secretary Floyd had an unsavory reputation about his personal integrity. There were also growing
rumors that Floyd, a Virginian, was in cahoots with several
rabid secessionists. Such concerns worked on Scott so much
that in December 1860 he transferred his headquarters back to
Washington, where he could keep a closer eye on things. He
was not in the capital long when he received reports of growing military problems. The situation of Major Robert Anderson
at Fort Sumter especially nagged him. Scott knew Anderson
well, and liked and admired the man. Scott believed South Carolina might attack Anderson's tiny garrison. If that happened,
Scott thought, a civil war would almost certainly result.

The crisis over Fort Sumter, lasting from December 1860 to
April 1861, forced General Scott to weigh a thousand military
options — almost none of them attractive.[5]

First of all, the fate of the capital itself was in doubt. It did not take much scrutiny to realize that here in Washington, the civilian population (many of its residents born in the slave states of Virginia or Maryland), the government, and even the military was permeated with people of doubtful loyalty. If it came to war, how would they react?

This question was more subtle than it seemed. A person's loyalty depends on family connections, friendships, income and wealth, age and life experiences, and whatever geographical spot a person thinks of as "home." Take Major Anderson. His childhood had been spent in Kentucky, his wife was a wealthy Georgian, and he and she still owned slaves in Georgia. On the other hand, most of Anderson's siblings now resided in Ohio, and his wife long ago had rented a suite in a posh New York hotel. During his long military career he had served both in the Deep South and in New England. During the months of crisis over Fort Sumter he was asked countless times where his loyalties lay. He thought long and hard about his answer. He concluded he had indeed been born in the South, but he had—as an adult—chosen the United States Army as a career. He felt sympathy with disaffected Southerners, he admitted, but he said he owed his allegiance to America. Robert Anderson had spent his adult years accepting a government paycheck, and as a man of honor, therefore, he felt his loyalty was to its flag. Period. Other honorable men with similar backgrounds—Robert E. Lee being the most conspicuous example—came to different conclusions. As it turned out, many individuals did not fully know in 1861 where their allegiance lay until forced to decide, by circumstances, which side to join. Painful decisions would be made at the last moment—once the war began.

Meanwhile, however, during the weeks before the war's opening guns, Winfield Scott had to do what he could to prepare for that increasingly likely prospect. Legally, he could not increase the size of his army; such a political decision was out of his hands. He could only make recommendations to his superiors. And even doing this was difficult because he had to deal with two administrations — Buchanan's, then Lincoln's. Scott understood that James Buchanan, a Democrat whose cabinet had many Southerners, would have a different perspective than the Republican Lincoln. But how different? Scott was uncertain.

Winfield Scott pieced together a plan of action — one he hoped would first be acceptable to the outgoing government, and then perhaps would be okayed by the incoming. He also had to figure out his options, which actions would be plausible, and the situation was changing almost daily. South Carolina seceded in December. Within a few weeks six other states were heading in that direction. In early February a Confederacy of the seceded states was announced. Other Southerners openly discussed the possibility of joining that organization. Scott knew all this.

Twisted around their stories were rumors. Scott had learned that leaders in both Virginia and Maryland were discussing the secession of their states. How real were their plans? How realistic were their options? He also had heard disturbing tales about the District itself. He had reports on his desk that secret conclaves were being held in Washington, where armed men spoke openly about initiating an uprising within the capital.

One of Scott's concerns sprang from the geography of the District. The decision to place the capital here had possessed a kind of democratic appeal. The spot would be a place, the Founders thought, which was indefensible, proving to the world that their experiment in government was genuinely open. Except for a few low hills — like the one the Capitol sat on — the District was essentially flat. It was also easily accessible from virtually anywhere in Virginia or Maryland — as the British army had gleefully proved in 1814 when they disembarked from ships a few miles north, marched across a portion of Maryland, and burned part of the capital to the ground. Winfield Scott had been a young soldier when that incident occurred. Now he was being asked to plan to defend this indefensible location, full of an unknown number of traitors who would be happy to join an assaulting army approaching from either the north (Maryland) or the south (Virginia).

Charles Pomeroy Stone, thirty-six, a clever West Point graduate and an acquaintance of Scott's from their days in the Mexican War, had resigned from the army, tried his hand as a banker, then taken a surveying position in the Southwest. Just after Christmas 1860, he was in Washington to drop off maps and reports and decided to drop in on his distinguished friend, General Scott, for a social visit. On New Year's Eve Winfield Scott was eating at Wormley's Hotel. He always enjoyed dining, but on this occasion he felt especially upbeat. He had recently learned that the temper of Buchanan's administration seemed to be changing. Secretary of War Floyd had just been fired. Old Buck, the president, was showing signs of spunk. Scott had an appointment that very evening at the White House to discuss military matters. Things were looking up.

Stone remarked that the old general seemed quite chipper. "Yes, my young friend," Scott replied, "I feel more cheerful about the affairs of the country than I did this morning." He paused for a moment, and elicited from Stone his opinion. As an ex-army man who had been in the capital only a few days, what did Stone think of its mood? Was the population here loyal? Stone said he believed most people he'd seen were loyal, but they did not have a firm hook to hang that loyalty on; they needed something concrete to rally around.

Scott liked this response. The next day, January 1, 1861, the general offered Stone a job. He asked him to take a temporary commission as colonel, to act as the Inspector-General of the District of Columbia. The position was somewhat anomalous, but important. An inspector-general of any political unit, like a state (or in this case, Washington), was a civilian who administered the region's militia. Scott was actually asking Stone to organize Washington's volunteer soldiers. At this moment the District only had a few militiamen, so Stone's first task would be to raise as many companies as he could. He would then supervise their organization, their training, their armament, and so on. If there was an actual revolt inside the District, Stone's men would shoulder much of the responsibility of putting it down. If the capital was attacked from outside, his militiamen would protect it. He would have the assistance of a handful of regular troops, including some marines at the navy yard, but their numbers would be paltry, unless things changed.

Stone accepted Scott's offer — and began immediately. He penned letters to forty prominent local citizens, asking each to organize a company of volunteers, drawing on only trustworthy men.

Like General Scott, Colonel Stone was particularly concerned about Lincoln's approaching inauguration. The president-elect was due to arrive soon and would take his oath on March 4. Rumors were rife that insurgents would attempt, at the very least, to disrupt the proceedings. On January 2nd, the *New York Times* reported: "It is now well-known that military companies have been organized and drilled for months past in Maryland and Virginia, and that the distinct object of their organization is to aid in the seizure of Washington City in the interests of the disunionists, or the prevention by force of Lincoln's inauguration. Some of the less prudent of their leaders boast in private circles that they have five thousand well-armed and organized men."

Clerks in most government departments were openly sporting secession badges on their lapels, little clumps of blue cloth. When departing prominent Southern senators or congressmen gave pro-secession speeches in Congress, the well-filled galleries broke into wild cheering. During February a House committee held hearings on whether "hostile organizations" threatened the District from within. General Scott testified. He told the committee he himself had already received over eighty death threats. The chief of the Capitol police admitted he owned land and slaves on the Virginia side of the Potomac and intended to depart and return to that state if it seceded. Many other witnesses described divided loyalties.

After a couple weeks of hearings, the five-member committee reported they had no positive evidence of a conspiracy to grab the capital, but this announcement was hardly reassuring.

In addition to supervising militiamen, Stone dealt with the nuances of loyalty in the District. In a sense he was serving as America's chief of intelligence. He lacked the manpower or, for that matter, personal experience, to act outside the boundaries of Washington, though he read Richmond's and Baltimore's newspapers, poring over them for hints of trouble. Mostly he focused on what he could control: his own volunteers and the federal buildings. He chose secret agents and embedded them inside each militia company. He discovered disloyalty — treason — in at least two. He relieved the commanding officer of a militia company calling itself the National Rifles, and took away its weapons. (A few weeks later most members of the National Rifles, led by their officers, marched across the Potomac and joined the Confederate cause. Stone had been correct about them.)

General Scott was able to transfer a few regular troops into the District, and by March 4, the day of Lincoln's inauguration, Inspector-General Stone had dozens of companies of volunteers on hand — as many as 3,500 militiamen altogether. Despite the rumors, the inauguration went off without a hitch. Immediately afterward, most of Stone's militiamen disbanded because the crisis seemed to have passed. Stone continued his work with the handful of volunteers that remained.

In March and early April Winfield Scott continued to worry about the safety of the District. Whatever Lincoln decided to do, Scott knew there would be reactions of some kind in nearby Virginia and Maryland.

On April 8, Stone was told to enroll four of his companies into federal service. These men would cease being strictly local militia. Each man must take an oath of allegiance to serve the federal government — which in effect meant Lincoln's administration. This distinction was subtle but important. Previously these men had volunteered to serve under local officers, for local purposes — in a sense, to defend their own hearths. Such membership had really only involved going to a few gatherings. In return they could wear uniforms, carry weapons, and consider themselves quite manly. On occasion they had marched about in public — perhaps strutting a bit — and been prepared to defend their homes and families against all "aliens." But to take a federal oath was very different. Each man would now be swearing to "support, protect, and defend the Constitution and Government of the United States against all enemies, whether domestic or foreign." And the oath stipulated that the man must attest that he was uttering these words "without any mental reservation or evasion." Henceforth he would have to accept orders from the president of the United States (and his designees, including federal army officers). What did this mean? Might he be asked to leave his home region? Might he be forced to abandon his job — and his income? If so, who would pay his rent? If he had children, who would care for them? Such questions forced each volunteer to take somber stock of his situation.

On the afternoon of April 10 a cluster of volunteers stood in an enclosed courtyard next to the War Department. A crowd of locals gathered to watch, a few of them hooting and scoffing. An army major, Irvin McDowell, stood before the militiamen and read the required oath aloud. He explained to them what the government had in mind and what would be required of them.

A few men chose not to take it, each for his own reason. Some were lifelong Democrats and felt odd about committing themselves to orders from an uncertain Black Republican like Lincoln. Some men with unsympathetic employers dared not endanger their jobs. Others had temporary family situations that demanded attention — sick children or wives. A few objected to the idea of being ordered away from the District, to some undesignated spot. Others, when faced by the ultimate choice, felt they simply could not swear to support the Union — no matter what. Each of such reasons was understandable.

———

By the night of April 11, Stone and the Union had signed up several fledgling companies. (Officially there was a difference between militiamen and volunteers. Militiamen had not taken the necessary federal oath. But when the war began, people on both sides tended to use the terms interchangeably.) Stone posted these men in key spots around the District. Some volunteers guarded certain selected federal buildings. Others waited at bridges and highways that entered town from either Virginia or Maryland. The duty of each man started at sunset and lasted till dawn. That first night, as Stone's volunteers tried to stay awake, Confederate guns at Charleston were opening fire at Fort Sumter. Stone's guards did not know it, but at dawn, as they staggered home or off to their regular jobs, the Civil War had begun.[6]

One can argue that the Civil War was eventually won in the Western Theater—that the war was decided out there, in places like Shiloh and Mobile, in New Orleans and Vicksburg and Missionary Ridge, and that the Civil War battles in Virginia were mostly bloody stalemates. This argument has merit, but the Union could have lost the war in the East. The Confederacy might have achieved its goal of receiving foreign support—particularly from Britain—if it conjured up something terribly dramatic, like the capture of Washington.

The whirlwind that, among other things, blew Mrs. Lomax and her daughters out of the federal capital, had been gathering for decades. Many factors energized the storm, but at its core lay the fear white Southerners had about the possibility of slavery's demise, about the prospect that Lincoln and his Black Republican brethren might attempt to free the slaves. Slavery was not simply a system of labor, as some Southerners pretended. It was a method of control. The concept of states' rights was a fabric with many layers, but deepest down, in its lowest reptilian recesses, it was wrapped in terror. Scratch a fervent states-rights advocate and he likely bled bigotry.

Abraham Lincoln was not entirely unsympathetic to such concerns. Though far less racially prejudiced than most white Americans, he recognized the depths of America's racial divides. Two days before the attack on Fort Sumter he chatted with a representative of a Colombian coal mining firm, the Chiriqui Improvement Company, and he broached to that businessman the possibility of sending to Colombia some of America's free blacks. During the coming war Lincoln would often speak of his plans to colonize African Americans somewhere outside the United States. He could never quite fathom the possibility of America integrating its races.

But the first issue Lincoln needed to resolve was not race. It involved South Carolina; on December 20, 1860, that state seceded. During the next few days she expropriated every federal property within her state borders—except Fort Sumter, sitting atop a tiny island in Charleston Harbor. Only a few score federal soldiers, led by the tired but honorable Major Robert Anderson, garrisoned that fort. By April 1861 Anderson and his men had run out of most supplies, such as candles to light their way through the fort's shadowy recesses at night, or soap to bathe. They had little fuel to heat their sleeping quarters or cook their food. Their health was deteriorating. They were almost out of food and therefore on the outer edge of starvation. Yet their determination in the face of being surrounded for months by hostile cannon, had caught the fancy of America's newspapers. Someone might debate the abstract pros and cons of secession, but almost no one could deny the gallantry of Major Robert Anderson and his command. Even Charleston's journals spoke admiringly of it.

Lincoln, however, did contemplate abandoning Fort Sumter, to avoid a dangerous confrontation with South Carolina. Most of his cabinet agreed, as did the nation's military leaders, including Winfield Scott. A few Republicans urged Lincoln to hold firm on Fort Sumter as a matter of principle, and of good politics. To withdraw Anderson would send a message, they said, that the new administration was weak. It could also stifle the goals of the Republican Party, only in existence a few years, and really still a loose coalition of elements not yet comfortable with one another. Railroad and tariff laws supported by important Republicans would be in jeopardy.

In Washington, most thought the fort would have to be abandoned soon. Sending provisions there might extend Anderson's tenure for a few weeks or months, but South Carolina might consider any assistance to Anderson as a belligerent act, a form of "coercion" (the term secessionists were using to describe any federal firmness). If the administration seemed an aggressor, this might cause the seven Deep South states which had just formed the Confederacy to become more truculent. And it might antagonize the so-called border states (the eight other slave states), nudging them toward their Confederate cousins. Men like William Seward, a quintessential Washington insider and the newly appointed secretary of state, considered the secessionist mood to be shallow, at least outside South Carolina. Seward thought that eventually, and quite soon perhaps, feelings of American patriotism in states like Alabama would reappear; the folks of the Deep South would remember their historical ties to America, and the economic advantages. On April 7, five days before the Confederacy opened fire on Fort Sumter, John Nicolay, the president's chief clerk, wrote his fiancée about "the excitement we have here now ... over the prospect of a war," but he remained confident. "I myself," he told her, "do not see the prospect in so gloomy a light. That there may be a little brush at Charleston or Pensacola is quite possible, but that any general hostilities will result from it I have not the least fear."[7]

Late in March, a few weeks into Lincoln's presidency, the president made his decision about Fort Sumter: he would stand tough; he would send its garrison supplies and food. An ex-naval officer named Gustavus Vasa Fox volunteered to lead a small fleet of ships (mostly hired commercial vessels) to Charleston Harbor. If South Carolina's authorities permitted, Fox would take the provisions into the harbor and drop them off at the fort. If a problem erupted Fox had on his ships a

couple of hundred soldiers (actually, raw and untrained recruits). In a crisis, Fox told Lincoln, those soldiers could reinforce Anderson's tired band.

With Lincoln's instructions in hand, Fox went to New
York to piece together his little armada. He hoped for secrecy,
but his optimism was foolish. Watchful men saw that something was going on at New York's docks, as hundreds of
barrels and boxes were being muscled aboard boats, and
newspapers reported this activity.

The government was obviously planning a military move.
But to where? Pundits opined that Lincoln was sending an expedition to Charleston; or maybe to Pensacola, Florida, where
another small federal fortification, Fort Pickens, also faced
Confederate forces; or to New Orleans; or to the open coastline of Texas. Some even theorized that Fox's fleet would be
moving against Cuba or Mexico. Such rumors found their way
into Southern newspapers. The governor of Louisiana wor-
riedly wired Confederate leaders about his concerns for New
Orleans: "Public mind here much disturbed at condition of this
place. Great fears of an attack."[8]

In fact, the Confederate leadership in Montgomery already
was aware that Fox's ships were heading to Charleston. They
knew because Lincoln told them. On April 6 Lincoln sent a
message to Francis Pickens, governor of South Carolina, saying that provisions were on their way to Major Anderson. The
federal government would not reinforce the garrison with
"men, arms, or ammunition" unless the delivery of the food
was interfered with. On April 8, when Pickens read this note,
he showed it to Brigadier General Pierre Gustave Toutant
Beauregard, sent by the Confederate authorities at Montgomery to supervise military operations in Charleston. Beauregard wired Jefferson Davis. Davis discussed the matter with
his cabinet, then ordered Beauregard to demand the fort's surrender, immediately. If Major Anderson refused, Davis said,
Beauregard was to "take" it.

———

Due mostly to nasty weather, Fox's first ships did not arrive outside Charleston Harbor until just before dawn on April 12. From that position they saw the Confederate guns open fire on Fort Sumter.[9]

President Lincoln had been spending the last few days trying to display an aura of tranquility, even insouciance. One day he unexpectedly dropped in on his wife's usual afternoon social gathering. He stayed to listen to a singer, and he chatted with guests, apparently quite calm. Underneath that veneer Lincoln was restive. He had recently had a private meeting with a Virginian, John B. Baldwin. Lincoln quietly escorted Baldwin to an unused bedroom where the two could talk privately, and locked the door to keep intruders out. According to later testimony the Virginian specifically told Lincoln that if the president tried anything with Fort Sumter, Virginia would secede. Lincoln recognized that if that happened, Washington would be in grave danger.

Perhaps he was thinking about this four days later, on April 8, when he dashed off a quick note to the governor of Pennsylvania: "I think the necessity of being *ready* increases. Look to it." On April 10 someone down in Charleston wrote the *Richmond Enquirer*: "The issue here is now certain. There will be an evacuation of Fort Sumter or a fight." That anonymous correspondent added: "The ball will probably open tonight." The following day a person in Washington wrote the same Virginia newspaper: "No one now doubts that the ball will open as soon the United States fleet attempts to enter the harbor of Charleston. All may look out for bloody work."[10]

On April 12 Beauregard wired Montgomery. "We opened fire at 4:30 A.M." The next day, Saturday, April 13, the news was becoming common knowledge. The *Baltimore Sun*, an afternoon paper, provided its readers extensive details about the assault. At one-thirty that afternoon, Governor Pickens wired Montgomery: "Sumter has raised the white flag."[11]

Washington, Sunday, April 14, 1861

It is not clear when Abraham Lincoln learned about the surrender of the fort—whether Saturday afternoon or evening.
His first reaction to the news also remains a mystery. But the
next morning, Sunday, he held an emergency cabinet meeting,
in which he and his chief advisers discussed the options.

Attorney General Edward Bates suggested an interesting
notion: instead of rushing into war, they could show the administration's seriousness of purpose by interrupting all mail to
the Confederacy and blockading ports in the Deep South, as
well as all traffic down the Mississippi River. The other men
in the room, including Lincoln, refused to accept Bates's cautious proposal.[12]

The Constitution specifies that only Congress can declare
war, but Congress was not in session, and could not assemble
quickly. Among other things, a national election would have
to determine every House seat and a third of the Senate's, and
this process would take time. One thing was clear: Lincoln
could legally act immediately, without waiting for congressional approval. A law passed in 1795, when George Washington was still in office, allowed a president to call on state
militias during crises. Traditionally militiamen were defined as
"state troops for state purposes"—that is, each governor retained personal jurisdiction over his own militia, and could
choose its officers, and direct its activities. But in a national
emergency the federal government could request military
assistance and the governors could lend their militia to
Washington.

Certain questions lingered. How many men should Lincoln request? Some in the room argued for 50,000, others for
100,000. Most of the cabinet assumed they might soon be asking for far more, but apparently they were concerned about
the uncertainty of public opinion, so they decided, after a brief
discussion, to compromise on 75,000. It turned out to be a
serious miscalculation, a number far too small, but these
decision-makers were still stumbling in the fog.

How many volunteers should each state provide? For that matter, which states? It would be fruitless to ask Francis Pickens or the governors of the Confederate states, but how about the eight other slave states? Would excluding those eight not suggest that the secessionists were correct about America being two "nations"? Yet, if Lincoln asked the border states for militiamen, their governors would inquire if the volunteers would be used to coerce the Confederacy.

And the president would need to specify how long he expected the militiamen to serve. After all, these men were really only civilians. They would be leaving their homes, their families, and, presumably, their jobs. Their lives would be disrupted. They had a right to know how long their service might last.

A more impenetrable question involved the cabinet's decision about Congress. On the day Lincoln took his oath of office, March 4, the House of Representatives, which had been in session since the previous December, followed tradition and adjourned. (The Senate continued to sit a few weeks, to "advise and consent" with the new president on his official appointments, but once that constitutional task was performed, they too adjourned.) Unless something untoward occurred, Congress was not slated to meet again until December. The administration had the playing field to itself. Except for a few pesky reporters and some lingering politicians (along with an endless queue of job-seekers), Lincoln and his advisers could contemplate what to do about Fort Sumter and such issues without having to waste time with explanations.

Constitutionally, a president may call Congress into session when "extraordinary circumstances" demanded it. This moment certainly qualified. Several factors seemed to make it imperative for him to call on the nation's representatives. Two of the enumerated powers of Congress were "to raise and support Armies" and "to provide and maintain a Navy." Another clause stated that Congress is supposed to: "provide for organizing, arming, and disciplining the Militia." Lincoln could have ordered Congress to come to Washington immediately, perhaps before May 1. Instead, his proclamation specified that Congress would not assemble until July 4, more than two months later. One might ask why he chose that date—other than the day's obviously neat symmetry, its patriotic implication. William Seward's son Frederick, in his biography of his father (based on personal observations as well as official documents), gives us a hint. "Congress," Frederick Seward writes, "would be loyal; but it would be a deliberative body; and to wait for 'many men with many minds' to shape a war policy in the debates of an extra session, would be to invite disaster." In other words, Lincoln and his cabinet purposely agreed on a relatively distant meeting time.[13]

(Other presidents have found it convenient to act without Congress looking over their shoulders. In 1950, for example, Harry S Truman, having just ordered his army into a Korean civil war without asking Congress's permission, was chatting with a dozen or so reporters. One newsman had just heard a senator say on the floor of the Senate that this step was a "police action," and therefore did not require a full congressional declaration of war. The reporter asked Truman if he himself would characterize these events this way, and Truman happily grasped the convenient phrase: "Yes, that is exactly what it amounts to."[14])

Amazingly, given the importance of these matters, our knowledge about that Sunday morning's cabinet session remains sketchy. No one there apparently kept notes. It seems likely Lincoln arrived with a draft of a proclamation and used this meeting to ask for reactions. He had been thinking about this subject for months. In the past few days he and the cabinet had discussed the federal laws allowing him to call up the state militias. We know that Lincoln personally wrote the proclamation, because John Nicolay carefully copied it, finishing this task sometime on Sunday between noon and two o'clock.

As finally written, the proclamation stated that given the crisis wrought by recent events, the president hereby summoned Congress into session, to assemble on the Fourth of July. The proclamation announced that seven states, separately and in combination, had been obstructing the laws of the United States, mentioning each by name: South Carolina, Georgia, Alabama, Florida, Mississippi, Louisiana, and Texas. Lincoln said he wanted 75,000 volunteers, men who could expect to serve for a period of only up to three months. The War Department, he said, would soon inform each governor of the precise number of militiamen called up.

The proclamation stated that the first task of the volunteers would be "to repossess the forts, places, and property which have been seized from the Union." Under the circumstances, this phrase certainly implied Fort Sumter, along with scores of other federal properties. Lincoln then mentioned another assignment: He declared that the volunteers would *suppress* the secessionist states. President Lincoln had an extraordinary feel for language. "Suppression" is a powerful word. In Memphis and Raleigh and Richmond, this would certainly mean "coercion" by a different name.

Lincoln knew the situation required soldiers, but he wistfully hoped the war might be limited, in scope and duration. He believed that in their hearts most Southerners remained loyal to America. His proclamation, therefore, asked people inside the Confederacy "to disperse and retire peaceably to their respective abodes." Did he really expect they might do so? It seemed unlikely a single Confederate state, having come so far, would change its mind. What did Lincoln assume would be the result of his proclamation in the other eight slave states? It is not clear.

Three days earlier, on April 11, only hours before the assault began on Fort Sumter, he had met with Governor Thomas Hicks of Maryland, a slave state, and assured the governor his administration had no intention of provoking the South. Then, on April 13, Lincoln met with three commissioners from Virginia, at a time when they probably did not yet know about the fighting in Charleston Harbor. They asked him what his intentions were in reference to the Confederacy. He reminded them that in his inaugural address he had promised to "hold" federal property and to collect taxes, but beyond that, he said, he had no intent to use undue force. Perhaps he was being disingenuous. Or maybe he changed his mind that very night, because his proclamation was certainly going to provoke many Southerners.[15]

What about Northern Democrats? Might they not think that Fort Sumter — and even secession — was Lincoln's fault, an unpleasant problem that Republicans ought to handle? George Ashmun of Massachusetts had much in common with Lincoln. Both were lawyers who had had lucrative practices representing railroads and other businesses. Each was an intuitive politician. Both had been Whigs who became Republicans. They had served together in the House (during Lincoln's only prior time in Washington), and both had opposed President James K. Polk's war against Mexico. In 1860 Ashmun had chaired the Republican National Convention in Chicago, which had nominated Lincoln. Ashmun, at fifty-seven, was only five years older than Lincoln. The two were not close friends, but Lincoln was fond of the Massachusetts lawyer, and this warmth was reciprocated.

Sunday afternoon, April 14, Ashmun went to the White House to visit the president. Although the chronology of Lincoln's activities that day is a bit murky, it seems likely the president had just left the cabinet meeting. He and Ashmun discussed the direction of events. The Massachusetts man was pleased to learn Lincoln agreed with him that the war, just beginning, must not appear like a Republican war or an abolitionist crusade — which it was already being called throughout the South. Both men thought the administration must reach out to Democrats.

Ashmun departed and went across town to the home of Stephen Douglas, Lincoln's chief opponent in the recent presidential race. Ashmun had known the Little Giant for years, since their time together in Congress in the 1840s. Douglas still felt thankful for Ashmun's support back in 1850, when the Massachusetts congressman had helped push a bill through the House to develop the Illinois Central Railroad, a project close to Douglas's heart (and his career and pocketbook). Now Ashmun hoped to use their old friendship to persuade the Democratic senator to confer with Lincoln about this crisis. But when Ashmun broached the idea to Douglas, the senator was not receptive. In addition to their years of bitter rivalry back in Illinois, Douglas felt stung by some of Lincoln's recent appointments. Ashmun emphasized that the president would welcome a conversation. (This comment suggests that Lincoln had initiated Ashmun's visit.) Douglas remained somewhat resistant. Then Mrs. Douglas intervened.

Adele Cutts Douglas was lovely, clever, warm, and accomplished. She was the senator's second wife. He had been a widower three years when he asked the young woman to marry him. He was twenty-two years older than she, and lately he had grown a bit slovenly, even seedy; he drank far too much. He did have fame and a pile of money, while she had neither, but her marital prospects within the elite society of Washington where she lived were excellent, so she must have seen something appealing in the squatty little man. She accepted his proposal. They had now been married four years; both seemed genuinely happy. Douglas had cleaned up his person, and his act.

He was still a powerful speaker and widely admired, at least in Northern Democratic circles. In a few days he would turn forty-eight, certainly young enough to contemplate running again for the White House. He was a fervent patriot; no one could doubt that. His ego, his ambitions, and his patriotism were in conflict. He had been talking with Ashmun about what he ought to do for an hour when Adele Douglas came in, listened for a while, then gently placed her hand on his shoulder and said he must go talk to the president. Her soft gesture of affection, along with her words, seem to persuade him.

It was eight o'clock and dark when Ashmun and Douglas arrived at the White House. Lincoln was pleased to see them. He handed the Little Giant a copy of the proclamation. Douglas read it, then said he considered it too feeble. Lincoln should be calling for more than 75,000 volunteers; he ought to be demanding 200,000. Douglas mentioned several other concerns he had, trouble spots the administration ought to keep in mind. He said he worried that Baltimore would be troublesome. If the railroads that served that city were cut, he said, this might prove disastrous. He had some specific suggestions.

Lincoln listened. Without Douglas in the pit with him, Lincoln's cause could be precarious. Douglas was the leader of the Democratic Party and had been a successful politician a long time. He had hundreds, perhaps thousands, of personal contacts, individuals who would tell him privately about the mood in precincts throughout the country.

At the end of their two-hour conversation Douglas promised his old adversary he would give the coming war his whole-hearted support. This was an important moment in American history. In a twinkling, Stephen Douglas had turned what was being called "Lincoln's War" into a national crusade. At this moment across America, other Democrats were coming to the same conclusion, but Douglas's public support probably made an enormous difference.

He was not just another politician. He was fiery and passionate. He now devoted himself to persuading his fellow Democrats to embrace the war as he had. During the next few weeks he rushed about, giving countless forceful speeches. He said those who opposed the war were clearly traitors (a word Lincoln hesitated to use). Douglas declared they should all be hanged. He wore himself to the nub. Then beyond. By early summer he was dead. He was a man of remarkable strengths and astonishing blind spots. Yet at this moment in his country's history, he served her well.[16]

Stephen Douglas was not the only politician to offer Lincoln support on that Sunday. The governor of Minnesota, Alexander Ramsey, happened to be in Washington. Early that morning, contemplating the breaking news about Fort Sumter, he rushed from his hotel to see Secretary of War Simon Cameron. Ramsey wished to volunteer the services of his state's militia right now. He caught Cameron as the secretary was leaving for that morning's crucial cabinet meeting. Cameron told him to put the offer in writing, which Ramsey immediately sat down and did. As a result Minnesota became the first state to volunteer its soldiers. The secretary of war thanked him and hurried off to the White House, Ramsey's promise in hand.

Other Northern governors would also be generally prompt and positive in their responses. Massachusetts, Rhode Island, New York, Ohio, and others would be eager to send troops.

The reaction in the border states was different. The governors of North Carolina and Kentucky both described Cameron's request for militiamen as "wicked." Tennessee's governor said the use of the troops would be unacceptable coercion. The response of the governor of Missouri, Claiborne F. Jackson, was more imaginative, or at least wordier. He called the administration's requisition "illegal, unconstitutional, and revolutionary in its object, inhuman and diabolical." Whether these politicians spoke for the majority of their constituents was not yet certain. But ominous signs were visible in most of the border states during those days. St. Louis, Missouri, was representative. A portion of that city's population remained loyal to the Union, but others in town agreed with Governor Claiborne Jackson. The city roiled in turmoil. The United States Army maintained an arsenal in town. If an enemy force pushed artillery to the heights above the city, the arsenal was likely to fall, and perhaps the entire state.[17]

CHAPTER TWO

The Firebrand

They may ring their bells now,
but they will soon be wringing their hands.
—ROBERT WALPOLE, 1739

Richmond, 122 miles from Washington, was a Southern hub. Although its population of 38,000 was far smaller than Charleston's and only a quarter that of New Orleans, its economic muscle gave it clout. It was a commercial center, sited at the fall line of the James River. Oceangoing steamers arrived at its wharves to pick up coal and ore brought from the interior. Its warehouses were stocked with pork and wheat and timber that had typically arrived on one of five railroads serving the city. Richmond was a manufacturing center, home to seven flour mills and the Tredegar Iron Works, which ran the largest rolling mill south of Pennsylvania, employing 900 workers.

As Virginia's capital, the city was accustomed to hordes of seasonal visitors. Many restaurants and hotels lined its streets, including the rather posh Spotswood, which opened its doors in late March 1861. Richmond's newspapers boasted of the capitol building, inspired by Thomas Jefferson, and of the broad avenues, lined with spreading linden trees. Wealthy citizens had erected fine brick homes near the tops of Richmond's eight hills (though local boosters claimed only seven hills, making her comparable to imperial Rome). A majority of the local poor found themselves crammed into sections near the river, with nicknames like Shed Town and Penitentiary Bottom. Foreign immigrants coagulated here — Irishmen and Germans, mostly — in all, numbering almost a third of the population.

A large portion of Richmond's laborers worked in the tobacco-processing industry, the original source of the town's prosperity. The city and its environs were home to fifty-two tobacco manufacturers, plus countless tobacco warehouses. Yet its biggest business — in terms of dollar volume — was the slave trade.

Slavery and race permeated Richmond's social and legal fabric. As with Washington, one cannot understand this town in 1861 until one grasps the importance of race and racism. Around the corner from the capitol building were a dozen slave dealers; another eight or ten had auction blocks a bit farther out. Advertisements in newspapers announced special bargains: assorted packages of men, women, and children. When an owner died, his or her estate was often purchased by interested buyers. The following notice appeared in a Richmond newspaper on Tuesday, April 16: "Trustees' Sale of valuable real estate, slaves, and household furniture." The announcement specified that the auction would include a three-story brick house, a piano, "and two Negro women slaves, Mima and Fanny, and the two infant children of the said Fanny, George and Ellick, and the future increase of such slaves."

Almost forty percent of Richmond's population was African American. Several thousand were free blacks, but most — almost a third of the city's people — were slaves. Richmond's free blacks worked as barbers and servants at the hotels; they acted as important cogs in the building trades: plasterers, carpenters, bricklayers; and they toiled in factories. Slaves ran the occupational gamut. The city government owned a number, employing them as janitors and firemen. The Tredegar Iron Works had many. Slaves also worked at the wharves, hoisting tobacco kegs onto waiting steamers; they pulled oysters from the James River; they were draymen, house slaves, and watermelon vendors along the main avenues. The following newspaper ads were typical: "A likely girl, about 14 years of age, accustomed to waiting in the house and nursing children"; "A servant boy, about 17 years old, raised on a farm, but with two years' experience in a tobacco factory"; "A smart mulatto boy, who is very handy in the dining room."

Richmond's legal code was firm about African Americans' behavior. Blacks were not permitted to smoke on city streets. Unless infirm or elderly, they were not allowed to carry canes after dark. The city prohibited gatherings of five or more African Americans, except at church services. Free blacks were required to carry passes in the evening. There were even ordinances banning behavior that seemed "uppity," like the use of "insolent" language. African Americans convicted of most infractions were punished in one of two ways. Either they were whipped, and thirty-nine lashes was normal; or they were sentenced to labor for one of the city's firms — generally performing construction work, like digging ditches or improving railroads, as part of a chain gang.

Over the years, such laws were actually enforced only sporadically. As in many Southern towns, during normal times there seemed little reason to waste police and court hours on insignificant matters. In 1861, with tensions wrought by secession and war, whites preferred thinking their slaves were happy and loyal, and newspapers gleefully carried tales of free blacks donating money to The Cause, or offering to serve the Confederacy's fighting men. A Richmond newspaper described the enthusiasm of a hundred Petersburg, Virginia free blacks, who volunteered to travel to Norfolk, carrying with them a Confederate flag, to build fortifications to defend that city from Yankees. According to the article, their black spokesman thanked the white ladies who sewed them the banner, saying he would personally like to plant it inside Fort Monroe. He also said, the newspaper claimed, that his hundred workmen were glad to perform the arduous labor "that is more suitable to our hands" than the more delicate hands of "white gentlemen." The article described how the hundred free blacks plodded to Petersburg's docks to the strains of "Dixie," and were cheered by "an immense crowd of darkeys."

Stories like this were common in 1861, but doubt lingered in the minds of many whites as to how blacks would really act in these uncertain times. Policing of Richmond's African American activity grew more vigilant. A listing of decisions of the mayor's court included these:

> Jack, slave of John D. Quarles, whipped for running his cart against that of James Britwell, and giving the aforesaid Britwell a specimen of vulgar lingo, when remonstrated with.
>
> Jim Murphy, colored, from Fredericksburg, no papers, whipped.
>
> John, slave of Henry Curtis, was whipped for having no pass and acting suspiciously.
>
> Nathan Willis, a free negro was sent to jail yesterday by the Mayor, in default of surety for his good behavior. Nathan had been induced to disport himself in an unseemly manner by reason of imbibing too much of the ardent. His "papers" were also ancient, and clearly demonstrated him to be an inconsiderate nigger.

Racism crouched, like a feral beast, at the heart of much of this. In July at least three white women would be jailed for "associating with negroes." In April the *Richmond Dispatch*, perhaps the city's most moderate newspaper, described a "most distressing calamity" that had occurred in Petersburg. During a sudden squall, four "very valuable negroes," fishing in the river, drowned. "The loss to each of their owners," said the *Dispatch*, "will be quite heavy."[18]

Richmond's population, and the resulting social mix, made it more volatile than it seemed on the surface. Its position in the heart of Virginia's Tidewater might have suggested it was as "Southern" as Milledgeville, Georgia. But it had far more dealings with the outside world, and with the North, than almost all other Southern cities. The recent tide of immigrants added an uncertain new element. John Brown's raid into Harpers Ferry, Virginia, made Richmond's leaders edgier. Into this tinderbox stepped ex-governor Wise, a man who could induce strong reactions.

Elizabeth Lomax was fond of Henry A. Wise. She had known him for years and considered him a charming old friend. One day in 1857, while he was still governor of Virginia, he dropped by her home in Washington. They chatted about her application to the War Department for monies because of her father's military service during the American Revolution. Wise was a handsome man with a high forehead and a slender, chiseled face. A few years younger than she, Wise had a mane that was only slightly gray, and his jaw was clean shaved. Flirtatiously he suggested she ought to give her request to the War Department personally because she had "the most lovely gray eyes with the longest lashes," and, he said, "when you look up at a man he is almost sure to grant any request." She giggled at the compliment but followed his suggestion—which succeeded— thus reinforcing her affection for Governor Wise.

Henry Wise might orate for hours on almost any topic— whether he grasped the subject or not. And he could be a spell- binder. Audiences were entranced by his theatrics, though after he sat down they often found it difficult to remember exactly what he had said or thought about a matter. This pro- lix tendency, noticeable for years, had grown pronounced by early 1859, during Wise's last year in the governor's office.

Fire-eaters like Edmund Ruffin disdained the Union and were unsympathetic with Henry Wise's cherished dream to be elected in 1860 to the presidency of the United States. Like Elizabeth Lomax, Ruffin was well acquainted with Mr. Wise. Ruffin, a highly respected Virginia agronomist and one of the South's most avid secessionists, had known him for years, and loathed him. Ruffin considered Wise an eccentric buffoon, a pompous windbag, and an ambitious weasel. Ruffin believed Wise's only emotional rudder was his frenzied scramble for fame and position. Ruffin thought Wise's most unforgivable trait was his tendency to waffle on whether Virginia's loyalty was to the South or to the Union.

Though Wise had made sure Brown was hanged for his crimes, Ruffin was outraged to read that the governor actually expressed admiration for Brown's courage. In Edmund Ruffin's eyes, finding anything admirable about the reprehensible Brown was heresy. Besides, thought Ruffin, the governor's presidential ambitions made his loyalty to the South dubious.[19]

In truth, both Ruffin and Elizabeth Lomax read Henry Wise accurately. The man could be charming. He had charisma, but was vain as a peacock, and erratic (or perhaps mentally flexible). In his younger days he had been thin-skinned, engaging in two duels and serving as a second in others. Elected to the United States House of Representatives at the age of twenty-six, he had retained that seat for eleven years. When appointed minister to France, the Senate refused to confirm him, though they later confirmed his appointment as minister to Brazil.

In early 1861 Henry Wise was only fifty-four, but looked older—tired and a bit grizzled. He had lived much of his life in Accomack County, perhaps the most isolated part of Virginia, thirty miles across the Chesapeake Bay on the Delmarva Peninsula. He now maintained a home not far from Norfolk. His third wife, Mary, resided there much of the year. She was quite ill, and he worried about her.

During the turbulent 1850s Wise tried to straddle most issues. He seemed mellower. The collapse of his presidential dreams in early 1860 left him unusually reticent. Then, in October of that year, when it became obvious Lincoln would be elected, Wise's behavior grew especially aberrant. The success of the Black Republicans, he said, "breaks the charm of my life. I am for Revolution—in earnest, to blood and fire." These words sounded fierce, but a few days later saw him backtracking. He declared himself still in favor of the Union. Yet shortly after that he reversed himself again. His mind grew more capricious. He proposed that groups of Virginia

Minute Men ought to be created. He did not clarify what they might actually do, nor how these bands would differ from the state's militia.

Three things about Wise's thinking remained fairly clear. First, he loathed John Letcher, his successor in the governor's chair. He considered Letcher not-quite-a-gentleman, and distrusted his stewardship during this crisis. Second, he felt contempt for Lincoln and the entire Republican leadership. He made the serious mistake of misjudging them, believing them — especially Lincoln — to be weak and timid. He thought they could be bullied or simply ignored. Third, during the winter months of 1860–1861 Wise started to contemplate the future. He and men like himself ought to consider methods that would give Virginia hegemony over America, if that was still possible, or at least over the South. At first Wise was unenthusiastic about the idea of a special state convention to discuss the subject of secession. But he finally accepted the notion, and in February 1861, when Virginia created such a body, he was chosen as one of its delegates.[20]

During the previous few decades political thinkers, especially in the South, had polished a method by which a state might consider secession. Voters would elect representatives to a special convention that would weigh the options. This body might simply vote to remain in the Union, or it might vote to secede immediately (as South Carolina's would do). If the convention decided the situation was too fluid to take immediate strong action, it could call a temporary recess and await developments. If Lincoln's administration did nothing unacceptable, the convention need take no action at all. On the other hand, if the convention concluded the situation warranted action, it could pass a tentative secession resolution, which would not be officially binding unless it was accepted by the voters in a referendum (as Texas's convention did). But there was another, more subtle choice, and this seems to have been Wise's original plan — his, and others'. A convention could propose a series of conditions — demands, if you will — which had to be met by the federal government for the state to remain in the Union. These proposals could carry great weight if other states joined the chorus — if the demands got the support of sister border states; if Maryland, especially, joined Virginia, since these two states bracketed the federal capital. Recently there had been much editorial chatter in influential newspapers like the *Baltimore Sun* and the *Richmond Dispatch* about the two states working together. Acting as a team, they could force the new administration to listen to reason.

The idea of a state convention had its appeal but seemed abstract and uncertain. Henry Wise juggled other options, far more dramatic options. He kept thinking about the fact that the federal government maintained three critical military installations in Virginia. Each was vulnerable.

One was Fort Monroe, more than a hundred miles southeast of Richmond. Like Fort Sumter, this fortification sat on a small island just off the coast, but it would be a harder nut to crack than Sumter. By itself Fort Monroe was potentially an important military bastion, but its very isolation kept it from being a vital focal point — at least immediately. Its garrison of a few hundred men was significantly larger than Robert Anderson's had been. Unlike Sumter, it could not be easily surrounded by guns and cut off from reinforcements, though a large body of bold men, slipping secretly up to it at night with ladders, might be able to grab it. In December 1860 Wise apparently met with other Virginians to discuss a foray against the place to snatch it.

Not far from Fort Monroe was a greater prize. Up the James River stood a fine naval base: the Gosport Navy Yard. (Henry Wise was particularly well acquainted with it, since his home sat near it.) Gosport, along with its storage buildings, held thousands of cannon as well as a bunch of naval vessels. If it and its contents could be seized, the results would be significant. Its artillery could be sent throughout the South to defend the coastline. Its ships could sail out the James and be used to block, like a cork, the mouth of Chesapeake Bay. Since Baltimore depended on sea trade, controlling access to the Atlantic could make Maryland's merchants amenable. If the entire Chesapeake came under Southern control, the rivers flowing into it could be controlled. Baltimore, sitting on the Patapsco River, would be vulnerable. And Washington, on the Potomac, could be bombarded.

Harpers Ferry was the home of the third federal military post within Virginia. Here was one of America's two major arsenals, with enough small arms on hand to supply a good-sized army, machinery to produce more, and with only about two score federal soldiers guarding it. If it could be captured in a surprise attack, several results could follow. Thousands of presently unarmed Virginians would immediately have guns. Overnight, these men would have turned into an army. Since the Baltimore & Ohio Railroad went through the town of Harpers Ferry, these armed Virginia volunteers could halt passing trains, hop aboard, and start eastward. The B&O line linked Harpers Ferry to both Baltimore and Washington. The volunteers could appear in either city within two hours.

With Harpers Ferry in hand and Baltimore concerned about its economy, Maryland might join Virginia's dance steps. If Virginia and Maryland formed a military alliance, it would seem that the District must submit. With the federal capital under control, any of several outcomes was possible. The Northern states might bow to the inevitable, and Virginia could broker an agreement between North and South, as she had often done in the generations after 1775. Or, if the North refused to accept this arrangement, Virginia could simply take her rightful place as leader of the Confederate South. British recognition would then appear inevitable.

All this might come to pass rather quickly and easily if a man of vision and resolve — Henry Wise, for example — took command. He apparently considered all these factors in his own haphazard, ill-organized way. During the twelve months that followed April 1860, after his national political ambitions collapsed, he transmogrified himself from a unionist presidential candidate to a militant revolutionary. Yet why and exactly when this took place is uncertain. His beloved wife's physical decline may have agitated his psyche, or emotionally released him. Another possibility is that one of his sons radicalized him: Obadiah Jennings Wise.

Jennings Wise (as the young man was called by those who knew him) was born in April 1831. He could be a fiery person. In 1859, for example, while his father was governor, he participated in a duel. By 1860, as editor of the *Richmond Enquirer,* he had grown into a rabid secessionist. Around Christmas of that year, just after South Carolina's secession, he wrote wild-eyed editorials that urged his state to seize Harpers Ferry and Fort Monroe and the Gosport Navy Yard—even Washington itself. But Jennings Wise the editor was not another shrill, ink-stained theorist, urging war while remaining discretely behind his desk, removed from military activity. In January 1861 he volunteered for the Richmond Light Infantry Blues, an old and highly prestigious militia unit.

It is uncertain whether the senior Wise's political frustrations pushed Jennings to greater frenzy or whether the young man's youthful ardor convinced his father. But by February 1861 Henry Wise had become the state's most influential secessionist.

Meanwhile Governor John Letcher was pleading for a cautious approach. He hoped a national compromise could be reached, that Republicans in Washington might forget their platform promises of the previous year. In this stance Letcher was not being unduly timid, as opponents like Henry Wise thought, but was reflecting the opinion of the majority of Virginia's voters. When the state convention opened in mid-February, at least two-thirds of its delegates were opposed to secession. Some, particularly those from the western counties of the state (where lived relatively few slaves), supported the Union without qualification. Most convention delegates, however, were conditional unionists — that is, they felt reservations about the Union, but if demands were met, would accept its continuation. Their lukewarm support of the Union was ominous. It meant they remained open to the concept of secession.

When the convention started holding sessions in February, the state legislature ceased meeting and turned over its chambers in the state capitol to the incoming delegates. From a distance the capitol seemed picturesque, but an observer described it as "grimly dirty on close inspection." During the early sessions, although a majority of delegates opposed Virginia's secession, gradually the pro-Union sentiment saw some erosion. In late March a unionist in Martinsburg, Virginia wrote in his diary: "The tone of the Convention seems to be giving way.... Hired bullies and hired mobs," he said, "besiege the Convention in its sittings, and follow the Union members to their lodgings, threatening assassination and lynch law." It did not seem a good omen when, on April 9, the convention voted 128 to 20 to recognize the Confederacy as a legal entity separate from the United States, thereby officially sanctioning the idea of secession.

But feelings of loyalty to the Union still remained strong in most parts of Virginia. On April 6 the voters in Portsmouth, Virginia, next to Norfolk, held a mayoralty election, and the unionist candidate won handily. In Richmond, unionists held a rally. Next to the speaker's dais stood a large American flag. When several young men holding aloft a Confederate banner strode in, they were swarmed by angry unionists. The Confederate flag was wrested from them and ripped apart, and the intruders roughly shown the door.

The convention was drifting toward adjournment without taking definitive action. Its discussions had grown desultory. Speakers droned about the wording of rather meaningless amendments to the state constitution. A vote to secede was voted down overwhelmingly, eighty-eight to forty-five.

Henry Wise was worried. The convention's temper still seemed far too unionist to suit him. Several secessionists, including Wise, met secretly and decided the convention needed goosing. They issued a circular about an upcoming Spontaneous People's Convention in Richmond. (One might ask how such a carefully crafted body could be called spontaneous, but the authors of the circular seemed to retain no sense of irony.) The conspirators printed multiple copies of the circular—perhaps using Jennings Wise's press—and distributed them across the eastern portion of the state. "Your presence," it announced, "is particularly requested at Richmond on the 16th day of April, 1861, to consult with the friends of Southern rights." It added: "Please bring with you a full delegation of true and reliable men."[21]

This assemblage, slated to open its doors on April 16, was intended as a last-ditch gamble, a radical attempt to overawe the unionist delegates. Its organizers did not imagine that events elsewhere were coming to a head so quickly. Virginia's secessionists had heard rumors that Lincoln's administration would back down on Fort Sumter, and perhaps Fort Pickens. It seemed the crisis might pass.

During the days just before April 16, about 200 "true and reliable" militants trickled into Richmond and settled into rooms at the city's hotels. Their presence was a sign of the weakness of the secessionist cause in Virginia.

Then all of a sudden circumstances changed. Henry Wise saw an opportunity and seized it.

On April 10 and 11, as a crisis in Charleston became apparent, the *Richmond Dispatch* used phrases like "war preparations" and "Victory or Death!" Such bombast seemed empty rhetoric. It still appeared possible that conflict could be averted. On April 12—the day Fort Sumter came under attack—the *Dispatch*, a morning newspaper that went to press about midnight the night before, contained hysterical articles about the nastiness of Northerners in general, and the evils of moderation in Virginia. The city's other newspapers were in agreement; forbearance equalled "submissionism."

At ten o'clock on the morning of April 12, the convention in Richmond opened its fiftieth day's session. Outside the air was misty. It had been raining almost a week. At first only a few delegates were present; others trickled in. (The barrage against Fort Sumter had already been going on for hours, but in Richmond they did not yet know it.) The early arrivals listened to a representative from Norfolk, a unionist, say he had received a petition from his constituents to vote for secession, but after examining the list of names appended to this document, he realized they represented the same voters who had long insisted on secession, so he was not inclined to change his stance. The discussion moved to other things, mostly dull procedural matters dealing with a proposal for a regional meeting of border states. Henry Wise used the opportunity to denounce delegates from the western part of the state who felt any connections to citizens residing in free states like Ohio. A vote was taken on one of ex-governor Wise's proposals; it was voted down, seventy-four to fifty-three. The delegates discussed their approaching adjournment for the summer months. Then they recessed for the afternoon.

When the evening session opened, the delegates returned to their discussion about the date in October when they might meet again. Suddenly Henry Wise announced he had important dispatches in his hand. War, he said, had begun in Charleston. The minutes of the convention show: *"Sensation."*

Then, amazingly, the conventioneers returned to the question about when they would meet in October. Wise made some minor proposal, which was rejected. An abstract and boring debate followed. The members finally agreed to rise for the day. Wise apparently never did read aloud the dispatches he had from Charleston.

But word about Fort Sumter had now spread to the streets

of Richmond. The telegraph office received a jumble of messages. Men rushed to the bulletin boards of the city's newspapers. Those standing nearest yelled out the latest reports as each item was tacked up, so eager folks farther back could hear the news. The early reports were scrambled, frequently inaccurate, but terribly exciting. The next morning's *Dispatch* contained a potpourri of overheated stories. One involved a nonexistent abolitionist plot to burn down the city of Charlotte, North Carolina. Another declared that Lincoln's expedition to Charleston had included "6,000 well-drilled, regular fighting men," and that the good people of Charleston had been forced, "in self-defense, to attempt the reduction of that fort which so long has menaced their homes and firesides." An editorial shrieked: *Abolitionism Demands Blood*.

Saturday, April 13

Emotional throngs crowded Richmond's streets. The convention opened its session at ten o'clock. Wise stood and read a message from Governor Pickens of South Carolina, saying "The war is commenced, and we will triumph or perish," and asking Governor Letcher what Virginia would do. (Hours earlier, "Honest John" Letcher had telegraphed Pickens that Virginia's convention, not he, would decide.)

Again, after an initial hubbub, the convention returned to mundane business. Its somnambulant discussions rolled on. One delegate, unable to control his agitation another second, shouted out that under the circumstances the state ought to secede immediately. He was ignored.

During that afternoon Richmond grew palpably tense. Saloons became jammed. Mobs milled about. Men who had drifted into town to attend Monday's Spontaneous secessionist convention added to the stew. Early in the evening the city received a report that Major Anderson had surrendered. The convention, after its afternoon break, reopened. Emotions now reached a crescendo. One delegate said he wanted to applaud the cotton states on their victory; another announced that he, on the other hand, wanted to applaud the Star Spangled Banner. A lawyer from the western counties named Jubal Early declared he was saddened that the American flag had been shot at and was sorry his friend Robert Anderson had been forced to give up Fort Sumter. Other delegates snapped back, saying that Early should keep such opinions to himself. Again someone made a motion that Virginia ought to secede, but the convention's chairman said the delegate was out of order. And so they adjourned for the evening.

Governor Letcher was scheduled to confer with a few of the convention's unionist delegates that evening, but the men of that committee were too nervous to brave their way through the frenzied crowds, which included countless armed drunks who did not want to hear anything negative about secession. The governor cancelled that evening's conference.

Hysteria had overtaken Richmond. An impromptu band of buglers and drummers hit the streets. Someone found a Confederate flag and waved it around. Thousands joined a procession that tramped here and there. They swirled over to the huge Tredegar Iron Works, whose owner was a fervent secessionist, and whose smelting fires during the coming years would greatly aid The Cause. The workers within unfurled their own Confederate banner. Orators standing in front of the factory shouted out that Tredegar-manufactured guns had been the ones that shattered Fort Sumter's walls. This news made the mob scream in delight; they felt their own city had participated in the victory in Charleston Harbor. The procession happily moved on. They stopped at an armory. Men ran inside and dragged out some cannon belonging to the Lafayette Artillery, a local militia outfit. People pushed the guns to a grassy sector in front of the capitol building and used them to crash out a hundred-gun salute. Some of the crowd wandered over to Governor Letcher's nearby residence and shouted his name. Musicians played "Dixie" and that other stirring revolutionary anthem, "La Marseillaise." Letcher appeared at his doorway. He peered at the mob through his wire-rimmed glasses, obviously ill-tempered. He said he saw no need for this demonstration. Many in the crowd, disappointed at his lack of fervor, booed and hissed—but moved on. Meanwhile, back at the capitol, speakers full of spirit and spirits stirred their audience to greater and greater gasping excitement. Some men ran into the building, dashed up the stairs, and raised the Confederate flag over the roof. The celebration continued. Flags fluttered from house windows. Rockets whooshed into the air. Torchlights glinted against the leaves of trees lining the avenues. Barrels of tar burned on street corners, spewing black clouds into the night sky. (Later in the evening Letcher quietly ordered the Confederate banner flying above the capitol pulled down and replaced by the state flag.)

The next day, Sunday, was far quieter. The city seemed hungover from its emotions of the night before. It being the Sabbath, the convention did not meet.

Monday, April 15

Richmond churned anew. The morning's papers contained a report that Lincoln would, this very day, issue a proclamation calling for volunteers from "the several States of the Union" to "suppress" the seven states of the Deep South. Details, the report stated, would be forthcoming from the federal secretary of war. None of the convention's delegates publicly mentioned this development during their morning discussions. Many considered the report a hoax. Someone wired Seward, whose name officially appeared at the end of the alleged proclamation, and asked about its validity. Henry Wise offered no statement—though in private even he said, "I don't believe it." (Up to this moment Wise had considered Lincoln and the Republicans too spineless to take action. He thought Washington, when it came to the brink of war, would back down and allow the Confederacy to go its own way.) While the convention awaited further clarification, its members agreed to recess. During that afternoon, men in Richmond huddled in excited confabs. Everything seemed in flux and far too confusing. A planned torchlight procession for that evening was postponed.

Henry Wise held a parley in his room at the Exchange Hotel with his son Jennings and several others. They were concerned about how the convention, as a unit, would react. The majority of its delegates might be too cautious or frightened to take a stand. Action was what the group in this hotel room wanted. The give-and-take of their discussion is now lost, but almost certainly they agreed on a coup, something bold. One of them sent a telegram to a hotheaded activist in one of Virginia's western counties, telling him to head immediately to Richmond. As soon as he arrived he was to come to the Exchange to confer with Mr. Wise. The recipient of this wire was a man named Imboden.

Thirty-eight years old, John Daniel Imboden was from the Staunton region of the Shenandoah Valley (called in Virginia, simply, "the Valley"). Henry Wise knew Imboden and respected his grit. This admiration was reciprocated. Two months earlier Imboden had written a friend: "Gov. Wise is the only real living embodiment of the true spirit which should animate Virginia at this time." When Imboden received the wire from Richmond, he left before nightfall. He was about to prove himself as doughty a fighter as Wise was a revolutionary.

Tuesday, April 16

Richmond's morning newspapers carried the report that Lincoln's administration was telling Virginia to send three regiments (2,340 men) to participate in the suppression of the Confederacy. Newsboys bellowed the news across the city's heart.

The *Examiner* said the report meant war against "the South." An editorial in the *Dispatch* frothed: "John Brown himself did not hate the South with a more deadly hatred" than Abraham Lincoln. "The purpose of these men," the *Dispatch* yowled, "is wholesale murder and massacre; we are to be invaded with fire and sword; the horrors of servile war, if possible, are to be added to those of civil war; our fields are to be laid waste, our houses destroyed, and if we resist, we are to be shot down or hung as rebels or traitors." As far as this newspaper was concerned, there *must* be no more argument, no more discussion. Henceforth anyone objecting to secession was guilty of treason. (When the topic was broached with Letcher, the governor mildly said he had not yet officially received Secretary Cameron's official message. Later in the day, after he did get it, he replied to Washington. He refused to send his state's militia, he said, "for any such use or purpose." As an aside to Lincoln he added, "You have chosen to inaugurate civil war." He promised that Virginia would react...firmly.)

Such was the mood in the city when Imboden arrived. On his way to the Exchange Hotel he encountered Henry Wise. The older man seemed tired — worn down by concerns about his wife's health and stressed by recent events — but glad to see him. Wise pointed out that Imboden, as captain of an artillery battery from Staunton, could prove extremely useful in the present crisis. He wanted the younger man to return home and gather together his battery company, then take them to Harpers Ferry. There, Wise said, he must capture the United States' arsenal. But it would take more than a few pieces of artillery to carry the arsenal, probably much more, so Wise also told Imboden to scour Richmond this afternoon and contact as many potential military leaders from the Valley as he could find. Wise said he wanted them in his hotel room at seven o'clock that evening. He was planning a war conference.

That night the Spontaneous convention opened its first session. A month earlier its organizers had fully expected they might have to apply force to get their way. They had been prepared to use soldiers, particularly Jennings Wise's militia unit, the Richmond Blues. If the Spontaneous conventioneers had decided that only dramatic action would benefit their cause, they felt prepared to arrest Letcher, even kidnap him. They were also ready to capture and hold unionist leaders of the state's regular convention. But now it turned out such revolutionary activities were unnecessary.

While the Spontaneous convention began its discussions, conspirators were holding a conclave in Wise's room at the Exchange. The men there agreed on the importance of the federal arsenal at Harpers Ferry. They recognized the critical factors: speed and timing. They knew the United States had a few soldiers guarding the place. It would be vitally important to reach the arsenal and capture it before its garrison could be reinforced, or alternatively, could destroy the facility. (It is not certain whether Wise revealed to the others in his room the full extent of his ambitions. Actually, he planned to use the thousands of muskets reportedly stored at the arsenal to arm militiamen, and he imagined them attacking Washington right away.)

For this coup to work, several elements needed to be in place — by the next afternoon at the latest. State militiamen must be involved — perhaps thousands of them. One of the plotters — perhaps Imboden — suggested the only way to guarantee success was to move quickly, and that meant trains. Messages were immediately dispatched to two railroad presidents living in Richmond. Sometime before midnight both businessmen arrived and agreed to collaborate. Their trains, they said, would be made available to rush Imboden and others toward the Valley. Tomorrow, more trains could be used to take Valley volunteers up toward Harpers Ferry.

But this left a problem. Officially, militiamen took orders from the governor — that is, John Letcher. Would Honest John agree? After all, his home was in the Valley. The members of the cabal might influence some militiamen, but maybe not enough. Letcher's support would greatly improve the chances of the coup's success. Even though it was already late at night, a committee of three — led by Imboden, a personal friend of the governor's — went to the gubernatorial mansion. They awakened him and laid out their plans. He rejected their request. He reiterated what he had said many times during the past two months: he would await the decision of the convention. If, or when, the convention passed an ordinance of secession, only then would he give the necessary orders.

The three-man committee returned to the Exchange, where they relayed the governor's irksome response. Henry Wise assured the cabal he would personally see to it that when the convention met the next morning (that is, in a few hours), it would vote immediately for secession. (Wise had gall; less than two weeks earlier the delegates had voted overwhelmingly against secession.)

The conspirators were still discussing their options when they received a wire that Washington had ordered a regiment of Massachusetts volunteers to go to Harpers Ferry. This message was inaccurate, but it spurred the energies of the men in the room. They frantically hammered out more details. They were now determined not to wait for Governor Letcher. Although Wise had no legal authority, he scribbled out some orders. With this slip of paper in hand, Imboden and several other men left to take the first steps toward what they hoped would be total success. They hurried to the city's armory and requisitioned guns and ammunition. The armory's sympathetic superintendent agreed. The Harpers Ferry assault was under way.

Henry Wise was not satisfied. At some point during the previous afternoon he had received a wire from Norfolk telling him that ships at the nearby United States naval base seemed to be preparing to move. He telegrammed Norfolk, saying those ships must be stopped. While the conspirators were meeting at the Exchange, men in Norfolk, led by William H. Parker, a state *inspector of vessels* (who had originally been appointed to that position by Wise) dragged three hulks into the river channel and sank them. This act was intended to accomplish two things: prevent reinforcements from getting into the navy yard and keep the ships already docked there from getting out — so they might soon be snared by the Virginians. If Henry Wise had his way, the Gosport Navy Yard was about to fall.

Even that did not end Wise's frenetic efforts. He also sent a message to South Carolina, pleading for soldiers. Governor Francis Pickens refused. He replied that he would not forward militiamen to Virginia since the request did not officially come from Letcher.

Wednesday, April 17

In the morning Henry Wise left his hotel and walked three blocks to the capitol. He was weary and emotionally drained. His tall, thin form looked more emaciated than usual. Lately his health had been shaky. In his haste to get to the convention as soon as it opened, to fulfill his promise to his fellow plotters, he did not take time with his appearance. His hair had a haystack look. Under his coat he carried a large horse pistol.

A few minutes after ten o'clock the convention began. It voted immediately to go into secret session. Henry Wise rose. He slammed his pistol onto the table, making sure it was in plain view. He glared about the room. An observer thought his very aura was electric — his hair springing from his head in all directions, his eyes mad with excitement. He announced that armed men were already hurtling toward Harpers Ferry. There would be blood flowing in the streets of that Virginia town this very night. And in Norfolk, he said, good Virginians were on their way toward the Gosport Navy Yard. The time for talk had passed. This was the moment for action. He was like a mad scientist in a grainy old movie, feverishly announcing he had created something... Stupendous.

The scene at the convention became chaotic. A delegate rushed to Wise and grabbed him by the hand, saying, as tears coursed down his cheeks, "I don't agree with you; I don't approve of your acts, but I love you, I love you." A few moments later, after some order was restored, the delegates voted on a reso- lution. It was eighty-eight for secession, fifty-five against. Governor Letcher was now free to order the militia to fight.

Henry Wise had kept his guarantee to his fellow conspir- ators. His gamble had worked. A single determined man had altered the history of his state—and his country. He had hardly operated single-handedly. If he had not acted, perhaps others might have done something similar. But they might not have succeeded as well, as efficiently.

It ought to be noted, however, that even his efforts—combined with the emotions bubbling up at this moment—changed the minds of but a fraction of the convention. Only about forty delegates altered their votes from the stand they had taken two weeks earlier. Less than 62 percent of the convention now voted for secession. Given the ferment, this is not a dazzling figure. It would be inaccurate to assert that all of Virginia was in favor of separating from the Union. Many of the fifty-five men who voted against the measure, mostly from the western counties, now returned to their homes, and within weeks that section seceded from the state of Virginia—thus West Virginia would be born. Also, according to the convention's ground rules, which had been agreed on weeks earlier, their vote to secede was not strictly valid. Officially a popular ref- erendum needed to confirm or deny the convention's resolu- tion. The electorate would get their say five weeks later, on May 23. And many things might happen during the interven- ing period.

Most people, however, chose to overlook this technicality. It seemed as though a mantle of legality now embraced the state's secession. Virginians who opposed it could even be por- trayed as outlaws and traitors. Elsewhere in the South, when the news of the convention's vote was announced, secessionists became ecstatic. Up to this moment only seven states had de- clared themselves separated from the Union, all from the Deep

South. In fact, except for South Carolina and Georgia, the Confederacy was merely a dubious Gulf of Mexico republic.

The addition of Virginia changed the profile of secession in several ways. To most Southerners, Virginia was by far the most respected state. It had been the Mother of Presidents: Washington, Jefferson, Madison, Monroe, and Tyler. Its notions about liberty had formed the backbone of both the Constitution and the Bill of Rights. On a practical level, Virginia's railroads could prove vital to the whole South, Richmond's industries were vibrant, and the wealth of the state's citizenry would be a welcome addition to the Confederacy. Perhaps most importantly, its willingness to join the Deep South would certainly influence the rest of the border states, those slave states that had not yet seceded.

Given these facts and heady possibilities, it was not surprising that folks in the Deep South celebrated the news from Virginia. At the Confederate capital, Montgomery's whites held torchlight parades. They fired a welcoming hundred-gun salute. Gleeful politicians gave speeches. In Mobile, the news reports from Richmond were followed by "immense cheering and frantic demonstrations." Roger Pryor, a young and charismatic Virginia politician and newsman, heard the news as he was going through Augusta, Georgia, on his way to Montgomery. A few days earlier, just before Confederate artillery opened fire on Fort Sumter, he had excited a crowd in Charleston by offering them his personal assurance that Virginia, his home state, would join the Confederacy as soon as blood flowed in Charleston. Now, in Georgia, hearing about Virginia's secession vote, he stood before another crowd and announced his great pleasure.

On the evening of April 17 a tired but happy Henry Wise gave a speech to the Spontaneous People's Convention. Observers thought it one of his best orations. In time he would be named a Confederate brigadier general and would faithfully serve The Cause, when health permitted, until the end of the war.

After that he would practice law. In truth, however, neither his military career nor his later legal business was very distinguished. But on April 16 and 17, 1861, he had served his purpose well. The question would now be whether his plans to win the war, perhaps in the next few days, would succeed.[22]

CHAPTER THREE

Cliffhanger

Thomas Jefferson visited Virginia's interior when the land was still a wilderness. He was enthralled. One thing especially caught his eye: the place where the Shenandoah River joined the Potomac. He glanced at the imposing hills looming above the intersection and, according to local tradition, immediately sat on a log or stone and jotted these notes: "The passage of the Patowmac through the Blue ridge is perhaps one of the most stupendous scenes in nature." He stared at the onrushing Shenandoah and the Potomac and was moved to a kind of poetry. "In the moment of their junction they rush together against the mountain, rend it asunder, and pass off to sea."[23]

Not long afterward, this site was chosen to become a federal armory. The government, realizing that the roaring rivers could provide the power needed to turn steel into guns, made arrangements with Virginia and purchased a large block of land: 1,669.5 acres, two-and-one-half square miles.

The silent forests rang with the sound of axes. Men came to work, and many brought families. They built dams and canals. They dragged in forges, then rolling mills and complex hydraulic machinery. They hammered out warehouses and barracks and private houses.

Harpers Ferry—along with Springfield, Massachusetts—became one of America's two great arsenals. Its facilities not only manufactured guns, but served as a storage facility for weapons and hundreds of kegs of gunpowder. In the 1850s the army stored about 90,000 muskets here (something ex-governor Henry Wise was aware of).[24]

In 1861 the town had a population of about 3,000 — including around 300 African Americans. Many people worked at the armory, of course, but others were employed by the Baltimore & Ohio Railroad, which maintained a depot in town and whose tracks passed over the wide Potomac just beyond the village, across a handsome covered bridge almost 900 feet long. Other townsfolk maintained the canal that stretched southeast, paralleling the Potomac, allowing anyone wishing to move heavy produce by water to bypass the river's rocks and shallows. Also in Harpers Ferry were people who earned a living from the town's taverns and hotels, well-to-do businessmen to scullery maids.

All these individuals worked and lived inside a natural bowl, with high hills towering on all sides, casting shadows across their village. Even on sunny days the town retained the ambiance of a Grimm fairy tale.

Maryland was just across the Potomac, and the border of Pennsylvania, the Mason-Dixon Line, was less than twenty miles away. Harrisburg (Pennsylvania's capital), was closer to Harpers Ferry than Richmond. Generally, when townspeople wanted to travel to Richmond, they took a B&O train to Baltimore, caught a connecting steamboat, and arrived at Virginia's capital by water. This might seem a roundabout route, but most folks in Harpers Ferry felt more connected to the people of Baltimore, or even Harrisburg, than they did to the Tidewater elite of Richmond.

The northern Shenandoah Valley had been rumbling about secession for a year-and-a-half, since John Brown's raid into Harpers Ferry, during which several locals lost their lives. Had Brown's plans borne fruit, the guns at the arsenal might have armed some local slaves, then more slaves farther south. In the fevered Southern rhetoric of the past year, John Brown's goal had been a vast race war, with rapine and murder. After the raid, documents were discovered in Brown's hideout in Maryland linking the raiders to supporters in New York and Boston. Boston had long been considered throughout the South as the heart of abolitionism. Emotional wounds in the Valley remained raw.

In January 1861 the armory's superintendent, Alfred M. Barbour, sent Army headquarters in Washington a worried message: "I have reason to apprehend that some assault will be made." What made Barbour anxious? Whom did he fear? Was it local secessionists who concerned him or — in light of the fact that a few weeks later he participated in Henry Wise's hotel-room cabal — was it a raid by abolitionists? In any case army headquarters took Barbour's warning seriously, especially in light of the recent rash of Southern takeovers of federal properties. It sent reinforcements: sixty-eight troops from Carlisle Barracks, Pennsylvania, about sixty miles away.

The soldier now in command of the garrison, Major Henry J. Hunt, did not like what he observed. The main arsenal and warehouses were spread out and vulnerable. His handful of soldiers could hardly defend more than one or two buildings. An enemy with a few artillery pieces could position them on the hills looming above, and bombard the armory at will. He noticed that many townspeople were openly hostile to his men. Most of the armory's employees seemed loyal enough, but they were unlikely to fight hard to defend the place. The situation was, he decided, ugly. Soon after arriving at this conclusion, however, he was ordered elsewhere to deal with other, seemingly more pressing, tinderboxes. The arsenal's garrison was reduced by a third.

In command now was Lieutenant Roger Jones, thirty years old, who had spent most of his military career on the frontier in Texas and New Mexico, dealing with what the newspapers of that era called "Indian problems." A professional soldier and a rather good one, Lieutenant Jones was sturdily built. He had a high forehead and pale eyes, a good straight nose and a bushy beard. He looked robust and a bit wintry, and was. If it came to a fight, he would understand what could be done and what could not. Like Robert Anderson at Fort Sumter, Jones and his forty-five-man garrison were about to face an overwhelming attack force.

Wednesday, April 17

Railroads and a rapid message system worked in tandem. Telegraph poles and their wires paralleled every rail line in America. To avoid accidents along isolated single-track lines, which most railroads still relied on, it was important to wire ahead every train's precise departure time. A railroad engineer, knowing another train was coming toward him, could pull his cars onto a parallel siding at an appropriate time, wait for the other to pass, then start again. Telegraph lines offered railroads a second advantage. At a depot it was important to know when a train was due to arrive and what it was carrying: how many passengers, what sort of freight. A stationmaster needed such facts to use his crews most efficiently, knowing when to rest them and when they should get prepared for intensive, often strenuous activity.

Telegraph wires near or at depots were often used for other matters: stationmasters sometimes forwarded along news and rumors.

Henry Wise and his fellow conspirators, having spent the night formulating their plot to capture the Harpers Ferry armory, had wanted speed and secrecy. They got speed but not secrecy, and this fact changed everything. Hardly had their meeting broken up when word of their proposed coup spread. After Imboden left the hotel at first light, he sent at least one man back to officers of the Staunton artillery battery, to tell them to get themselves ready to move. Those nearly one hundred men lived in homes all across Augusta County. There was no way their scurrying activities could have remained secret. Friends and neighbors became keenly aware something exciting was afoot. The population of the Staunton region had been generally opposed to secession. Now many people demanded to know what was going on. Was it true, they asked, that Governor Letcher or the convention had declared secession? If so, why was this fact not public knowledge?

Meanwhile Imboden boarded a train in Richmond, heading for the Valley. People in Staunton knew of his approach and something of his mission. They were also aware his train would need to pause at depots along the way to take on additional water and wood. His primary stopping place would be the Gordonsville station, approximately halfway between Richmond and the Valley. Given the turmoil in Staunton as crowds on street corners shouted questions at one another, Imboden's brother George was urged to wire Gordonsville to ask his brother about the situation. George did so.

When Imboden's train reached Gordonsville, John A. Harman, who was also on the train, happened to read George Imboden's incoming wire. Harman, too, had participated in the all-night planning session in Wise's hotel room and was returning to his home in Staunton. With the telegram in his hand, he noted the time: noon. Aware that Wise had guaranteed the conspirators he would squeeze an immediate secession resolution from the convention, Harmon concluded by this time it must have been accomplished and he calculated Governor Letcher would have, by now, announced that fact. Without consulting Imboden, Harman decided to answer the question, using Imboden's name. As a result, by lunchtime much of the population of Staunton knew about secession and the proposed foray against Harpers Ferry. Given the telegraph system, in which individuals representing all shades of political opinion manned the keys, this information rapidly spread elsewhere—including northward to Lieutenant Jones, who was about to learn of the menace rattling toward him.

Imboden turned out not to be the primary actor in this phase of the drama. John Letcher had been reluctant about secession until this moment, but as soon as the convention passed its resolution, he took hold of the reins. He sent telegrams and messengers westward, ordering militiamen to move on Harpers Ferry. The fact that he was from the Valley was probably important. Given the built-in suspicions western Virginians had about their Tidewater counterparts, if an easterner like Henry Wise had been in office, a gubernatorial call for volunteers might not have been greeted as positively.

Letcher's messages caused waves of excitement. For example, fifty miles from Richmond was the tiny hamlet of Louisa Courthouse. That afternoon, the governor's proclamation arrived there. The Louisa Blues, the town's tiny militia company, was told to assemble and head toward Harpers Ferry. They lacked proper uniforms and enough weapons, but in a few hours almost all of them were waiting at the little railroad depot where, they were told, a train would pick them up. A minister intoned over their bowed heads a prayer to the God of Battles. Women waved damp hankies. Older friends and relatives wished them luck. The train arrived, and off they sped.

Scenes like this were being duplicated across Virginia. In Charlottesville, home of the state's largest college, two companies of infantrymen gathered and departed as their families waved good-bye. In Staunton, militia leaders told a throng clustered at the station that their boys would "do or die." A great cheer arose. Tears were shed as the train drew away.

Few, if anyone, seemed to realize they were really going off to war—certainly not the Civil War that was approaching. They thought this a crisis, not a war. To them, this incident would only be of short duration, something they would handle briskly and cleanly, that would bathe them in glory so that friends and family would envy them when they swaggered home.

The attack on Fort Sumter several days earlier, like a strong wind, had begun to whip up emotions in Virginia, but by itself it did not energize most Virginians. In Lexington, Governor Letcher's home town, students at the Military Institute raised a secession banner when they first learned about Sumter. Then local workmen elevated an American flag on an even taller pole. This led to some cursing and pushing between the two sides: ruffled feathers and perhaps a few bruises. The tone in town remained tense and divided for three days. But on April 16 the laborers came and cut down their own flagpole, and the American flag. Why? What had changed?

As in Richmond, it was not Fort Sumter that caused the emotional turnaround; it was Lincoln's proclamation. Until Lincoln asked for volunteers to "suppress" the Southern rebellion, the conflict between the Republican administration and the Confederacy felt to most Virginians like a family squabble. The presidential proclamation, however, seemed intrusive.

Slavery was not an important economic or even social issue to most whites living in the Valley. But words like "home" did matter. Lincoln's proclamation made it seem to many Virginians that a great tidal wave was hurtling in their direction. This onrushing force of Northerners (outsiders) would have to be held back, by a dam built of human flesh if necessary. Militiamen, called up by Governor Letcher, could not protect the entire northern border of the state, hundreds of miles long. They would have to focus on just one or two places. Harpers Ferry was the first.[25]

The volunteers who sprang to arms can be compared to citizens of good will performing a civic duty, acting, in effect, as a large posse. Consider Turner Ashby of Fauquier County.

Turner Ashby would become a kind of Robin Hood to many Virginians, a romantic and mystical figure on horseback, riding through the countryside to succor the people of his region. He seemed a chivalric man — a fabulous rider on a wonderful steed, a quiet man who spoke little, a warrior, but a compassionate soul who cared deeply about family and hearth. In a way Ashby's persona became Virginia's version of the later western hero. His early death in the war only added to his immortality. Some Virginians still speak of him with reverence.

In fact, Turner Ashby, thirty-two, was a merchant by trade who never traveled far from the house in which he was born.

His small store provided him a reasonable income. He bought fifty acres nearby and grew tobacco. He owned ten slaves. His intellect was, at best, average, but he was a hard worker. He was compact of body and of medium height. His hair and eyes were dark, his skin swarthy, his lower face covered by a thick black beard. He was a serious person, completely humorless, a quiet-spoken man who said little and wrote clumsily. He appeared gentle, but only up to a point. His mind remained rigidly conservative, even reactionary. He admired, perhaps emotionally needed, order. He hated anything that threatened to alter the world he knew. To preserve that world, he made himself into a vigilante.

Ashby disliked Irishmen. When some Irish workmen building a railroad not far from his store fought among themselves and with locals, the railway's owner asked him to step in. Ashby, bearing a note from the influential railroad man, went to Richmond, spoke to the governor, was granted the militia rank of captain, and provided with guns. Leading a squad of like-minded men, he rode to the camp of the workmen and told them he would kill them unless they behaved. They leapt into line.

Another person who drew Ashby's wrath was a local farmer, a Northerner by birth and the only openly declared Republican in the region, who employed free labor on his dairy farm. Ashby ordered him to leave the state or be tarred and feathered. The farmer departed.

When John Brown brought his raiders to Harpers Ferry, Ashby raised a cavalry company called the Mountain Rangers. They arrived at Harpers Ferry too late to be involved in nabbing Brown, but they made themselves useful during the weeks thereafter, guarding several fords across the Potomac, making sure no more abolitionists or other outsiders came to disturb the region's tranquility and order. Henry Wise, governor during this period, saw something in Ashby: an emotional sturdiness. Other Virginians agreed; shortly after Lincoln's election, a statewide militia group elected him its vice president.

On April 16, 1861, Turner Ashby happened to be in Rich-mond. When Imboden was searching for sympathetic compa-triots to attend the gathering at Wise's hotel room, Imboden persuaded Ashby to come. There is no evidence the laconic Ashby contributed to the discussions, but the next morning, when Imboden started for Staunton, Ashby boarded another train and began heading, by a different, more direct route, to-ward Harpers Ferry. If he was anything, he was a man of action.[26]

Thursday, April 18

Turner Ashby, along with two other men, stepped from the morning train at the Harpers Ferry depot, not far from the ar-senal. One of his companions was Alfred Barbour, who had for some reason recently resigned his position as superintendent of the armory, and whose purpose now was to rouse the local workers to support the Virginia militiamen when they arrived. Accompanying these two men was James Alexander Seddon, a wealthy planter and respected Richmond lawyer. Seddon was slender, courtly, and bookish. Exactly why he came is un-certain, perhaps to suggest by his presence that Barbour and Ashby's mission had the support of the Tidewater elite. The three men told bystanders near the depot that Governor Letcher had declared Virginia no longer part of the Union, that his official announcement would arrive at the telegraph office by midafternoon. Immediately the town—already tense and uncertain because of sensational rumors during the past twenty-four hours—grew frenzied. Folks gathered on corners to discuss what might happen. Turner Ashby's very presence stirred excitement. The fact that he was here seemed to prove that a military force must be coming to seize the arsenal.

Lieutenant Jones, at the armory, also learned of this. He had already received a telegram from army headquarters in Wash-ington that three trainloads of Virginia militiamen had been spotted heading toward the Valley, and he had ordered his tiny garrison to begin shredding boards in the armory's carpenter shop to create wooden chips that could be useful in igniting fires. He had the straw pulled from six mattress bags, then had them stuffed with gunpowder. He placed these bombs in strategic spots, where they could do the most damage. He made sure that the 15,000 muskets near at hand were gathered together and surrounded by flammables. (Henry Wise and his fellow plotters had been wrong about one thing. Harpers Ferry had indeed once held about 90,000 guns, but no longer; most had been transferred elsewhere. On the other hand, Lieutenant Jones, who had only been at the armory a short time, did not realize one of the outer warehouses contained several thousand muskets. Jones failed to destroy these, and they would eventually be found and distributed to Virginia's militiamen.)

It took all day for the lieutenant's garrison to complete their preparations. Jones asked the arsenal's civilian workmen to assist them. A few volunteered—including a large man named Jeremiah Donovan, who stood at the main gate with a musket, keeping his eyes peeled for any approaching enemy. Other workers offered to act as pickets on the main road into town and took off in that direction.

A few miles south of the armory, beyond a glowering hill called Bolivar Heights, was a minuscule hamlet named Halltown. Virginia militiamen began clustering there. Their officers were unsure what to do. They had not yet received official orders from Governor Letcher to attack Harpers Ferry. Most of these men, local fellows, were not enthusiastic about secession. Although told by Ashby and Seddon to assault the federal position, they were disinclined to do so without concrete orders from Letcher. So they waited. One observer made a rough count of their numbers, and calculated about 340. This seemed a sizeable enough force, but these men were completely untrained in warfare. Most were neither bloodthirsty nor angry. Almost all had brought along guns of one sort or another, fowling pieces many of them, but not much ammunition. They had found a single six-pounder cannon, which they had dragged to this spot. They had no desire to fight to take the armory — especially against professional United States regulars who were, it seemed certain, well armed and entrenched. The militiamen lingered near Halltown during the late afternoon, nervously awaiting reinforcements. Ashby felt impatient and showed it.

A rider on a mud-spattered horse finally galloped up, carrying an order from Richmond. The leader of the militia force read it, nodded with satisfaction, and said, "Now I can act with a clear conscience." Off the little army started down the road toward Harpers Ferry. It was about eight o'clock and getting dark. One of the group described the scene: "The stars twinkled clear and chill overhead, [and one could hear] the measured tread of the men and the occasional half-whispered word of command."

Suddenly from the darkness came a voice challenging them. They halted immediately. Officers hurriedly shouted orders to load muskets. It is a difficult feat during daylight hours to pour loose powder into a gun barrel, then jam a cartridge down with a ramrod. At night, it takes extraordinary coordination, and time. The click-clack slither of ramrods lasted a while, followed by the nervous cocking of musket locks. The men at the front of the pack drew out bayonets and snapped them into place. What had seemed a bit of a lark, a pleasant walk on an April evening, had just grown serious.

The militiamen crept cautiously forward, but whoever had shouted at them was gone. The men pressed ahead. Twice more during the next hour they were challenged by hidden watchers. Each time they halted. At one point they actually saw pickets, four members of Jones's garrison. The militiamen shouted at the federals to halt or else, and took them captive. (During the confusion of the next few days, the four federal soldiers made their escape.)

Civilian emissaries from Harpers Ferry came out on the road and excitedly told the militiamen that the troops at the armory had been reinforced by an unknown number of townsfolk. The Virginia volunteers were now perhaps a mile or so from the armory. In the murk, their officers paused to contemplate their next move.

At the armory, Lieutenant Jones's men staggered about with heavy kegs, laying trains of gunpowder. Jones planned to destroy as much as he could, then cross the Potomac, and if all went well, keep going until they arrived at Carlisle, Pennsylvania. He hesitated because he was not positive that the army had not already sent him reinforcements. If they had, those troops would be arriving by train at any time. (Jones had probably heard the same rumor the militiamen had, that a Massachusetts regiment was approaching. In fact this prospect was not entirely absurd. Half a dozen regiments of Lincoln's volunteers were at this moment moving southward from states in the North. One could assume they might entrain through Baltimore. Six miles beyond that city was a small station called Relay House, where the tracks split. If a regiment at Relay House boarded a train going westward, rather than south from there to D.C., they would soon arrive in Harpers Ferry. Given the national importance of the arsenal, it was understandable why Jones could believe army headquarters might have ordered reinforcements this way. He wanted to wait as long as possible, just in case.)

About ten o'clock a sentinel he had placed on the road ran back to say militiamen were only a few minutes away. Jones decided he could stall no longer. He ordered torches applied to the trains of gunpowder.

His garrison then started, marching rapidly toward the covered railroad bridge that crossed the Potomac to Maryland. In the darkness the men marched in two parallel columns. Within a few minutes they were beneath the bridge's roof. They moved hurriedly through its shadowy gloom. A cluster of townsmen followed them, shouting imprecations, taking a few potshots in their direction, then racing away when Jones's men threatened to stop and open fire.

The small garrison passed over the bridge and continued, stumbling along throughout that night and the next day. They were worried that Maryland secessionists might try to stop them, so they did not linger. They had brought no provisions; the men grew weak with hunger. Thirty miles they walked. By the time they arrived at Carlisle, Pennsylvania, they were exhausted beyond measure.

Back at Harpers Ferry, as Jones's garrison hurried across the bridge, buildings burst into flames behind them, followed by a great crash of explosions. Splinters of window glass spattered the streets.

On Halltown Road, where militia officers were contemplating the options, they were startled by the first thunderous detonations and the sight of two balls of flame rising into the night sky. Turner Ashby spun his horse around and galloped into town, along with a few followers. Clomping behind him into Harpers Ferry came the militia infantrymen. They entered bedlam. Men, women, and children caromed about, toting or dragging stuff, preserving things from the fires. Some clasped armloads of muskets or bayonets they had saved, others pushed wheelbarrows filled with precious plunder: barrels of molasses or flour or pork, stuff too valuable to go to waste. Some of the armory's workmen who knew their way around the facility manned pumps and doused the flames at the factory where gun stocks were turned. The machinery used to make gun parts was saved, and later turned out to be quite helpful to the Confederacy.

At first, there was some discussion about chasing after the federal troops, but a rumor that Jones had mined the bridge made the volunteers decide to wait until morning. The next day the bridge was carefully examined and found to be safe, but the federals were long gone.

Within a day or two a sizeable army of militiamen had gathered in Harpers Ferry. They might have crossed into Maryland, but Jones's quick thinking, destroying the muskets and much of the gunpowder, meant the Virginians were less well armed than they might have been. Yet Virginia soon had a force here of several thousand armed men, less than two hours from Washington by railroad. Trains passed them occasionally, heading in that direction. The militia officers might have flagged these trains down, climbed aboard, and headed toward the virtually defenseless capital.[27]

Several factors stood in the way. By law, militiamen could not be ordered out of their state. Governor Letcher was not inclined to challenge this rule. A second matter — ironic as it seems — involved states' rights. If Virginia militia crossed the Potomac, this act would have put them on Maryland soil without invitation. In the atmosphere of the time, doing this seemed unacceptable — at least to many Virginians, who were still unsure about the concept of secession.

(It ought to be noted that a county sheriff in Maryland, just across the river, wired his state government in Annapolis that gangs of Virginians did cross the bridge on Saturday, April 20, a day after Harpers Ferry was taken, and were searching for weapons, house to house. The sheriff said he officially complained to the Virginia commander, Kenton Harper, and was promised such activities would cease — so long as no Northern troops came to the region. Kenton Harper did write to Richmond that he had "effected an understanding with the Maryland authorities," so Virginia's foray into Maryland had been brief. Nothing more was heard about this for the next two weeks.)

In a sense, citizens of Virginia had heard that the protective dam along their northern boundary might break — where it had almost cracked when John Brown had crashed against it. They had gone to the danger spot, had reinforced it with their bodies acting like sandbags, and were now satisfied. Many militiamen in Harpers Ferry, not thinking to bring food with them, did the next best thing: they got drunk. Confusion reigned. An adjutant general, theoretically responsible for keeping track of military details, wrote his wife: "I hold an office whose duties are new to me." He admitted to her that although he was supposed to know such details, he had not a clue how many militiamen were actually in the town.[28]

CHAPTER FOUR

ten-*HUT!*

When the rebels fired on Fort Sumter,
their shells traveled remarkable distances;
one flew north and exploded under me.
I landed in the ranks of the 3d Maine.
—UNION SOLDIER ABNER R. SMALL

The march was a continuous ovation—
ladies lined the streets of the town
and showered flowers upon us—
every delicacy the country could afford
was spread before us,
and we imagined ourselves heroes.
—CONFEDERATE SOLDIER WILLIAM W. BLACKFORD[29]

Most Americans considered their militia systems either risible or, as one person declared, "a public nuisance." Then came 1861. North and South, men volunteered in a rush. Their reasons varied. Some were unemployed workers seeking an income. Others wanted to avoid stressors at home—carping parents or unexpectedly pregnant girlfriends. Some, Huck Finn-like, just wanted to light out, to see the world and have adventures, to escape the humdrum. Some got caught up in the excitement of the moment and became intoxicated by the energies swirling around them. Flags seemed to be everywhere, and bands, and stirring music. Mesmerizing speakers offered political or religious pep talks. "God is on our side," they might announce. Or: "The enemy threatens our existence, our very hearths." Fort Sumter fell in mid-April, a time when the sap rises, and, it is said, the libido. Donning a uniform could make a fellow look manly — as wondrous and admirable as a peacock, his feathers a-spread to attract impressionable hens. Here and there, young ladies harmonized a ditty, "I am Bound to Be a Soldier's Wife, or Die an Old Maid." And weeping elderly gentlemen really did hand small bundles of hard cash to total strangers, simply because those young fellows were wearing uniforms and boarding trains heading toward the war zone. Excited throngs lined streets and leaned out upper windows to watch regiments march past. They waved flags and handkerchiefs, they threw hats in the air, they flung flower petals at departing heroes.

Across the South, as troop-carrying trains whistled past fields of cotton and ripening crops, black field hands, caught up in the moment, stopped what they were doing and ran toward the tracks, smiling, waving, and shouting.

This was powerful stuff. It was hard not to get hypnotized by it. Seldom does life offer an average person chances to be lionized as a hero. Everywhere, school boys found classrooms confining. One student at Oberlin College in Ohio told his brother: "War! and volunteers are [our] only topics of conversation or thought. The lessons today have been a mere form. I cannot study. I cannot sleep, I cannot work." A few hundred miles south, a freshman at the University of Virginia felt similar stirrings. He saw placards everywhere bellowing "War! War! War!" He wrote in his diary: "No studying today."

Never in America's history — before that moment, or since — has there been anything to duplicate this outburst of unbridled excitement, not even during the headiest, naïve days of America's entrance into the First World War. In New York City, the acerbic diarist George Templeton Strong could not suppress his emotions. He saw "the national flag flying everywhere; every cart horse decorated." As a middle-aged family man he would not be expected to join the army, but on the mid-April day when the first New England regiment marched through New York on its way to save the national capital, he left his law office to watch. Afterward he jotted down his reactions: "Immense crowd; immense cheering. My eyes filled with tears, and I was half-choked in sympathy with the contagious excitement. God be praised for the unity of feeling here! It is beyond, very far beyond, anything I hoped for. If it only last, we are safe."

A Virginian, Herbert Henry Hawes had moved to New Jersey years earlier. Now, in April, he sent a letter to family members back in Virginia: "As I write, I hear the drum & fife — by which a company is marching to the [train] cars, on their way to Washington. You have no idea of the rapidity with which this enlisting is going on at the North." He tried to account for it. "There is no ill-feeling against the South, but there is not one man in 10,000 who will not give his life and fortune to put down Secession."[30]

With a few exceptions, the generation of 1861 had no clear concept of war's realities. The most recent national conflict, the Mexican War, had been prettied up in the press and by politicians. Few commentators mentioned the large portion of deaths during that contest resulting from unromantic causes — dysentery and like diseases. No one spoke of the rapes and other atrocities committed by American soldiers.

Equally important, almost all leaders, North and South, misread the potential for their opponents to care deeply, to act with determination. Virtually no one, not even wise old heads like Winfield Scott, foresaw the immensity of the coming savagery. The virtual mania that now embraced so many had been unpredicted. The ferment was astonishing, and today, can hardly be explained.

It is easy, in our far more cynical era, to conclude that the passions resulted from little more than mob mentality — a spasm of mindless emotions that would inevitably soon pass. Yet idealism played a large part. James M. McPherson has written an excellent examination of this topic. His book, *For Cause & Comrades*, reminds us that many of the earliest volunteers on both sides were motivated by what used to be unashamedly called "higher values": duty and honor. He concludes, after analyzing thousands of letters and journals, that matters of conscience played a major role during the war's initial weeks.

Anyone who examines the private papers from that period will discover that patriotism was a powerful motivator of the first volunteers, though Southern volunteers differed noticeably from Northern troops in what their patriotism involved. The turmoil of the coming war would later create a broad Southern affection for "the South," but in April 1861 that concept was mostly a romantic abstraction, found in newspaper editorials or political posturing. During the early weeks of the war comparatively few young men from Georgia, say, or South Carolina spoke of defending the South — to say nothing of that brand-new entity, the Confederacy. Southern volunteers whose motives could be labeled patriotic were ready to fight for their states, and nothing much more than that. Most of them really only volunteered to defend something far closer: their friends, their families, their little communities, places where they knew almost everyone. To them, that was what they meant by "the South." (This fact is not surprising. In mid-April Robert E. Lee referred to Virginia as his "country.") When most Southern volunteers spoke more broadly than their specific states, they talked of defending such abstractions as "homes" or "hearths."

On the other hand, Northern volunteers did refer in their letters to "the Union." Nowadays that term — like "secession" — seems terribly dated. Can we really believe that sensible young men would choose to fight for something as vague, as academic, as "the Union"? The simple answer is: yes. To grasp what Northern volunteers meant by that term, mentally translate it into the present-day word "America," with all its nuances. Ask yourself if the very existence of America was being threatened today, whether many citizens would not avidly rush to defend it.

By 1861 "the Union" was a phrase that had been used for decades to represent the nation as a whole — its culture, its history, and its future — as opposed to certain negative connotations being given to the term "United States" by secessionists. To most Northerners, it must be said, their concept of America would really only have meant those local things they were used to — things like friends and family and the local culture they assumed represented the whole country. In that way they were much like Southerners volunteering to defend their hearths.

After the Civil War was over, once the fighting became a distant memory, it would be hard for younger people to understand the emotional impact of the word "Union." That was the main reason for the popularity of Francis Bellamy's 1892 Pledge of Allegiance: to remind youngsters what the Civil War had been about, why their grandfathers had fought it.

In April 1861 the psychological pressures, the desire to volunteer immediately no matter what the costs to oneself or one's family, were difficult to disregard. Take the case of William W. Blackford, from an obscure county in southwestern Virginia. A college-educated engineer, he was a thirty-year-old father of four children, the oldest of whom was still under five. He had a good income and a loving wife. After John Brown's raid in late 1859 he dabbled a bit in military matters. He bought a book on drilling and joined a local cavalry unit consisting of about a dozen locals. He hardly took this hobby seriously. During the 1860 election he opposed secession, and he accepted Lincoln's election, when it occurred, as perfectly legal. But in late April, when he learned about Lincoln's proclamation, he considered it outrageous. A day or so after reading it, he happened to be in his local town and found himself signing up for one of Virginia's brand-new military units. He was immediately assigned a barracks, and began drilling. He did not return home for a long time, not for a single day — though his wife visited him a few times at his barracks. He soon departed with his unit to move nearer to the enemy. He would not lay eyes on his house for the next four years. His story was far from unusual.

As for the feelings of Northerners, consider the young men from Ogdensburg, New York, who joined a local unit that eventually became a company in the Sixteenth New York Infantry Regiment. The area of Ogdensburg, in the northernmost sector of the state, lies shivering against the chilly waters of the St. Lawrence River, and its population was sparse. Even before Governor Edward D. Morgan called for volunteers on April 18, men of the isolated New York counties that bordered Canada began preparing to fight.

A local newspaper editor, Henry R. James, was one of the first in this region to hear about Major Anderson's surrender of Fort Sumter. He was at his office when he received the news, and, on the spot, he printed a sheaf of "enrolling papers," took them, along with the telegram about Fort Sumter, and rushed outside. He found a sturdy box and carried it to the intersection of the tiny hamlet's two main streets. He plopped the box down and mounted it. Folks, sensing his agitation, gathered around. He read the telegram aloud, then handed out the enlistment papers he had just printed. Men in the crowd hurriedly signed them.

A few miles away, in Potsdam, New York, a speaker pointed at an American flag and asked his listeners to go with him to uphold its "honor and glory", forty eight men signed up. In Chazy, New York, the owner of a lumber company asked his workmen to go to war with him; forty agreed and elected him their captain. Franklin, New York women knitted socks for their heroes. The men of nearby Depeyster gathered at a local tavern. Fifteen signed a muster roll. They had few weapons and no uniforms. A few days later, as they marched to the railroad station, they halted in front of a store specializing in men's hats, whose owner handed each volunteer a gingham checked cap — the first symbol that they were, somehow, part of an army. And so it went.[31]

After Cameron's request, the very first of Lincoln's volunteers to arrive in Washington reflected this amateurish stage of the war. They constituted five ill-assorted, and largely unarmed, companies from Pennsylvania. Their trip to the capital involved an ordeal that would have far-reaching implications.

On the day Confederate guns opened fire on Fort Sumter, Pennsylvania's legislature happened to be in session. Its members had been hearing rumors about the prospect of bloodshed in far-off Charleston, or some other locale in the South. Their recently-elected Republican governor, Andrew Gregg Curtin, had been pressing Lincoln to be firm. Curtin had just presented his legislature a bill to reorganize the state's militiamen and better equip them. He was sure a war was coming. On the evening of April 12, the state's legislators were actually discussing this measure when news arrived by telegraph about the attack on the federal fort. This information was announced to both houses and caused a sensation. An opponent of the bill jumped to his feet and announced he was changing his vote to yea. A few minutes later both houses overwhelmingly passed the proposal. Curtin was waiting in the legislature's executive chamber, and as soon as it was brought to him, he signed it. He hurried to Washington to tell Lincoln about Pennsylvania's wholehearted support.[32]

Residing in the small town of Pottsville, Pennsylvania, were the first Northerners to volunteer. On the evening of April 11, a few hours before Confederate guns opened fire on Fort Sumter, about forty members of the Light Infantry of Pottsville, a militia company, happened to be holding a meeting. A local businessman named Henry Cake had been financing this group for years, supplying them uniforms and a building they could use as an armory. If they planned a parade and too few members could participate, he hired temporary "soldiers" to march with them. He had just been in New York on business, where he had read stories of the prospects of a military incident somewhere in the South. He cut short his visit and hopped a train for home. As soon as he reached Pottsville he hurried directly to the armory, where he told the men the rumors he had heard. He suggested they pass a resolution offering to defend Washington. One man made a legal objection, reminding them that, by law, they could officially only serve the state of Pennsylvania. Someone else said they ought not restrict their offer to the national capital, but should promise to defend the Union. The group agreed to both points, then passed a resolution that they immediately wired off — one copy to Harrisburg, the other to Washington.

The next morning, April 12, the men of the Pottsville Light Infantry sent a four-horse omnibus to scour the community for others who might want to join. In the wagon sat three men. One played a fife, another banged a drum, a third rose to speak about their cause. Above them flew an American flag. Though unaware as yet that Fort Sumter was already being battered by Southern cannon, the three were splicing together one of the building blocks that would soon be defending America. By that evening the Pottsville Light Infantry numbered a hundred. More than half these men had had zero military training, had never marched a step. This meant they had no idea about how to drill — about the pace of a marching step or the spaces that were to be maintained between ranks. They were virtually a mob, not an army. Few owned weapons; some had never even held a gun, to say nothing of shot one.

In Washington, Secretary of War Cameron received the Pottsville telegram. He replied right away, accepting their offer. By itself, Cameron's answer meant little. Whether the Pottsville volunteers would serve would be up to Harrisburg, fifty miles from the little town.

On Monday morning, when Pennsylvania received Cameron's official request to send regiments, someone wired Pottsville: bring your company to Harrisburg. Similar messages were being sent to other militia units in central and eastern Pennsylvania. By Wednesday evening, April 17, five of these companies had arrived in the state capital. Most of the men from Reading and Lewistown and Allentown were as innocent of military matters as those from Pottsville. And these volunteers certainly looked unprepossessing. Only a fraction wore anything resembling a uniform. Some had on neat business suits; others wore overalls. They were a motley crew. Their only weaponry consisted of a few assorted pistols and sabers, along with thirty-four muskets and no ammunition. As a group they lacked any command structure.

Early Thursday morning each man learned he must take an oath to serve the federal government. Doing so, he would be mustering himself into national service. Henceforth he would no longer be a state militiaman. These volunteers would become Lincoln's soldiers. Southern newspapers were already characterizing such men as swinish mercenaries, the dreaded mudsills of Northern cities. According to editors in Richmond and Charleston and Nashville, therefore, these few hundred men were no longer Pennsylvania clerks and farm boys; they were "Yankee murderers, thieves, and rapists."

The 460 volunteers who took the oath boarded a train to Washington. The first stage of their journey—the eighty-nine-mile trip from Harrisburg to Baltimore—would probably run smoothly, but in Baltimore things might go awry. Since Maryland was a slave state, a portion of Baltimore's white population would feel connected to that institution and might be determined to maintain its existence. Whether such factors would throw Baltimore into chaos was yet unclear. Maybe the authorities there could control things. Aboard their train, the Pennsylvania volunteers were heading into a potential cauldron.

On Monday, April 15, Baltimore's major newspaper, the *Sun*, was full of articles about the crisis. One story, datelined New York, said that on Saturday the Albany legislature had passed a bill raising money for its militia. Another item stated that Rhode Island's Democratic governor, William Sprague, had offered Lincoln his state's artillery plus an infantry regiment that Sprague said he personally would lead to the federal capital. In Boston on Saturday, according to the *Sun*, militia officers had crowded forward to beg the state of Massachusetts to accept their companies. On both weekend days, the *Sun* said, mass meetings of outraged citizens had gathered in Philadelphia.

Word about Lincoln's proclamation reached Baltimore early Monday morning, before the *Sun*, an afternoon newspaper, went to press. Thus one of its editors had the opportunity to write a column about it; he called the proclamation "ultra" and "warlike."

The *Sun* presented itself as above partisanship, but it could not hide its sympathy for the Confederacy. While the newspaper avoided advocating Maryland's immediate secession, it openly embraced the right of secession. It considered the Confederacy a reality — a fait accompli. The *Sun* noted that any attempt to undo that new, self-declared "government" must be considered "coercion." And coercion would constitute a hateful Republican plot. In the *Sun*'s view, Lincoln's proclamation was mean-spirited and divisive. As a later editorial stated: "The Sumter business is no sufficient cause for war." According to the *Sun*, Lincoln and his administration were only trying to stir things up to keep their new party from splintering apart.

As to the city of Baltimore, the newspaper admitted that the populace seemed agitated by all the reports. On Friday, April 12, the *Sun*'s classified page had included two small ads. One had sought "able-bodied, unmarried men, wishing to go [fight with the] South." The other had urged readers to join the United States Cavalry, whose pay, the advertisement proudly declared, ranged from twelve to twenty-eight dollars a month. Both notices had been submitted before the onset of war. Then came the stories about Fort Sumter — described by the *Sun* as fighting "between the Confederate and Federal governments." Saturday afternoon's edition offered a screaming headline: OPENING OF CIVIL WAR, followed by animated descriptions of the bombardment.

The level of passion in Baltimore exploded that Saturday. Feelings remained high on Sunday. Little incidents caused flare-ups. One man was arrested for threatening to assault a visitor from North Carolina who had a secession cockade pinned to his lapel. A ship at the docks, whose home port was Richmond, flew some sort of secession flag. A group of Baltimoreans boarded the vessel and demanded the banner be taken down. It was. But the captain of the ship was not present, and when he returned, he raised it again. The police were called to maintain order.

By Monday and Tuesday the mood of Baltimore seemed a bit less boisterous, but the appearance of calm was deceiving. The Confederate recruiting office was deluged with applicants. On Monday thirty young men left by steamer for Norfolk to join the army of Virginia. On Tuesday seventy more volunteers applied for Confederate service. As an indication that the city was divided, a federal recruiter in town was also besieged by men anxious to volunteer.

An election was hurriedly conducted for delegates to attend a Southern Rights Convention in the city. A hundred men were quickly picked. They held their initial session on Thursday morning (the day the first Pennsylvania volunteers were going to pass through the city). The assembled delegates were told of the approaching train and its passengers—and that those Yankee troops would be arriving in a few hours. The conventioneers agreed that they would not prevent the passage of the Pennsylvanians through the city, but then they left the chamber and began to agitate the city's population. Some of them raised a Confederate flag at an important intersection in town, then fired a hundred-gun salute. Sometime thereafter a few citizens decided to fire a small swivel gun in a fifteen-gun salute—to honor the fifteen American states with slave laws, these fifteen for decades having been considered a virtual unit called the "slave states." The enthusiasts had only gotten off two rounds when a group of workmen from a nearby shop charged them, grabbed their popgun and threw it in the river.

Late that morning, as the train carrying the Pennsylvanians entered Maryland, someone in Baltimore wired northward an ominous message: mobs had taken over the city's streets. As a result, twenty miles from Baltimore the train pulled onto a siding and came to a halt. The volunteers wondered why they had stopped. Their leaders alighted and walked to the front where they spoke to the engineer. He said he was under orders to stay here because of the prospect of violence if he entered the city. The spokesmen for the Pennsylvanians explained that Washington was in danger, that they had to go there immediately. They asked: was the telegram from Baltimore accurate or just a rumor? The telegram might be an attempt by sinister forces to prevent the volunteers from getting to the national capital. The officers said they were prepared to take this train right now if its crew refused to continue. The engineer and conductor reluctantly agreed to press ahead.

The officers returned to their companies and wandered through the cars, talking to their men. It was imperative, the officers said, that they reach Washington. When they arrived in Baltimore, the volunteers ought to avoid any action, any words, that might cause an incident. This train, the officers explained, did not continue all the way to Washington. In fact they would have to get off these cars in the northern part of Baltimore and march through the city, more than a mile, until they reached another station. If they made it that far unscathed, they would board a different train, which would carry them the last leg to the capital. It seemed likely the march would be hazardous. Almost certainly they would be hooted at, sworn at, maybe spat on. They might have rocks and bricks thrown in their direction. They might even be fired at. Such things would be provocative, of course, but the volunteers must try to ignore them. It was vital they not get bogged down in Baltimore. The whole future of the United States might depend on what they did — and didn't do — in the next few hours.

The Pennsylvania volunteers had two unexpected advantages. Because of the attack on Fort Sumter a few days earlier, the War Department had become uneasy about the status of Fort McHenry, which guarded the entrance to Baltimore Harbor. The tiny garrison at this fort, the War Department had decided, ought to be reinforced, and a forty-man company was ordered there. By chance, these regulars were aboard the same train from Harrisburg that the Pennsylvania volunteers had taken. This meant these professional soldiers, well disciplined and fairly well armed, were on hand, and they offered to escort the volunteers from the first station to the second, staying on their right side throughout the march, only leaving after the Pennsylvanians had reached the second station, when the regulars would turn and head for Fort McHenry, less than two miles away. Also, by coincidence, one of the five Pennsylvania companies wore overcoats and carried sabers. To an undiscriminating eye, these men could pass for regular troops. With luck and grit the Pennsylvanians might just make it through Baltimore.

The march turned out to be an ordeal. A mob did await them. The crowd did hoot and hector. Some happily cheered for Jeff Davis. Some groaned at the mention of Abe Lincoln. A few threw paving stones. A Pottsville private was hit in the head with a brick flung from a rooftop. People of the crowd did grab the coattails of a few volunteers and yank at them, but this was mostly an annoyance. The mob might have done worse, but city policemen were on hand, walking along with the volunteers.

At the second depot civilians in the milling crowd espied among the volunteers a sight that caused a ripple of rage: a uniformed black man. His presence meant, some in the mob instantly decided, that the rumors were true: Lincoln and his Black Republicans intended to arm the "niggers," just like the hated John Brown had tried to do. Lincoln's announcement that he wanted to coerce the Confederacy would mean a servile revolution—rape and murder by rampaging black slaves. One member of the mob intended to put a stop to this, right now.

Nicholas Biddle was the African American in question. He was indeed wearing a uniform, and was also armed—though only with a small knife he carried in his pocket. He was not a real soldier, however, and had not taken the muster oath in

Harrisburg. His presence here resulted from his occupation: he was a paid valet of one of the Pennsylvania officers and was accompanying his employer in this role. Biddle was about to become one of the early casualties of this war.

A Baltimore thug leaped from the crowd, brass knuckles gleaming against his fist, and cracked Nick Biddle on the forehead. Blood poured down the poor man's temple, while his unidentified assailant scuttled back into the crowd in triumph — and disappeared. Biddle was outraged and wanted to go after his attacker, but his companions reminded him about their orders.

A few minutes later the Pennsylvanians boarded freight cars. A few in the mob clambered onto the train and tried to kick holes in the roofs. Others frantically attempted to rip up the tracks in front of the engine or uncouple it. Two of the Pennsylvanians finally felt they had taken enough. They jumped out and offered to fight. The crowd may have appreciated this sign of truculence. At least no one stepped forward to accept the challenge, and the two soldiers got back into their car as the train started to leave the station.

It was almost sunset when the Pennsylvanians arrived in Washington City. As they stumbled from the train and began to stretch their legs, they seemed to observers to be far from potential saviors of the nation. Major McDowell greeted them and directed them to their temporary quarters in the Capitol. The army had decided to put them up in the empty chamber of the House of Representatives.

The volunteers went to bed hungry. The army failed to have any provisions ready for them, or weapons. The next day, Friday, April 19, they were given some coffee, some bacon, and hardtack. Their military life had begun.[33]

CHAPTER FIVE

The Sixth Massachusetts

If the trek of the volunteers from Pennsylvania represented what the United States might expect in the next weeks and months, the country—as it had been constituted more than four score years earlier—was almost certainly doomed. Luckily for the fate of America others were on their way—including an unusual lawyer from Massachusetts who would help save his country.

Benjamin Franklin Butler was almost shockingly ugly. Although not exactly obese, his body was soft and gooey. At forty-three years old, he looked as doughy as a two-hundred-pound sack of suet. His hair had already receded to the farthest ranks of his pate, and he kept his sideburns and the mane at the back of his head long. A sorry mustache hung below his nose, but he was otherwise clean shaven. Deep bags sagged below both eyes. He also had an unfortunate condition known as strabismus, in which his left eye crossed, squinting somewhere off toward the right.

He had entered the world in 1818, the youngest of six children born to Charlotte Ellison Butler of New Hampshire and John Butler, an enterprising semi-pirate who worked the Caribbean and died there of yellow fever, having never laid eyes on Ben, his youngest son. John Butler's death left Charlotte in straitened circumstances. For a time she farmed out several of her children, including Ben, who was born sickly and seemed unlikely to survive. In 1828 she gathered her brood together and moved them to a new mill town, Lowell, Massachusetts, thirty miles or so north of Boston, near the border of New Hampshire. There she opened a boarding-house. The Butlers of Lowell were near the bottom of the town's social structure. But the boy read, voraciously, and this habit stimulated his mind and his imagination.

During his early years Ben remained scrawny and odd looking, but he proved quick witted, a trait that would some-day make him rich. He was also extraordinarily combative — though because of his puny physique, he used intelligence as his weapon. Like many awkward boys, he was enthralled with the notion of becoming a soldier. He even dreamed of attending West Point, but failed to receive the necessary con-gressional appointment. He became a lawyer. He had enor-mous energy, could work endless hours, and applied himself with great vigor. For a case involving insanity he studied medicine. For another suit he practiced iron working at a machine shop. His first clients were often mill girls employed in Lowell's textile factories. This brought him into conflict with the powerful owners. He demanded the reduction of the workers' fourteen-hour shifts, and won. He relished such battles. When only twenty-seven he was admitted to practice before the United States Supreme Court, one of the youngest lawyers to attain that privilege. He eventually married and fa-thered four children. He grew immensely wealthy and, some-what ironically, even became part owner of one of Lowell's factories.[34]

He also dabbled in politics, finally focusing on it with in-creasing energy. He was elected to the Massachusetts House, then its Senate, where he sat for a while, its only Democrat. He ran for the governorship, unsuccessfully. In 1860 he was a delegate at the Democratic National Convention. There he voted for Stephen Douglas for the first seven ballots, then switched his support to Senator Jefferson Davis, voting for the Mississippian on the next fifty ballots — Davis's most loyal, if improbable, supporter.

Fifteen prominent Democrats, including Butler, agreed to meet as a committee if the Republicans won that November, planning to gather in Washington in late December. On December 23 Butler arrived in the capital. South Carolina had just seceded. He sought out the other members of the ad hoc committee but discovered that their original purpose now seemed irrelevant. Only seven of the fifteen were in town — most brought here by the opening of Congress three weeks earlier. These seven apparently never met as a group, but Butler spoke to each individually. One evening he talked to Jefferson Davis. Their conversation was strained. They spoke about the topic on everyone's lips: secession.

"Will you come with us?" Davis asked — as Butler later recalled their conversation.

"No," Butler replied, "I shall go with my State because of my allegiance to the United States."

Davis seemed deeply moved by this thought. "It is possible, then," he said, "that we shall meet hereafter as enemies."

Another person Butler encountered in the capital was an old friend. This unnamed man led him to a long, low shed in Georgetown. Inside were almost a hundred armed men practicing military maneuvers. "We are getting ready," the friend said, "for the 4th of March": the day of Lincoln's inauguration. Butler suddenly realized that secession was not just an abstract theory. It carried the prospect of violence. Here in Georgetown, he thought to himself, was a gathering army that intended to stop the Republicans, if they could — to assassinate Lincoln, apparently. He left the capital immediately to warn authorities in Massachusetts.

Ben Butler held the rank of brigadier general in his state's militia, and had been the senior officer in 1860 when Massachusetts held its annual militia encampment with a gathering of about 6,000 men. Now he believed the time had come when their services might be needed. A severe winter storm prevented his train from reaching Massachusetts until January 3, by which time the recently elected governor named John A.

Andrew had officially taken office. Andrew, a Republican, held no fondness for the Democrat Butler, so Butler decided it would be prudent to ask someone to intercede on his behalf, and he chose Edward F. Jones — not only a solid citizen, but the colonel in one of Butler's regiments, the Sixth Massachusetts, representing Lowell and other nearby towns. Jones agreed, and the two men went and spoke to Governor Andrew. The governor listened but said he had a concern. This whole secession matter — and by this time several states in the Deep South had taken such steps — seemed like it might be connected to party politics. He, Andrew, had been hearing that many Massachusetts militiamen — in particular, Butler's men — were Democrats. If it came to a military crisis, as Butler was suggesting, and these militiamen were called to protect a Republican president, could Democrats be trusted?

Andrew's uneasiness was reasonable. For years many Massachusetts militia units had acted as virtual organs of the state's Democratic party. A year earlier the Democratic governor, Nathaniel P. Banks, had reorganized the militia, and Andrew suspected that Banks and Butler's militia involvement at the previous summer's encampment had been at least partly political (and almost certainly it had). It seemed prudent to be sure of the loyalty of the state's soldiers before arming them and sending them off.

During the next few days every militia company in Massachusetts called on its members. Each man was asked: If it came to a crisis, would he be willing to support a Republican president? Furthermore, would he swear he was ready to leave the state and his job and family and other obligations, if it came to it, to support his country? Those who said no, for whatever reason, were scratched off the rolls. The result was that by early February, Massachusetts, unlike almost all other Northern states, had an accurate record of men prepared for action — with all that it might imply.

Jones's regiment — the Sixth Massachusetts — seems to have been the first to finish the assigned questioning. On January 19 its officers agreed to a resolution that tendered the regiment's services, whenever or wherever they might be needed. A week later the state legislature passed its own measure, offering the federal government (that is, President James Buchanan) "such aid in men and money as he may require, to maintain the authority of the national government."

Southern states like South Carolina had for weeks been raising troops, so they had a head start. Massachusetts was not going quite that far, but it was getting prepared. Its state legislature sent copies of their resolution to the governors of virtually every other state. Weeks before Fort Sumter was attacked, the North was slowly awakening. Almost no one in the South noticed it, and few in the North, but a giant was stirring.

On the morning of February 5 Colonel Edward Jones, commander of the Sixth, along with Ben Butler, went again to speak to Governor Andrew. Jones was worried. His militiamen were mostly working men with families. Few had enough disposable income to purchase extra equipment for themselves, and they lacked many items necessary to well-equipped soldiers. Two of his companies possessed no uniforms whatsoever; the other six made do with those they had, even though their uniforms were for parades, for show, not active field wear. On any campaign these clothes would quickly fall apart. Although the Sixth had muskets of one sort or another, many of their guns were old, and the ammunition of some muskets would not fit the guns of others. The men also had no knapsacks, haversacks, blankets, tents—or other gear that would enable them to camp out if it came to a real campaign. Butler, owing to his recent trip to Washington, emphasized that the men of the Sixth had no overcoats, which might be significant if they were asked to go to Washington to guard the March 4 inauguration.

The Sixth Massachusetts was in far better shape than many militia groups at the time—the five companies of Pennsylvanians, for example, who would soon arrive in Washington, or countless Southern units—but supply issues were very real. In their parlors, reading articles about far-off battles,

American civilians had no grasp of logistics. They had a problem imagining the complexity of outfitting an army. In 1861 most civilians would have been puzzled by the significance of a message one professional soldier sent his headquarters during this period: "Send as fast as can be procured 2,500 [horse]shoes and 100 pounds of horseshoe nails, and six sets of shoeing tools." Nails and shoeing tools would have seemed far too mundane for most civilians to deem important. Yet, as the old saw reminds us, kingdoms have been lost for the want of such seemingly trivial things.

Governor Andrew did what he could. He asked his legislature to provide funding for the needed items. Although some state newspapers howled that Butler had a vested interest in seeing his soldiers get overcoats, since one of his companies manufactured them, a contract between the state and the company was agreed on — the coats were made, and the militiamen received them. The other items Jones asked for did not appear so quickly. But when Lincoln's inauguration came off without a hitch, Massachusetts's legislature sighed happily, concluded the war scare was over, cancelled all its other emergency appropriations, and adjourned.

The date was April 11. Although Boston's journals had been blaring feverish rumors about the crisis that was expected momentarily somewhere in the South, the state's legislature saw no reason to remain in session. Few events from those days are as revealing as this — that the good politicians of Massachusetts, clearly wanting to do the right thing, did not foresee the chaos that would fall on them and the entire nation a few hours after they adjourned and headed home. This discrepancy reminds us of the powerful difference between a prospect and a reality.

Governor Andrew, unlike his legislature, remained uneasy about the recent news reports. On Saturday, April 13, he wired Washington, asking the War Department if he could tap the federal arsenal in Springfield for two thousand rifled muskets. (His request, it should be noted, was not based on his concern about the safety of the national capital; it stemmed from Andrew's anxiety about two empty federal forts near the mouth of Boston's harbor, which he thought might be taken over by "lawless men." He wanted to station militia in both forts.)

But war had already begun in Charleston. And on Monday, April 15, Secretary Cameron's telegram, requisitioning the nation for volunteers, arrived in Boston. Ben Butler happened to be in the city handling a court case when he was given a note. He read it, rose to his feet, and asked the judge for a postponement. He said it was critical he start getting troops ready to save Washington. The time was four forty-five; he wanted to catch the five o'clock train back to Lowell. The judge agreed. Off Butler rushed. (Apparently the court case, whatever it was, was never resolved, at least according to Butler's self-congratulatory autobiography.)

The next morning, Tuesday, Butler boarded the train at the Lowell depot to return to Boston. Plans and ambitions danced in his head. He was only one of several Massachusetts militia commanders, but it was his goal to lead the first volunteer regiments to Washington. His motives were mixed. No doubt he felt a desire to perform his patriotic duty to help save the nation. But he seems to have had an additional incentive. As an extremely ambitious politician, he was keenly aware that military glory had helped elect four of America's sixteen presidents. Why not himself? If he moved quickly, he might take troops to Washington and arrive there before any other militia general. If the national capital was kept safe, he could then claim to be its savior. And who could calculate what benefits might accrue?

In theory he commanded four militia regiments. During the previous three months he had seen to it that each was relatively prepared. None of the four could be considered especially well armed, or well drilled, but — compared to other such units in Massachusetts or elsewhere in the North — they were fairly ready to go. A question lingered: would these four regiments be the first ones Governor Andrew sent, with Ben Butler in command?

Butler later insisted he wired Henry Wilson, one of Massachusetts's two senators, who was in Washington at the time, and asked him to speak to Secretary Cameron on his behalf, and that when Wilson did so, Cameron agreed that Butler was the very man to head Massachusetts's first troops. This story is almost certainly bogus, a product of Butler's preening. Governor Andrew, not Cameron, would appoint the commander of the state's first volunteers, and the governor was not only a Republican, he neither liked nor trusted Butler.

It is uncertain when Butler formulated his plan of action and whether the events of that morning were as accidental as he later claimed. According to his autobiography he was sitting on the train going from Lowell to Boston when he noticed James G. Carney, president of a Boston bank. It only then dawned on Butler, he would later claim, that the legislature was not in session at the moment, and could not practicably be brought back for some days, at the very least. He also knew that state law stipulated no treasury monies could be used to fit out or transport troops without legislative authorization. Time was wasting. The nation was in peril. As the train chuffed along, he spoke to Carney and asked him if his bank would lend Governor Andrew funds to cover this temporary crisis. Butler later said: "I also asked him if he would recommend my detail as brigadier-general." Carney agreed to the loan, and said he would even contact other bankers in the city and urge them to do the same. When the two men arrived at the Boston station, Butler accompanied Carney to the banker's office and waited while the man wrote a note on official bank stationery. Butler stuffed it into his pocket and sped to talk to Andrew.

Once inside the governor's office he opened his remarks by saying he wanted to be appointed to lead the first troops to leave the state. The governor replied that this was unlikely. He said he had two other men in mind, both militarily senior to Butler. In fact, Andrew noted, one of those two was sitting just outside the office, and Andrew intended to select him for the post. Just then the state treasurer hustled into the room. He announced that the state lacked available funds to send *any* volunteers, and could not do so until the legislature convened. That would certainly mean a delay of days, maybe weeks. The federal capital could be captured by rebels during that period. Butler presented the governor his note from Carney.

A few hours later Governor Andrew made it official: Ben Butler would be leading the first troops to Washington. This appointment allowed Butler to label himself a brigadier general outside Massachusetts, though it should be noted his title only gave him authority over Massachusetts troops, not those from any other state.

He was hugely energized. He instantly appropriated a room in the State House and began sending a flurry of messages to company and regimental commanders. The essence of the note was this: get ready immediately.[35]

Upon receiving Cameron's request, Andrew had immediately asked Washington how to send troops. He was told to forward them to the capital by train. The next day, Winfield Scott wired the governor with a change of plans. He wanted at least one regiment, maybe two, to head to Fort Monroe on the coast of southern Virginia, which meant those men must proceed there by ship.

The weather in Boston was nasty. Rain fell in torrents, interspersed with sleet. Parts of the state lay under a blanket of gray winter snow. Despite the conditions, men rushed about, flinging clothing into bags, kissing their families goodbye, boarding trains. Some scuttled off to Fall River, on the coast. Two partial regiments boarded ships, one on Wednesday, the other on Thursday, each heading toward Fort Monroe, as Scott had requested.

Other volunteers, arriving in Boston, were told to stay inside Faneuil Hall to await orders. Militiamen trickled in. By late Wednesday afternoon, Colonel Jones's Sixth Regiment was prepared to leave. They marched from the Hall to the railroad station, and started the long train ride toward Washington. Among other stops, their route would take them through Baltimore. What they might encounter there was, as yet, unclear.[36]

CHAPTER SIX

Mobtown

Baltimore had gone through an enormous growth spurt in the decades before the Civil War. The census of 1790 listed its population as 13,503. Then in a single decade it doubled, surpassing Boston. Between 1830 and 1860 Baltimore and Philadelphia competed for which one could call itself America's second largest city after New York.

What caused Baltimore's dramatic expansion? The city's merchants were extraordinarily energetic. When they faced competition from outsiders — the Erie Canal in New York, steamboats up the Mississippi — they proved themselves robust and flexible. In 1813 they launched their first steamboat, and within thirty years their fleets, with their flat bottoms, dominated trade in Chesapeake Bay and its scores of rivers. The Bay virtually became Baltimore's proprietary lake, and the Bay's southern mouth gave the city easy access to the Atlantic. For a while the city billed itself as "America's breadbasket," taking grain from Maryland's farmers, grinding it in her mills, and annually sending off tens of thousands of barrels of flour to slaveowners — some living along the Bay's outer perimeter, others as far away as the Caribbean. In 1827 Baltimore's merchants also chartered the very first American railroad, which eventually became the Baltimore & Ohio. By 1861 its 513 miles of tracks linked Baltimore to Wheeling on the Ohio River, and therefore to the entire western trade. The B&O's tracks also tied the city to Washington and farther south. In 1852 the railroad completed its Camden Street Station in the southern part of town—the largest railroad depot in America.

The city needed plenty of strong hands to perform the work. It encouraged immigrants from Germany and Ireland to come, and they arrived in droves, tens of thousands of them. The census of 1860 showed that more than a quarter of the city's 212,418 people had been born in Europe (which does not count their children, born in America, but who generally maintained close ties to their ethnic roots).

Many arriving Germans soon moved away from the city, drifting into the interior, but a large number stayed and settled into Baltimore's life. They formed societies like the Germania Club and the Concordia. They developed singing groups and literary and gymnastics clubs. The richest Germans melded with the city's elite and even began speaking fondly about Southern rights, but the great mass of the city's Germans (and their offspring), often shopkeepers, opposed slavery and remained strongly loyal to the Union.

Maryland boasted that it had America's oldest record of toleration of Catholics, and Baltimore was home to thousands of families of Irish descent. By 1860 the city's many Hibernian societies offered Irish American families steamboat picnic excursions in the Bay.

The city was also home to a great many African Americans: 25,000 free blacks, and over 2,000 slaves. Most of the steamboat workers were slaves, the property of shipowners. They hustled as roustabouts at the wharves; slave stokers and deckhands formed the backbone of ships' crews; and black chamber maids and dining room waiters looked after the passengers.

Baltimore was a complex metropolis, not easy to characterize. It contained eighty synagogues and churches of virtually every type. It had twenty active temperance societies, and more than two thousand places serving booze (giving Baltimore one drinking establishment for every hundred residents: man, woman, and child). The city was sprinkled with fine parks — especially Monument Square, near where most of Baltimore's gentry lived. It also had good hotels. Even Charles Dickens, who found little in America to like, praised Barnum's City Hotel (which had no connection, it might be noted, to P. T. Barnum of New York). The seven stories of this hostelry towered above the central city. Its dining room, famous for crabs and venison, terrapins and wild duck, made sure a liveried black waiter stood behind each guest's chair.

But the city had long been famous, or infamous, for something else: an ugly tendency toward violence. Eruptions had often exploded during its colonial years. Perhaps it was Baltimore's heterogeneity. The fact that the city had welcomed Catholics may have resulted in antagonisms more than toleration. One factor was competition between Irish immigrants and free African Americans for jobs at the city's factories — with the usual results of hostility and spasms of violence. By 1815 Baltimore had acquired a nickname, Mobtown, a moniker stemming from one particular event. A local editor had opposed the War of 1812. His house, though defended by more than a score of prominent friends including Robert E. Lee's father, Richard Henry "Light Horse Harry" Lee, was attacked by an angry crowd and virtually destroyed. The maddened mob beat and tortured the defenders, killing one. Richard Henry Lee never fully recovered from the brawl. When members of the mob were tried for the crimes, they were acquitted by sympathetic local courts. Stories about this action, and the follow-up trials, created the city's unsavory reputation. Baltimore's notoriety was further intensified by more riots in 1835 (focusing on several prominent bankers). Newspapers across America now used "Baltimore" and "Mobtown" interchangeably.

During the 1850s the city's reputation reached its nadir. Gangs of thugs took control of most wards and dominated several of the city's volunteer fire companies. These bands adopted colorful names: Plug-Uglies and Red Necks, Gladiators and Black Snakes, Blood Tubs and Spartans. Some of the gangs were relatively small. Others numbered in the hundreds. They were in fact proto-fascist packs with close ties to political organizations. They terrorized voters; they beat citizens with brass knuckles and clubs; they used their fists and knives and guns to murder rivals. Their political violence lay like rancid slime atop the normal levels of urban crime. The city lacked an adequate, professional police force — though it ought to be said, few cities in the world of that era had one.[37]

Concerns about Baltimore's volatility altered Lincoln's schedule in February 1861. On his way east to his inauguration, traveling from Springfield, Illinois, he stopped along the way to present himself to audiences throughout the northern tier of the United States. After New York he continued on to Philadelphia. He planned to leave the City of Brotherly Love and continue west to Harrisburg, where he would address Pennsylvania's legislature, then board a train for Washington. This last leg would take him through Baltimore, and therein lay the rub.

Samuel Morse Felton was fifty-one years old, bespectacled, a bit chubby, and respectable. A civil engineer by trade and inclination, he had been president of the Philadelphia, Wilmington, and Baltimore Railroad for a decade when, in January 1861, an old friend of his, Dorothea Dix, called on him. Miss Dix was a person of substance, internationally recognized for her ceaseless activities as a medical reformer. She had devoted the previous two decades to humanizing the care of the mentally ill. A New Englander, her tireless travels nourished friendships with many acquaintances in the South. From them, she learned of a possible plot to kill President-elect Lincoln before he could take his oath of office. She heard that secessionists in Maryland were patrolling the two main rail lines heading southward into Baltimore: the Northern Central out of Harrisburg, and Felton's line out of Philadelphia. She warned Felton about the rumors. He listened politely but considered her concerns overwrought. Then a few days later he heard a similar story from a second person and decided he had better investigate. He contacted a detective.

Allan Pinkerton, in his early forties and Scottish by birth, had started a detective agency in Chicago. For nine years railroads had occupied most of his attention, gaining Pinkerton a reputation for toughness and competence. This reputation was the reason Felton asked him to come to Philadelphia for a talk.

When the detective arrived Felton explained the assassination rumors. Felton was also nervous that mobs might damage his railroad line. He offered Pinkerton a handsome retainer. The detective promised to investigate the situation. He said he would assign operatives to snoop around Baltimore, and, if possible, join some pro-South militia units there.

Pinkerton personally spent more than a month skulking the city's streets. It did not take him or his colleagues long to encounter assassination talk. Pinkerton chanced upon a man named Cypriano Ferrandini, once a barber at Barnum's Hotel, whose customers represented the city's elite. Ferrandini proudly told Pinkerton that he was patching together a group to kill the president-elect when Lincoln came through the city.

On February 21 Lincoln arrived in Philadelphia on schedule. His entourage included his wife Mary, their children, and several men quietly acting as unofficial bodyguards. Pinkerton spoke to Lincoln, telling him what the detectives had unearthed. The two men knew each other from their railroad connections in Illinois. Lincoln heard Pinkerton out but remained unconvinced. Then later that evening Lincoln had another visitor: Frederick W. Seward, acting as an emissary for his father, the soon-to-be secretary of state. Young Seward's message was that the threat in Baltimore was real, and dangerous.

The two warnings, coming back-to-back, persuaded Lincoln. Felton and Pinkerton suggested he continue his planned trip to Harrisburg. There he would give his speech, but instead of then attending a party, he should secretly return to Philadelphia and board one of Felton's trains.

And so it transpired. Lincoln slipped out of Harrisburg, returned to Philadelphia, and started south. His train, one of Felton's, rattled through Baltimore in the middle of the night while the president-elect slept. He arrived at Washington about six o'clock in the morning and went to his hotel. His actions were not particularly sneaky, merely prudent, although he soon concluded that the ruse had been unnecessary. However, he was chagrined when he learned that his wife was badly frightened after her train—the one that had come directly from Harrisburg, and which he had been slated to ride—was searched in Baltimore by some loud-mouthed goons. They stomped through the cars, shouting that they wanted to get a gander at the Republican leader. "Where is he?" they growled. "Trot him out." "Let us see him." When Lincoln heard about this, he mildly commented that the searchers were merely being obstreperous. (Mary was not as forgiving.) Lincoln was more concerned to hear that a large friendly crowd had gathered in Baltimore to greet him and been disappointed.

It is now impossible to know with certitude whether Pinkerton was correct, whether assassins had indeed been waiting at the Baltimore station. There certainly was much chatter throughout the South in those weeks about killing Lincoln. Perhaps the talk was hot air, perhaps not. Whatever the truth, some opposition newspapers used this incident to make fun of him. Opponents in Baltimore riled audiences in the city, saying that Lincoln had insulted their town.[38]

By mid-April 1861, Baltimore was in an uproar, and most of the state of Maryland was equally crazed. For much of the previous decade the state's politics had been noxious. During the 1850s the American Party (better known as the Know Nothings) had controlled Maryland's political machinery, combining the stench of anti-Catholic bigotry with xenophobic patriotism.

The governor of Maryland in 1861, Thomas Holliday Hicks, was a political hack. Three years earlier, Hicks, a farmer from the Eastern Shore and a rather obscure Know Nothing state legislator, found himself unexpectedly elected to Maryland's highest office. A chunky man, mentally sluggish and not overly courageous, he now seems amazingly like the title character of the 1937 movie *The Wizard of Oz*. Hicks and actor Frank

Morgan's Wizard character shared certain qualities, like shifti-
ness, as well as moments of unexpected wisdom. By 1861 Governor Hicks's position had grown untenable, since his Know
Nothing party had virtually dissolved, denying him any base
of support.

The state's Democrats consisted of an uneasy alliance of
three elements. Its traditional leaders included pro-Southern
slaveowners, particularly planters from the counties bordering
the Potomac and on the Eastern Shore. Lately certain law and
order businessmen had joined them. They wanted the elimina-
tion of Baltimore's gang violence, plus a legal means to control
Maryland's unruly workmen. The third part of the Democratic
party were rabid racists, increasingly uncomfortable about the
state's large free black population.

By 1859 Democrats controlled the state legislature and,
ignoring Hicks, began shoving through laws. Among other
things, they cheerfully adopted measures putting pressure on
the state's African Americans. The legislature provided weapons
to the state's militia companies (most of them officered by fellow Democrats) enabling them to crush any obnoxious activities of either slaves or free African Americans. The legislators
had the gall to offer free blacks the choice of becoming slaves,
if they wished.

Reformers in the general assembly also pushed through
laws giving the state almost total control over the city of Baltimore — including its police. The legislators even ousted Baltimore's delegates from the general assembly on the rationale
that they must have been elected by corrupt voting. The reformers handpicked the five members of Baltimore's just-
created police governing board, which in turn chose the city's
new police marshal, George Proctor Kane. Marshal Kane, a
successful businessman as well as a slaveowning Democrat,
had the assignment to bring order to Baltimore, to reduce its
violence, and to crush its gangs. He was honest and energetic.
He cleaned up the police department with vigor — throwing
out the most corrupt policemen, replacing them with men he
could trust.

A stipulation of Maryland's new Metropolitan Police Act specified that no Republican could become a Baltimore policeman, at any level, and Kane especially relished firing men with Know Nothing connections. Soon Baltimore's police department reflected the attitudes of Kane and the police board. In general the policemen believed in social order, meaning they kept tabs on the city's African Americans and Irish immigrants, and sympathized with the city's pro-South activists.

During October 1860 Baltimore held a municipal election in which a reformer named George William Brown became the new mayor. He carried every ward; even Know Nothings voted for him. Baltimore seemed ready for some serenity. Brown and his Citizen Reform Association were determined to wrest control of their town from the gangs.

The presidential election took place a month later. Only nine percent of Maryland's electorate voted for either Lincoln or Douglas, the two main candidates in much of the country. In Maryland, as in Virginia and Tennessee, the race was between John Bell, the candidate of the Constitutional Union Party, reflecting a Whiggish cautiousness; and John C. Breckinridge, who represented the Southern rights wing of the splintered Democratic party.

The results are not easy to decipher. Know Nothing voters, with no candidate of their own, opted for Bell. The state's pro-South faction voted for Breckinridge, and so did the reformers. Bell and Breckinridge ran virtually neck and neck, though in the end Breckinridge carried the state by an eyelash. One can debate the meaning of these results, but one thing is clear: Republicans were despised throughout Maryland. Lincoln had no popular base there.

The capital of Maryland was the sleepy coastal town of Annapolis. In April 1861 the legislature was not in session. With the announcement of Lincoln's April 15 proclamation, Governor Hicks had two reactions — both of them, as it turned out, correct. He refused to call the legislature into session on the grounds that it might act emotionally (even though this decision placed much weight on his flabby shoulders). And he went from his official residence in Annapolis to Baltimore to see if he could affect events there.

On Hicks's appearance in Baltimore, the governor's fifty-man official guard serenaded him — with, among other tunes, the "Star Spangled Banner." Their officers also called on the men to give "three cheers for the Union," and they did so, with apparent gusto. But problems were a-brewing.

On the evening of April 18, not long after the five hapless Pennsylvania companies had passed through the city, several events occurred. Word arrived that Virginia, Maryland's sister state, had seceded the day before, and rumors spread that Harpers Ferry was under attack. At a meeting of Baltimore's Southern Rights Convention, the delegates strongly opposed allowing any more Northern volunteers to pass through the city. They adopted a resolution that the movement of such troops to Washington was "uncalled for by any public danger." They promised to "repel, if need be, any invader who may come to establish a military despotism over us." The mood of this gathering was not promising. Neither was a note that Marshal Kane had sent the local agent for Felton's rail line, asking peremptorily whether it was true Felton planned to bring troops "to war upon the South," a phrase indicating a belligerent attitude. Felton was at that very moment in fact making arrangements to shuttle volunteers toward Washington.[39]

Senator Charles Sumner of Massachusetts arrived in Baltimore that evening, registered at a hotel, deposited his bags in his room, and left to visit a friend in town. Sumner was a well-known abolitionist and Republican. Among other things, he was famous for having been the recipient of an 1856 beating. He had been sitting at his desk on the Senate floor writing, his head down, when a young South Carolina congressman, Preston Brooks, stepped up behind him holding a gutta-percha cane (the kind often used to discipline disobedient slaves). Brooks looked down at the Yankee's head, suddenly lost all self-control, and began hammering Sumner repeatedly on the head and shoulders. The senator tried to rise, but his desk trapped his legs. Finally he fell, bleeding and senseless, onto the Senate carpeting. Brooks's cowardly act was rejoiced in some Southern quarters, but it transformed Sumner into a heroic symbol in many parts of the North.

Now, four years later, when Sumner arrived in Baltimore, word spread through the city about his presence. A large, unfriendly, vocal crowd gathered outside his hotel. "Bring him out!" they shouted. The mob threatened to burn the building if he did not appear. Police or boredom eventually caused most of the crowd to wander away. Still, a few remained, lurking nearby, so when Sumner did return, he was hurriedly ushered in through a side door. The manager pleaded with him to leave, but the senator had nowhere else to sleep, so he spent the night at the hotel, occupying different accommodations from those originally assigned him. He had planned to depart on the next day's midmorning train to Washington, but prudence and pressure from the hotel's management caused him to rise at four o'clock, slip out a private door, and take a carriage through the darkness to the depot before anyone saw him. It was April 19.[40]

Meanwhile one of Felton's trains was heading southward from Philadelphia. It moved slowly, its thirty-five cars a heavy load for a single engine to pull. Squeezed into it were the men of two separate military groups. One consisted of a Pennsylvania unit that represented the Philadelphia region. Like the men of the five Pennsylvania companies who had passed through Baltimore the day before, these Pennsylvanians were almost completely unarmed. The other group of volunteers was the Sixth Massachusetts.

The previous couple of days had passed pleasantly enough for these Massachusetts troops, if somewhat exhaustingly. Take the example of one of its companies. Early Wednesday morning (two days earlier), its men had gathered at their home armory in Worcester, Massachusetts, forty miles from Boston.

A large crowd coming to see them off jammed the building. One person showing support was Emory Washburn, an ex-governor of Massachusetts, now a law professor at Harvard and a local resident. Dangling from his arm hung a basket, piled high with Bibles. He handed one to each volunteer, uttering a few encouraging words. The soldiers at the armory learned their train was finally ready at the depot and marched toward the station. Townsfolk crowded the streets, yelling encouragement as their boys passed—off to save Washington and preserve the Union.

Their ride to Boston took two hours. There the throngs were larger. The Worcester troops mixed with men from Lowell and Acton, from Groton and Stoneham and Lawrence. All were handed gleaming new Springfield rifles. Few had ever held such wonderful things. Governor Andrew ceremoniously presented Colonel Jones the regiment's official colors and made a stirring, patriotic speech. Other speeches followed.

What with one thing or another, it was seven-thirty that evening when the more-than-700 men of the Sixth started toward the Boston station. The air had grown noticeably chilly, but the horde at the depot was huge and vocal. More yelling, more huzzahs, more shouts of good-bye, more tears. Bells clanged. Fireworks shot into the night. Some exuberant souls in the swarming crowd blasted pistols skyward to express their excitement. The train's engineer gave a mighty blast on his whistle and off they went.

Two hours earlier one member of the Sixth, Corporal Sumner H. Needham of Lawrence, found time to jot a quick note to his wife. His regiment, he told her, would be leaving for the capital soon. He was not sure whether they would be stationed in Washington or be ordered to some other dangerous place. Nor did he know how long he would be gone; the Sixth had signed up for three months, but he hoped to be home earlier. He told her he knew she was unhappy about his departure, yet the venture he was embarking on was important. Still, he wanted to tell her: "My heart is full for you, and I hope we may meet again. I shall believe that we shall. You must hope for the best and be as cheerful as you can." In forty-three hours Corporal Sumner Needham would be fatally wounded in Baltimore.

During the night, as their train was hurtling westward to Springfield, Massachusetts, then south through Hartford and New Haven, the volunteers could see from their windows that masses of folks along the way, knowing they were coming, had built bonfires. Flames flickered along the tracks to light their way, and men and women, huddled next to the warming fires, windmilled their arms as the train passed, grinning and shouting encouragement — words the soldiers, of course, could not hear.

It was almost eight in the morning when they arrived in New York. They climbed from the cars, and were escorted to one of three different hotels, where they were provided with mighty mounds of breakfast food. Afterward they marched down Broadway. Looking about, they were astonished. They had never seen anything like it. It seemed as though they were moving through a vast, cacophonous red-white-and-blue cavern. Flags fluttered from almost every window. Horns blared, people of all ages screamed in joy just to watch them pass. A volunteer, writing home that night, called it "one of the wildest scenes of enthusiastic excitement it was ever my fortune to witness."

It should be remembered that this was Thursday morning, April 18. The war — sudden, unexpected, and obviously critically important to the nation's future — had started only a few days earlier. Emotions had skyrocketed. New York's newspapers that morning were crammed with stories about incidents in cities North and South, from Charleston to Philadelphia. To ratchet the tension up further, a ship, the *Baltic*, carrying Major Robert Anderson and his exhausted Fort Sumter garrison, was just now steaming into New York's harbor, and the city was preparing to embrace those battered champions about whom the nation had been reading the past four months.

The Sixth marched to a dock and boarded a ferry, which carried them across to New Jersey, where they found another train. The people of New Jersey also greeted them with joy. Private John B. Dennis ogled the females who crammed into the galleries. "Their enthusiasm," he would later recall, "exceeded all bounds; they became so carried away that handkerchiefs, gloves, pieces of ribbon, and even curls were cut from their heads and thrown down to the boys, while the band played the national airs, and patriotic songs were sung. And amid such a scene, which made every man there proud to be a soldier, and to have so much loveliness to fight for, the train pulled out of the depot." One of his comrades wrote his sister about the trip: "When we left Boston it was snowing, and the next day we were traviling through a country where the grass was as high and green as it is in our place in the first of June." He liked the bucolic look of this land. "The cattle were all in the field," he told her, "and the trees were in bloom. The wheet was six inches high in some places, and the farmers are near done planting."

Across New Jersey the Sixth sped — urged on as they passed through Newark and Rahway, Princeton and Bordentown, by more thousands of supporters, the firing of cannon, the waving of flags, drums a-drumming, and bands playing. All this energy, one Massachusetts man thought, could only mean good things. "We feel confident," he wrote home, "that there will be no fighting, and that we will be at home again in less than three months." He did not consider it ominous that soon after his train passed Trenton, he and his comrades were handed ten cartridges each. (The implication of these cartridges did apparently dawn on Private John Brady, a member of one of the Lowell companies. He became unglued. According to the regiment's official report, Brady was "taken insane" and permitted to leave the train at one of the smaller stations in southern New Jersey, to return home.)

The rest of the Sixth arrived in Philadelphia about eight o'clock that evening. They had been on the road now over twenty-four hours. Most had slept a bit, off and on; others had been too excited at their first time away from home. They were escorted up Philadelphia's Chestnut Street to the Girard House, which had been emptied in honor of their arrival. About eleven o'clock they were told to rest.

As the regiment tried to sleep, their commander, Colonel Jones, was having an uncomfortable conversation about the rude treatment the first Pennsylvania companies had received in Baltimore a few hours earlier. Those with whom Jones now conferred had learned by telegram that people in Baltimore were planning to halt any more troops coming through their city. Colonel Jones and the others discussed the options. Someone suggested a couple of alternative methods of getting to Washington, water routes that would allow him to bypass Baltimore. Jones listened, but decided that those routes seemed uncertain and far too time consuming. The federal government was in danger, Washington needed help, now, and he intended to provide it. He issued orders to rouse his men.

Drummers at the Girard House beat a call to action. Weary volunteers struggled to their feet. They tramped down Chestnut Street and boarded the train awaiting them. It was one-thirty in the morning when it started off.

The date was April 19, 1861. To borrow Lincoln's phrasing, exactly four score and six years earlier the American Revolution had begun on the village green of Lexington, Massachusetts. Now men, mostly from the same region of Middlesex County (at least one of whom was a direct descendant of Lexington's Middlemen), were heading toward their own moment of destiny.[41]

CHAPTER SEVEN

Patriotic Gore

There is some considerable difference between
"playing soldier" and the "soldier on duty."
—W. D. G., MEMBER OF THE SIXTH MASSACHUSETTS

Dulce et decorum est pro patria mori
Sweet it is, and proper, to die for one's country
—HORACE, *ODES,* CA. 8 B.C.

Friday, April 19, 1861

Tempers in Baltimore simmered throughout the morning. Respectable citizens, representing much of the city's elite and calling themselves the National Volunteer Association, held a meeting. Although they disagreed a bit about tactics, they opposed any armed Northerners passing through their city. The pathetic, unarmed Pennsylvanians had stirred up too much disorder the day before. Meanwhile a huge rally filled Monument Square not far away. The rhetoric there was less subdued. Orators screamed out their loathing of Lincoln and his Black Republicans. No more Yankee troops, they shrilled, could go through town. Mayor Brown addressed the throng. He announced that he, too, was completely opposed to "coercion," implying he considered that Lincoln's proclamation planned the coercion of the South.[42]

A few hours earlier, just before dawn, the train from Philadelphia had entered northern Maryland. Most of the Sixth's volunteers were curious. Few had ever visited a slave state. They stared at the people they passed. An enlisted man from Worcester thought the faces looked "sullen." Unlike folks they had seen the past two days, these individuals showed no evidence of joy — no bonfires, no rockets, no flag waving, no cheery smiles. This boded ill.

Their train, on a ferry, crossed the wide Susquehanna without incident. It was probably just after this that Colonel Jones learned that Baltimoreans planned to physically resist their passage. He walked slowly through the cars, preparing his troops for what they would soon face. He made sure they still had cartridges for their Springfields. He ordered them to load their guns. (The complex process of loading a rifle would have been daunting to men who had never done so, and, no doubt, as their train rattled along, rookies received instructions from comrades.)

Jones had a bad feeling about Mobtown. Among other things, he worried his volunteers might do something provocative. He was well aware of the 1770 Boston Massacre, when a handful of British soldiers had opened fire on an angry mob pelting them with stones and chunks of ice. He knew his troops would soon be crossing Baltimore slowly, from one station to another. He believed — incorrectly, it would turn out — that the Sixth would be making this crossing on foot. This movement, he thought, would take time. Getting his men off the train, lining them up, marching them more than a mile through unfamiliar streets, then boarding another train — assuming one was waiting for them — would take at least an hour, probably more. He knew it was important they not get bogged down. He kept in mind his assignment: to reach the federal capital quickly, since, as he understood it, Washington might be attacked at any moment. He wanted nothing to occur in Baltimore to interfere with that goal. He even advised his regimental band not to play provocative songs.

He told his men as he walked through their cars: "You will undoubtedly be insulted, abused, and, perhaps, assaulted, to which you must pay no attention whatever, but march with your faces square to the front, and pay no attention to the mob." They must remain controlled, even if the mob hurled "stones, bricks, or other missiles." They must not fire their weapons—unless fired on first. And, even if fired on, they should remain disciplined, awaiting orders from their officers. And if they did shoot, they must only aim at those individuals shooting at them. They must not fire indiscriminately. Colonel Jones was asking a great deal. History often tells of incidents when professional policemen or veteran soldiers become unglued when sworn at, when spat on, when threatened, when battered with rocks. These Massachusetts volunteers had been store clerks and farmers only two days earlier.[43]

The train whistled as it pulled into President Street Station and braked to a halt. The time was just before eleven in the morning. A crowd waiting at the depot was not huge; at that moment, it numbered perhaps 250 or so. Some hooted at the sight of the volunteers, taunting them. Nothing more.

But the soldiers did not immediately march away from the station, as Jones had assumed. Instead, workmen at the depot prepared to move the train's cars, one by one, with the volunteers still aboard, to Camden Street Station. The process was supposed to go like this: The engine would be uncoupled and moved off a bit. The rolling stock would then pass through a cumbersome process. Each car was separated from the others. Four horses were led to it and harnessed to its front, using a special contraption. A track had been laid through this part of the city, connecting President Street Station (used by Felton's Philadelphia, Wilmington, and Baltimore Railroad) to Camden Street Station, almost a mile-and-a-half away (serving as the mother hub of the Baltimore & Ohio). These two railroads had an arrangement whereby they sometimes used each other's cars for a fee, to avoid the expense and aggravation of unloading unwieldy materials like coal and wheat and having to cart it through Baltimore. Moreover, passengers sometimes remained in their cars so they would not have to worry about transferring their luggage and slogging from one depot to the other in the rain or snow, though more typically the cars served as omnibuses, crossing town with the passengers inside them, who then alit and boarded a waiting train at the other station. (When Lincoln went through Baltimore two months earlier he had slept through this part of his journey, so had been on one of the cars that passengers could stay on all the way from Philadelphia to Washington.)

The two depots were almost precisely east-west from each other, with a stubby arm of the harbor lying between them. The horses pulling a car would first plod northward from President Street Station for four blocks. The track then turned to the left onto Pratt Street. The Pratt Street portion of the trip, a mile in length, led the cars past the harbor and docks on the left, with tied-up sloops and steamers, schooners and scows. On the right was Marsh Market, a large, open-air emporium selling fish and other foodstuffs; then blocks of warehouses and brick buildings with small shops on the ground floors and rented rooms above. Dingy saloons, huddling coarsely here and there, were frequented by begrimed stevedores and sailors. Near the end of the Pratt Street track was a nice establishment called Maltby House. Between Marsh Market and the Maltby, almost two dozen streets and alleys, coming from the heart of the city, opened onto Pratt Street. Just past the harbor, the track pulled left off Pratt onto Camden Street. A block down Camden sat the new, large B&O station.

The system always held the prospect of delays. Although the teamsters who maneuvered their nags were generally adept at their jobs, they had only a limited number of horses: fewer than forty, it seems. This meant they could only move eight to ten cars at a time before sending teams of horses back to pick up more cars. This particular trainload, with so many cars, would require far more complications, with the men of the Sixth Massachusetts filling the first dozen cars and the Pennsylvanians jammed into a score more. The Baltimore teamsters and horses would have to work hard. Transferring all these volunteers and their baggage would require at least four trips, using increasingly exhausted horses. The process might take six hours. (This was assuming sufficient B&O trains were ready at Camden Street Station — and there weren't.)

If a passenger stepped from the train at President Street Station, he could walk to the depot on Camden Street in a half-hour or less. It would not be an entirely pleasant jaunt, even if the weather was hospitable. He would have to dodge street vehicles along the way and listen to workmen cursing on the docks. He could expect to step over or around a number of impediments. As with any docks, Pratt Street had the usual detritus of the sea trade along its edge: boxes and barrels to be laded into the holds of waiting ships; anchors in a clump that looked like a challenging game of Pick-up Sticks. On this particular day, paving stones and sand lay piled near the intersection of Pratt and President. (The city was resurfacing Pratt Street. That very morning, in fact, laborers had started early working on this task. Carts creaked slowly up and down the avenue, carrying materials. Most of the drivers were African Americans.) A watery stream from the interior of Maryland, called Jones Falls by Baltimoreans, entered the harbor where Pratt and President intersected. A bridge — a wooden structure — enabled traffic to cross it. This, too, was being updated. Shoring timbers were strewn about.

Late morning. Shops were open for business. Housewives and slaves, purchasing food supplies, wandered the stalls at Marsh Market. Most seemed unaware that two thousand Northern volunteers had just arrived at President Street Station, five blocks away.

City officials were equally in the dark. The previous afternoon, after the Pennsylvania companies had stumbled through town and departed for Washington, Marshal Kane and Mayor Brown, among others, heard rumors that more troops might be arriving in a few hours. But when none appeared, they concluded the railroad men who ran the two lines coming south into the city had decided not to carry volunteers through Baltimore. The officials believed they would at least be informed well in advance of any new military arrivals. They were wrong; Felton did not trust them and purposely had not, a few hours earlier, telegrammed the city when he sent more troops toward them.

But about eight o'clock that morning, someone along the railway did wire Baltimore the news, most likely a telegrapher in Havre de Grace. Who received this surreptitious message? The answer is unknown, but almost immediately crowds began gathering at both major depots. Someone connected to the Baltimore & Ohio Railroad contacted Marshal Kane and asked for protection. Kane was keenly aware the B&O was the city's most important business, and he was happy to do what he could. He rushed to Camden Street Station, the southernmost of the two depots in question, and sent messengers to his policemen to head there. By nine o'clock he and about forty of his men waited. His purpose at this moment, obviously, was to protect the B&O's property, not the volunteers, who would be arriving almost a mile-and-a-half away, at President Street Station.

No one at Camden Street Station knew how many troops were coming on Felton's train. The Massachusetts regiment by itself was fairly large, actually consisting of eleven companies, not the traditional ten, and it was accompanied by a band, traveling, because of their clumsy instruments, in a baggage car behind the rest of the regiment.

(Weeks later a grand jury would review the events of this day. Witnesses would claim they saw Kane with George Konig, a well-known local goon and Democrat, walking arm in arm just the day before. As we will see, Konig was at the center of some of the coming violence. Whether Marshal Kane was a friend of Konig was irrelevant to the events of April 19. Kane was about to act forcefully for peace. He probably opposed the presence of the Massachusetts volunteers, but he was anxious to preserve order and to maintain the property of the B&O.)

About ten o'clock that morning three members of the city council entered the law office of Mayor Brown. They were troubled. They bore a note from Kane saying, somewhat cryptically, that more Northern troops were due to arrive, and that the police chief suspected trouble. (It ought to be recalled that less than an hour earlier Mayor Brown had told a rally on Monument Square he opposed coercion.) The mayor rushed to the nearby headquarters of the police board. Kane had already departed, but the city's chief solicitor, George M. Gill, was there, as well as some police commissioners. The mayor told them he was heading to Camden Street Station, and said they could join him. He jumped into his carriage and raced off, accompanied only by lawyer Gill. When they arrived at Camden Street Station they saw that the crowd at this spot was growing large and noisy, and impatient.

Youngsters on horseback rode down Pratt Street to the other station to see what was going on there. A little after eleven a boy galloped back to announce that a train from Philadelphia had indeed pulled in, and it seemed to be stuffed with Yankee troops. Teamsters, he said breathlessly, were attaching horses to the cars; the first group ought to appear at any moment.

The first car trundled into sight about eleven-thirty. A portion of the crowd snarled curses at Yankee invaders and yawped their affection for the Confederacy, cheering Jeff Davis. The car had its blinds drawn so that the troops inside were not immediately visible, but when the first uniformed Yankee stepped out, the mob surged forward. Only the presence of Kane and his policemen, forming a human barricade between the crowd and the soldiers, kept things in hand. As a result these troops remained unscathed as they walked over to a waiting train and stepped inside one of its cars. Under Jones's strict orders, they tried to ignore the imprecations and the taunts and those in the crowds who brandished knives and pistols (though some soldiers quietly cocked their guns, just in case). The second car arrived, then the third. And so on. A few had their windows broken and dings on their sides from rocks flung at them. But given the emotions, this damage seemed small. The volunteers quickly disappeared from view when they boarded the new train. Events seemed to be going smoothly, all things considered. Mayor Brown felt pleased. His satisfaction was premature. After the first eight carloads arrived at Camden Street Station, several things occurred, almost simultaneously.

First, the policemen learned that a group of local men, southwest of the station, were attempting to yank up the rails to prevent Yankee troops from getting out of Baltimore. Kane ordered a squad of his policemen to check out the accuracy of this rumor and to stop the destruction of railroad property. If necessary, the police were to go as far south as Relay House, about eight miles away. (For the next hour or two some of Kane's policemen scurried along the rail line. They frequently did find desperate locals ripping at tracks. The policemen also found places where rails had been blocked by timbers and the like, and they tossed these impediments aside. The departure of this squad of policemen from Camden Street Station weakened Kane's available police force there.)

Meanwhile a car on Pratt Street began to be assaulted with great violence by a mob. In the space of less than five minutes, a tense but controlled situation spun into madness.

A member of this mob, Ernest Wardwell, in his midteens, has given us a splendid eyewitness account. Earlier that morning he had been sitting in his classroom. He and his fellow students had felt an uncertain air of edginess. All of a sudden they heard fire bells outside clanging, followed by street noises cascading into the school through the windows. The principal, seeing that further education was impossible, dismissed the students, advising them to go home immediately. As Wardwell grabbed his hat and raced toward the door, his friend Henry Cook said, "Come on Ernie, let's see what's going on." The two ran toward the bedlam. They joined an "immense crowd" near President Street Station (the eastern depot), and were instantly part of a jammed-together mass of sweating flesh. They could see a train's car slowly moving along, pulled by a team of horses. Civilians crowded around it screaming in rage, their faces distorted. At first, Wardwell would recall, "I was paralyzed with fear." But in a trice he found himself caught up in the frenzy and was yelling too, as loudly as he could. He saw men in the mob throwing things at the cars, and, wishing to join the fun, he searched for something to fling but was disappointed to find nothing with the proper heft. In a few moments he had gone from schoolboy to a crazed inhabitant of a pulsating mob. He had become a mindless, out-of-control thing.[44]

The Massachusetts men aboard this car had also been struggling to maintain emotional balance. Major Benjamin F. Watson, the Sixth's second in command, was among them. Like Colonel Jones, Major Watson had thought the regiment would be marching to the other depot, and was thus a bit startled after a few minutes at the station to look out and see that his car stood at the front of the train—that is, that all those cars preceding it had disappeared. He was contemplating the implications of this fact when four horses were attached to his car, and off it jolted. The noisy mob outside was growing by the second (and now included young Ernest Wardwell).

The car moved four blocks, and the horses were swinging onto Pratt when the volunteers inside felt a distinct bump. They came to a halt. The mob, frantic now to stop their passage, had placed obstructions on the tracks. Major Watson jumped out to investigate, saw that the car's wheels had jostled off the rails, and wondered what to do. The throng crammed close to him. Quick-wittedly he pressed a passing team of horses into service, and somehow—while the crowd jeered—got the wheels back into place. The car, jolting into motion, began.

Watson would describe what then happened. "The starting of the car was the signal for volleys of stones and other missiles, and occasional shots." Bottles, pieces of iron, paving bricks smashed against its sides. Windows on both sides crashed inward, splinters of glass and slivers of wood knifed through the air, ripping at the men's uniforms and skin.

The civilian driver at the front was visibly nervous, and Watson stepped forward and stood next to him, hoping his presence would act as a steadying force. One of his soldiers was injured by an incoming missile. Officers ordered the anxious militiamen to lie down. The faces outside, as one volunteer would remember it, seemed "wild, terrible, and venomous." Some troops wanted to retaliate, but Watson reminded them about Jones's orders that they must not fire unless someone shot at them first. Suddenly a shout came from the middle of the car, and Major Watson looked back. A private put up his hand. Blood ran down his arm, as, strangely, the soldier calmly showed he had just had part of his thumb shot off. "I then gave the order," Watson would recall, "to fire at will."

Sixty-four rifle-toting infantrymen jumped up from their crouched positions and started firing frantically in the general direction of their tormentors. These men called themselves the Washington Light Guard. Officially they constituted K Company of the Sixth Regiment. Two days earlier they had been civilians, most of them workmen by trade — house-builders or printers, silver-platers or masons. At least one was a reporter. Almost all were from Boston proper, not one of its outlying towns. Almost none had ever handled guns. Their aim was poor.

Those who remembered how to reload their weapons were in the act of doing so when the car stopped a second time. While Major Watson's attention had been distracted, the driver had unhitched his horses and skedaddled. The major ran after him. The swarming crowd here was so thick the driver found himself slowed down and, amazingly, Watson caught up to him, about fifty feet from the door of the now-stalled car. Rifle fire from the men inside kept the mob away a few moments while Watson successfully wheedled the driver to return with his horses.

The car started a third time. Workers at the wharves and docks on the left gaped from a few feet away. People atop the buildings on the right pelted it with stones that clanged off its roof. It had almost reached the place on Pratt Street where it would have turned left toward Camden Street Station when some in the crowd, seeing its approach, finally succeeded in ripping up rails. The car had to halt, again. The men of the Washington Light Guard quickly filed from it, lined up as best they could, and hustled hurriedly toward the depot, less than 200 yards away.

Colonel Jones, quite worried at the sounds of gunfire, was waiting. He told K Company to board the train. He peered in the direction of the other station, far out of sight, and wondered where the rest of his regiment was.[45]

Things, already bad, were about to turn far worse.

As the car carrying Major Watson and his crew successfully escaped, some Baltimoreans made efforts to prevent more Yankees from getting through. Up to this moment, events had transpired haphazardly. Now, certain individuals took charge. Exactly who they were is not certain. But likely they were prominent city merchants who knew the wharf of the city well. They began issuing orders. Burly stevedores — most of them African Americans — were ordered to drag the eight heavy anchors, piled along Smith's Wharf, onto the tracks that went along Pratt Street. Nearby paving stones were added to this heap, along with timbers scheduled to be used as struts on the bridge and a cartload of sand. Men also grabbed picks and shovels from the road-construction site, and pried up the tracks. No more cars would pass this spot.[46]

At the far station the troops of the four remaining Massachusetts infantry companies sat nervously in their cars, awaiting horses to take them. Suddenly two local citizens claiming unionist sentiments ran to the front car. Inside was Captain Albert S. Follansbee and C Company, one of two drawn from the population of Lowell. Two weeks earlier they had constituted a militia unit humbly calling itself the Lowell Mechanic Phalanx. Follansbee, thirty-seven, had somber eyes, receding hair, and a bushy brown beard. He listened carefully to the two citizens excitedly saying the track ahead was blocked, that his car would never reach Camden Street. He made a quick decision. He sent a message to the car directly behind his that he intended to march, and he ordered his company to pile onto the platform.

Within minutes, the 260 volunteers of the remaining four Massachusetts infantry companies were standing at the depot, knapsacks weighing against their shoulders. The men tightly gripped their weapons. (No one thought to inform the band members, huddled farther back in their baggage car, that the infantrymen were departing.)

Captain Follansbee, acting in temporary command of this ad hoc battalion, led off. He had no clear mental picture about which direction he should take and was forced to ask a policeman to give him guidance. The volunteers trailed behind him. They had not proceeded more than a few paces when they found themselves confronting a hundred or more men walking directly at them, led by George Konig, the politician and saloon owner. The smirking Konig bore a staff in his arms from which dangled a Confederate banner of some sort.[47] He or one of his sidekicks yelled that the "white niggers" from Massachusetts would never live to reach the other station. Follansbee ordered his men to press forward. As they neared the barkeep, Konig and his companions spun around and strutted off before them — waggishly compelling the Yankee troops to march behind the Southern flag. The New Englanders heard themselves been called "Yankee dogs" and "nigger-stealers," "cutthroats" and "murderers," "jailbirds" and "scum" — and worse.

This procession only moved together a block or two. Several Union supporters in the watching crowd decided to end the farce. They ran at Konig to wrest his flag from him. They succeeded in ripping it from the pole, but were physically prevented from carrying it away. This scuffle, near the intersection of President and Pratt, pricked the rage that had been percolating. Then, brickbats and bottles spun through the air like angry hornets. People at upstairs windows and on rooftops flung household objects down on the passing soldiers: lumps of coal, pitchers and dishes, jars of nightsoil. Some found their marks, glancing off the volunteers' shoulders and heads. Soldiers were knocked to the ground. Most staggered to their feet. One man, his head fractured just above his left eye, did not get up. Others who went down were pounced on, stomped, and hammered with rocks. Those still able to walk pressed on. They reached Pratt Street and turned left. Here they discovered that someone had removed planking from the bridge, but they hop-scotched across the remaining stringers and reached the other side. They then saw, several blocks away, the barricade that had been flung together across the tracks.

Follansbee ordered his men to pick up their pace. The volunteers began to double-quick, trotting now. The sight of these running troops churned the mob into a paroxysm of frenzy — as the sight of a jogger moving away can encourage dogs to chase after and nip at the runner's legs. The shrieking voices intensified. Apparently many in the crowd assumed the guns the soldiers carried were unloaded. From both sides, the mob kicked and shoved at the troops, trying to knock them down, attempting to grab their rifles. Civilians fired pistols from short range at the soldiers. A volunteer felt a bullet pierce his thigh. Another tumbled to the street, shot in the nape of his neck.

Somewhere near the barricade, Follansbee stopped, turned to the volunteers behind him, and yelled "Fire!" In the cacophony few of his men heard the order. Perhaps twenty soldiers obeyed. Some would later claim they only aimed at the people pointing guns at them. In a few cases, maybe so. One civilian shot by the soldiers was James "Mickey" Clark, who had suddenly emotionally snapped. Seeing a Yankee officer, Clark screamed into his face, hit him, yanked a soggy chaw of tobacco from his mouth, and flung it. The officer raised his pistol and shot the crazed Clark in the eye. Other troops fired with less discrimination. One observer said he saw the volunteers running, haphazardly shooting rifles over their shoulders without aiming. These men were unschooled in military matters. It would be absurd to assume they would use their weapons with the discipline of well-trained regulars.

The bedlam reached a crescendo, the noise echoing off the buildings on either side. The leather boots of the Massachusetts volunteers thumped on the cobblestones, shouts and curses coming from all sides. The meat-whacking *fumphs* of fists hitting cheekbones and shoulders, of thick shoes kicking against legs and torsos. The BANG! of gunfire. Screams — of rage and fear. And shouts of pain from men whose flesh had just been torn by bullets or knives.

Then out of nowhere, it seemed, a well-dressed citizen appeared at Follansbee's side. "I am the mayor of Baltimore," the man murmured, and shook the captain's hand. It was indeed George Brown. He was breaking the promise he had made earlier on Monument Square; he had come to still the violence, to assist the soldiers in getting through Baltimore.

A few minutes earlier, when Major Watson and the Washington Light Guard had staggered into Camden Street Station, they had said that more troops were trailing somewhere behind them. The mayor was startled by this news. He had assumed the crisis was over. He sent a companion to alert Marshal Kane as to what he planned, and strode off toward the noise. He saw the anchors piled on the street. Nearby stood five policemen who had been trying unsuccessfully to get them moved — prevented by the mob. Brown decided to use his authority. He ordered the anchors pulled away — presumably by the same African Americans who had dragged them here from the wharf. The mob chose not to defy their mayor. Brown watched as the anchors were shifted from the tracks, then, believing that cars could again move on Pratt Street, he began heading toward the chaos.

Almost immediately he encountered the volunteers coming toward him, shooting wildly as they hurried. After introducing himself to Follansbee, Brown urged the captain to stop his men from jogging. It was their pace, the mayor said, that was causing at least part of the trouble. Follansbee insisted his troops had done nothing to provoke this violence, and Brown said he understood: "You must defend yourselves." Follansbee thereupon ordered his column to revert to a normal marching pace. As the troops slowed down, Brown wheeled next to Follansbee and offered to walk alongside him. The mayor hoped his presence at the front would calm the mob. He heard people around him saying, "Here comes the mayor." He was optimistic, but far too sanguine. He had only accompanied the volunteers a block or two when he grew aware that the mob behind them had once again increased their attacks. He saw some troops firing into the crowd. At one point he waved his umbrella and shouted, "For God's sake, don't shoot." He apparently had changed his mind about the Massachusetts men having the right to defend themselves.

Several soldiers, including Follansbee, would later claim they observed the mayor grab one of their rifles and fire into the mass of civilians. He would deny this, saying he had only been handed an empty Springfield rifle which had fallen to the ground, and that he then left the marching soldiers to carry this abandoned weapon into a store for safekeeping. He did admit he had already decided to leave the volunteers, since he was accomplishing nothing. They said/he said. The truth is foggy.

Neither Mayor Brown nor Captain Follansbee, at the head of the column, were aware that volunteers about a hundred yards farther back were receiving the worst of the attack. A sergeant, Timothy A. Crowley, became a sort of magnet for missiles. Assigned to carry the regimental colors, he stationed himself almost precisely in the center of Follansbee's procession, with members of his color guard marching near him. This cluster became a focus. Rocks grazed Crowley's head. One stone mashed just between his shoulder blades, eventually resting atop his knapsack, a sort of hitchhiker until a marcher behind Crowley brushed it off. Two brickbats smacked against the flagstaff, but the sergeant held on more tightly and kept marching. Except for bumps and bruises, he somehow remained mostly unhurt. Those behind him were less lucky.

The first to die was Private Luther C. Ladd, born in New Hampshire on his father's farm. At the age of sixteen, bored with farm life, wanting something different, Ladd had headed to Lowell, where he found a job in a machine shop. Now, on Pratt Street he was struck in the head by some heavy object and crumpled to the ground. A person snatched his gun and shot him in the leg. Sympathetic unionists in the crowd picked him up and carried him to an infirmary. People there tried, without success, to stop the bleeding. Ladd was a handsome boy, seventeen years old, and dying. The good-hearted Baltimoreans wanted to know why he had come to this place. Perhaps delirious, Private Ladd gave his answer. "The flag," he murmured, "the stars and stripes." At least those were the words observers later recalled. (When his body was returned to Boston and examined, a newspaper said: "His face was somewhat swollen, and gave much evidence of rough usage" — that "usage" being the battering the mob had given him as he lay on the pavement, his lifeblood pouring onto the cobblestone street.)

Corporal Needham, a plasterer from Lawrence, the letter writer who had urged his wife "to hope for the best and be as cheerful as you can," was shot in the neck, then smashed by the crowd and kicked to a pulp. He lingered in Baltimore for eight days before dying of his wounds.

Private Charles Alfred Taylor had recently joined the company. Few of his companions, after he died, could recall much about him. Someone remembered he was an artist of some sort — a "decorative painter." Sergeant John Ames of Lowell, thirty-seven and married, was also murdered this day. So was twenty-two-year-old Addison O. Whitney, a spinner at one of Lowell's mills, shot in the chest.

Five soldiers altogether. Except for Corporal Needham, who had been marching near the front of the pack, the others were members of D Company, the Lowell City Guards, which trailed along directly behind Sergeant Crowley and his regimental flag. Ten other troops from this company received wounds of one sort or another.

Behind this group, at the end of the regiment, came Captain John H. Dike's company from Stoneham. A quarter of these men were also wounded during the march, including their captain (who would be robbed of a thousand dollars inside a small purse he was handed in Boston for the use of the entire company).

In total, forty members of the Sixth Massachusetts were killed or wounded badly enough that they were listed as having received medical care. Those officially "wounded" had broken bones, had been shot or stabbed, or smashed with rocks or fists or boots so severely that blood gushed from at least one—and often several—gashes. Many other volunteers received contusions on their shoulders from thrown missiles, or bruises on their knees from stumbling, but they were not officially listed as casualties of the incident.

It could have been much worse. During a normal battle in the coming war a casualty rate of under 6 percent was called moderate or even light. On the other hand, in this case such a percentage would have only reflected the regiment as a whole. The casualty figures for the four companies facing the brunt of the assault would have been deemed "rather heavy." As for the two rear companies, they suffered a 25 percent casualty rate. Using the usual military standard, these numbers would have been labeled "devastating."

As Follansbee's battered men, still moving, stumbled along, several factors coincided. Marshal Kane appeared with two score policemen. They charged past the Massachusetts troops and formed a line between them and the mob, each policeman holding a drawn revolver. Given the extraordinary level of violence in that vicinity, it was a gutsy move. Some policemen were immediately hit by stones, but Kane's action saved many lives — on both sides.

While the policemen stood like a wall, Follansbee and the front of his column arrived at another partly erected barricade, and kept going. They did not realize it but they had just been lucky. On the far side of this mound was a cannon. Members of the mob had found it somewhere, and were apparently in the process of loading it with something. The unexpected appearance of Follansbee's soldiers bearing down on the gun crew, bayonets in front, caused the putative artillerymen to scatter.

Only a block or so then separated the front of the ad hoc battalion from the depot. Another wave of rioters roared toward them. Gunfire was again exchanged, as well as some fisticuffs. (This may have been where Corporal Needham received his fatal wounds.) Then this phase of the battle was suddenly over.

Colonel Jones waited impatiently by the train. He ordered the new arrivals to board the cars. The time was just before one o'clock.

The Sixth had been in Baltimore less than two hours. Railroad officials on the scene and city authorities urged them to lower their cars' shades and get moving. The regiment had been able to bring along most of its wounded — though not all. If they departed immediately, they would be leaving behind their baggage, and the band members, who were trapped somewhere back there, abandoned to some uncertain fate. But the railroad men assured them that this train could not carry any more men than it already had on board. Besides no one could be sure that Kane's policemen had been able to clear the tracks south of the station.[48]

The agents of the Baltimore & Ohio Railroad were half hysterical. The presence of Yankee troops aboard their cars offered the prospect of complications for the company, whose hundreds of miles of tracks lay inside slave states. During the previous few hours these officials had received disturbing news. Virginia's convention had definitely voted to secede, and thousands of Virginia militiamen had taken over Harpers Ferry this very morning. The B&O would have to tiptoe carefully now around this political minefield. If the railroad was seen to favor either camp in this confrontation, the other side might retaliate.

Three years earlier the company had acquired a new president, John Work Garrett. A fat, fairly bright forty-year-old, Garrett was a member of one of Baltimore's most prominent families, with strong ties to both commerce and banking. In his heart he was probably loyal to the Union, but his sympathies were with the South. In 1860 he had said about his railroad: "It is a Southern line." But he had uttered that sentence when the topic was merely abstract. Reality now was trickier. For example, he and other B&O leaders had to be concerned that Virginia militiamen in Harpers Ferry might choose to burn the important wooden bridge there, instantly stopping all major east-west traffic on the line. A large portion of the B&O's income was derived from carrying freight — coal from western Virginia, for instance — through Harpers Ferry.

An additional complicating factor came into play. The Baltimore & Ohio's chief rival was the Pennsylvania Central, whose tracks paralleled those of the Baltimore-based company but lay a hundred miles to the north, allowing it to pass through free states like Pennsylvania. Lincoln's new secretary of war, the man whose orders shifted Union volunteers from place to place, Simon Cameron, was part owner of the Northern Central Railway, a subsidiary of the Pennsylvania Central. A cynic might assume Cameron would use his position to benefit his own railroad at the expense of the B&O. After all, whenever troops took trains from one place to another, they paid for their passage. Colonel Jones, for example, had just handed the B&O hard cash to carry his regiment from Baltimore to Washington.

With the prospect of tens of thousands of paying passengers, no railroad in the United States wanted to overlook the prospect of making a profit. But the B&O's officials wondered, at what cost? Their immediate concern involved information they were getting from their men along their line south of Baltimore: that maddened Marylanders were making efforts to prevent the Sixth — or any other Northern troops — from arriving at Lincoln's capital; that hooligans seemed to be ripping up rails faster than Kane's policemen could replace them. The valuable bridges owned by the B&O were also vulnerable. A few miles south of Baltimore was a hundred-foot wooden span called Jackson's Bridge. If burned, the Sixth might not get to Washington (though it was possible the volunteers would simply march past that detour and insist they be picked up by another B&O train on the far side). Freight, however — cannon and ammunition — could not be moved so easily.[49]

Under the circumstances, in the push-pull of all these factors, the B&O's master of transportation in Baltimore, William Prescott Smith, decided that although he could not prevent the Sixth from using his train, he wanted them out of town as fast as possible. Once they departed, his superiors could determine their next steps. As the last of Follansbee's procession tottered into the station, therefore, Smith pleaded with Colonel Jones.

Jones was outraged by what had just happened to his men. He may also have been anxious about his band members, who were nowhere in sight. Jones told Smith that many of his troops were nearly crazed with rage, and he considered taking them back down Pratt Street on an errand of revenge or to clear the way for the band. His official after-action report would offer no hint of this intention, but Jones's superior, Ben Butler, would later insist Jones had only been stopped from taking that action by a message he was handed from General Scott, which said: "Let there be no possible delay in your coming." Meanwhile, the B&O's master of transportation, Smith, continued to beg Jones to hurry. "For God's sake, give the order for the cars to move; the mob is already trying to tear the tracks up in front of us. If you don't, no one of your men will leave here alive."

———

Jones made his decision; his troops would depart. He ordered his men to pull down the curtains over their windows. The train began to move. Crowds still milled near the station, kept slightly away by the presence of policemen, but threatening just the same. The colonel hoped to keep his angry volunteers, rifles still gripped in their fists, under reasonable control.

Once the train was chuffing down the tracks, civilians along the way started heaving rocks. Shards of glass spattered the interior of the cars and rained down on the troops. At least one Baltimorean, perhaps several, climbed on top of one of the slowly moving cars and bashed at the roofs. Civilian ambushers, hiding behind trees, fired at the passing train—though without effect, since the marksmen cautiously stayed far back. At one point down the tracks the train was forced to halt where rails had been torn up. While this problem was being fixed, wary troops stood alongside those making repairs, watching clumps of Marylanders grouped not far off, shaking their fists and offering rude salutations. At this juncture the conductor told Colonel Jones he refused to go any farther. Jones reminded the man he had paid for this trip and insisted on his right to have it, adding, if the conductor refused, the Sixth would expropriate the train and run it themselves. There was no more trouble.[50]

Fifteen-year-old Ernest Wardwell had failed to find a rock to throw at the soldiers, and, then, feeling an odd sense of sympathy for their plight, he had joined their march as they walked past him. He even carried one of their unloaded rifles. For reasons he could never understand, when the Yankee soldiers boarded the train, so did he. He became their mascot. Months later, back in Massachusetts, he officially mustered into another regiment and eventually rose to the rank of captain.

The infantrymen of the Sixth were gone. The crisis in Baltimore, however, was far from over.

CHAPTER EIGHT

Malice and Compassion

I still believe that people are really good at heart.
—ANNE FRANK

The number of civilians killed or wounded in Baltimore on April 19 is fuzzy. Unlike soldiers, who were listed on official rosters and can therefore be somewhat tracked, acquiring details about that era's citizens is problematic, at best. During that day many of Baltimore's injured were cared for at home, or not at all, so it is impossible to offer numbers with any confidence. Some historians have estimated that twelve citizens were killed and at least a hundred more wounded. One historian, Matthew Ellenberger, has analyzed the dozen Baltimoreans he says were killed this day. He checked the city's tax records and found only one of them listed there, which suggested to him that the vast majority of the mob as a whole were propertyless people.[51]

But most of Ellenberger's sources were newspapers, and therefore questionable. Even in quiet times, the journals of that era were notoriously slack. During the emotional days after these events, Baltimore's newspapers, depending on their political leanings, inflated the importance of some incidents and denigrated or ignored others.

Periodicals from other cities may have offered slightly more reliable information, but they also must be read cautiously. A major Philadelphia paper, the *Public Ledger*, for example, carried an item about two civilian casualties in Baltimore. One, it said, was "a boy" named William Reed. The article described him as a seaman on the oyster boat *Wild Pigeon*, tied at the Light Street Wharf, and that he was shot in the abdomen. The *Ledger* added that he "was crying, at last accounts, in the hold of the schooner." Another "boy," Patrick Griffin, it said, was "shot through the bowels" while standing in the doorway of a hotel, watching the spectacle. Several questions come to mind. Whose guns shot these two? Reed, on the boat, would have been in direct line of anyone firing from the roofs of the buildings toward the Yankee volunteers; but Griffin was probably (though not necessarily, given the confusion in that sector) pierced by a Massachusetts ball.

The word "boys" typically referred to young males, but it was also commonly used in newspapers to denote African Americans of any age. We therefore do not know their race, if that makes any difference. What was their eventual fate? In that era, getting shot in the abdomen or bowels generally resulted in a lingering and painful death, but neither individual seems to have been listed as among those civilians killed (though American newspapers in 1861 seldom deigned to notice the suffering or demise of African Americans). Like so many of the civilians killed or injured this day, what actually happened to those two "boys" is now lost.

The single most-talked-about casualty of April 19 was a dry goods merchant named Robert W. Davis. In terms of social standing, he represented the upper tier of the city's population.

Late that morning Davis and a companion, a young lawyer and part-time newsman, Thomas W. Hall, strolled down the tracks south of Baltimore out of curiosity. They had heard that people were ripping up the rails and wanted to see if this story was accurate. They walked less than a mile, saw nothing, and turned around. At some point they were joined by three acquaintances. The reporter Hall would later testify that he and Davis had no knowledge of anything happening on Pratt

Street or near Camden Street Station, insisting they were entirely "ignorant at the time of any bloodshed, or that any collision with the people had taken place" along Pratt Street. If one were to believe Thomas Hall, he and his companions were merely five jolly young gentlemen out on a peaceful jaunt, entirely unaware of the extraordinarily noisy nightmare occurring not far away — a ludicrous claim.

These five men were four blocks below Camden Street Station when the Sixth's train, leaving the city for Washington, passed them. Davis stood perched on some railroad ties near the tracks. Policemen were in the vicinity, about 200 yards away, still protecting the rails from anyone wanting to interfere with the train's departure. Davis and his pals, according to Hall's testimony, saw a few Yankee soldiers inside the cars and cheerfully shouted hurrahs for Jeff Davis and the Confederacy. Davis derisively waved a loosely held kid glove at the passing Massachusetts volunteers. If Hall's testimony was accurate, the little group was acting no more threatening than sports fans cheering the home team and booing the opposition. According to Hall, only after the young merchant Davis was shot — "I am killed," he said to Hall — did his companions fling stones at the disappearing train.

Colonel Jones's recollection, written three days after this incident, was different. He reported that as the train was picking up speed, "a volley of stones" hit the cars. One volunteer, the colonel said, then fired a rifle from the window of the car, killing William Davis. Jones said he investigated the incident, speaking to "reliable witnesses" who assured him that Davis was one of those heaving rocks at them. Jones admitted, even if Davis had indeed thrown a stone, this action would not have justified the Massachusetts soldier shooting him — but, Jones sighed, given the experiences of the past two hours, his men "were infuriated beyond control." (The fact that Davis had one of his kid gloves off, and not the other, might suggest he had removed one glove to pick up a rock.)

Everyone agreed: the fatal shot, and perhaps several other rifle balls, came from one of the last three cars. This almost certainly meant the volunteer who shot Davis was one of those who had marched with Captain Follansbee, probably a member of the Stoneham company, the last to arrive at the station. Although none of its men had been killed in the melee on Pratt Street, a quarter of them had received wounds so severe they needed medical attention, and had to be left behind, abandoned on Pratt Street to an uncertain fate. Among these was their commander, Captain John Dike (the officer who was robbed of the company's entire money supply).

The men of the Sixth were not hardened veterans. Guns were new things to them. A normal person, half demented by raging emotions, often wants to strike with whatever weapon comes to hand—a paving stone or a rifle. This fact does not excuse the shooting. An unnamedMassachusetts soldier did in fact murder Davis, and a court-martial ought to have determined the soldier's fate. But this did not happen; so far as the record shows, no one in the Sixth was punished for any infraction on the passage through Baltimore.[52]

The effect of Davis's death is interesting on several levels. His untimely demise was extensively covered in local newspapers and the city held an inquest into it. The next day the *Sun* described him as "a gentleman of irreproachable character, fine intelligence, and great popularity in mercantile circles." But officials made little effort to discover the identities of most of the civilians severely injured, or even killed, during the violence. This dichotomy nicely reflects the class prejudices of the times.

A member of Baltimore's city council would later admit "an intense excitement" now rocked the city, lasting at least forty-eight hours. He confessed the explosion of emotion, particularly because of the murder of Davis, grew "beyond control."[53] But what, specifically, was he referring to?

Anyone writing analytically about this era of Baltimore's history must deal with differences between the words "crowd" and "mob." The term "crowd" is neutral—it refers to an assortment of people. The second word, "mob," implies disorder, and is derogatory, revealing something about the person using it. Just as "horde" (as opposed to "army") implies that the group in question is undisciplined and not the right sort of folks to invite to a family barbecue, the pejorative word "mob" not only implies a large group, but suggests mindless, faceless individuals who, in some way, are animalistic. Members of a mob are seen as emotionally unbalanced and uncontrollable. From a social viewpoint they tend to represent that class sometimes called "rabble" or "riffraff" — at least to the person using the term.

What kind of people formed Baltimore's crowds on this occasion? Were they the hysterical goons described by Massachusetts volunteers? Or were they merely truculent pro-South roughnecks, as some thought, or even just fervent secessionists? Or were they simply local folks who resented armed outsiders marching through their streets — and in that sense, typical Americans?

One thing is clear: To call them a "mob" is accurate, but simplistic. Analysts have long tried to piece together what happened that day in the streets of Baltimore. Except for a few fanatical pro-Southerners, almost no one, in the city or outside, held the New Englanders responsible for the violence. (Since many Americans in 1770 had blamed British troops for the Boston Massacre, the fact that most Southerners rebuked Baltimoreans for the savagery on Pratt Street probably derived from the city's prior sinister reputation. For Baltimore, generations of chickens had come home to roost.)

Did the situation along the one-mile stretch of Pratt Street turn bloody because of what city officials later called "a sudden impulse," or was it organized? The answer seems to be: both. In the crowd were prominent merchants and lawyers who were pro-South leaders — men like Judge T. Parkin Scott and politician William Byrne. (The judge had spoken at a rally the night before, where he exhorted his listeners to take action against incoming Yankees.)

An historian, Frank Towers, has analyzed the rioters, identifying 159, using magistrate's reports, tax and census records, newspaper accounts, and grand jury investigations. He has concluded: "The most common occupations for rioters were merchant, clerk or other commercial pursuit, followed by a smaller number of immigrant workers." So far as Towers could determine, the wealth of the average rioter was more than ten times that of the typical working-age Baltimorean. While Professor Towers's methods are meticulous and impressive, many of his sources, by necessity, consist of court cases and committee hearings. Witnesses called to give testimony would probably not have been a true reflection of the typical member of the mob. A court wanting to clarify a confusing event relies heavily, if possible, on articulate observers. This usually excludes the addled, the illiterates, the dullards, the mentally sluggish.[54]

One problem with confidently drawing a clear picture of these events is that no one can positively know how many people were involved. Estimates of the numbers range from a mere few hundred to ten thousand. Individuals scampered from one locality to another during these events. Some people participated by throwing objects from rooftops or windows, but never came downstairs to join the jumble of humanity in the streets. And, of course, there were all those curious persons drawn to the growing din. Pratt Street and the docks were a well-known center of the city's economy. This was an era in which crowds enjoyed public spectacles. In 1858 the open-air debates between Senator Stephen Douglas and the lawyer Abraham Lincoln had attracted immense throngs who stood patiently under a blistering sun for hours listening to the two candidates orate. Part of the crowd on April 19 consisted of sailors and dockworkers aboard the tied-up ships, men with front row seats to this theater.

An analysis ought to begin by dividing the civilians into broad types. It seems plausible that most were like young Ernest Wardwell—drawn to the scene by curiosity. Some of these, on arriving at the turmoil, would have become emotionally involved, viewing the Massachusetts troops as outsiders, and therefore "not-one-of us." But most of the simply curious would not have participated on one side or the other. Instead, they would have remained bovine — an audience at a Punch-and-Judy show, perhaps rooting for this side or that, mildly excited by what they saw, their mouths agape, yet not profoundly moved.

A fair-sized portion were Union supporters. These people participated in a number of quiet ways. They assisted certain volunteers, offering advice about how to escape the dangerous elements; they provided medical attention; they hid frightened or wounded soldiers. Union supporters also stood as observers, feeling silent affection for their country, but not acting. How large was this element? It is impossible to know. When strong emotions roil a large crowd, those who are angriest, those willing to take the strongest and harshest positions, are obviously dangerous. Under such circumstances, wise individuals remain cautious.

How can we characterize those who openly and actively opposed the Massachusetts volunteers? We know, as Professor Towers reminds us, that many came from the city's respectable element. Given the geography of the events on Pratt Street, lying as it did next to the docks, it is not surprising that a number of young merchants were drawn in. These men had commercial businesses — in the steamship trade, for instance — which would have kept them in contact with slaveowners on the Eastern Shore or slave interests in Virginia or the West Indies. Many had friends or family members farther south. In their hearts they were Southerners, comfortable with their image of the Confederacy (a newly created organization they knew little about), loathing the hated abolitionist Black Republican administration of Abraham Lincoln, which they fervently despised, sight unseen. Within the next few months some of these men would leave Baltimore for Virginia, to join what would be called the Maryland Line — Confederate soldiers who proudly marched behind a Maryland banner into battles.

An interesting subgroup of this commercial element consisted of scores of men employed by the city's federal Customs House. (Professor Towers discovered "at least eleven Customs employees" who participated in the violence on April 19.) Baltimore was a major international port, which had customs agents to review the lading of incoming ships and to collect tariffs. These officials were appointed by the federal government. For more than a decade Democrats had controlled the White House, and the local Customs House had long served as the center for Baltimore's Democratic Party, a fact that had been particularly true when the Know Nothings filled most municipal offices. The brawling Know Nothing gangs like the Plug Uglies underscored the importance of the Customs House, which seemed the last bastion of sense and respectability. During the period between 1858 and 1860, agents there had worked with the reformers. It had been in their minds a moral crusade, with the agents fighting, fist against fist, against Know Nothing gangs. Know Nothingism was gone by 1861, at least in an organized sense, but emotions were still frayed. Since a number of national Republicans had once been Know Nothings, all Republicans were seen as immoral enemies. Recently, Customs House agents in Baltimore had learned that Secretary of the Treasury Chase, one of those Republicans was appointing new agents to replace them. Since March there had been incidents when Chase's appointees arrived in town. (During coming weeks several appointees were threatened with murder if they tried to perform as customs agents. A man from western Maryland, Henry Hoffman, arrived in the city a few days after April 19. He had sat in the United States House of Representatives, and Chase had named him collector of customs in Baltimore. But after observing Baltimore's paroxysms of frenzy, and sensing the hostility toward all things Republican, he decided it would be unwise to remain, and returned home to wait until the city calmed down.)[55]

To be sure, many of those in the April 19 crowds were less respectable, or at least less middle class, than customs officials. Baltimore, like several other American cities, had been suffering an economic slowdown since 1857. Things had begun improving in early 1860, but then, starting in the autumn, the economy suddenly staggered downward — perhaps because of uncertainties connected to Lincoln's election. With Republicans coming to power, what changes, some city businessmen wondered, might be in store?

Commerce slowed — both at the docks and the railroad stations. This meant wealthy merchants felt pinched in their wallets. Two banks in Baltimore failed. Several large businesses started laying off workers late in 1860, and continued doing so in 1861. Factories and foundries and canneries saw their markets weaken, and they fired laborers. Unemployment became rampant, reaching about 25 percent. In early March the city's Poor Association was assisting at least five thousand residents. Wives and children went hungry. Economically, the city was in a crisis.

The police arrested on April 19 many rock throwers, but then let almost all go, fining most of them a pittance for breaking a city ordinance against hurling missiles. Neither the newspapers nor court records nor the later recollections of city officials offer a clear profile of this element of rioters. One expert in Maryland's history, William J. Evitts, decided that most rioters were ruffians, drawn from "the unemployed, the street gangs, the fire-house clubs, the riff-raff, and drunks, and on-leave sailors." Evitts offers no proof for his assertion, but we can assume he was probably correct — if for no other reason than such elements are commonly found contributing to rock-throwing mayhem.

But consider what did *not* occur on April 19. There apparently were no attacks by white mobs against African Americans. Nor did observers mention youngsters throwing manure, readily available on horse-busy streets — even though such behavior was common in mid-nineteenth century America during civil disturbances. The rioting of this day, therefore, was turbulent and bloody, but it did not quite tip into anarchy; it retained a focus that can only be described as political.[56]

A frantic search for guns seems to have started as soon as the very first shots were fired on Pratt Street. The jeering crowds could no longer think the Massachusetts troops carried no bullets. Civilians began breaking into nearby shops that sold weapons, sometimes offering to pay for these items on the spot, sometimes shouting empty promises over their shoulders about returning to pay while sprinting out the door. Exactly how many businesses or armories were cleared of their weaponry during the next twenty-four hours is uncertain. But many were. By nine o'clock that evening, men wandered Baltimore's streets with guns in their hands, on the lookout for Yankees, or any-one who might sympathize with them. (The mayor issued a wistful proclamation the next day, asking citizens who wished to contribute their privately-owned guns to step forward.)

About two o'clock that afternoon some men, including a few local militia officers and policemen, ran into the main office of the telegraph company. Their leader carried a hatchet. He de-manded to know which of the several telegraph wires dangling out the window went north. None of the employees said a word. The man walked to where the wires trailed outside, chose one at apparent random, and cleaved it. He and his com-panions departed. A few minutes later the telegraphers spliced the severed wire. They remained mum about this repair work, and during the next several hours messages (including several originating in Lincoln's War Department) clandestinely sped northward, through the city. (It was not until the next evening that all wires from Baltimore to the North were completely shut down.)[57]

A sordid spate of violence during the afternoon focused on federal soldiers who, unfortunately, remained trapped in the city after the Sixth's departure. Some of these Union men were the Massachusetts regiment's band members; others consisted of Pennsylvania troops.

The two dozen bandsmen were the first to feel the mob's wrath. When their train had first arrived at the station, the mu-sicians opened the large sliding doors on both sides of their car, giving them a cross-breeze. Soon their presence was noticed. A few Baltimoreans slipped up to the car, announced they were friends, and said that if the musicians waited here quietly, they might not be disturbed. But as the crowds near the depot grew larger, the band members felt increasingly vulnerable. People clustered near the car and cursed them, calling them, among other things, "damned Northern paupers." Others shouted that they were dead men, that they would not live to leave the city. The musicians quickly slammed the door facing the street. All this happened very quickly, during the minutes after Follansbee and his group started off.

The band leader, Drum Major R. P. Winn, decided he had better seek police protection. He hopped from the car. He observed, a few blocks away, Captain Follansbee's men turning the corner onto Pratt Street. He saw missiles flung from the roofs and windows of the buildings, and one of the volunteers brained by some object and collapse on the street. He saw the shooting begin and men on both sides falling. But he did not observe any policemen, so he decided to consult with the commander of the Pennsylvanians, Colonel Small, about what ought to be their next step. Small happened to be standing nearby, and the two searched for a railroad agent to request that their train be moved back a bit, to carry them away from the obvious danger. They did find a railway official, but he refused.

Meanwhile, events at the baggage car turned frightening. A bandsman named John Nutting left the car to find Winn, but he had hardly reached the street when he was charged by angry men with clubs. He turned back and saw that a mob was assaulting the baggage car as well as other cars behind it where the Pennsylvanians sat. Chased by howling thugs, Nutting reached the baggage car's open door and clambered aboard. The attackers, just behind him, tried to follow. The musicians hit and kicked at the invaders, but the mob was too large, too determined to get within. The situation in the shadows of the car became a nightmare, like scenes from a movie about ghouls. The mob broke through the roof and shrieked down that they would bring gunpowder to pour into the hole. The musicians, realizing they were inside a potential tomb, flung themselves from the back door, a few of them clinging to their instruments, perhaps to use as weapons or from an instinctive desire to preserve these precious articles.

Instinctively they raced northward along the tracks, using the train as a wall to hide their passage, and another train that happened to be standing on their right to hide them on that side. But then they emerged at the rear of the trains, and the mob caught sight of them. The crowd threw rocks. Every musician was hit somewhere on his person. One band member saw two policemen standing together and rushed to them for safety. "Run," the policeman told him, "run like the devil." And off the bandsman sped again. (A young drummer, an eighteen-year-old French lad, became separated from his companions. He flung off his military overcoat, ripped the telltale stripe from his pants, and ran off again. Somehow, he succeeded in boarding a steamer heading north, and a few days later found his way to Lowell.)

The rest of the band were saved by two Good Samaritans. About half a mile from the station the musicians bumped into a "rough-looking man" whose name was Philip Laupus. A person of German extraction and a tobacconist by trade, he was a part-time musician himself. "This way, boys!" he said to them, "This way!" His little tobacco shop on Eastern Avenue was near a narrow alley, and he directed them toward it. In its dim recesses was a brick building, and standing in the doorway was a large, brawny woman. Her name was Ann Manly (or Manley). This building belonged to her. The city listed the place as a tavern; in fact, it was a whorehouse and she was its madam. She was also a staunch unionist. As each musician arrived at her door, she shook his hand and told him to run up the stairs behind her. As the last one entered, he was struck in the back of the head with a stone and fell, senseless, to the ground. She lifted him and carried him, still dazed, upstairs. She and the prostitutes helped clean their wounds and bandaged them. She gave them food and water. Somehow she found enough civilian clothes for all twenty-two. The men offered to pay; she told them not to insult her.

As the musicians rested in this unusual haven, Philip Laupus, the tobacconist, snuck to a nearby police station to seek assistance. He left word there for Marshal Kane and returned to Ann Manly's establishment. A few minutes later Kane appeared, accompanied by forty of his policemen. He said he would personally take the band to the nearest police station, where they would be safe.

Before leaving, the bandsmen fervently thanked their hostess, the other women, and Mr. Laupus. At the station house they found Drum Major Winn, who had been brought here earlier. For the next three hours they hid at this police station, even dining on crackers, cheese, and lager beer. In the early evening, escorted again by a protective force of Kane's policemen through crowds of pugnacious citizens, they returned to President Street Station and boarded a train that started northward, heading toward Philadelphia.[58]

The trials of the Pennsylvania volunteers on Felton's train were messier. How they found themselves in this predicament involved a series of accidents.

Their commander was Colonel William F. Small of Philadelphia, a forty-one-year-old moderately successful politician. He had fought in the Mexican War, and afterward maintained his connection to the state militia, particularly two Philadelphia regiments (each actually a mere nubbin of a proper-sized regiment). One of the two units was made up primarily of men born in Germany or of German extraction (considered by most Americans a military asset). The other contained a few veterans of the Mexican War, but neither group was well trained or equipped.

On January 28, 1861, in light of recent events in South Carolina, Small wrote President James Buchanan, a fellow Pennsylvanian, offering the services of his two regiments, referring to them as the Washington Guard, and declaring himself their brigadier general. He told Buchanan that his militiamen could start their service by garrisoning arsenals and other federal buildings in the Philadelphia area, thus freeing up regulars who could be used elsewhere. He added that, after his men had some experience under their belts, they could be "ready for the field in a few weeks, or even days." No record tells us what, if anything, Buchanan thought of the offer.

By mid-April, Small's men, who had received no additional training or equipment in the intervening weeks, were quite unprepared. Few, if any, had uniforms. When Governor Curtin ordered Small to take his men to Washington, the colonel, aware of their lack of preparedness, originally planned to entrain them inconspicuously through Baltimore at night. After they had arrived in Washington, he thought, the Army would provide them with clothes, weapons, and other equipment. He was more concerned with speed, with getting to the capital in time to save it, than he was with preparing for the trip there. He did not take into account the possibility of snafus.

Small's men were ready to leave Philadelphia at ten o'clock in the evening, but one of the cars developed a problem. This caused a delay. Then before they could depart, the Sixth Massachusetts arrived and were put aboard the train on cars attached to the front.[59]

Exactly how many men constituted Colonel Small's command is unclear. Some sources thought 1,200; others estimated far fewer. Since they constituted only ten companies (six in one regiment, four in the other), a reasonable guess would be about six or seven hundred. (Later in the war these same men would come to form the core of the Twenty-sixth and Twenty-seventh Pennsylvania Regiments.) No matter how undersized Colonel Small's command, the B&O train that would eventually take the Sixth Massachusetts from Baltimore to Washington, at thirteen cars, was far too small to have also taken the Pennsylvanians. So even under the best of circumstances, Small's volunteers would have been stuck in Baltimore.

At first, as they waited at the President Street station, almost no one in Baltimore knew of their existence. But this situation would not last.[60]

As we have seen, Colonel Small did try, unsuccessfully, to persuade railroad agents to move their train back from the station. While outside the anonymity of the cars, Small suddenly realized he was in danger. Seeing a mob approach him, he tried a ruse. He turned aside, pretending he was merely a merchant examining goods at the depot. As he stood there, the crowd squeezed past him, searching angrily for Yankees.

The Pennsylvania troops were in regular passenger cars and were more visible than the band members. When stones suddenly crashed through the windows and the shouts of the mob engulfed them, the Pennsylvanians felt trapped. Spontaneously, without thought, they jumped from the train. In their civilian clothes, once they had scattered, they had little to hold them together. Suddenly they were nothing but hundreds of terrified men in a strange city, a place where everyone seemed ready to harm them. Self-preservation took hold. Here and there a few buddies stayed together, but many fled as individuals, trying desperately to disappear into milling crowds. Some succeeded. Some did not, and suffered the consequences.

Officially their only fatality was an enlisted man named George Leisenring, a member of Small's staff, a twenty-six-year-old German-born clerk. By chance he was sitting in the last seat of the rear car when the mob burst in behind him. Before he could move, one thug stabbed him in the back and another in his side. He was later pronounced dead in a Pennsylvania hospital. That is all we know, not even how his corpse reached Philadelphia.

Almost certainly there were other deaths among Small's volunteers, perhaps as many as five, but their names have been lost because the two regiments never reached Washington, so they were never officially mustered into the federal army and listed on a register. These men died in the service of their country, as unnamed members of a Pennsylvania unit. They were never even paid for the few days they spent trying, unsuccessfully, to reach Washington to save the federal capital.

We do know that thirteen Pennsylvanians were injured severely enough that they received professional medical care. The commander of the four "German" companies — Lieutenant Colonel William Schoenleber, forty-five — was cut above and below his eye. One of his captains had his thumb chopped off, and a lieutenant was stabbed repeatedly. But the collapse of their organization meant that no accurate records about their fate or whereabouts exist. Some never returned home; they may have been killed or simply run away.

A number of Small's men were lucky enough, or organized enough, to reach cover at a police station, where they received protection. Others found safety inside empty freight cars. Throughout that evening, police officers continued to escort Pennsylvanians to a train and surreptitiously slip them aboard, the same train the musicians would finally board. As it started chugging slowly northward, it stopped occasionally to pick up fugitive stragglers from the brigade, frightened men stumbling along the tracks, heading home. This bedraggled assortment reached Philadelphia about nine o'clock Saturday morning.[61]

Other Pennsylvanians appeared in the city as late as Monday, or even later. Twenty-eight of them had banded together and started on foot. They were twenty-two miles north of Baltimore when accosted by a crowd of armed Maryland vigilantes, who marched them to a jail. As one Pennsylvanian recalled the incident, the vigilantes were "secessionists with revolvers pointed at our heads, calling us names which would not be fit for publication." Inside the prison, they listened to a mob gathering outside, threatening to lynch them. The next morning the sheriff informed them the town's citizens were, at that moment, conferring on whether to kill them immediately. Later he came back and said they were being released, but on condition that they had to start walking immediately toward Philadelphia, sixty miles away.

As these weary men tottered northward, vigilantes on horseback rode before them, tooting horns. Citizens gawked as the procession passed. The Northern troops were given neither water nor sustenance. They muddled along, desperate to reach their home state, to cross the Mason-Dixon Line, to find safety. Eventually, Sunday morning, in Pennsylvania, they found a church and begged for assistance. Its pastor treated them kindly.

In rural Louisiana, at a small Catholic academy calling itself Poydras College, whose students came from well-to-do Creole families, the school's English literature teacher was a young man named James Ryder Randall, twenty-two, born in Baltimore. On Sunday, April 21, two days after the riot on Pratt Street, he read about it and learned a classmate of his had been wounded. That night Randall could not sleep. He felt deeply troubled by the story. It seemed to him that hordes of cruel Yankee soldiers had slaughtered unarmed civilians in Baltimore. He rose from his bed and sat at his desk. By flickering candlelight he scratched out some words to express his emotions.

It was common practice in that era, particularly in the South, to put feelings into poetry and to offer the result to local newspapers. Someone — probably Randall himself — sent his rhyme to the *New Orleans Delta*. On April 28, the *Delta* printed his rather overheated efforts. Among its several stanzas were these lines:

> The despot's heel is on thy shore,
> His touch is at thy Temple's door,
> Avenge the patriotic gore
> That fleck'd the streets of Baltimore,
> And be the Battle Queen of yore...

Other Southerners wrote doggerels about the events in Baltimore, but for some reason Randall's efforts caught the fancy of editors. A number of Southern newspapers reprinted the poem. Inevitably it appeared in Baltimore's own press. Folks there appreciated its sentiments and its throbbing pulse.

Among the enthusiasts were three young women: two sisters, Jenny and Hetty Cary, and their cousin Constance. The Cary family, originally from Virginia, was prominent and fairly well-to-do, related to the Randolphs and Jeffersons. Mrs. Cary, the mother of the two sisters, ran a fashionable girls' school in Baltimore. Due to Virginia's secession, the family's allegiance was with the South. (Late in the year, the three girls would design and sew what would become the famous battle flag of the Confederacy. Hetty Cary, considered a great beauty, according to the standards of the time, would move to Richmond early in the war, become engaged to the handsome Confederate officer John Pegram — a good and gallant man from an aristocratic Virginia family, though a rather mediocre soldier. Hetty and John would marry in January 1865, three weeks before he was killed in battle.)

In early 1861 the three Cary girls were members of a young women's glee club calling itself the Monument Street Girls. Hetty suggested they turn Randall's poetry into music. Her sister Jenny thought the college song "Lauriger Horatius" (itself drawn from "O Tannenbaum") would almost perfectly match the rhythms. Jenny sang the result at a meeting, and it was a hit. Soon afterward the song was published locally, and not long after that, a music teacher realized that the nine stanzas could fit the more impressive "O Tannenbaum," by punching in the refrain "My Maryland" again and again.

Randall's hackneyed lines lacked polish, but his sentiments were sincere and had sinew. His poem about the parlous events in Baltimore on April 19, 1861 — in its new musical form — became one of the Civil War's most recognizable tunes and, though dated, remains Maryland's state song to this day.[62]

CHAPTER NINE

Controlling a Maelstrom

Baltimore, April 19, 1861, afternoon and night

Right after the Sixth departed, Governor Hicks and Mayor Brown wired Lincoln: "A collision between the citizens and the Northern [*sic*] troops has taken place in Baltimore, and the excitement is fearful. Send no troops here. We will endeavor to prevent all bloodshed." They added that they had already called up their militia and therefore would not need any federal assistance to keep control. Hicks and Brown suspected this telegram would not be sufficient. They decided they needed more to persuade the president to stop sending volunteers through Baltimore. To carry a separate message, Brown chose three envoys, each a distinguished citizen — one a politician, the other two lawyers. This second note cautioned Lincoln that the people of Baltimore were "exasperated to the highest degree by the passage of troops." The mayor said he was convinced the only way to pass through his city was to "fight their way every step." He begged the president to order no more troops to come this way. "If they should attempt it," he warned, "the responsibility for the bloodshed will not rest upon me." Hicks appended his own comment, stating, "I fully concur." Hicks and Brown told the three envoys to use all their persuasive powers on Lincoln. The B&O arranged a special train, and the trio departed that evening. They arrived late; the president was asleep and would not see them until morning.

Meanwhile Baltimore's leadership felt a need to take some action. Even while the mob was storming Colonel Small's poor unarmed troops, officials were announcing a mass rally at Monument Square, to begin at four o'clock. Thousands came. The state flag was prominently unfurled and remained the only banner in sight. Ten men spoke. With the exception of Hicks, whose roots were elsewhere in the state, each was an important cog in the city's or county's highest economic or political circles. They urged their listeners to let the authorities handle things. Mayor Brown informed his listeners that he and the governor had already told the president not to send more troops. He said he felt confident and asked Baltimore's populace to maintain the good name of the city. (At this mild reproof the mayor received a few boos.) Hicks rose and announced, "I will suffer my right arm to be torn from my body before I will raise it to strike a sister state"—presumably meaning Virginia, but implying other Southern states. Most speakers on this occasion expressed greater passion. Severn Teackle Wallis was typical. In his mid-forties, Wallis, a respected lawyer, would later be the first president of Baltimore's bar association. His present duties included acting as legal adviser to the police board. (He also happened to be the grandfather of the yet-unborn Wallis Simpson, the woman for whom Edward VIII would abdicate his throne.) Mere talk, he shouted, seemed unnecessary, adding: "If the blood of citizens on the stones in the street does not speak, it is useless for man to speak." He admitted his heart was with the South.

Another orator emphasized the city's "murdered citizens." One speaker, who had once represented Baltimore in Congress, entertained the masses with a kind of pep rally. Are you "Yankees?" he screamed. "Noooo!" they yelled back. Were they Southerners? "Yayyyyy!" they roared.

Eventually the speakers were done and the thousands in the audience drifted away. Some may have gone home for the rest of the day, but that evening other orators gave stirring speeches at different venues—including the large open space in front of Barnum's Hotel. This was stimulating stuff. These perorations seemed to suggest that the city's most important citizens were on the case, and Baltimore's people could rest easier — and remain law abiding. At least that was what the leadership hoped.[63]

The next day's newspapers, however, noted that certain elements stalked the streets that night, guns in hand, looking for Yankees. About nine o'clock a mob gathered at President Street Station. They had heard guns were stored there — and they wanted them. They broke windows and kicked in the door. A terrified night watchman assured them the place contained no weapons, but they refused to believe him. He suggested they look around. They selected a committee, which searched the station. When they failed to find anything, they stomped off. Marshal Kane learned about this and other incidents. He did not like this turmoil, this tendency toward lawlessness. He fumed. The social current was whipping out of control, and it seemed possible more Northern troops might be coming toward them at any moment. If, or when, these men arrived, Kane was convinced a bloodbath would rock his city. He sent a wire to an acquaintance, Colonel Bradley T. Johnson, who commanded a rather sizable militia force in Frederick, Maryland, fifty miles west of Baltimore: "Streets red with Maryland blood; send expresses [telegrams] over the mountains of Maryland and Virginia for the riflemen to come without delay. Fresh hordes will be down on us tomorrow. We will fight them and whip them, or die." (Colonel Johnson would arrive the next day with some militia.)

Marshal Kane was a person of integrity, a man of courage. A native of Baltimore, the police chief was forty-one years old. For the previous two decades he had devoted his enormous energies to the improvement of his city. He had been a leader in modernizing her fire departments; he had recently been active in setting up an insurance company, serving as its first president. As a humanitarian he had raised money in 1847 for victims of the Irish potato famine. He had accepted command of

Baltimore's 398-man police force because he felt an obligation to erase the unsavory image of Mobtown. For months he had been working hard at this task, and had generally succeeded, the gangs being much less evident now, the streets far safer. On April 18 he had worked feverishly to assist the first five Pennsylvania companies through his city's streets. On the 19th he personally saved the lives of hundreds of Massachusetts and Pennsylvania volunteers. In a sense this chubby, bearded grain merchant, only a temporary police chief, was the central hero of the day. Without his forceful actions, the chaos and bloodshed would have been far worse.

But Kane's message to Bradley Johnson revealed his real feelings. He considered Lincoln's volunteers as "hordes," as faceless monsters. Baltimore was *his* city; the Union troops were outsiders. He blamed their presence — and, therefore, indirectly, President Lincoln — for the blood in the streets. His intention — at least when he sent that wire — was to "fight them and whip them, or die." This man, who had done so much to prevent violence, now seemed to be promising it. It is likely, of course, that his words were only a releasing of strong emotions. He had slept little during the previous two nights. He had just witnessed the apparent destruction of his dream to improve Baltimore's reputation. He loved his town. Things had appeared to be going well of late, at least in terms of law and order. The sight of the mobs pushed him over the edge. Since he thought of himself as something of a Southerner, he could not find it in his heart to blame pro-Confederate agitators like T. Parkin Scott — men who were attempting to convince the populace to join Virginia in secession.

During the evening of April 19, Marshal Kane, after ensuring the safe departure of most of the Massachusetts band and the Pennsylvanians, attended a quiet gathering at the home of one of the city's more prominent citizens. He had only been there a few minutes when one of his officers came to report a new, and sinister, development. The president of the Pennsylvania

Central Railroad, J. Edgar Thomson, had just wired his representative in Baltimore that more Northern troops would be leaving Pennsylvania shortly, and that one of their goals would be to teach Baltimore's mob a lesson. Kane and the others in the room were shaken by this news. They broke into two groups. Some—including Charles Howard, chairman of the police board—went to police headquarters to confer about the situation. Kane, accompanied by E. Louis Lowe, an ex-governor of Maryland and one of the speakers at that afternoon's rally in Monument Square, went to the mayor's house to talk to Brown. They believed that Governor Hicks was staying at a hotel, and they intended to speak to him later.

It seemed obvious to Marshal Kane and the others that the best way to avoid further bloodshed was to prevent the passage of more Northern troops. The easiest way to accomplish that would be to obstruct somehow both railways coming from Pennsylvania—the one from Harrisburg, the other from Philadelphia. The two rail lines had to pass over several rivers to reach Baltimore. Each crossing meant a bridge, a wooden structure that could be burned. But if a person intended to destroy bridges, it would be smart to do so well north of the city, to keep Lincoln's troops as far from town as possible. A quick analysis told these men that the bridges across Back River, Gunpowder River, and Bush River would be good choices. Each was fairly far away, yet their relative proximity to Baltimore made them readily reachable by those who wanted to damage them.

Kane's policemen could perform some of the destruction, particularly if Mayor Brown okayed using them, but Hicks would eventually have to be included. Militiamen in the city might be tapped. Kane and his companions neither liked nor trusted the Know Nothing Hicks, yet it was critical to get his permission for their plan for two reasons. The bridges in question were outside Kane's jurisdiction, or Brown's, so their demolition would necessitate a state order. Also, using militiamen required the governor's signature, as, by law, he was their commander in chief.

Kane and Lowe arrived at the mayor's residence, and were told by his brother that Brown had retired. It was about midnight. The visitors said they must see the mayor, immediately. When Brown appeared, Kane described the disturbing telegram about the approaching Yankee troops. The mayor instantly understood its ominous implications. He, too, recognized the importance of the bridges. (Several hours before this, Brown had even raised the notion with Hicks, though the governor had then rejected it, declaring he had no authority to approve such a drastic measure as burning bridges. Hicks was disinclined to destroy private property—especially the property of wealthy and important men like Samuel Morse Felton of the Philadelphia, Wilmington, and Baltimore Railroad, and, even more, Secretary of War Simon Cameron.)

Governor Hicks was unaware of it, but Cameron was already feeling considerably cranky. The presidents of the two railroads in question (Felton's and Thomson's) learned early in the afternoon about the Baltimore rioting. They had sent a joint communiqué to Cameron saying they considered it "impracticable" to send any more volunteers through that city. About this time they had received a message from Hicks stating that "no troops can pass through Baltimore." They had also heard—perhaps directly from Garrett, the president of the B&O—that his trains would now "refuse to transfer" any more of Lincoln's volunteers. Given these developments, Felton and Thomson sent a follow-up telegram to Cameron, to ask for his instructions. Cameron was not in a good mood. His reply was testy: "Governor Hicks has neither right nor authority to stop troops coming to Washington. Send them on, prepared to fight their way through, if necessary." The secretary of war was not going to allow either a weak-spined politician like Hicks or the Baltimore mobs to dictate terms to Washington.

It is likely Cameron conferred with Winfield Scott about the situation, because at some point during the day General Scott sent a wire to Philadelphia that Pennsylvania's militia must move as quickly as possible to protect the rails, the telegraph lines, and the bridges — all the way to Washington. A confrontation about bridges was approaching. The question was going to be: which side moved quicker?[64]

In Baltimore that evening Mayor Brown told Kane something surprising: the governor was not at the Fountain Hotel, as Kane had assumed; he was right here, in this very house. Hicks was in bed, Brown said, asleep, feeling unwell. (The governor had slept little during his previous four days in Baltimore, and he was indeed probably exhausted. But he may have come to Brown's house out of a sense of caution. He had received several death threats. He probably considered it more prudent to spend the night at the mayor's residence than at a public hostelry.)

Hicks would later deny any knowledge about, or connection to, the destruction of the bridges, but was certainly lying. Four eyewitnesses agreed about the following: Brown and his brother, along with Marshal Kane and Louis Lowe, went to Hicks's bedroom. During the ensuing conversation, two other men somehow wandered in and listened. The mayor told the governor about the ominous telegram. Brown said Northern troops would be drawing into one of the city's stations in a few hours. As he saw it, if that happened, a battle between the citizenry and Lincoln's soldiers would be inevitable. The mayor would later recall that he said, "The only way to avert the calamity [is] to destroy the bridges"; and he would remember Hicks's response as something like: "It seems to be necessary." While Hicks's words seemed supportive, they were also obviously vague. The mayor pressed the governor harder. The bridges in question, Brown emphasized, were outside his personal jurisdiction, so Hicks would have to give his approval. Would he do so? The governor wriggled uncomfortably. Destroying railroad property, he said, was serious business; he wasn't sure he had the authority. He wanted time to consider the matter at length. But the group surrounding him in this bedroom refused to allow any wriggle-room. The governor was a well-known equivocator. In normal times — politics being the art of the possible — such temporizing, or squirming, would have been understandable, and perhaps admirable. But these were far from normal times. A civil war — especially in a border region like Maryland — tends to force a person to take a stand. The group reminded Hicks that Yankee troops could be on them in as little as three or four hours, and the Northerners might well be in the mood for revenge. At this moment, they said, the streets of Baltimore were being stalked by hundreds of armed, emotional men. Things could rapidly get worse. Would not the governor grant his permission to burn the bridges?

Mayor Brown's brother would remember the following exchange:

Hicks said, "I see nothing else to be done."

"But, sir," replied the mayor, "I cannot act without your consent. Do you give it?"

Though Hicks would later tell the legislature he never agreed to the action, witnesses confirm he now caved. Yes, he said, burn the bridges.[65]

This conversation was critical to Baltimore, and maybe to American history. The men in this room felt frantic about the city's fate. One cannot blame them. It was their town, one of the largest cities in the United States, and probably the most volatile.

Troops were indeed moving toward them from various parts of the North, or were getting ready to do so. If someone did not perform immediate acts of destruction, if the railroad bridges were not burned this very night, before dawn, bloodshed in Baltimore would almost certainly have reached great, perhaps epic proportions.

Yet it is not unreasonable to ask: would that have changed the war? During the next four years the nation would suffer hundreds of thousands of deaths. Would a few thousand in Baltimore have changed things? Would the citizens of Maryland have been more or less inclined to leave the Union? Would the population north of Maryland have become horrified by the realities of civil war so early in the conflict, or might they have grown more determined? How about people in the South — especially Virginia? At the moment, the Virginians had their own problems to worry about, though there were individuals in that state who felt strongly inclined to aid their sister just across the Potomac. There was already a sizeable, and growing, army at Harpers Ferry that could board trains and be in Baltimore in two hours. Also, there was Washington to worry about. If serious fighting broke out in Baltimore, the federal capital would lie vulnerable for a longer period.

On the other hand, if Marshal Kane and his companions did burn the bridges, and trains were prevented from getting to Baltimore, might not this action alter the direction of the Civil War? Inevitably, the District of Columbia would be cut off for an indeterminate period. Isolated from the rest of the country, Lincoln and his administration might fall to a sudden attack from Virginia, supported by Southern sympathizers inside the capital. Lincoln had announced his proclamation four days earlier, but all he had received so far were perhaps empty promises from several governors, a few score regulars, some unarmed militiamen from Pennsylvania, and the battered Sixth Massachusetts. During those same four days Virginia had seceded and her soldiers had captured a major arsenal not far from the capital, and they were threatening to seize Gosport, whose fall might result in the Chesapeake Bay becoming a virtual Confederate lake. The importance of this moment — the severity of the crisis — can hardly be exaggerated. Much would depend on what happened during the next few hours.

As soon as Hicks showed his approval (by a word, perhaps only a nod), Kane and Brown rushed to police headquarters. There ensued a brief conference with members of the police board, Kane's official superiors. Mayor Brown explained the situation, his proposed solution, and the fact that Governor Hicks had just concurred. Everyone agreed the bridges had to go.

Before dawn two teams left Baltimore. One consisted of militiamen. George Hume Steuart, who was seventy years old, had been a leading militia figure for decades. He personified the city's elite. Extremely well-to-do, he lived in a fine mansion near the center of town and owned many slaves. He had helped defend Baltimore in 1814 when the British attacked it. His son — George H. Steuart, Jr. — graduated from West Point (second from the bottom of his 1848 class), and was now a captain in the United States Cavalry. Both Steuarts sympathized with the South. (Two days later Steuart, Jr., would resign his commission; he would join the Confederate army, become a general and fight at Gettysburg, among other places. Steuart, Sr., would himself shortly leave Baltimore for Virginia, and he would spend most of the war years there.) After the Sixth Massachusetts had passed through Baltimore, Steuart, Sr., announced he would use militiamen to "suppress the insurrection and riot going on in the streets of the city, and to preserve good order and quiet." But his health was a bit shaky, and another soldier took command of the city's militia: Isaac Ridgeway Trimble, a West Point graduate (1822), who, at fifty-eight, was more than ten years younger.

It was Trimble that night who led a platoon of militia up the tracks of the Northern Central, toward the southern border of Pennsylvania (the Mason-Dixon Line). A dozen miles above Baltimore, near a village named Cockeysville, they stopped at a narrow wooden bridge and damaged it — making it unusable until it received time-consuming repairs.

Another team, consisting of about forty policemen led by Marshal Kane, commandeered the morning mail train just north of the city as it approached from Philadelphia. They rode it back up the line. Using turpentine they burned four bridges, including a major span that crossed the estuary of Gunpowder River. They also seized two telegraph offices and forced their adolescent key operators to join them. The team considered going as far north as Havre de Grace, to seize Felton's ferry there, but, at the last minute, decided it was not worth the dangers; and that Yankee troops could probably hire other steamers easily.

Kane and his men did not get back to Baltimore until late in the afternoon. The middle-aged police chief was probably dog tired.

As all this was transpiring, Governor Hicks roused himself early in the morning, boarded a train, and hustled south to Annapolis, the state capital, thus separating himself from the activities of the bridge burners—at least in his own mind. He fooled no one. Few in Maryland liked him; most thought him feckless. Lincoln considered him, at best, a convenient puppet.

Hicks's position was untenable. The *Richmond Dispatch* declared him part of Lincoln's Black Republican coterie—and therefore "a double-dyed traitor" to the South.[66] Unlike Virginians Robert E. Lee and Governor John Letcher, whose efforts for their state, and the Confederacy, had since then been accepted, even praised, Hicks was in a double bind. If he had moved his state toward secession, his actions would have enraged almost all Northerners, and he would have been labeled a traitor to the Union. It is hard not to feel sympathy for the man.

Saturday-Sunday, April 20-21, 1861

Two days after the Sixth passed through Baltimore, David Hunter Strother, a resident of Virginia, arrived in the city. As he walked from the railway station to his lodgings, he found himself accosted by strangers who asked him who he was and where he came from. When they learned he was a Virginian and that he had recently been at Harpers Ferry, they asked excitedly about events there. They said they heard that Jeff Davis was on his way toward Washington with an army of 50,000, but they admitted they were uneasy because a Yankee army, a hundred-thousand strong, they thought, was about to pounce on poor Baltimore, to punish her for her actions on April 19. Would not Virginia send soldiers soon to give them succor? Strother chose not to explain that he remained a unionist. "Throughout the city," he wrote in his journal, "everything evidenced alarm and excitement. Men and boys were running wildly about, armed with swords, horse-pistols, fowling pieces, bowie knives, and every imaginable weapon of offense." He noticed crowds gathering in front of hardware stores and any other store that still had potential weapons. It was a Sunday and these establishments were closed and locked, but he saw mobs break the doors and ransack the shops. "Axes, scythes, hatchets, sword-canes, pitchforks were distributed to the eager and half-frantic mobs." He also realized the thieves were happy to grab other plunder: whiskey, tobacco, jewelry, and cash. "To these proceedings, the city police appeared to make but a demonstrative resistance, occasionally firing a volley from their revolvers in the air, which only served to increase the turbulence of the mob."

At least three factors were now at work, churning the city's mood.

One was fear. As citizens had told Strother, it seemed likely that thousands of Yankee soldiers would soon appear. Lincoln had called for volunteers. During the previous few days, every train coming south had carried newspapers from Philadelphia and New York that had hastily written descriptions of the violence on Pratt street—accounts portraying patriotic Massachusetts youngsters, on their way to save the national capital, being brutally attacked and murdered by Baltimore's worst thugs. These newspapers depicted great excitement up north, of Northern governors issuing militant pronouncements. Even rural Northern hamlets, it appeared, could provide vivid tales of fervent patriotism: flag-waving, hot speeches, young men running to join the colors, marching feet and brass bands and the whistles of departing trains. In Baltimore, anyone glancing at such articles had to feel as though a great earthquake had rumbled and a vast tidal wave of armed men was — at this very moment — hurtling headlong in their direction. Clerks at Baltimore's half-dozen newspapers pinned these articles to bulletin boards out on the streets. Crowds gathered around, nervously scanning the clippings.

The adage that reminds us that pain depends on whose ox is gored is applicable. Among Baltimoreans, the tragic death and wounding of their own citizens had been shocking. Many people of Baltimore considered the pounding that the Sixth Massachusetts volunteers received was justified. North of Maryland, a far different attitude prevailed. There, the men of the Sixth represented all Americans, and their bloodshed had been wrought by faceless brutes. Northern editorials, written Friday evening, demanded retribution. The writers no longer focused solely on the defense of the federal capital. They wanted troops passing through Baltimore to wreak havoc; they wanted vengeance.

Each news item, whether reasonable or ludicrous, became fodder for heated conversation on street corners. The rage the North aimed at Baltimore was disturbing and terrifying. To most Baltimoreans, there seemed no question that Lincoln's hordes would be arriving soon; the only debate involved how many. Not surprisingly, estimates about the size of the approaching army swelled. Individuals took a certain relish in taking a number — 20,000 perhaps — and doubling it.[67]

The populace of Baltimore prepared to defend themselves. There were ugly incidents involving attempts to locate even more weapons. Some actions seemed more personal, and probably represented old resentments. An unfortunate storeowner named William P. Wright, the proprietor of a china shop, was visited at work by a gang that smashed most of his merchandise — either because Wright was thought to harbor unionist sentiments, or because this was a convenient excuse for something else he had said or done in the past.

There were other acts of lawlessness, as angry men who prowled the streets, savoring old enmities, practiced vigilante justice. On Saturday afternoon a large crowd gathered outside a Baltimore establishment called Turner Hall. During the period between 1840 and 1860, Germans arriving in America usually settled near one another. They often created organizations where they could meet and relax with other German speakers, things like the Turner clubs. During the 1850s Turner clubs were formed in New York, Houston, Indianapolis, San Francisco, and Springfield, Massachusetts, as well as a hundred other places — including Baltimore. Although their main purpose was social, most Turners had an irrepressible love for physical activity. (The German word *turnverein* means an athletic or gymnastic club. *Turners* derives from the German word for "gymnasts.") They hiked, they sang, they walked on their hands, they did cartwheels for the sheer joy of it. And in politics, they tended to oppose slavery. During the election of 1860 Turners nationwide voted for Lincoln and other Republicans.

How Baltimore's Turners voted in 1860, however, is impossible to determine; but that Saturday in April, the mob attacking their meeting hall was obviously politically motivated. The *Sun* later said rumors had spread sometime around noon that a militia company of Turners calling themselves the Turner Rifles intended to offer their military services to Washington, and that they allegedly kept a stash of guns at their hall. A pack of angry men, at least thirty in number, broke into the hall, but found it empty. Out of sheer cussedness, they ransacked it anyway, stealing what they wanted and vandalizing pictures, dishes, and furniture. They departed the premises before police (tardily) arrived. (Looking back, one can label those thugs protofascists.) An hour or so later, about a dozen blocks from Turner Hall, another mob, or perhaps the same one, gathered outside the offices of *Der Wecker*, a German-language newspaper, its name ironically meaning "alarm." The mob shouted that they would crash their way inside and kill the publisher unless he hung a secession flag outside. This time the police arrived and moved the crowd along, but a few hours later a gang came by and shot out the newspaper's windows. *Der Wecker's* editor and publisher, and others who worked there, went into hiding.

Given this atmosphere, the plight of Fort McHenry, less than two miles from the center of town, was precarious. A small fort built in 1797 to defend the city from outside invaders, it was now manned by a garrison of about sixty troops, the most visible federal presence in the region. From a civilian viewpoint, Fort McHenry seemed imposing. Its brick walls loomed high above a dry ditch. It was known to house forty pieces of heavy artillery. And, after all, its ramparts were the very ones made famous by Francis Scott Key's stanzas about stars and stripes.

In fact it suffered serious weaknesses. Its guns had potential, to be sure, but their mostly wooden carriages had been allowed to fall into disrepair. The fort's commander, Captain John C. Robinson, would later say his guns would have been "of no more use than so many Quaker guns [fake artillery, often made from carefully sawed tree trunks, designed to fool potential attackers]."

The garrison hardly felt hostile toward the local population. Its officers had traditionally mixed freely with Baltimore's leading citizens. They attended parties and dances; they sometimes married local belles. Men like Brevet Colonel Robert E. Lee, who had resided with his family in Baltimore for three years while modernizing the city's defenses, were feted by the city's elite. The fort's enlisted men also mingled with civilians, becoming friendly with young ladies in the city, as well as tavern keepers and merchants.

Over the years Baltimore had spread slowly outward toward the fort, so that homes and commercial establishments could be found quite near its walls. It would be easy for attackers carrying ladders to trot right up to it. And if enough men had sufficient courage (whether derived from rage or liquor), they could clamber up those ladders and fling themselves over the walls. Captain Robinson certainly thought so. Sometime on Saturday he wired Army headquarters in Washington, saying he was sure the fort would be attacked within a few hours. He said, without much confidence, he thought his garrison could hold out.

Robinson and his men were well aware of what had happened at Fort Sumter. Sumter had had the advantage of being situated on an island in the harbor, yet, seven days earlier, it had fallen quickly. Fort McHenry's garrison, reading accounts of that attack in local newspapers, bought extra provisions in the city's markets so they could not be starved into submission as Fort Sumter's men had nearly been. They also frantically began filling sandbags. Luckily they had been reinforced by that small contingent of regular artillerymen who had accompanied the very first Pennsylvania volunteers going through town. These new men immediately pitched in.

The garrison laid timbers around their primary magazine. They poured gunpowder into eight-inch shells and cut short fuses for these bombs. If attackers came, the garrison would stand on the walls, light the fuses, and toss these hand grenades into the ditch. The men of the garrison also carefully placed a brass field piece — smaller than their other cannon, but far more maneuverable — so that it pointed down the main road leading toward them from the center of the city. They aimed another gun, stuffed with canister, to face the sally port, through which an attacking force might push. Finally they loaded an antiquated mortar and pointed it in the general direction of Monument Square. It was so old they could not be sure if it would even fire, or whether it would explode when they yanked its lanyard.

Shortly after dark a messenger arrived at the fort, bearing a note from Charles Howard, president of the police board, with an ominous warning: "You may be annoyed by lawless and disorderly characters approaching the walls of the Fort tonight."

This news would hardly have surprised Captain Robinson. He had gone into town earlier in the day to purchase some things. He had worn civilian clothes so as not to excite any reaction, but a local man warned him to return to the fort, and accompanied him along the way, presumably to guarantee his protection. What was disconcerting in Howard's message was its next phrase: "We propose to send a guard of perhaps 200 men to station themselves at Whetstone Point," a few blocks from the fort. The purpose of these men, the note stated, would be to stop and arrest "disorderly persons." Captain Robinson was unconvinced. It seemed imprudent to permit 200 armed men to approach that close to the fort's outer walls. Nor was he comforted to be assured verbally by the messenger, John W. Davis of the police board, that these 200 protectors were members of the Maryland Guard. In the past few weeks Robinson had already met several officers of that militia unit. He did not trust them. He suspected (correctly) their loyalties were with the Confederacy. He told the messenger he would not permit the militiamen any closer than a Catholic chapel about three-quarters of a mile away.

Then he said something that shook Davis. After displaying to him some of the fort's defenses (and none of its weaknesses), Robinson pointed at the mortar aimed at "the heart of the city." He declared that if the Guards came any closer than that Catholic chapel, he would open fire — implying he intended to shoot both the militiamen and blast harmless civilians far out in the city. The latter prospect stunned Davis. Would Robinson, he asked, really give that order? Yes, Robinson replied; regrettably, he would. The messenger, incensed by this threat, blustered: "I assure you, Captain Robinson, if there is a woman or child killed in that city there will be not one of you left alive, sir." Robinson said he was willing to take that chance.

In his recollections, John Robinson — who would rise during the war to the rank of major general — said he was convinced the only thing that really saved Fort McHenry was the unexpected appearance that very night of a steamer carrying

Northern volunteers. By the next morning rumors in the city were rife that the ship had dropped off 800 reinforcements. Seeming to confirm the rumor was the appearance on McHenry's outer esplanade of a string of military tents.

Actually, the steamer *Spaulding* had indeed been carrying hundreds of Massachusetts volunteers, but it was taking them to Fort Monroe. The only reason the ship had stopped was to pick up fuel for its engines, coal that the navy kept stored there. After taking on the fuel, the vessel had departed, the Massachusetts troops still aboard. As to the mysterious tents, Robinson had ordered them erected as soon as he got a whiff of the rumors about reinforcements. Since the fort was cut off from all contact with the city, the public did not discover their mistake for ten crucial days.

When Charles Howard, head of the police board, wrote his own account of the Fort McHenry matter, his position was different from Robinson's. In it he asserted that his board and the Maryland Guard had been genuinely sincere in their desire to protect the fort that weekend. His report stated that the Maryland Guards remained in the fort's sector for "several nights," and, he thought, it was their efforts that kept the fort safe. The reality is now murky.[68]

During that weekend Baltimore's leaders, having prevented further train travel from the north, took other drastic actions to isolate the city. They saw to it that telegraph wires going north were cut, this time effectively. The mail normally arriving by train from northern states was mostly interrupted because of the destruction of the bridges (though a few items like newspapers were brought in by wagon). On Saturday morning, several outsiders who seemed possible "spies from the North" were arrested, and only released when it turned out they had been trapped in the city by the bridge destruction. To prevent a surprise naval raid by Yankee ships, the harbor buoys were hauled up.

Among other things, Baltimore ceased to receive much news about what was occurring in the outside world. Whether this ignorance sedated the population or increased its edginess is unclear.

Travelers from the North could still get to the city, by horseback or carriage or even on foot, and Southern steamers were permitted to hire pilots who guided them safely to the wharves. But all this was clumsy. The police commissioners were asked if at least one ship would be allowed to run each day between Baltimore and Philadelphia, to carry passengers and the mail, including Northern newspapers, to the city. The commissioners said no. Businesses locked their doors and waited for the crisis to blow over. Their employees, inevitably, found it hard to purchase food or pay their rents. Within days this situation would become explosive, but, for the nonce, Baltimore's leadership felt it critically important to barricade the city from the North to maintain order.

On Sunday morning, by official order, even telegraph poles north of the city were chopped down — in case someone tried to repair the snipped wires. The authorities also took control of telegraph lines going southward. Henceforth anyone wanting to send a telegram had to get specific approval from Marshal Kane. Early the next week the city's leaders relented slightly on the total embargo. Although the list of items not allowed to be sent from the city included foodstuffs, coal, and munitions, the authorities permitted fishing vessels to come and go, and even released a shipment of oysters to be sent by rail to Chicago. But most business remained stalled.

Washington, D.C., was now in a state of semi-isolation. As a result, Lincoln's administration remained unaware of the deteriorating situation in St. Louis, where the majority of Missouri's officials were hostile to the Union. A small detachment of federal soldiers guarded an army arsenal in the city. Opposing them were hundreds of armed and determined secessionist militiamen. On Sunday morning, April 21, Francis P. Blair, Jr., a local congressman and a brother of Lincoln's postmaster general, Montgomery Blair, decided to inform Washington of the dangers. He did not trust the key-operators at the St. Louis telegraph office, so he crossed the Mississippi River and set up a temporary station on the eastern side. From there he wired Lincoln's government and described the situation. Unless something was done soon, he said, the arsenal would be captured, then the city of St. Louis, and all Missouri, a slave state, would likely join the Confederacy. Traffic on the Mississippi and Ohio rivers, he suspected, might be interdicted. Iowa, Minnesota, and southern Illinois (where there was already strong pro-Confederate sentiment) would be affected.

This telegram did not reach the federal capital because of the severed telegraph lines; the message only made it as far as Pennsylvania. By chance, Major Fitz-John Porter had just arrived in Pennsylvania on another mission, as an emissary of Winfield Scott. When shown Blair's telegram, he responded. Acting as though he possessed the authority to speak for General Scott, he wired various individuals in St. Louis. They moved quickly. Porter's quick thinking probably saved the day for the St. Louis arsenal, and maybe for Missouri.

As to Maryland's militiamen (representing wards within Baltimore, plus others arriving from elsewhere in the state), these men were slowly and methodically wrapped up like yarn and controlled by the city's leaders. This process was touchy. After all, the authorities had requested military assistance. But as Saturday advanced, the town seemed to the authorities far too inundated with armed and fidgety men. Some Maryland volunteers arrived by train, but a mounted company clattered in from Towson, less than ten miles to the north of town. Two companies of militiamen from Easton, across the Chesapeake on the Eastern Shore, came by steamer. According to the *Sun,* even "200 and 300 of our most respectable colored residents made a tender of their services to the city authorities." Mayor Brown thanked these African Americans for their offer and said he would let them know. (The *Sun* also quoted a local citizen who had just returned from Virginia; Richmond's slaves were enthusiastic secessionists, and "their hearts are with the South.")

Beginning Saturday, the city's elite took charge of Maryland's incoming volunteers. The militiamen were fed. They were organized and drilled. They were assigned barracks, which was both an act of humanity, to protect them from the elements, and a method to reduce the amount of mischief they might otherwise commit. Having them march about or perform tedious guard duty was also a handy way to distract them, to give them something to do. Marshal Kane announced that henceforth no unauthorized military groups would be permitted to march or parade.

The strategy of using drilling to control a potentially lawless mob of militiamen came from a South Carolinian in town, Colonel Benjamin Huger, a lifetime soldier. Months earlier, in Charleston, he had watched storm clouds develop in his native city and had sadly departed. Before leaving he had spoken to his good friend, Major Robert Anderson, in command of the small federal contingent, and the two old comrades had shaken their heads at the unfortunate and mindless turn of events. Huger had even suggested that Anderson take his command to that empty fortification in the harbor, Fort Sumter. Departing South Carolina to stay with his wife's family in Baltimore, Colonel Huger took an official leave of absence from the army. He was a genial chap, well liked by all, and he was now painfully aware he could no longer hide from secession. He planned to resign his commission and join the Confederate army, but before he packed, Baltimore's leaders asked for any military advice he might offer about the militia in town. He replied, "If we don't give these fellows plenty to do, gentlemen, they will give us plenty to do!"[69]

The city's authorities were concerned about more than just the militiamen. With many shops and businesses closed, several banks announced over the weekend that they did not intend to open their doors on Monday. This underlined the potential for serious problems. Workers with no work could grow antsy and dangerous. On Saturday Mayor Brown ordered all drinking establishments padlocked. Most taverns accepted this demand, but at least one saloon keeper was arrested for ignoring it. Marshal Kane issued a proclamation setting a six o'clock curfew; idlers found on the streets after that hour would be arrested. Kane even prohibited musical bands from marching or playing their instruments publicly. It was his intention, he announced, "that the city be reduced to a state of quiet and repose."

The need for social control was made especially obvious Sunday morning.

In the respectable wards of town, families ate Sabbath breakfast and dressed for church. The sky was clear and blue, and sunshine warmed the cobblestones. Carriages were made ready. Churchgoers departed to attend eleven o'clock services and assembled sedately in their pews.

Suddenly word spread through town that a huge horde of Northern troops was nearby, preparing to swarm across Baltimore. The outsiders may have already broken inside the city limits. At five minutes to eleven the city's main clock pealed a call to arms. Hearing that urgent tolling, entire congregations rose to their feet and rushed up the aisles toward the church doors. Children grew goggle-eyed. Women shrieked in hysteria at the thought of their menfolk fighting or themselves being raped by rampaging Yankees. Some ladies fainted. Within moments the streets were jammed with a shouting, bustling population. Drums rumbled in armories throughout the city, calling all militiamen to arms.

It took a while to sort out the facts. It turned out that a few minutes after ten o'clock, an excited rider named Gist Cockey had galloped up to police headquarters. He was from out of town, and had seen "five thousand" armed Yankees coming from Pennsylvania and getting off their train after they discovered the bridge burned near Ashland. All these troops, he announced, were now temporarily camped on his father's farm near Cockeysville, about fifteen miles or so northwest of the city.

The young man's information was at least partly accurate. Governor Curtin of Pennsylvania had continued to mass militiamen in Gettysburg and was forwarding them as soon as they could be considered even vaguely organized. Lincoln had asked for volunteers; Curtin was supplying what the president had asked for — in this case, about two thousand or more men, under the loose command of a state militia officer named George C. Wynkoop. Like Curtin's earlier troops, these men were mostly unarmed and without uniforms or training. And since the governor expected them to shortly be in Washington, where they would be provisioned by federal authorities, he failed to supply them with sufficient food or tents.

At the time folks in Baltimore were rushing about in terror at the prospect of invasion by a host of Yankees, the poor Pennsylvania militiamen in Cockeysville were already suffering acute hunger and feeling vaguely mutinous. Three of these men would soon be dead from lack of nutrition or illness. Meanwhile they waited at their increasingly soiled campground, uncertain about their next step.[70]

In Baltimore, volunteers rushed to offer their services. Street peddlers hawked secession badges — clumps of satin or even cardboard — and these quickly sold out and were pinned to coat lapels. Bands strenuously played "Dixie," which, the *Sun* declared exuberantly the next day, "has become the national air of the South already." Hundreds of locals drifted northward toward Cockeysville, going higgledy-piggledy, by any conveyance available, to meet "the enemy." Most carried some sort of weapon — fowling piece, rusty saber, navy pistol, axe, a sword cane or two, even a thick stick to serve as a club. Some rode horses, others tumbled into buggies and wagons and carriages. Their intention, so far as can be determined, was to slow the movement of the invading army, to act as guerrillas if necessary.

Baltimore's leaders, perhaps wanting to seem still in control of events or wishing at least to maintain some rein over their citizenry, tried desperately to find arms for those volunteers remaining in town. Marshal Kane again begged all citizens who owned weapons to turn them in to the police. A few citizens did. Ross Winans, an extremely wealthy local manufacturer and strong Confederate supporter, provided 2,000 pikes that his factory had produced. But less than half the city's volunteers were able to acquire genuine weapons; others had to be satisfied with wielding kitchen knives or pitchforks. They wanted more. By early afternoon places rumored to still have weapons were raided by crazed mobs. Hardware stores and foundries, particularly those owned by Germans or anyone suspected of unionist feelings, found themselves under attack.

By midafternoon Sunday the situation in Baltimore was again approaching anarchy. Brown and Kane were doing all they could, but were feeling overwhelmed.

Much now depended on the actions of President Lincoln. And he seemed far out of his depth.

CHAPTER TEN

The Yard

President Lincoln's worries were multiplying. He had announced his proclamation on Monday, April 15. By Friday, four days later, he was aware of Virginia's secession and the fall of Harpers Ferry. Maryland, he knew, was a dangerous powder keg. On Saturday, as he pondered what to do about Baltimore, another problem emerged at the Gosport Navy Yard. Washington, sitting as it does on the Potomac, had to be sensitive to events in the outer Chesapeake Bay. What happened at Gosport could tilt control of the Chesapeake and seal the fate of the national capital.

Gosport's history had begun centuries earlier.

The weather of the North Atlantic is notoriously unpredictable and treacherous. During the early seventeenth century European sailors, crossing the ocean, desired more than simple sandy landfalls; they needed safe harbors. They wanted the Atlantic's gale winds behind them, muffled by islands or promontories. They also wanted to feel confident that any waters below their keel this close to the mainland were good anchorages, neither rocky nor too shallow. They required nearby fresh water to drink and, if possible, a local population amenable to trade. Preferably their harbors would be connected to rivers providing access to the interior: to timber and pelts, and once fulltime settlers arrived, to farm goods and freshwater fish. Dutch and English sailors, French and Spanish, those who bumped into the North American continent, discovered many serviceable harbors sprinkled along the Atlantic coast. Initially these were only stopping places, but eventually they became towns, then cities. Some, like Boston and New York and Charleston, were near the ocean. Others — Philadelphia, particularly — were inland, far from the Atlantic winds. One of the best sanctuaries was the Chesapeake Bay, because its waters were protected by a thick landmass — a peninsula over 150 miles long and more than fifty miles wide, dangling like a thick beard down from Pennsylvania. This land shield eventually held parts of three states — Delaware, Maryland, and Virginia — and acquired the nickname Delmarva, though usually was called the Eastern Shore by locals. The peninsula is flat and sandy, and contains short rivers like the Choptank and Wicomico. Tiny islands sparkle like diamonds along its interior coastline. While most of its shoreline and rivers are too shallow to offer docking places for ocean-going vessels, small boats easily sail along its inner edge. Across the Bay from the Eastern Shore lies a superb haven for men of the sea. Here dozens of wide rivers flow from the interior. Great ships arriving from all over the world have no difficulty entering Chesapeake Bay's gaping mouth, with its channel more than ten miles across. Once inside the Bay, a virtual inland sea, such vessels can continue northward almost 200 miles — even farther if they keep going up the Susquehanna River into the heart of Pennsylvania, all the way to Harrisburg. Alternatively they can tack into dozens of other rivers and anchor or dock against their banks.

In 1861 steamships departed from Baltimore several times a day, following regular routes to Annapolis, thirty miles south — not only Maryland's state capital, but the home of the Naval Academy. A passenger from Baltimore could debark here, perhaps discuss matters with a state legislator, then head to the town's railroad station and board a train that could take him to nearby Washington. Or he could choose to buy passage on a steamship and go from Annapolis to the Potomac, then on to the national capital. Or if he steamed farther south, on his right he would pass rivers like the Rappahannock and the

York. A few miles before exiting the Bay to enter the Atlantic, he could espy from the deck of his ship, off the starboard bow, a cape several miles wide. A large brick fortress sat at its end, easily visible to passing ships, its guns glowering outward at any enemy who might approach too near. This was Fort Monroe — the largest military bastion in North America, one of the greatest forts in the world. Winfield Scott considered Fort Monroe of vital importance. If pressed, he would assert that the federal government could afford to give up places like Fort Sumter, and even all Texas, if necessary. But not Fort Monroe — not at least without a fight. Its position, so close to the mouth of the Chesapeake Bay, made it vital in his mind. To lose it could mean the entire Bay might be forfeited. Baltimore (and perhaps all Maryland) could be lost; and maybe the Potomac River, even the national capital.

The waters just off Fort Monroe were called Hampton Roads. A steamship — perhaps a passenger ship from Baltimore — could pass the fort, and instead of heading left out into the Atlantic, could swing right and enter the James River, whose deep waters could carry this vessel on the same route the 105 English settlers took in 1607 when they sailed into that river, continuing twenty miles, dropping anchor, and creating a settlement they named Jamestown. By 1861 a ship traveling up the James might steam until the river's waters were too shallow to proceed higher. If so, it had arrived at the docks and warehouses of Richmond. Or it might anchor farther downriver — perhaps at Petersburg. Or it might tie its lines at the town it came to first on the James: Norfolk.

In 1861 Norfolk was a sea town. Its population depended on trade, on building or repairing ships, on carting goods between docks and warehouses, on filling and serving tankards of rum and plates of oysters, on providing beds to weary travelers. Norfolk actually sat on the southern bank of a narrow inlet from the James politely called the Elizabeth River. Directly across this stream was a smaller town named Portsmouth where sat the greatest American naval base of that era, the

Gosport Navy Yard. Just as General Scott had worried for months about the fate of Fort Monroe, the Navy Department in Washington had been stewing over Gosport.

Even before the American Revolution, the British navy had recognized this locale's potential and had started erecting a marine yard here, calling it Gosport, after a dockyard back in England. In 1800 the American government contacted Virginia's governor and said the new United States Navy would like to purchase land there to erect a major naval base. A deal was struck. By the 1820s the navy proposed to build its first dry dock at Gosport. Since the region suffered no heavy frosts and possessed handy building materials for sailing ships, and because the waters of the James were deep, and with Fort Monroe only a few miles away to offer protection, this site seemed ideal. By the 1850s the Gosport Navy Yard employed 1500 workmen and had the largest dry dock in the Western Hemisphere. The yard had a huge crane (called "shears") that performed major repair tasks, a foundry, a good hospital, gas lighting, and an excellent boiler shop to construct or repair steam engines. The navy had also expanded its presence in the region, moving some materials to a spot across the Elizabeth River called Saint Helena, a section of Norfolk. Here the Yard stored much of its ordnance (including, in early 1861, 2,800 barrels of gunpowder). Gosport also had on hand over a thousand naval guns — many of them massive artillery pieces, some of the largest in the world. If the Confederacy captured them, it could sprinkle them along its coastline and up the Mississippi River, making assaults against her far more difficult.

In addition to all this hardware, in early 1861 the navy had ten vessels docked at Gosport — a quarter of its entire naval force. Since a significant portion of America's military ships were at sea, far from home — in Caribbean waters, for example — the warships at Gosport actually represented almost half the navy's readily available military might. Six of these vessels were rather obsolete sailing ships, and in rough shape, but the other four — especially the forty-gun steam frigate

Merrimack—were relatively modern. The situation of the *Merrimack* was particularly worrisome. With her steam engines she was one of the best military ships in the world—potentially fast and muscular. She had recently been brought to Gosport after a few years at sea to have her engines replaced. At this moment she stood empty and quiet, her mechanical parts strewn across a nearby dock. Workmen at the navy yard intended to repair her eventually, but there seemed no rush. Other ships that had arrived earlier had priority.

The navy had an additional problem: not enough sailors. The number of its trained seamen was small, and most of these were at present serving far away. A handful had been in New York earlier in the year, but Lincoln's decision to send expeditions to Fort Sumter, and to Fort Pickens in Florida, scooped up most of those. The Navy Department would be hard-pressed to find the manpower to sail all its ships out of Gosport if it became necessary or desirable to move them somewhere else.[71]

In early 1861 the most delicate issue at the Gosport Navy Yard involved the ticklish matter of how Washington ought to treat the state of Virginia. The need to be circumspect with the Southern states had haunted President James Buchanan, especially in the five-month period between Lincoln's election and inauguration. Buchanan believed, if he acted forcefully, he could worsen relations with Southerners. Even when secessionists expropriated federal properties in the Deep South, including arsenals, Buchanan refused to react with much vigor. It seemed possible that the seceding states were merely in a surly mood, made testy by Lincoln's election. Perhaps this situation was like a marital squabble. Given time and a calm approach, the other side might relax and remember the benefits of being part of the United States. Besides, most of Old Buck's advisers convinced him the government lacked sufficient military punch to act vigorously.

During this period Lincoln—first in Illinois, then after his arrival in Washington and before his inauguration—offered

virtually no concrete suggestions. When asked if he were willing to compromise on the major issue of "slavery in the terri-
tories," which had been much discussed of late, he replied:
absolutely not. But he never clarified what he actually intended to do once in office. He occasionally said publicly that
he would "collect the tariff" and "hold federal properties,"
though how he would accomplish these things, he left un-
stated. One might ask, for example, exactly how he intended
to go about collecting the tariff in the port city of Charleston,
previously a major center of American tariff collecting. The
official collector in that town had long since ceased performing that function, which meant that imports arriving at
Charleston's docks paid no tariff duties to Washington. Making firm speeches about tariffs might allow the president-elect
to sound resolute, but murkiness remained. Nor was the tariff
question merely an abstract issue. Approximately two-thirds
of the federal government's income came from these taxes on
incoming goods. Without this money, how could Washington
pay its bills? (How could it, for one example, hire more seamen?) And by early April 1861 this tariff matter affected more
than the seven states of the Confederacy. Virginia remained in
the Union. Norfolk was a major American port. The federal
government maintained customs collectors there. Would Lincoln make an issue of tariff collection in that city? He almost
certainly would need to. And this would inevitably cause a
flurry of problems in that town, less than a mile from the
Gosport Navy Yard.

Abraham Lincoln was as sensitive about the delicate status
of Virginia as Buchanan had been. From the time of Lincoln's
arrival in the capital, almost two weeks before his inauguration, he had attempted a policy of appeasement with Virginia's
leaders. He was told by men like Seward—and he believed it
to be true—that most Virginians remained good unionists. He
assumed they would continue to be so as long as he did not rile
them by some unacceptable action. His task would be to calculate what would be acceptable. He received much advice—
mostly contradictory and confusing. It is hard now to parse

Lincoln's thinking at that time. Many observers, then and since, have examined the tea leaves of his words and come away befuddled. But this much seems clear enough: like an untrained enlisted man ordered to dismantle a land mine, Lincoln handled Virginia very daintily. When he sent provisions to Major Anderson at Fort Sumter, he hoped those two matters — affairs in Charleston and Virginia — would not clash. How silly he was.

Then came the Confederate attack on Fort Sumter, and his follow-up decision to ask for volunteers. Did he realize this request would kill any chance of continuing his appeasement of Virginia? The question is an important one. If Lincoln, on Sunday, April 14, had a suspicion that his proclamation — which would be announced the next day — would cause an immediate explosion in Virginia, he ought to have moved more warily, to have made careful plans about how to deal with issues that might arise there. It is unlikely he could have done anything in advance to save the arsenal at Harpers Ferry, but he certainly could have handled the status of Gosport better.

A phrase, slightly bowdlerized, about the inner workings of bureaucracy says: stuff runs downhill. It is an accurate description about how things work in most organizations. The attitudes of those at the top tend to be reflected by people beneath them. Flunkies generally adopt the methods and mood of management. Attitudes of honesty or of chicanery, suspiciousness or caution, kindness or cruelty are embraced by subordinates.

In this way Lincoln's original concerns about the sensitivities of Virginians were bound to be reflected by those below him in the hierarchy. He seemed determined not to ruffle Virginia's feathers, so the members of his administration reacted accordingly. As for the fate of Gosport, this policy, at the very least, was dubious, perhaps stupid.

Gideon Welles was secretary of the navy. In a sense Welles had been an odd choice for the position. His connections to the sea were sketchy, and he had never been an administrator of any large institution. His background had been mostly in Connecticut, and involved journalism. He had been editor and part owner of the *Hartford Times*, a good regional newspaper. He had dabbled in politics, and to repay him for his efforts Andrew Jackson had made him a local postmaster. In 1845 President James K. Polk appointed him head of the Navy's Bureau of Provisions and Clothing. Welles performed this assignment honestly, though without noticeable distinction. In the 1850s he had become a Republican, and in 1860 had backed Lincoln over Seward. The choice of him as secretary of the navy was, therefore, based on politics, not naval expertise. Lincoln obviously wanted to pick someone from New England to sit in his Cabinet; Welles, who had supported him, was that person. Curiously, Welles eventually grew into the position. He was hard working, intelligent, and had a strong enough personality to control the immense bureaucracy that blossomed during the war years.

As for Gosport in 1861, Welles recognized its importance from the beginning. He knew the situation there was dicey. After all, the Yard was in the farthest southeast corner of Virginia. Everything that happened on the base would be watched. Each morning local workmen would rise from their beds outside the navy yard and walk through its main gate. Each evening they would return home, where they would describe what they had seen and heard. The smallest changes would be analyzed and interpreted endlessly. Since part of Gosport's materials were housed in Norfolk, there was constant traffic each day back and forth across the Elizabeth River. Furthermore, steamers regularly traveled between Norfolk and Richmond or Baltimore. Welles could hardly assume doings at Gosport could remain unnoticed. If a naval vessel at the dock had a few guns trundled up its gangplank, Richmond and Baltimore newspapers would ponder the implications.

Years later Gideon Welles's diaries were published. Since he was a skilled journalist, the entries were articulate. They were also opinionated and often acerbic. He did not mince words. But his diary from mid-April 1861 until mid-May was uncharacteristically cryptic. One entry stated he asked Winfield Scott for troops to guard Gosport, and the general had replied—quite properly—that, although Scott was sympathetic, he did not have manpower to spare. (Scott only had a few hundred soldiers available, and those not already assigned to critical spots like Harpers Ferry and Fort Monroe were necessary to protect Washington itself.) Gosport was of course important, but dealing with it would be Welles's problem. Besides, Scott told the secretary of the navy—and the old general knew that region of Virginia well—if it came to real fighting, Norfolk was indefensible.

Welles decided to take the matter up with the president. Lincoln listened to the secretary's concerns about the naval base, and to Scott's analysis. Lincoln had previously ordered Welles to make "no important or extensive changes" at Gosport, at least without consulting him first, and on this occasion he told the navy secretary, according to Welles's diary, that he concurred with General Scott. In fact, Lincoln said he thought putting soldiers at the naval base would be "inexpedient and would tend to irritate and promote a conflict." He added emphatically, according to Welles, that "any extraordinary efforts to repair the ships with a view of removing them and the public property would...exhibit a want of confidence and betray apprehensions that should be avoided."[72]

Assuming Welles's recollections of this conversation were accurate—and there is no reason to doubt it, as the rest of his diary is generally confirmed by independent data—Abraham Lincoln was the person most responsible for the fastidious handling of Gosport Navy Yard. When things collapsed there a few days later, newspaper editors—and, later, historians—seldom put the onus on Lincoln; they blamed the naval officers involved. It is true that charges against a few high-ranking officers would be partly deserved, but President Lincoln could have ordered more forceful action in Gosport, especially on Sunday, April 14, once he decided to issue his proclamation. But because he continued to tiptoe around all things Virginian, the Gosport problem weighed heavily on those who had to bear its burden.

Since August 1860 the commandant of the yard had been Captain Charles S. McCauley, sixty-eight. (Normally, a commandant of a navy yard or even a fleet bore the title, if not the official rank, of Commodore.) McCauley had had a distinguished career. If the army or navy in that era offered reasonable pensions, men like McCauley would probably have resigned from the service. Instead, the navy maintained a tradition of appointing older captains to supervise its navy yards, the positions being respected and undemanding—in normal times, sinecures. (But the naval base at Pensacola, Florida, had been commanded by such an officer, Commodore James Armstrong, who, early in 1861, had meekly handed that important military bastion to a small militia force without putting up a fight. The navy yard in the District of Columbia was commanded by Commodore Franklin Buchanan. Lincoln attended the wedding of the commodore's daughter only a few days before that officer departed Washington to join the Confederate cause.)

One issue for leaders like McCauley was that their sources of information generally came from locals. McCauley would occasionally receive snippets of advice from the distant Navy Department in Washington, but on a day-to-day basis those he spoke with were almost entirely people who lived within a mile or two of the base. Most of his young officers, with families who were natives of the region, had sympathies that were, at best, divided. The newspapers McCauley read were penned by local editors. The parties he attended were hosted by well-to-do nabobs like Henry Wise, men who had become his friends. McCauley would have been shocked to realize that the governor of South Carolina, Francis Pickens, had been receiving secret messages for months from local spies about the Gosport Navy Yard and about McCauley's attitudes and activities.[73]

When Henry Wise stood and addressed the Virginia convention on the morning of April 17, announcing he had organized an expedition to take over Harpers Ferry and implying he had also arranged an assault on Gosport, it is hard to find many of his fingerprints on that naval base. Wise did telegram contacts in Norfolk as part of his plot to foment a secessionist coup in Virginia, but we have little other evidence of him continuing to tamper with events there.

We do know that on April 18, Governor Letcher issued an order to one of Henry Wise's young relatives, William Booth Taliaferro, who happened to be in Richmond. Taliaferro, thirty-eight, a member of a prominent Virginia family, had attended both Harvard and William and Mary. He had participated in the Mexican War and in the suppression of John Brown's raid. Now, Governor Letcher's orders were that he should leave immediately for Norfolk, a hundred miles down the James River, to take command of that area's militiamen. With those troops, he was to attempt to take over Gosport. Letcher said he did not know how large a force this task would require, but assumed it would probably take five thousand men. Taliaferro left that evening.

Letcher did not feel sanguine. It seemed unlikely that Taliaferro could round up enough men to accomplish the mission Letcher had in mind. (Letcher also wired Francis Pickens, asking the South Carolinian for any extra manpower he might have on hand now that Fort Sumter had fallen. Pickens turned the request over to the Confederate leadership in Montgomery. Within a few days Montgomery forwarded a few hundred troops from Georgia to Norfolk, but by April 23, as these first Confederate troops arrived in Virginia, their presence was no longer needed; the fate of Gosport had already been decided.)[74]

After Gustavus Fox's expedition departed New York, heading for Fort Sumter, Gideon Welles, in Washington, grew edgy. A crisis, he thought, would almost certainly erupt as a result of events at Fort Sumter. Gosport seemed exceedingly vulnerable. On April 10 Welles sent a personal note to McCauley. It read:

> In view of the peculiar condition of the country, and of events that have already transpired, it becomes necessary that great vigilance should be exercised in guarding and protecting the public interests and property committed to your charge. It is therefore deemed important that the steamer *Merrimack* should be in condition to proceed to Philadelphia or to any other yard, should it be deemed necessary, or, in case of danger from unlawful attempts to take possession of her, that she may be placed beyond their reach.
>
> Indeed, it is desirable that all the shipping and stores should be attended to, and should you think an additional force necessary, or that other precautions are required, you will immediately apprise the Department. In the meantime exercise your own judgment in discharging the responsibility that devolves on you.
>
> It is desirable that there should be no steps taken to give needless alarm, but it may be best to order most of the shipping to sea or [to] other stations.
>
> Please keep the Department advised of the condition of affairs, and of any cause for apprehension, should any exist.[75]

McCauley was being told to do nothing that might "give needless alarm," though he probably ought to "order most of the shipping [to head out] to sea," especially the *Merrimack*. How he was to accomplish this, under the circumstances, was unclear. As Welles was aware, McCauley still lacked sufficient sailors to man all the ships at the yard. And the *Merrimack's* engines remained in pieces, scattered about.

The next day—April 11, one day before the attack began on Fort Sumter—Welles sent a flurry of excited messages. He told McCauley to get the sailing ship *Plymouth* moving immediately; it was being transferred to Annapolis. He followed that wire with a second note to McCauley, this one emphasizing the urgency of the *Merrimack,* which he wanted moved out of there as soon as it could be gotten ready. McCauley replied to the Navy Department that he had spoken to his chief engineer and been told the *Merrimack* could not be made ready for sea in under a month.

This same day Welles ordered the commandant at the New York Navy Yard to transfer 200 seamen to Norfolk, "without delay." The officer in New York replied apologetically a few days later that thus far he had only been able to hire sixty-three men, but he would try to fill the secretary's request. He later reported he might have enough men ready by the 20th or 21st. (It would turn out to be too late.)

Also on the 11th, Welles ordered Commander James Alden to hurry to Gosport and speed the *Merrimack* away from there as soon as it was shipshape. For some reason, Alden took his time.

Even after sending all these messages, the navy secretary remained unsatisfied. The next day he ordered his engineer-in-chief, Benjamin Franklin Isherwood, thirty-eight, to Gosport. Isherwood's assignment would be to examine the *Merrimack's* condition, to see if he could do anything to expedite her removal. Clearly, as Lincoln's naval expedition approached Charleston Harbor, Welles sensed a crisis looming.

Engineer-in-Chief Isherwood steamed to Gosport, and in just over two days performed a remarkable naval feat. (His report described his reaction on first examining the *Merrimack*: "The engines were in a wretched state. All the braces were out of the boilers, having been removed with a view to the substitution of other and larger ones, and the entire machinery was in a disabled condition.") By pressing the yard's laborers to work around the clock, he was able to install enough of the dismantled engines so he could announce on April 17 that the ship could be moved the next day. By this time Commander Alden had finally appeared. He and Isherwood somehow rustled up more than forty men to stoke the *Merrimack's* steam engines, and the ship was ready to go. All that was needed was McCauley's permission.

McCauley hesitated. He was acutely aware of Welles's obvious anxiety about the *Merrimack,* but he had an additional, and antithetical, concern: the navy secretary's previous reminders to cause no "needless alarm" among the local population. McCauley was convinced the populations of both Portsmouth and Norfolk were ready to explode. Although he had not yet learned that the Virginia convention had voted in favor of secession—since that decision had been made secretly only the day before—he was certainly aware that hundreds of local civilians were marching around Norfolk with guns. They had been doing so for weeks, forming militia companies whose numbers were growing. The movements of these military units were overt. In fact, from McCauley's own residence on the base he could distinctly hear the frequent arrival of reinforcements by train. He caught the whistle of the incoming engines and the gleeful shouts of the arriving militiamen. (He did not realize that much of this commotion was a ruse. A man named William Mahone, head of the local railroad, was backing one of his trains quietly from the depot then bringing her noisily in again, as men stood by the station joyfully yelling out fake salutations.)

McCauley had also learned on the night of April 16–17, hours before Virginia's convention voted to secede, that tugs had slipped into the James River, dragging three old ships and sinking them in the channel several miles below Norfolk. (The lead tug, *Teaser,* had just arrived in Norfolk—its master, William H. Face, having been ordered there from Richmond—though ordered by whom is unclear.) McCauley even knew that someone had removed the channel's buoys. It seemed plausible that moving the *Merrimack* or any other fairly large ship from the yard was now problematic. At least this is what McCauley's young officers told him.

McCauley was also informed by sailors on the *Cumberland,* tied up by the Elizabeth River's edge, that from their masthead they had observed earthworks being built just downstream from the navy yard. If big guns were placed atop those earth-works, the game would be near checkmate. No more ships would be able to enter or depart without permission. This prospect was the last straw for the commandant. He decided to ignore Welles's previous order against stirring up the locals. He agreed that a volunteer officer should go and inform the Virginians that if they did not cease building that earthwork *immediately*, naval artillery would open fire on the city of Nor-folk. Construction on the earthworks ceased.

What to do with the *Merrimack* — to say nothing of the other ships at the yard — remained unsettled. McCauley had reserva-tions about moving any ship unless absolutely necessary. His own inclination was to act cautiously, but he was also under ex-plicit orders from Welles — and implied orders from Lincoln — to do nothing to prod the Virginians. Removing ships from the Yard probably would be considered provocative. He also was uneasy about whether it was still possible to maneuver ships out the James because of the scows sunk there and the buoys having been snatched away. Some of his officers said they thought it could be accomplished, but if any ships were dam-aged on a shoal and sank, he would be held responsible.

Good leadership requires, among other things, the ability to extract the best choices from a variety of contradictory advices. In retrospect one can see that McCauley erred on the side of caution. It turned out ships were able to escape the navy yard. But until the attempt was made and proved successful, he could not have been certain. Also, there was another factor. As long as the *Merrimack* remained tied to the dock, her guns — facing both inward toward the navy yard and outward at the Eliza-beth River, and all the way across the stream toward Norfolk — could serve as a deterrent to anyone wishing to attack. Since his primary responsibility was the defense of this base, the *Mer-rimack* could perform an active role in assisting him.

Besides, McCauley's boss, Secretary Welles, still remained uncertain as to how best to proceed. On April 16 Welles wrote McCauley a confidential note. In light of the attack on Fort Sumter, Welles now urged "additional vigilance and care." But as to the *Merrimack*, Welles seemed less certain than he had been a few days earlier, when he had ordered Alden and Isherwood to speed that vessel from Gosport. Welles was aware the ship was almost ready to move, but added: "It may not be necessary, however, that she should leave at this time, unless there is immediate danger pending." Welles did urge that the *Plymouth* be moved away from the docks and suggested that another sailing ship there, the *Dolphin*, also be taken from the yard.

Confusing the atmosphere even more, Secretary Welles had grown so suspicious of the communications system in Virginia that he handed this note to an officer named Captain Hiram Paulding to hand-carry to Gosport. This would involve a cumbersome process; it was three days before Paulding presented the new message to McCauley — and by that time, everything at the yard had changed.

As the unfortunate McCauley, pestered with advice from all sides, tried to calculate what best to do at Gosport, the mood in Washington, many hours up Chesapeake Bay from Norfolk, was no calmer. Lincoln was conducting almost constant cabinet meetings by this time. The situation just across the Potomac in Virginia was obviously parlous and growing worse by the hour. General Scott had received reports that trainloads of militiamen were chuffing northward through Virginia. Presumably these soldiers were on their way toward Harpers Ferry, but this was not certain; they might be heading directly toward Washington. Just then, somebody cut the telegraph lines south of Alexandria.

One afternoon during a cabinet meeting, Gideon Welles was informed that someone was waiting outside to speak to him. The secretary stepped from the room. Commander Alden stood there, obviously emotional. According to Welles's diary, Alden declared that Commodore McCauley, at Gosport, "seemed stupefied, bewildered, and wholly unable to act." (Isherwood at some point during this day also spoke to Welles about Mc-Cauley; the engineer said he suspected the commodore was sodden with alcohol. No one else mentioned such a possibility, and we can assume Isherwood confused tension and exhaustion for intoxication.) Welles listened to these criticisms. He was unimpressed with Alden's own character, considering him, at bottom, a timid man, "not endowed with great moral or physical courage." Welles had hoped Alden would inspirit the elderly commandant of Gosport, but instead the younger man had rushed back to Washington to whine. Despite Welles's reservations about Alden, the secretary asked the officer to explain to the entire cabinet what he had just said. Commander Alden entered the room and repeated his charges against Mc-Cauley and his concerns about the Yard.[76]

Gideon Welles then went to Scott to plead again for troops to send to Norfolk. The general remained unconvinced that ordering soldiers to the navy yard would accomplish anything, but since the last time Welles had made this request the situation had changed. Scott had just learned that two Massachusetts regiments were at sea. He assumed, but could not be positive, that they were heading toward Fort Monroe, as he had requested.

Scott knew little about these regiments—for instance, where they were at this moment, where they were headed, how well trained they might be. He assumed, as state militia, that they had probably done some drilling in the past, but this would hardly have made Scott sanguine about their military abilities. He had been told something about the equipment they carried — their muskets, their blankets, and so on — but he suspected they were little better than a mob. He himself had written America's three-volume bible on military drilling, which emphasized the complexities of learning the manual of arms and how much time and attention would be required to acquire by rote the smallest detail; so he recognized the discrepancies between casual militia training and true military drill. Only a day earlier, when the first Pennsylvanians had appeared in Washington, calling themselves a "regiment," they turned out of be only half the requisite size. If those Pennsylvania volunteers were any reflection — and Scott had a feeling they were — he was not hopeful about the quality of Lincoln's volunteers. (Actually, at the very moment he was speaking with Gideon Welles, the first Massachusetts volunteers were approaching Fort Monroe. The battered Sixth Massachusetts was in transit from Baltimore.)

Secretary Welles would not be put off this time. He had come directly from the cabinet meeting, striding across the lawn of Executive Square. He informed Scott that the cabinet and Lincoln were worried about the status of Gosport. The administration had just agreed that Welles must order the *Pawnee* to the Yard (along with some marines stationed in Washington). The government was willing to take this step even though the *Pawnee* was the sole war vessel now patrolling the Potomac and protecting the District. Lincoln's acceptance of its departure suggested to Scott the level of the administration's anxiety about Gosport.

Scott decided he had little choice. He wrote a note to an army engineer, Captain Horatio Gouverneur Wright, an intelligent West Point graduate living in Washington, working on federal building projects — a stolid, trustworthy, forty-one-year-old. Scott ordered him to Gosport, traveling on the *Pawnee* along with the navy's marines, over whom Scott had no authority. Wright, said Scott, was to offer his engineering services to Commodore McCauley, in designing and executing some sort of defense system for the navy yard. Since the *Pawnee* would be steaming past Fort Monroe on its way to Gosport, Scott proposed that Wright "call at Fort Monroe and consult Colonel [Justin E.] Dimick on sending a portion of its garrison to assist in the defense of the navy yard. If two volunteer regiments [the ones from Massachusetts] shall have joined him, he may spare one of them for that purpose perhaps."

But General Scott remained nervous, unsure of what Dimick was now facing at Fort Monroe. After all, Fort Sumter, also a seacoast fortress, had been attacked a few days earlier. It seemed possible Fort Monroe would be next. Scott advised Wright that Dimick's decision must be based on what he, the commander at Fort Monroe, considered best for his situation, not the concerns of the navy about Gosport. If Dimick perceived *any* threat coming toward him from the surrounding population, he must use caution.

Winfield Scott was not easily spooked. The wariness of this message is an indication of the old general's uneasiness.[77]

That night — Friday, April 19 — Captain Wright boarded the *Pawnee* at the Washington Navy Yard. Between fifty and a hundred marines joined him. (For the previous two days Welles had also been hoping to obtain additional marines from the Philadelphia Navy Yard, but had just learned this was impossible because the private steamship company that he expected to transport them refused to send one of their unarmed vessels into harm's way. So Welles — and Gosport — had to make do with what was on hand.)

Captain Paulding would also be aboard the *Pawnee*, carrying his orders from Welles to take command of all naval personnel at Gosport, including the marines. If possible Paulding was to move whatever ships he could out of danger. Second, he should save the navy yard, if that could be done. If not, he was to destroy it, to keep the base out of the hands of the "insurrectionists."

Saturday, April 20, 1861

The *Pawnee* took almost a day to reach Fort Monroe. It arrived in midafternoon. By chance, both Massachusetts regiments were already there, the second one having just steamed in a few hours earlier. Its volunteers had been at sea for days. Most were woozy from seasickness and rancid from lack of hygiene; all were stiff from inactivity. These men constituted the Third Massachusetts.

Captain Wright rushed into Fort Monroe with Scott's message for Colonel Dimick, the fort's commandant. Three hours later, David W. Wardrop led his 348 men of the Third Massachusetts Regiment (actually six companies, and therefore only a battalion), out of the fort and aboard the *Pawnee*. Wardrop was glad his men had been chosen and not those of the Fourth Regiment; he wanted his Third to have the honor. At 6:45 P.M. the *Pawnee* headed for Gosport, fourteen miles upriver. The men of the Fourth stood along Fort Monroe's parapets and yelled resounding cheers as the warship passed by. Their comrades in the Third shouted triumphantly back.

The foam of the Bay sprayed against the steamer's deck as the ship pressed against the tricky currents. It was darkening now, but a half moon lit the clear sky. Upriver several miles, near the junction of the James and the Elizabeth, the sailors noticed man-made obstructions in the river: sunken boats, their masts jutting above the water. The *Pawnee* steamed cautiously past the hulks, then hurried on.[78]

The infantrymen noticed that the sailors started double-shotting the cannon facing the port side. The volunteers themselves were each handed twenty-five cartridges, ordered to load their rifles, and told they were heading toward Gosport, less than an hour away, that rebels might have artillery on the river bank to blow them from the water. If that turned out to be the case, their officers told them, their job was to try to pick off the enemy gunners. Most of the Massachusetts men, like so many of Lincoln's volunteers, had never previously fired a rifle.

The men aboard the *Pawnee*—the marines, the 349 Massachusetts volunteers, Captain Wright of the army, Hiram Paulding of the navy—did not know it, but they were too late. Several hours earlier Commodore McCauley at Gosport had already made a crucial decision about the Yard.

McCauley felt entirely cut off from Washington. Strangers were wandering, unhindered, around his yard, picking up arms here and there and walking off. Most of his staff officers had skedaddled, as had the majority of the yard's workmen and some of the base's marines. If he wanted to count optimistically, McCauley suspected he retained the support of perhaps sixty marines, but this handful would have to guard the huge navy yard and all its buildings and docks, as well as its several miles of walls (not counting the materials across the Elizabeth River in Norfolk that had almost certainly already been lost). He could also lean on the support of the approximately four hundred seamen on board both the *Cumberland* and the *Pennsylvania,* although the first duty of those sailors would be to their ships, not the Yard.

Given the continuing whistles of what seemed to be incoming trains carrying enemy troops, and rumors that Norfolk already had 5,000 armed men on hand, with more arriving almost hourly, McCauley was becoming frantic. The fact that Taliaferro commanded, at most, five hundred essentially unarmed Virginia volunteers was inconsequential. McCauley was forced to react to the evidence he had available. Like all leaders in such sticky situations, he was essentially a slave to whatever intelligence he was receiving. One of McCauley's chief sources of information was the man in charge of the Yard's marines, Lieutenant Colonel James Edelin. Although Edelin remained loyal to the Union, he was so nervous about the situation in Norfolk that he only visited that town to pick up funds from a bank to pay his men. He later admitted, "I deemed it dangerous to go there." Edelin had an informant, an ex-workman at the Yard, who told him the insurgents had five thousand men under arms. Edelin imparted this (dis)information to McCauley.

McCauley, therefore, was not reacting timidly, an elderly man jumping at shadows, no matter what people would later say. His responsibilities were enormous. His superiors — Secretary Welles and Lincoln — had emphasized far too often that he must act with cautious prudence, and they had offered him far too little real support.

McCauley still hesitated to destroy naval property. He had been in the navy for well over fifty years, since his midteens.

Purposely damaging government equipment felt unseemly. Friday night he probably slept restlessly, hoping for some advice or orders from Washington, some change. But on Saturday morning everything appeared about the same, but worse. He was told that insurgents seemed to be placing cannon near the mouth of the Elizabeth River to prevent ships from leaving. This news, though false, pushed him to a decision. Given the certainty that rebels had already dropped obstructions in the river and were preparing to place more, McCauley, alone in his responsibility, made his decision.

In the early afternoon of that Saturday, April 20, he ordered most of the unmanned ships at his yard scuttled. He intended to keep them out of the hands of the insurgents. (One, the *Germantown*, being worked on, was sitting beneath the huge crane's shear legs. He said this heavy contraption should be allowed to fall onto the ship, and the monstrous thing was dropped, shattering the *Germantown*'s masts and hull.)

Scuttling vessels required men to board the ships and open several critical entry ports. Once this was done, while those ships settled gradually into the river, the men McCauley had available also tried to disable as many of the ships' guns as they could, spiking most of them (ramming metal rods—slender files called rat tails, or, after they ran out of these tools, using extra-long nails—into the guns' vents or touchholes, near the tails of the barrels). Relatively light guns were flung over the sides. Within the Yard, men ran about destroying other pieces of equipment.

By nightfall most of this work had been done, at least as much as McCauley's crews could accomplish. Under his orders they had left the buildings untouched—the barracks, the hospital, the storage places. He finally boarded the frigate *Cumberland*, flagship of Commodore Pendergrast, and said he was prepared to leave.

He had been aboard but a few moments when sailors on deck started scrambling, frantically preparing to repel invaders.

For the previous few days the crews of the *Cumberland* and the *Pennsylvania* had been watching for any hostile steamers approaching, coming downriver from Richmond. The chaotic situation at the Yard had added to the tensions. For almost a week crewmen of passing boats had shouted catcalls at the federal sailors, promising their approaching doom. It was well known in naval circles that an aggressive antagonist could destroy his enemy's ships by pressing burning hulks against them.

The time was eight o'clock; it was almost totally dark. Suddenly a lookout shouted that he saw a vessel approaching. Perhaps this approaching ghostly boat was one of those hulks, about to burst into flame just before ramming the *Cumberland* or the *Pennsylvania.* Or possibly the incoming vessel contained armed pirates, Virginia volunteers, who would swing themselves across like buccaneers when they crashed together.

Drums beat to quarters. Artillerists ran to their pieces. Orders were given to the gun crews: prepare to fire. Gunners lit their matches (narrow cords that could be lighted and plunged into the vent holes to ignite the gunpowder within); they stood by their guns, waiting. An officer on the *Cumberland,* standing at the ten-inch pivot gun on the forecastle, aimed this cannon at the approaching intruder. He took his gun's lock string (lanyard) in his hand, ready to pull. Sailors stared into the dimness, their ears attuned to catch every sound: the lapping waves, orders from their own officers, any shouting by an enemy. Someone on the *Pennsylvania* called into the darkness: Ahoy there!

The approaching ship seemed to offer no response. (Actually, it was the *Pawnee.* Someone aboard her did carol out her identity, but a land breeze was blowing straight downriver, and these words were lost to the anxious men waiting on the *Cumberland* and *Pennsylvania.*) A second query was yelled. Again this elicited no response. Almost certainly, those waiting thought, this must indicate an attack. The officer at the ten-inch forward gun shouted to his superior, "Should I fire?" "No," came the reply, "we will hail her once more."

In the murk, either because of someone's bellowing or keen eyesight, the seamen on the *Pennsylvania,* anchored a bit downstream and therefore closer to the approaching vessel, realized the intruder was a friend. They began cheering. They called to the *Cumberland* not to fire, the new ship was the *Pawnee.* The crew of the *Cumberland* exploded in shouts of happy relief, and welcome.[79]

(The incoming *Pawnee* was also observed by citizens in nearby Portsmouth, where many of the yard's workmen resided. Catching sight of this vessel, thinking it was here to save the Yard, a bunch of the Portsmouth civilians who felt loyal to the Union excitedly began cheering, too.)

A few minutes later, an officer of the *Pennsylvania* boarded the *Pawnee,* along with Commodore Pendergrast and Mc-Cauley. Paulding, down from Washington, described his instructions from Welles: henceforth, he was in charge. He also said that Captain Wright of the army had been ordered by General Scott to give all assistance, and that the volunteers from Massachusetts might be useful. He inquired about the situation here.

In many ways McCauley was probably greatly relieved. His responsibilities had been lifted from his shoulders, transferred to Paulding. He gave his replacement a synopsis of what he knew and understood, including the situation at the Yard — the scuttled ships still sinking, the purposely broken equipment, the disabled guns. Then he departed and went to his quarters in the Yard. He told his young son, who was at the residence, that he intended to remain here — to "go down with the ship," as it were.

Paulding's first thought was for the scuttled ships. Were they already too full of water, or could they be saved? Might they be pumped out? A quick check provided the answer: they were past an easy solution. In time, maybe a day or two, they could be made relatively shipshape. Hiram Paulding, sixty-four, exhausted from constant, fatiguing duty during the previous few weeks, made his own important decision. He concluded it was too late to save the ships, as Secretary Welles had wanted. And he would not attempt to preserve the navy yard. As he saw it, his duty was to continue the destruction

McCauley had started and depart with whatever ships and men he could.

Did Paulding make a mistake? He had on hand three warships, with their many cannon that he could use to pound Norfolk and Portsmouth on either side of the Elizabeth River. With the reinforcements he had brought (the extra marines, the seamen, and the troops from Massachusetts), he had a sizeable and rather well-armed military force. A few hours away, at Fort Monroe, were more reinforcements — and, it seemed likely, even more volunteers would soon be arriving at the fort. He still had full possession of the navy yard and all its potential weaponry. He could almost certainly hold out here indefinitely, no matter what the reputed size of whatever force of ill-trained insurgents might be in Norfolk.

In his report Paulding would say, "It was apparent that the yard could not be held by our available means of defense." No doubt he had been convinced by what he had just been told by the naval officers around him, by his own observations, and — more subtly — by his own inclinations. But he was wrong. (Although poor McCauley would, most often, be blamed for abandoning the Yard, Captain Wright's report admitted that, when they arrived, McCauley insisted he was personally "disposed to defend[ing] the yard and property to the last." Wright noted it was Paulding who, after reviewing the situation briefly, disagreed, and decided to destroy whatever he could, and leave.)

For Paulding to turn his back — or, to be more accurate, America's back — on the navy yard, even though he might save a few of its ships, was fraught with danger for the Union. Gosport was a marvelous naval base. Once the rebels entered its gates they would instantly acquire many invaluable things (to say nothing of the éclat they would have gained, which in turn might garner them support from teetering states like Maryland, or even interested foreign countries like Great Britain). The Confederates would almost certainly be able to repair some of the ships Paulding would be leaving behind.

And using the Yard's facilities, they could construct others. They would, in addition, possess innumerable cannon that would provide them with enormous power — either defensive or offensive. With Gosport and its equipment, the rebels could threaten Fort Monroe at the mouth of the James, and maybe even be able to close the Chesapeake Bay. In that case, if nothing else, the merchants of Baltimore, barred from the Atlantic trade, might throw their support to The Cause. Washington, trapped on the Potomac, could fall. These eventualities were not merely vague possibilities. Several were virtually guaranteed.

McCauley, feeling isolated and virtually abandoned and under siege, had some rationale for his concerns about his yard. Paulding did not have this excuse. All he might have said in his defense was that his vague orders from Welles suggested that his primary assignment was to save ships, and, if necessary, to destroy the navy yard. He also knew the administration was frightened about the District of Columbia. The *Pawnee* had been viewed by Lincoln and his cabinet as an important protective device to patrol the Potomac, to guard the District from an assault by Virginians. Welles had made this very clear: the Secretary wanted that warship back, immediately. So Commodore Paulding, considering his options, decided to do what McCauley had done: destroy stuff. For the next few hours, in the darkness, Gosport became the scene of rapidly moving men, preparing destruction.

A hundred seamen from the *Cumberland* were sent with sledge hammers to further damage the cannon that had previously been spiked. The sailors first tried to knock off the guns' trunnions. Each cannon had two trunnions — short, bulbous appendages protruding from the barrel's sides. The trunnions fit into slots in the carriage, on which a gun was nestled. Spiking a gun only disabled it until someone came along and removed the metal object hammered into its touchhole. Extracting a spike could generally be done fairly easily, normally taking only a few hours. But knocking off a trunnion would make the gun impossible to aim until it had been repaired, which typically required that a gun be sent to a metal shop to have new trunnions installed.

These protuberances might look vulnerable, but in this case they proved sturdily resistant. Again and again the federals slammed their sledge hammers against these short stumps, to little avail. No one had thought to bring cold chisels. (Paulding's report said the crews were unable to dislodge a single trunnion; another observer thought they may have destroyed a few. In fact, the officer in charge of this operation would later testify that, although he and his men could not damage the new Dahlgren guns at the Yard, they were able to wreck many older guns.)

A second task of destruction that night was more successful. Seven ships—even the four that had been scuttled, whose upper portions (masts and parts of their decks) remained above the waterline—were doused with turpentine and oil. Trails of gunpowder were laid in long rows leading to these vessels. The men in charge of this operation were under strict orders not to ignite the trains until nearby ships like the *Cumberland*, which would carry them all to safety, had moved clear, out of danger. Timing would be critical. The doused ships must not be set afire until everything else was made ready, and until the tide had risen enough to allow the deep-keeled *Cumberland* to sail safely away from her moorings. Most of the men who laid down the gunpowder were recalled to the ships. Only a few men were left to light the trains. Their signal would be a rocket, shot from the *Pawnee*. In the darkness, the arsonists were to wait stealthily by the delicate lines of gunpowder and watch for that sign.

Meanwhile other men rushed about the Yard, preparing to blow up or burn facilities like the storehouse and repair shops. (By accident, the marine barracks burst prematurely into flames. The scurrying parties simply ignored this fire and kept on with their work.)

Another team made a concerted effort to wreck the dry dock, potentially the most valuable single military asset the federal government possessed. The army engineer, Captain

Wright, who understood construction, and a naval commander, John Rodgers, led a band of almost fifty men, forty
of them from the Massachusetts regiment, the others, seamen
off the *Pawnee*. When this group arrived at the monstrous gran-
ite dry dock, they realized their task would be formidable. In
the darkness Wright decided their only chance lay with a large
pumping gallery, an essential piece of the machinery used to
drain water from the dock so that keels of propped-up ships
could be worked on from below. Despite the dim light inside
the recesses of the dock, the men hurriedly built a makeshift
platform next to the pumping gallery and placed on the platform a full ton of gunpowder. They then ran a trail of gunpowder up to the surface. The two officers agreed to stay and
light the train themselves. They ordered their companions to
return to the ship, except for one seaman, whose assignment
was to watch for the rocket signal from the *Pawnee*.

All these activities did not go unnoticed. A spokesman for
Taliaferro in Norfolk appeared early on and spoke to Commodore Paulding. He said that General Taliaferro—in an
offer of delightful audacity given the weakness of the Virginia
forces—would permit the *Cumberland* to depart unscathed if
the destruction of "public property" ceased immediately. (It
must be remembered that to men like Taliaferro, the ownership of federal facilities like Gosport reverted to its resident
state as soon as that state seceded. For months now, such had
been the rationale of secessionists throughout the South. Using
such logic, what Paulding was attempting was an act of vandalism—the destruction of Virginia's property.) Paulding's report would say he told Taliaferro's emissary that Union cannon
would fling balls at the defenseless city of Norfolk if any Virginians fired at the federals.

Finally everything seemed as ready as it was going to be. Then
McCauley's youngest son appeared at the *Cumberland*. His father—his father, he blubbered—absolutely refused to leave.

Paulding ordered an officer to go to the residence of the old seaman and advise McCauley that the entire yard was about to explode in flames, and it would be wise to come now. Reluctantly McCauley gave in, eventually appearing from out of the darkness.

At 2:25 A.M. the *Pawnee* pulled away from her place against the wharf. She did not yet give the signal. The *Cumberland* still had to get to safety. It took that ship an hour-and-a-half to slip her moorings and drift out into the Elizabeth River, then slowly, carefully, inch down toward the James. Paulding ordered the *Pawnee* to fire the signal rocket. It was 4:20 A.M.

Inside the navy yard men saw the rocket leap into the sky. They lit their matches and applied them. In seconds things began to burst into flame, simultaneously, across an expanse as big as a small city. The masts and spars of great warships became candles, and the rigging sparkled translucently. Buildings appeared to explode, their windows shattering. Glowing flakes spun into the air and floated in wind currents like great raptors. The sky turned red and yellow, becoming as bright as high noon, the leaping flames in stark contrast to the clouds of billowing black smoke. The roar of the fires could be heard for miles. The heat was intense.

Wright and his two companions, standing by the dry dock, found themselves trapped by the conflagration. They had planned to race to the water and take a small boat out to one of Paulding's ships, but they discovered this impossible. So they spun in the opposite direction, toward the yard's main gate. It, too, was ablaze, but they raced through the flames. On the far side they spied a small dory and jumped into it, and started rowing down the Elizabeth River. But the flames behind them revealed their presence to Virginians on the Portsmouth side, who opened fire. The three Union men altered their direction and rowed toward Norfolk, realizing they stood no chance to escape, and deciding to surrender to Taliaferro. They thought that he, as a representative of the governor, might be more lenient than baleful civilians in Portsmouth. It turned out to be a wise decision. According to Wright's later report, Taliaferro received them "kindly," and even put them up in one of Norfolk's better hotels. The next day he forwarded them to Richmond. Governor Letcher was also considerate. After a three-day sojourn in Richmond, the governor escorted them to the train station and saw them off, so as to ensure their safety as they passed through the city's streets.

Commodore Paulding had his own problems during the night of the Gosport fire. A few determined insurgents had snuck downriver during the night and added more barriers to the hulks they had previously sunk, even while Paulding's men were laying gunpowder through the Yard. These Virginians hoped to trap the federals, and nearly did so. Just before dawn, the *Cumberland* got caught in the obstructions. The smaller *Pawnee* made it down the channel, but it took the sailors on the *Cumberland*, plus the ropes of another vessel, which steamed out from Fort Monroe, to yank the great warship loose from the trap.

News about Gosport spread quickly. The tenor of the various reactions was to be expected. On Tuesday the *Norfolk Herald* called the conflagration a despicable act of pure vandalism, terming it, among other things, "devilish...villainous... demon-work."

In the North the reaction was astonishment. The captures of Fort Sumter and Harpers Ferry, along with scores of other small federal properties, seemed bad enough, but none of these losses compared to that of the Gosport Navy Yard. After all, Major Anderson had only had a garrison of around seventy men and the defenders of Harpers Ferry had been a smaller handful. But the Yard—with all its guns and warships and many hundreds of defenders—had been deemed almost invulnerable. On Thursday afternoon, approximately thirty-six hours before it fell to the secessionists, the *Washington Star* had spoken about its status with unbridled confidence. Now, with

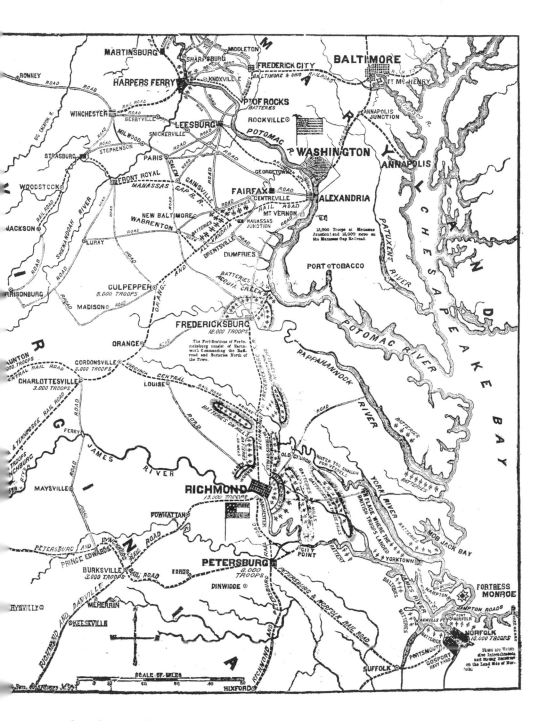

The Chesapeake Bay, the scene of action
during the first weeks of the Civil War.
Courtesy of the Library of Congress

In 1861, as Abraham Lincoln took the oath of office on its steps, the unfinished state of the Capitol dome imitated the newness of the nation and the new administration.
Courtesy of the Library of Congress

Henry Wise was arguably the most significant
Virginian in mid-April, 1861. His zeal not only
levered his state from the Union, but threatened
the very existence of Lincoln's government.
Courtesy of the Library of Congress

A *Harper's Weekly* on May 11, 1861, shows the burning of the United States arsenal at Harpers Ferry on April 18, 1861. After this, Washington was isolated from the west.
Courtesy of the Library of Congress

Fort Monroe.
Courtesy of the Library of Congress

Map of Fort Monroe and vicinity. Fort Monroe and the Gosport Navy Yard formed a critical military marriage. Winfield Scott understood that these two bastions were designed to work in tandem to protect the mouth of the Chesapeake. *Courtesy of the Library of Congress*

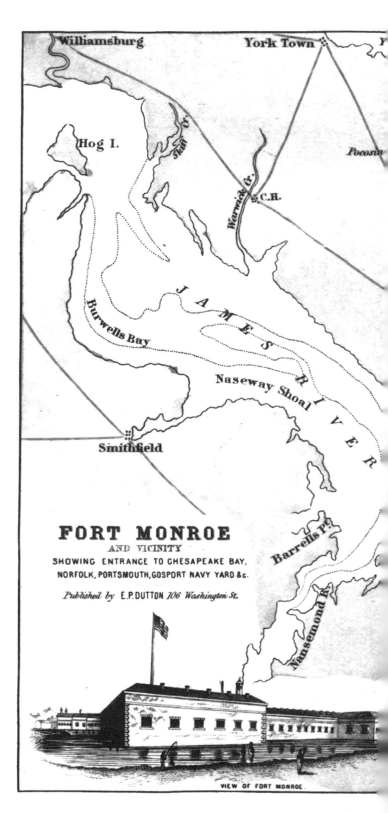

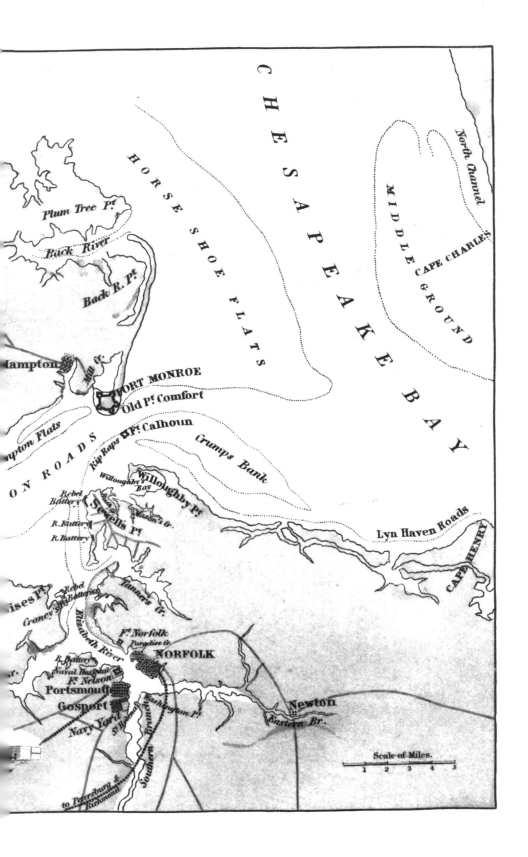

C H E S A P E A K E   B A Y

North Channel

M I D D L E   G R O U N D

CAPE CHARLES

H O R S E   S H O E   F L A T S

Plum Tree P.ᵗ

Buck River

Back R. P.ᵗ

Mill Cr.

Hampton

FORT MONROE

Old P.ᵗ Comfort

pton Flats

O N   R O A D S

Rip Raps F.ᵗ Calhoun

Crumps Bank

Willoughby's Bay Willoughby P.ᵗ

Rebel Battery

Mason's Cr.

Craney's P.ᵗ

R. Battery

R. Battery

Lyn Haven Roads

CAPE HENRY

Rebel Batteries

ises P.ᵗ

Tanners Cr.

Craney Id.

Elizabeth River

F.ᵗ Norfolk

Paradise Cr.

NORFOLK

R. Battery

Naval Hospital

F.ᵗ Nelson

Portsmouth

Gosport

Navy Yard

S.ᵗ Helena

Washington P.ᵗ

Southern Branch

Newton

Eastern Br.

to Petersburg &
Richmond

Scale of Miles.

1   2   3   4   5

Secretary of the Navy Gideon Welles would
eventually prove himself an able administrator, but
he fumbled badly during the war's early weeks.
Courtesy of the Library of Congress

The USS *Pennsylvania* in flames. The
Federals purposely destroyed several of
their own ships at the Gosport Navy Yard.
The conflagration, visible for miles, signaled
that Washington might be blocked from
assistance arriving by water.
Courtesy of the Library of Congress

Ben Butler was probably the Civil War's most controversial figure. Though far from a good general, he served his country well for several critical weeks in April and May of 1861.
Courtesy of the Library of Congress

The 7th New York marching down Broadway on its way to war. America's best-known and most-respected militia regiment strived to reach Washington before the capital could be captured by rebels.
Courtesy of the Library of Congress

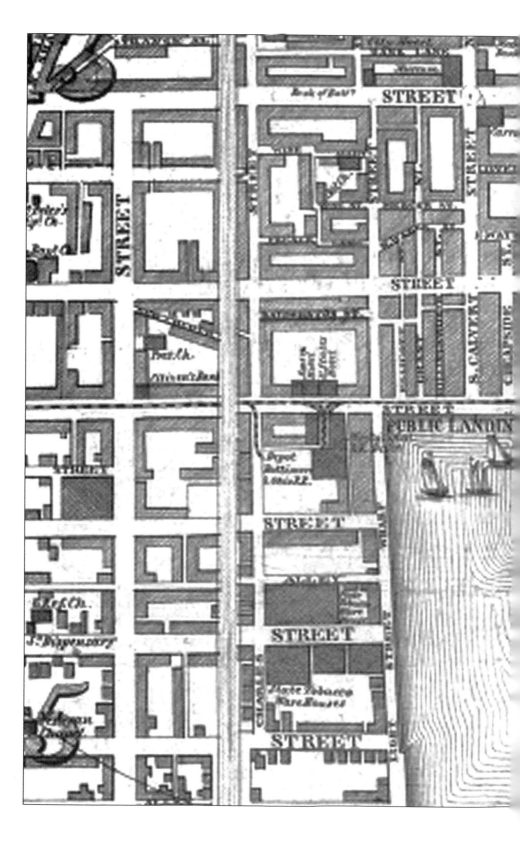

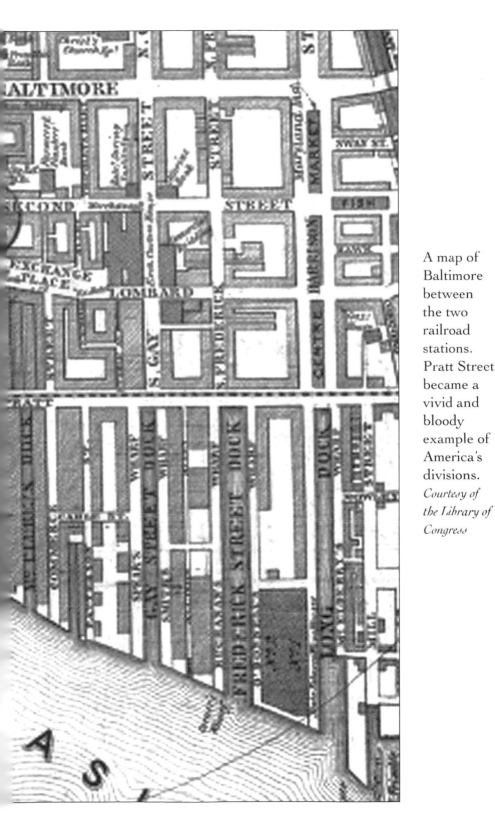

A map of
Baltimore
between
the two
railroad
stations.
Pratt Street
became a
vivid and
bloody
example of
America's
divisions.
*Courtesy of
the Library of
Congress*

Currier and Ives produced this dramatic re-
creation of the Baltimore Riot, which took place
on the anniversary of 1775's Battle of Lexington.
Courtesy of the Library of Congress

The 8th Massachusetts in the Rotunda.
Lincoln's administration was unprepared
for its saviors and was forced to billet
them in various Federal buildings.
Courtesy of the Library of Congress

The arrival of the New York 71st at the Washington, D.C., railroad station. Most Washingtonians felt enormous relief at sight of the Northern volunteers.
Courtesy of the Library of Congress

This 1862 map was suppressed during the war
because some in Washington thought it too revealing.
General Scott and President Lincoln felt squeezed,
in April 1861, by their precarious position.
Courtesy of the Alexandria Library Historical Collection

its loss, Horace Greeley's *New York Tribune* expressed outrage, announcing its destruction an unrelieved disaster, a terrible military defeat.

In retrospect the loss of the Yard turned out to be far more than a setback. Its huge supply of gunpowder helped the Confederates win battles like Bull Run. Its cannon were used to defend countless Southern bastions and thereby greatly lengthened the war that was only just beginning.

One fact ought to be noted: despite the melodramatic appearance of the flames coming from the ships and a few buildings, much of the navy yard went entirely unscathed. Most of the residences were untouched. Many thousands of shells and cannonballs, which had been thrown into the river, were easily retrieved. Valuable timber, copper, anchors, chains, and canvas were saved. More importantly, the foundry, the boiler shops, and almost all the machinery were intact. Within days Virginia workmen would be hammering and sawing inside the machine shop. Also, the important dry dock had been saved by the quick-thinking action of one Virginian, C. F. W. Spotswood— who had just resigned his United States naval commission. He rushed into the yard as soon as he saw the flames, went to the dry dock, recognized the danger, and flooded it enough to douse the slow-burning fuses. And although most of the ships had been damaged, several were repairable—including, of course, the *Merrimack*, which would be raised, clad in metal plates, and, as the *CSS Virginia*, would battle Lincoln's *Monitor* to a standstill in less than a year.

No matter how one analyzes these events, the Union's loss of Gosport was a disaster. Many men were blamed for it. McCauley took the brunt of the abuse. Certainly others, like Paulding and Secretary Welles, deserve some censure, probably far more than the unfortunate McCauley. Ultimately, however, the fault was Abraham Lincoln's. For weeks he had followed a policy of appeasement of Virginia. In this regard he was as diffident and cautious as the reviled President Buchanan had been. Lincoln had gone out of his way to make no sudden moves there, so as not to provoke the Virginians into secession. To prove he meant them no harm he had refused to order Welles to take actions that might have saved Gosport — until it was too late. In fact, it is possible the Virginians might also have taken Fort Monroe had General Scott not firmly insisted it be strengthened.

It seems fair to note Lincoln's culpability. As Harry Truman famously noted about the proper stopping place for "the buck," responsibility for such disasters belongs to the resident of the White House.

An alternative and not unreasonable defense of Lincoln's actions and inactions would be that he may not have been able to take any other route. Once he had made the decision to send assistance to Fort Sumter, the Confederacy was going to attack Major Anderson. As soon as Fort Sumter was assaulted, Lincoln was convinced he must react militarily. Hence his proclamation. This in turn was the excuse that men like Henry Wise in Richmond had been waiting for, and Virginia's secession was virtually inevitable. After that, events moved very quickly.

By Sunday, April 21, as word about Gosport spread to Washington, men like Lincoln understood the dire situation. Baltimore, forty miles to the north, had already closed down. The fall of Gosport, to the south, might mean that Chesapeake Bay was also closed.

If things did not improve, and fast, the District — and perhaps America, as a single political entity — might be doomed.

CHAPTER ELEVEN

And in Washington

Every eye is now turned to Washington City,
in anxious expectation of the events
which seem to be impending in that quarter.
—PHILADELPHIA *PUBLIC LEDGER
AND DAILY TRANSCRIPT,* APRIL 22, 1861

On Christmas Eve, 1861, eight months after these events, General Irvin McDowell sat in the basement of the Capitol, testifying to a congressional committee. He was here primarily to talk about the disaster at Bull Run that had taken place in July near Manassas, but the committee also wanted his opinion on whether he thought any danger now existed for the capital. The committee was aware McDowell had been stationed in Washington the previous March and April, often representing the Army when volunteers arrived, officially greeting them and mustering them into federal service, so he was well acquainted with the recent history of the capital's military strengths or weaknesses. When the committee asked him about the present dangers, he reassured them. The Confederates, he told them, would not dare attack Washington with defense lines the District now had, ten to twenty miles south of where he was speaking. In fact the enemy, he said, had probably never entertained any such notion. Or at least, he said, they had not contemplated an assault, "since the blue times last

April." McDowell did not need to clarify what he meant. In December 1861 Washington was safe, but she had not been in the first days of the war—just after Virginia's takeovers of Harpers Ferry and Gosport. Back then, he thought, she *had* been in grave danger.[80]

News about the attack on Fort Sumter fell on the District of Columbia like a mortar shell. During the previous few weeks Washington's hotels had been jammed. The triumph of the Republicans, their arrival at the White House, had meant a fresh distribution of federal fruits. There would be lucrative positions aplenty. A new administration also involved new contracts— the purchase of thousands of different items, from stationery to ships' screws. Handsome profits would be pocketed.

To be sure, in the hotels' saloons during the March days just after Lincoln's inauguration, one could occasionally hear, amidst the wet splattering of tobacco juice, bothersome things. Men wrestled with the concept of secession, trying to calculate what it meant and how it might affect the nation, and themselves. By April there was talk about naval movements, but few guessed the reality. Pessimists might grumble, but the hostelries remained full. Almost certainly, it seemed, war would be averted. Reasonable men would find reasonable solutions. Remarkably, the staff at the White House remained apparently sanguine. The day before the attack on Fort Sumter, Lincoln's chief secretary, John Nicolay, wrote his fiancée that she should not be "alarmed at the 'rumors of wars' which you hear from this direction. There is some idle gossip about danger of a demonstration being made by the secessionists against this capitol [*sic*]." But he did not visualize that occurring. In his mind the Confederates would need to keep their troops close to home. They "will scarcely make an attempt so foolhardy as that of attacking this city."[81]

News about the Confederate assault on Fort Sumter altered the optimism. Though, if one were to believe the District's newspapers hawked by shouting newsboys Monday morning, the reality of war had still not entirely sunk in. Charleston seemed far away. Even Lincoln's proclamation had surprisingly little immediate effect on the District. Maybe this unpleasantness would come to nothing.

But little by little the capital's hotels started emptying. Steamers, departing either north or south, were crowded with nervous passengers. The train station near the Capitol grew noticeably busy. This pattern accelerated as the week wore on. A New York reporter who had been in Washington a month earlier returned to the District and was shocked by the changes. His first day back he went to Willard's for dinner. "I was surprised to find the halls and public sitting-rooms almost empty, and still more so when the office clerk, in answer to my question, 'What's the news?' said, 'Well, as you have been away, it will be news to you that we are going to shut up this hotel tomorrow, and this meal will be the last you can be served from here.'" Willard's, Washington's "great caravansary," which had been crammed with a thousand guests a few days earlier, now contained fewer than fifty patrons. News from Virginia — especially the convention's vote in favor of secession and the military takeover of nearby Harpers Ferry — prodded people toward action.

Thursday, April 18, 1861

During the day word caromed through the District that Virginia had seceded. Army carts, filled with ammunition, clattered here and there, distributing musket cartridges to infantrymen and cannon shells to gunners stationed at the Washington end of Long Bridge, peering warily at the hills of Virginia. Meanwhile, at the Capitol, burly workmen unloaded timbers and concrete to block up the building's major doors and windows. Iron plates, purchased for the unfinished dome of the Rotunda, were lugged into place to form breastworks in the porticos.

General Scott was especially uneasy about the vulnerability of the White House. In 1861 most of the federal executive branch was squeezed into four buildings clustered closely together on a single grassy rectangle near the Potomac called President's Park or Executive Square. Here sat the Executive Mansion (the official name of the White House); a few yards from its West Wing stood the War Department and the Navy Department. Just off the East Wing was another large structure, with the State Department housed at one end and the Treasury at the other. Pathways tied all these buildings together. It took only moments for the long-legged president to stride from his office to, for example, the War Department, where he could confer with Cameron about the latest rumors; or to the Treasury, to speak to Secretary Chase. If the enemy thrust into the capital, this rectangle, especially the Executive Mansion, would be a natural target.

The idea of an assault on Washington made Scott fidgety. He had been able to transfer hundreds of regulars to the capital, and in theory Charles Stone still commanded thousands of District militiamen (though how loyal they were or stalwart they would remain if it came to a real attack was doubtful), but the recent events in Virginia and Maryland were worrisome. Scott decided to transfer his personal apartment from rented rooms on Sixth Street, more than ten blocks from President's Park, to another location just around the corner from the War Department. These new quarters, owned by a Mrs. Duvall, had a large yard where the army maintained a guard each night. One observer would later recall that whenever the general left his quarters, "dark-visaged men would be seen on the corners of the street, intently scrutinizing him." Sometimes stray bullets, fired by unseen persons, would smack against the brick walls of the general's headquarters.[82]

On April 18, the day the government learned about Virginia's secession vote and the likelihood of a follow-up attack on Harpers Ferry, General Scott ordered Major David Hunter to take command of the Executive Mansion's guard detail. Back in February, Hunter, a professional soldier and West Point graduate, had accompanied the presidential party from Illinois to the capital, acting as a military bodyguard. Now his services were expanded. To begin with, Scott told him, the number of men guarding the White House had to be dramatically increased.

Within hours Hunter had the services of two volunteer companies — a total of approximately one hundred men. Most of them had only come to Washington seeking jobs, and were staying in hotels. In the past few days two individuals had each organized a "company" of volunteers to protect the government, without pay or promises.

One was Cassius Marcellus Clay of Kentucky, fifty, a hard man. Although from a slave state, he was a fervent and outspoken antislavery exponent, and was one of the few Southern Republicans. In 1843 he was shot while giving a speech. Yanking out a bowie knife, he attacked his assailant, cutting off the man's nose and one of his ears, and gouging out his eye. At the 1860 Republican convention Clay came moderately close to being the party's vice presidential candidate. Now, Lincoln had selected him to be minister to Russia (where the Kentuckian would, years later, play a key part in Seward's Folly, the purchase of Alaska from the Russians).

He was in the capital, preparing to leave for Europe, but, because of the crisis atmosphere, he decided not to depart yet. He was determined to use his charisma to raise a company of action-ready fighters. He sported three pistols and a large, nasty-looking knife called an Arkansas toothpick, and immodestly called his followers the Cassius Clay Company. One of its members, Adam Gurowski, later ruefully recalled that he and the others drilled and patrolled as clumsily as "Falstaff's heroes," though Gurowski believed that in an emergency they would have "fought well." Major Hunter assigned Clay's group, quartered at nearby Willard's Hotel, to act as a reserve backup in case the White House was attacked.

The primary White House defense force, for a short time, was the creation of another romantic character out of America's West, James Henry Lane, forty-six. Thin-faced, unkempt, and intense, Lane was a member of a prominent midwestern family. In 1855, after a successful career in Indiana as a lawyer and politician, he moved to Lawrence, Kansas, the heart of that territory's antislavery Jayhawker faction. It was a bloody time. Lane was a fiery orator and pugnacious fighter. Like Clay, he had fought in the Mexican War, and in civilian life he had shot and killed a neighbor. In early 1861, when Kansas became America's newest state, Lane was chosen as one of its senators. He had just arrived in Washington. During this crisis he patched together a band of tough fighters, mostly fellow westerners, and called them his Frontier Guards. Major Hunter, who had served at Leavenworth, Kansas, knew Lane personally and recognized his resolve.

At dusk on the evening of April 18, Lane and his crew of about fifty men arrived at the White House. He carried an enormous sword. Most of the others held government-issued muskets. They ensconced themselves in the East Room. Nicolay would later describe the scene: "Under the light of the gorgeous gas-chandeliers, they disposed themselves on the brilliant-patterned velvet carpet." They cracked open a wooden box of ammunition and took out cartridges. They drilled a bit, trooping back and forth on the frayed, stained carpet, then settled down for the night. These colorful ruffians only remained that night and the next, but they left an indelible impression on those at the White House. One of Lane's men later claimed that during their two-day stay, President Lincoln, his wife Mary, and some cabinet members started to enter the East Room, but were threatened with cold steel and ordered away, "perhaps jocosely."[83]

Friday, April 19, 1861

During the morning Lincoln learned that Harpers Ferry had been attacked, and that the small federal garrison had burned much of the arsenal and retreated. Throughout the day the president also received updates about the bloody passage of the Sixth Massachusetts through Baltimore. Others in the District learned about the Baltimore incident through the grapevine. By late afternoon a crowd of Washington denizens began gathering near the railroad station. They waited — some out of curiosity, many with growing anxiety. The *Star* estimated their numbers in the thousands. About five o'clock they heard a train whistle. A ripple of excitement shivered through them. If nothing else, this whistle indicated that rails north of the city had not been ripped up, as had been feared; trains could get through. The crowd stared up the tracks, northward, along Delaware Avenue. They were startled by what they first observed: the whistle had come from only a single engine, traveling by itself, flying a signal flag of some sort. When it squealed to a halt, the crowd shouted to its engineer, wanting to know what his solitary car meant. He announced he had been sent on ahead as a kind of scout, to check the tracks along the way; two other trains were just behind him: the regular passenger train from Baltimore, which usually arrived about this time, and another one carrying the Sixth Massachusetts. Five minutes later the first train, the one with civilians, came into sight, then the other carrying the volunteers. The trains' engineers energetically yanked their whistle-cords, partly because this was normal practice when entering the busy Washington streets two blocks from the Capitol, partly from sheer excitement. They had made it!

One member of the Sixth would recall: "Old men and old women who were loyal to their country threw their arms around our necks and kissed us, and with great tears streaming down their cheeks, blessed us and called us their deliverers." Colonel Jones ordered his men to line up in a column next to the tracks. Those volunteers not too injured from the riot marched with whatever dignity they could muster, rifles leaning against their shoulders.

The extraordinarily shy Miss Clara Barton, a thirty-nine-year-old government clerk, watched the Sixth pass. A native of Massachusetts, an ex-schoolteacher, a spinster, as unobtrusive as one of the glassed-in exhibits at the Patent Office where she worked, Miss Barton had stern brown hair, just starting to gray, and a face as round as a turnip. Although timid and high strung, something inside her stirred — the tribulations of these Massachusetts troops, of boys from her home state, probably. As the wounded men, groaning in pain, came from the cars, many on stretchers, she immediately, instinctively, began caring for them. Most were carried to a local infirmary, but within a day or so she took many wounded into her house. And she saw to it that others, too numerous to fit into her little place, received proper medical attention. Outside the Sixth, few noticed her efforts.

Clara Barton had discovered her life's calling. Daily, after seeing to the care of the wounded, she came to where the healthy members of the Sixth were quartered, providing them with cooked food, reading aloud to them from their local newspapers, scurrying about town to make sure they had simple necessities like towels and needles. She quit her job at the Patent Office. Given her intense shyness, she often found the human contact trying, but her will was so strong she defeated her own demons — though she would suffer periods of nervous collapse. With no training she made herself a nurse — more, a medical specialist. She, a solitary woman in her forties, dressed in black, would spend much of the war caring for the badly wounded and dying, accepting the fact of their vomiting, their bleeding, the stench of their gangrene. Years later, after seeing more terrible results of combat in Europe, Clara Barton would drag the somewhat-resistant United States into the Red Cross, the thirty-second country to join that organization.

She once said the important thing is not whether you wish to do something, or even if doing it is bearable; what counts is only "the need, and how to meet it." Of all the stalwart people of this era, this small, awkward, nervous, wrenlike maiden lady was certainly one of its greatest heroes.

(Earlier this same day, Dorothea Dix, a far older and more experienced medical specialist, well known for her activities, had quietly visited the White House and offered her services. These two individuals, coming to the war from different angles and emotions, would perform magnificently. They did not compete with each other; that was not the way of either woman. They simply served, with energy and devotion, each in her own style. It is interesting that, in a sense, both these wonderful women entered the Civil War on the same day.)[84]

After the Sixth Massachusetts left the depot and marched through the cheering masses, they were directed to the Capitol itself. They wearily climbed its stairs and entered the Rotunda by the East Portico. Someone pointed the way toward the Senate chamber, and they clanked into its gaslit interior, still vaguely echoing the secession debates from a few weeks earlier. The men of the Sixth were exhausted. Many bore bruises and scabs where brickbats or fists or boots had struck them. They slumped onto the Senate's cushions. Some instantly fell asleep. Others wandered the room, staring at the names on the desks of the men who had recently sat here: Jefferson Davis, William Seward, Charles Sumner, Stephen Douglas, the others — Northern and Southern, the great and the very far from great.

In a few minutes President Lincoln entered, accompanied by a small entourage. The tired Massachusetts volunteers watched the tall form slowly move about the chamber, shaking the hand of each man he found awake, saying a few words of good cheer, thanking them for coming. He smiled warmly.

Suddenly, unexpectedly, a woman began to sing. Apparently she was the only female in the room, the wife of the state geologist of Wisconsin. Why she was there is unclear, or what her motives were at this moment. But the words she sang were known by all, and one by one the men in the room rose, and joined her in repeating Francis Scott Key's famous question: "Oh, say can you see, by the dawn's early light, what so proudly we hail'd at the twilight's last gleaming?" And some men wept.

A few moments later, Lincoln departed. (Ben Butler of Massachusetts would later claim that Lincoln, before leaving, took Colonel Jones's hand in his great paw and shook it firmly.

"Thank God, you have come," he said, according to Butler, "for if you had not, Washington would have been in the hands of the rebels before morning." It is an interesting tale, but probably untrue. Lincoln certainly felt anxiety at this moment about the prospects of Washington, but he seldom volunteered his concerns to others.)

The men of the Sixth returned to their cushions. Their empty stomachs grumbled. They had left almost all their supplies in Baltimore. Amazingly, no one in Washington now thought of providing them with food. The same confusion and inattention to detail that twenty-four hours earlier had caused the poor wretches from Pennsylvania to go to bed without provisions still bedeviled Lincoln's war effort. It would be the next morning before victuals were finally brought to the Sixth, the "saviors of the nation's capital."[85]

Even the confident John Nicolay was beginning to reveal a certain uneasiness. That evening he wrote his fiancée: "We have rumors that 1500 men are gathered and under arms at Alexandria (seven miles below here) supposed to have hostile [designs] against this City and an additional report that a vessel was late this evening seen landing men on the Maryland side of the river. All these things indicate that if we are to be attacked at all soon it will happen tonight." It was eleven o'clock. Nicolay suddenly learned from some source that Secretary Cameron expected, at the very least, a "brush" with the enemy before morning. Continuing his note, Nicolay told his fiancée this gossip, but added: "I do not think any force could be brought against the city tonight, which our men could easily repel, and therefore do not feel seriously alarmed, although the apprehensions of danger are pretty general."[86]

Before midnight a company of District militiamen marched to Washington's main telegraph office. Operators manning the keys there were ordered to leave immediately. For the next twelve hours not a single wire was sent from this office in any direction. The tapping of increasingly concerned queries came in from Richmond. No reply was offered. Saturday afternoon an official censor arrived at the office. Questions arriving from Richmond were now answered, "It's none of your business."[87]

Three days later the Sixth marched from their quarters in the Senate and formed a square. Major McDowell stood in the middle and uttered the words each man was required to swear: their oath of allegiance. After he finished, Colonel Jones stepped up to McDowell and quietly said he suspected a few of his troops had not actually uttered the oath. McDowell turned to the group and asked whether any of them had second thoughts; whether any, in fact, had not repeated the necessary words aloud. Five men stepped forward. A cry of rage came from their comrades, several of whom rushed at the doubters as if to pummel them. One of the five explained he could not; he had a wife and six children. The other four said similar things, though one relented and agreed to take the oath after all. His four comrades were banished. "The mark of Cain," McDowell sneered, "is upon you here and [at] home." He turned his back on them.[88]

Monday, April 22, 1861

Over the weekend, signs of tension accumulated in the capital. Almost the entire student body of Columbian College, blocks from the Capitol, left town. The price of food edged upward. Few stores had any more guns to sell. Business declined. The Washington Theater closed and locked its doors, admitting that almost no one was attending performances. There was a shortage of paper; the *Star* dropped its issues to a single sheet. The District's churches felt the tension. On Sunday the Presbyterian minister in Georgetown included the names of Jefferson Davis and Aleck Stephens in the usual blessings. Members of his congregation confronted him with their objections, and he offered to resign. His resignation was accepted.

On Sunday evening, when the news about Gosport reached the capital, matters came to a head. Washingtonians felt isolated and trapped. Theoretically one might still receive mail brought by wagon, and one might still contact family or business acquaintances in the North by sending a wire to Ohio, which might successfully make the circuitous route to a city like Philadelphia. Also, one could board a Baltimore & Ohio train and travel westward to Wheeling. But this would take you through Harpers Ferry, where gimlet-eyed Virginia militiamen were known to be scouring every railroad car.

It seemed likely there would be bloody fighting in the streets of the District, and soon. If nothing else there might be looting and other lawlessness. When enemy armies enter a city, civilians, especially women and children, are not safe. There was talk about impressing all government employees into military service. This rumor spurred clerks, particularly those with Southern sympathies, into action. It also affected military men stationed in the District. This crisis exposed the loyalties of many people. Under the circumstances it was difficult to waffle. Some results were tragic. A clerk at the Treasury later recalled: "One distinguished officer, a valued friend, met me, chatted gaily for a few minutes, shook me warmly by the hand, went home and shot himself. While one was telling me of this shocking tragedy, ten minutes afterwards, another friend, just around the corner, had done the same thing."

On Monday morning, April 22, government departments were swamped with resignations. The early trickle became a gusher. One train left the station that morning, heading toward Baltimore. It had only three passenger cars and these were jammed.

Frantic families turned to alternate means of transporting to move themselves and their belongings: baby carriages, wheelbarrows, drays, pushcarts. "A long procession hastened up 17th Street in disorder," one resident observed. They were determined to reach Rockville, Maryland, just beyond the District's border, on foot. They had the appearance of refugees or fugitives in all wars — droopy countenances, slumped shoulders, frightened eyes.

These departures had reverberations. With so many families moving out of town, property values plunged. The value of stocks slid. Before leaving, many people went to their banks to extract deposits. Others wanted banks to convert currency into gold or silver. The value of federal bank notes dropped precipitously, since bankers began accepting cash only at a fifteen percent discount. And the rush to the banks caused a rumor that one unnamed bank did not have enough specie on hand and intended to close its doors, at least temporarily. Other residents ran to banks to remove their deposits. (A clerk at the Treasury quietly took the federal bonds he had on hand and locked them in the Department's vault.)[89]

In the Senate chamber, members of the Sixth Massachusetts wrote letters home. An enlisted man told his sister they had been sleeping with their weapons, expecting an attack at any time. "We were," he said, "call[ed] up two different nights and received ammunition and we expected to march out and fight." One of his officers, Alpha B. Farr, the normally unruffled adjutant of the regiment, wrote: "There is great excitement here. An attack is expected at any time." Another member of the Sixth tried to maintain a stiff upper lip: "We fear an attack upon the capitol [*sic*] in a few days. I hope it will come soon and that this matter of secession will be settled at once."

Articles in the *Washington Star* did not calm the citizenry. One issue of the newspaper announced that Virginia secessionists had placed cannon along the Potomac somewhere below the District, and that these guns could prevent any aid from coming by that route. The newspaper also listed other rumors the editor considered unnerving — including a tale that just outside the District sat an 8,000-man army of bloody-minded Marylanders, most of them mounted, ready to pounce.

The next day the *Star* asserted that 3,000 Virginia troops were within "striking distance" of Baltimore, that they were simply awaiting an invitation from Maryland to cross the Potomac and join the 15,000 secessionist troops there.

Foreign diplomats stationed in the capital grew nervous. Some contemplated the propriety or wisdom of placing some symbol above their legations to indicate that these buildings and their occupants held diplomatic immunity. The Prussian envoy was disconcerted to learn that he possessed not a single flag from home. In his panic at the prospect of rampaging Confederates ransacking his residence, he hired a painter to write, in German, the phrase, *The Prussian Legation* over his door, perhaps hoping that the foreign words, like a clove of garlic, would repel attackers.[90]

When Winfield Scott learned of the fall of the Gosport Navy Yard, he reacted quickly. All of Chesapeake Bay was in danger, and Washington could be threatened from a new direction: attackers steaming up the Potomac.

Scott had already decided to beef up a nearly empty army post, Fort Washington, twelve miles down the Potomac on the Maryland side. A few days earlier, in a meeting of the cabinet, someone had asked the old general about the usefulness of that decayed War of 1812 fort. "I think, Sir," replied Scott, "that Fort Washington could now be taken with a bottle of whiskey. At last accounts, it was in [the] charge of a single old soldier, who is entirely reliable, when he is sober." The somnolent, bibulous days at that fort were now over. Soldiers arrived. The fort's guns were loaded and aimed toward the river. All ships attempting to pass it would be stopped and searched for enemy troops, or munitions, or provisions.[91]

The Washington Navy Yard was another problem. On Monday morning, April 22, many of its highest-ranking officers resigned, several crossing over to Virginia. How many of those remaining were actually loyal was uncertain. The *Pawnee*, which had been docking there, had not yet returned from its Gosport venture. Scott considered this navy yard to be a critically important post, situated as it was on the southeast corner of the District. The previous Friday his soldiers had seized four civilian steamers owned by a Virginia firm, the Washington & Fredericksburg Steamboat Company. These four ships normally plied the waters of the Potomac and nearby rivers, carrying passengers heading from the capital to Fredericksburg, Virginia, and farther south. Scott ordered these ships transferred to the Washington Navy Yard, where they would be armed with heavy guns. This was, he said, to be done "in the most expeditious manner possible." (The two militia companies led by Jim Lane and Cassius Clay that had temporarily watched President's Park were sent to the navy yard to guard it.)[92]

Another issue the army dealt with that Monday involved food, especially flour. With an attack on the capital appearing likely, the District's military men, and perhaps even its civilian population, might need sustenance for a long siege. Georgetown's flour mills drew Scott's attention. On Sunday the general's intelligence staff learned that thousands of barrels of Georgetown flour were being loaded onto schooners, to be shipped south. Secretary Cameron himself hurried to the quartermaster's department and ordered the officer in charge to round up vehicles. By Monday everything was ready. With soldiers on horseback leading the way, a motley collection set out: army-issue wagons, drays, carts, even tired vehicles normally used to haul ice or furniture. This procession rumbled through the streets and appeared in Georgetown before most of that town's residents understood what was happening. The long line of vehicles went to the wharf first. A ship, the *Hamilton*, was tied there, laden with 2,000 barrels of flour. A nearby tug was just firing up to push the *Hamilton* into the channel. Scott's troops sprang aboard and announced they were taking the flour. Men hurried from the wagons and started unloading the ship. The procession started again, this time to a warehouse that held another 3,000 barrels. Arrangements had already been made with its owner to purchase his stock for a fairly reasonable price of about $7.50 a barrel. (Flour in the

District had recently sold for as little as $5 a barrel, but the price of flour on the open market would soon more than triple.) The procession moved to other warehouses. All day and through the night, carts and wagons rattled between Georgetown and Washington City. The government soon had tens of thousands of barrels of flour stored in the basements of the various federal buildings that could serve as defense posts.[93]

By that evening, April 22, Washington resembled a ghost town. Except for the clatter of hoofbeats as military couriers galloped past, or the tramp-tramp of uniformed militiamen, the District seemed eerily quiet. Government offices were vacant. Houses were abandoned, their window blinds left wide open, even their windows ajar, as dead-looking as bleached skulls.

It had been only a week since Lincoln's proclamation was released, but they had been seven momentous days. As news from Virginia, especially Harpers Ferry and Gosport, trickled in, the District trembled. A rebel assault seemed likely.

Years later Charles Stone would describe a conversation he had with General Scott on the dangers Washington faced. It was part of Stone's routine to drop by the general's headquarters to report anything that might have happened overnight at key locales like Long Bridge and Chain Bridge. But on that Monday, when he stepped into Scott's office, the general was furiously writing and only paused long enough to glance over his spectacles and tell Stone to return at four-thirty, when they would dine and talk.

   At the appointed time Colonel Stone arrived. Scott showed where Stone should sit at the table. A servant brought in soup, and without another word the two officers spooned it into their mouths. A roast duck was brought. General Scott offered Stone instructions on how to carve a fowl. More silent eating. Finally Scott told the colonel to pour them both some sherry from a decanter. The two men sipped from their glasses, and the general summarized the situation.

> Gosport Navy Yard has been burned!
> Yes, General!
> Harpers Ferry bridge has been burned!
> Yes, General!
> The bridge at Point of Rocks [about thirty miles up the Potomac, in Maryland] was burned some days since!
> Yes, General!
> The bridges over Gunpowder Creek beyond Baltimore have been burned!
> Yes, General!
> They are closing their coils around us, sir!
> Yes, General!

Scott was just blowing off steam and thanked Stone for listening. "Your very good health, Sir," Scott said, and drained his glass. "Now, how long can we hold out here?"

Stone estimated ten days.

The two officers discussed their options. Stone claimed to have 4,900 District militiamen under his command (as inspector-general of the District). He thought these "soldiers" might be sufficient. Although his men patrolled eighteen miles of exterior lines, he did not expect the enemy had more than 5,000 troops available at this moment. So from wherever the attackers came, his volunteers could just pull slowly back to certain "centers."

Scott asked him to be specific, and Stone listed each center by name: the Capitol, of course; and the large buildings on President's Park; plus the Patent Office and the Post Office, and even City Hall. Stone said he thought his men would fight hard because they would be defending their own homes.

Scott listened. Finally, the old general declared that the plan was too ambitious. The government did not have sufficient manpower to defend that many centers. Forget the Capitol, he said; he thought it unlikely that even the rebels would burn down that landmark, or the Supreme Court. Nor could City Hall be safely defended. The only place that counted, Scott said, was Executive Square. And within it, the most defensible structure, as he saw it, was the Treasury. Scott said he wanted all the executive seals to be taken there and deposited inside its vaults. If the situation came to it, the troops would retreat to that place, where they would fight a last-ditch battle.

According to Stone's later recollections, Scott added something else. He wanted Lincoln and his cabinet to remain with the troops. "They shall not be permitted to desert the capital!"

Did in fact the old general actually utter this line, which suggests he suspected that the entire administration would run away if the situation became too hot? There were rumors that ships like the *Pawnee* had been kept tied up near the White House, at the Seventeenth Street wharf, to spirit Lincoln and the cabinet out of town if the situation were to collapse. An argument could be made that doing so would be wise. Washington might fall to the rebels, but as long as Abraham Lincoln remained free, he could claim that the government of the United States still existed.

Scott had given more years to the defense of his country than almost anyone in the history of the United States. He had served her, not only long and loyally, but extremely well. He had performed heroically and with audacity and cunning in the War of 1812, the Indian Wars, and brilliantly during the Mexican War (in which he had taught a generation of young officers how to fight). As a soldier, few American officers have ever performed as capably as he. His distinguished career ranks him with a handful of great American generals: George Washington, John Pershing, Douglas MacArthur, perhaps a few others. He had immense prickly pride, but there has never been any question that he served his country with all his heart, and this had often meant taking orders from unworthy men in positions of political power. He might grumble or dawdle, but he eventually obeyed. If Stone's recollection was accurate (and Stone did not publish it until 1884, long after Scott's death),

then perhaps the general was speaking emotionally, but not seriously. Or, perhaps he really was contemplating some action
to keep the politicians in the national capital—by force if necessary. It would have been a revolutionary act, but these were
revolutionary times.[94]

General Scott and Colonel Stone—along with many, many
others in Washington, civilian and military—were preparing
for a coming onslaught. But were Southerners—particularly
Virginians—planning such an attack?

CHAPTER TWELVE

The Curious Marriage of Great Britain and Ben McCulloch

De l'audace, encore de l'audace, et toujours de l'audace.
(Audacity, more audacity, and always audacity.)
—GEORGES JACQUES DANTON, 1792

Richmond, April 19, 1861

Most adult white Richmonders seemed gleeful. With the convention's secession vote now public knowledge, with Harpers Ferry liberated from the grasp of Black Republicans, with the weather finally dry and pleasant after the long rainy spell, a celebration seemed appropriate. So Richmond held her second torchlight procession of the week. Some citizens considered it the grandest celebration the city had ever seen. Bands played martial and sprightly airs. Roman candles arced golden radiance into the darkness. Here and there, marchers paused to listen raptly to jubilant speakers who assured them everything was wonderful. One orator shouted, "I predict in less than sixty days the flag of the Confederacy will be waving over the White House."

"In less than thirty days," someone in the throng yelled back.

"On to Washington!" the crowd screamed.[95]

Great Britain, mid-April, 1861

In a sense the American Civil War was something of a puppet show. Whenever Union and Confederate armies fought,
politicians on both sides would slyly eye the European audience, checking it for reactions — thumbs up or thumbs down?
From the war's earliest moments, men like Jefferson Davis
believed the Confederacy's greatest hope was to gain the support of England. Most Southerners were fairly confident that
any conflict between Southern boys, supposedly inured to the
harshness of nature and to handling guns, versus Northerners, thought to be primarily shop clerks or immigrant peas-
ants, would certainly result in a Southern victory, eventually.
But everything would be easier if Britain became involved,
sooner rather than later. At the very least, she could supply
the Confederacy with sufficient weaponry. Better, far better,
would it be if Britain and the Confederacy formed an alliance.
Other countries like France might join — if nothing else, simply
to enjoy spanking that headstrong adolescent, the United
States.

For years Southern politicians and Southern editors had
asserted that English mill owners (in regions like Lancashire)
would always need, and demand, a continuous flow of Deep
South cotton. In 1858 a senator from South Carolina, James
H. Hammond, said what many Southerners believed: "What
would happen if no cotton was furnished for three years? I
will not stop to depict what everyone can imagine, but this is
certain: England would topple headlong and carry the whole
civilized world with her, save the South. No, you dare not
make war on cotton. No power on earth dares make war upon
it. Cotton is King."

To put it less floridly, Southern leaders were convinced
that British politicians, voters, and businessmen would embrace the South — out of necessity, if nothing else. Some Englishmen might not like slavery, it was true. An obscure British
judge in the early 1770s had apparently been the first official

in the history of the world to declare slavery illegal. And since the 1830s the British navy had actively interrupted the international slave trade coming out Africa. Leaders in the Deep South, however, felt confident that practical Brits, when forced to decide between dubious idealism and their pocketbooks, would see the light.

Was this wishful thinking or did this notion have some basis in fact?

Several factors came into play.

Was the supply of Southern cotton vital to the British economy? Yes. Not only were English mills and mill-towns quite dependent on cotton textiles, so were railroads and banks, as well as a hundred professions connected to the sea trade — from powerful merchants to nameless sailmakers and draymakers, among many examples. Great Britain could purchase some cotton from other sources, like Egypt and India, but those regions could not supply enough. Nor did all their cotton have quite the quality of the best Southern cotton. On the other hand, the weather during the past few years had been especially kind to Deep South cotton plantations, and as a result, English warehouses were stuffed to their ceilings with cotton bales. It would be at least a year before a noticeable shortage cut into production of British cotton textiles.

Was the British antislavery movement still politically formidable in 1861? The answer would seem to be yes and no. That movement still retained influence, though it had lately lost some of its earlier vigor.

Did British politicians need to consider other, less obvious factors? The matter of Canada, for example, ought not to be ignored. If England sufficiently annoyed Lincoln's government, the American president might order an attack on Canada, and perhaps take it over. And there were elements inside Canada that would welcome that opportunity. Also, if Britain aided the Confederacy, English trade in the Caribbean and with Mexico would be vulnerable to Lincoln's navy. And there was grain. America's Northern states supplied England with relatively inexpensive foodstuffs that helped feed British workers. It might be unwise to annoy Northern farmers too much.[96]

Whatever decision British leaders arrived at would not be easy. Under such complex circumstances, the attitudes of three specific Englishmen would be critical.

Richard Bickerton Pemell Lyons (generally referred to as Lord Lyons by much of the American press, which continued to knuckle its forelock at European titles) was Britain's minister in Washington, the present-day equivalent of ambassador. In early 1861 his messages home could profoundly affect the opinions of his superiors in London, so his reaction to events was important. Lyons, who turned forty-four on April 26, was a polished and experienced diplomat. A cool but tactful man, he had served in the United States since 1859, a period of swirling emotions. He found most Americans not to his taste; they seemed excitable and potentially violent. He did not trust William Seward, or like him. But neither was Lyons fond of the cockiness of many of the secessionists. He believed several things. The Confederacy, he was sure, was a fact, even though the new American president might consider it a fiction. Abe Lincoln, Lyons thought, would almost certainly be unable to glue the United States back together. But Lyons also considered it in Britain's best interest — for the moment — to remain neutral and await events. (For his part, Secretary of State Seward felt uneasy about the Brits. His advice to America's new minister to London, Charles Francis Adams, was to watch England's leaders with care; what they now did, Seward said, could "ruin" the United States.)

John Russell was Britain's foreign secretary and therefore Lyons's immediate superior. Russell had served as prime minister between 1846 and 1852. Topping his slender, frail body burned an extremely good mind. He disliked bloodshed. He refused to encourage emissaries of the Confederacy, when they came to talk to him, but in his heart he believed it best for all concerned — Britain and the two sides within America — to stop fighting. The easiest solution would be for Lincoln to accept the Confederacy. On January 10, 1861, he wrote: "I do not see how the United States can be cobbled together again by any compromise." He even considered some sort of British intervention — for the sake of peace.

Russell's boss was Prime Minister Henry John Temple Palmerston, seventy-six, a capable statesman with forceful opinions about many topics. He had long served as foreign secretary, and believed he fully understood the subtleties of international matters. He had observed during his lifetime how often European countries split apart or merged together, so the concept of secession did not seem all that remarkable. As to the situation in America, Palmerston did not like Americans, their republican form of government, or the Irishmen who had recently been pouring into that country. He saw little reason to hide his disdain. He opposed slavery but noted that both sides in the American conflict insisted slavery was not the reason for their dispute. (The leaders of both North and South, wishing to avoid any connection to this scalding emotional issue, found it convenient to focus on political abstractions like states' rights, and the legality of secession. The apparent disinterest of America's leaders in slavery permitted Palmerston to base his decision on practical issues rather than idealistic matters.)

On January 1, 1861, just after Palmerston learned of South Carolina's vote to secede, he told Queen Victoria that the United States was already essentially dissolved. And when, in February, other states, along with South Carolina, formed a formal governmental pact they called the Confederacy, Palmerston was sure the issue had resolved itself. Palmerston was positive that Jefferson Davis's government was a reality, not an illusion. Reasonable adults, Palmerston might have said, do not whine about facts, they accept them.

What Palmerston and Russell and Lyons did not understand was Lincoln's unwillingness to consider the Confederacy a viable entity. Lincoln even refused to refer to the conflict as a war, since that implied combat between relative equals. In his view the Union was not only undissolved; it was in fact indissoluble. He continued to employ the term "rebellion."

To British leaders Lincoln's attitude seemed unreasonable, but until the American president came to his senses, London was in a quandary. It is significant that on April 15 Lyons sent a confidential message to his government: Washington, he said, seemed worried the federal capital might soon be captured.

Examining official documents can be like wistfully staring at tea leaves, hoping for an insight. One senses, however, that in April 1861, if the secessionists captured Washington, the game—at least as far as the British government was concerned—was up.

Given these stakes, was a Confederate seizure of Washington a real possibility?

Assume Jefferson Davis moved troops swiftly northward from the Deep South, using trains to carry them to Richmond. His army, joined by Virginians, could certainly have numbered 20,000. Between April 20 and April 25, this force might have leapt across the Potomac before Lincoln had sufficient manpower to defend the capital. Even if Lincoln and his cabinet escaped, what would have been the likely results? Maryland might well have joined the Confederacy. Then the British government, followed by the French and others, would probably have officially recognized the Southern regime. After that? Lincoln might have been impeached. Northern governors might have expressed outrage, but a sense of gloom could have become so pervasive that a lengthy war would have proved difficult, if not impossible. Hindsight, it is often said (generally mistakenly) said, is twenty-twenty. Yet in this case an argument can be made that the Confederacy could have won the Civil War during its first two weeks by a sudden and dramatic assault on Washington. Was that prospect conceivable in Montgomery?

At his office in Alabama, Jefferson Davis felt overwhelmed by problems of supply and internal bickering. The Confederacy already had a large army. Davis had asked his seven original states to raise a hundred thousand men, and tens of thousands of Southerners had immediately volunteered, had been organized and armed, and were already leaving their hometowns. Thousands of Confederate soldiers were in Charleston when Fort Sumter fell. Thousands of others were camped near Pensacola, preparing to assault Fort Pickens. By mid-April, the Confederacy already had 35,000 men under arms, with more being organized almost daily.

Jefferson Davis was a bright West Point graduate who had performed heroically during the Mexican War, and he had served in Washington as an active secretary of war, then as a senator from Mississippi with a keen interest in army affairs. Of all contemporary American politicians he had the most experience in military matters. Like Napoleon, he could combine political leadership and the ability to command armies in the field. Many Southerners believed this would happen. "Nothing," the *Richmond Enquirer* editorialized on April 13, days before Virginia seceded, "is more probable than that President Davis will soon march an army through North Carolina and Virginia to Washington." Northerners thought the same. The *New York Tribune* asserted: "President Davis has an army of 25,000 men on the march to Washington." The *Baltimore American* declared that the Confederate president was "on his way to Richmond with 100,000." Twenty years later, John Nicolay, Lincoln's personal secretary, recalled that in early 1861 the administration knew Jefferson Davis had tens of thousands of soldiers and 100,000 "serviceable arms." Years afterward, Ben Butler would say he still did not understand why Jefferson Davis had not attacked Washington in April 1861. According to Butler, the thousands of troops the Confederates had in Charleston alone could have entrained north to the Potomac in little more than a day, then crossed to Washington "without opposition."[97]

Southern spokesmen added fuel to the rumors about such prospects. On the evening of April 12, 1861, while Charleston's guns were still firing on Fort Sumter, the Confederate secretary of war, Leroy Walker, stepped out into the fine night air of Montgomery and spoke to an excited throng agog with

Southern patriotism. He opened his remarks prudently, admitting that no one could be positive what would result from the events in Charleston. Then his tongue, tangled by excitement, betrayed him. He announced that in less than three months the Confederate flag would fly over Washington. Perhaps even over Boston. His listeners yelled themselves hoarse.

During the next few days newspapers across the South shouted their agreement. The Milledgeville, Georgia, *Southern Recorder* declared: "The government of the Confederate States must possess the city of Washington." Any other option, it thought, was unacceptable: "The District of Columbia cannot remain under jurisdiction of the United States Congress without humiliating Southern pride and defeating Southern rights." The New Orleans *Picayune* said: "The first fruits of a Virginia secession will be the removal of Lincoln and his Cabinet." In North Carolina, which had yet to secede, the *Goldsboro Tribune* and the *Raleigh Standard* said that volunteers from their state were eager to march on Washington.

In Virginia many citizens believed that, while outside assistance to capture the federal capital would be acceptable, Virginians hardly needed any help. The *Richmond Examiner* was confident the people of Virginia "pant for the onset" of an attack on Washington. The newspaper believed it understood the mood of all Virginians: "From the mountain tops and valleys to the shores of the sea there is one wild shout of fierce resolve to capture Washington City at all and every hazard. The filthy cage of unclean birds must and assuredly will be purified by fire."[98]

How exactly was this to be accomplished? Opinions varied. It seemed possible, of course, that Jefferson Davis would biblically lead a great host onto the federal capital. But maybe all that was needed was a rapid thrust across the Potomac from some nearby spot like Harpers Ferry (north of the District), or Alexandria (a few miles downriver). The *Washington Star* received each morning the latest edition of Alexandria's primary journal, the *Gazette,* and reprinted items of interest. On Monday afternoon the *Star* reprinted a story from that morning's

Gazette: not far from central Alexandria, it said, was an encampment of 1,200 to 1,400 Virginia volunteers, their numbers
growing each day.

If an army was about to attack Washington, and Jefferson
Davis was too busy with Confederate affairs to command it,
who would? Several names were bandied about. General
Beauregard, the Hero of Fort Sumter, was often mentioned. It
seemed only logical that he might lead northward the victori-
ous troops who had battered Sumter into surrender. But news
reports from Charleston indicated he was still in that city.

If not Davis or Beauregard, then who? The most common
answer was a man named McCulloch.

Ben McCulloch was a national legend. Though now almost
forgotten, in 1861 he was a celebrity whose name carried almost the same half-mythic luster as Sam Houston. During the
early months of 1861, newspapers North and South carried
countless tales about how Ben McCulloch was putting together a great army to cross the Potomac, grab Washington,
and deliver it as a prize to the Confederacy. The *New York Post*
asserted, even before Fort Sumter, that McCulloch had been
scouring Maryland and Virginia for weeks, signing up volunteers to launch an attack on the capital as soon as war began,
and that thus far he had lined up 5,000 or more. On April 20
the *Vicksburg* (Mississippi) *Whig* announced that McCulloch
and a five-thousand-man army in Virginia were about to take
Washington.[99] Was there anything to this?

Benjamin McCulloch never received much formal education,
but this was because of where he spent his childhood, not the
poverty of his parents. His father was a graduate of Yale,
his mother the daughter of a fairly wealthy Virginia planter.
The senior McCulloch was not exactly shiftless, but between
1812 and 1830 he drifted with his wife and children (who
numbered, eventually, thirteen) from North Carolina, to Tennessee, to Alabama, and back again to Tennessee. Mostly he
farmed. Meanwhile young Ben hunted and fished. He espe-

cially enjoyed shooting bears. He once claimed he'd never killed fewer than twenty in a year, and that one year he slaughtered eighty of the beasts.

In Tennessee the McCullochs were friendly with two locals, Sam Houston and Davy Crockett. When both men departed for the northern Mexican province of Texas, Ben, twenty-two, told his pal Crockett he would join him there. But McCulloch became ill on his way to Texas and was forced to stop for a while. Thus he missed the earliest days of the American uprising there. By the time he reached Texas, Santa Anna had taken the Alamo and Crockett was dead. Ben stayed in Texas and soon proved himself a stony fighter. He battled Mexicans and Indians and fought at least one duel. He worked as a surveyor, a Texas Ranger, and a federal marshal. At one point he journeyed to the gold fields near Sacramento, where he served as a sheriff.

Such exploits made good copy. Newsmen liked writing about him. His activities during the Mexican War even led to a book that exalted him: *The Scouting Expeditions of McCulloch's Texas Rangers*. Before the "West" had reached the status of myth, Ben McCulloch exemplified certain traits many Americans considered part of their national character. He and his manly ways placed him in a long line of frontier heroes, such as Daniel Boone, Davy Crockett, Jim Bowie, and Natty "Hawkeye" Bumppo, the lead character in James Fenimore Cooper's immensely popular *Leatherstocking Tales*. McCulloch even looked the part. In 1861, at forty-nine years old, he stood five feet, nine inches, was as thin and wiry as a riding crop, had a weather-beaten complexion from years of Texas sun, piercing deep-set eyes, and a full mustache and beard. He looked tough, and was.

In February 1861 his name was splashed across the front pages when General David Twiggs, the commander of all federal troops in Texas, surrendered his entire force (the largest single unit in the American army) to Ben McCulloch without a fight. Within days rumors spread that the rugged lawman intended to lead an armed force to Washington to prevent the inauguration of Lincoln. (Actually McCulloch remained in Texas until mid-March.)[100]

What happened next is cloudy. Someone in the Confederate government wanted to utilize his expertise or renown. On March 4 Secretary of War Walker wrote him from Montgomery, asking him to raise a regiment of cavalrymen to protect the western frontier of the Confederacy from Indian and Mexican raids (now that Twiggs's soldiers had been forced to abandon the region). McCulloch was not interested; he wanted to be more than a border guard, and gave Walker's offer to his younger brother Henry. He then departed Texas, reportedly on a mission to acquire a thousand modern rifles, though this seems a curious use of his talents. We know he traveled at least as far north as Richmond, where he did contact Samuel Colt, a longtime friend, to purchase a thousand revolvers (not rifles).

Other than hysterical headlines, is there any evidence that McCulloch was contemplating attacking Washington?

Newspapers of that period normally covered all local visits by prominent individuals, and often listed their hotels, as well as their comings and goings. This reportage was that era's equivalent to the society page. On April 1 the District's newspapers, which daily checked the hotel registers of the better hostelries, listed an "H. McCulloch" at Brown's Hotel, which catered to Southerners. This person might have been Ben using a slight alias, but more plausibly was his brother Henry, who may have accompanied him to get weapons. (It seems possible, but not likely, that the rumors that ensued were triggered by the appearance in Washington of Henry McCulloch — or maybe even some other person with that last name.)

Another piece of evidence comes from Alexandria, just across the Potomac from the District. According to the April 4 issue of the *Alexandria Gazette,* Ben McCulloch was now in their town — and had also been in Washington during the previous few days. The paper said he was departing on that morning's train for points south. It is possible the newspaper made a mistake about the presence of Ben McCulloch, but this seems unlikely; the *Gazette* would have been proud that such a famous Southern hero was in their midst.

Then two days later the *Washington Star* asserted that McCulloch "was seen to emerge yesterday morning [April 5] about daybreak from the residence of a gentleman of the First Ward of this city [Washington]," and that he then rode off. (It was commonly believed McCulloch had long maintained some sort of relationship with Lucy Gwin, the attractive daughter of California's proslavery senator, William M. Gwin, who had a home in the District's First Ward. Although the dates of the stories in the *Gazette* and *Star* are in slight conflict, the discrepancy was but a single day. Combining these two sources, one might deduce McCulloch spent at least one night at the Gwins' house in Washington, then crossed to Alexandria, where he boarded a train or steamship for Richmond. A few days later Richmond newspapers did announce that he left their city on April 8, heading toward New Orleans. We do know from his private correspondence that he was in New Orleans a week later. According to Thomas W. Cutrer, his most diligent biographer, the Texan wrote letters from New Orleans's St. Charles Hotel in mid-April, so we can be confident he was *not* involved in any Virginia plot to take Washington at that time.

Several factors seemed to have caused the hysteria. McCulloch's reputation as a Texas Ranger and as a scout laid the groundwork. It seemed plausible that such a heroic figure might gallop into Washington leading a posse of horsemen. This prospect — romantic or terrifying, depending on one's point of view — no doubt led to the original rumor that he intended, early in the year, to prevent Lincoln from taking his oath of office. Then when he did in fact show up in Virginia, and probably in Washington, during the first few days of April, it did not require a mental leap to imagine he was preparing an assault, scouting the terrain. The prospect that this dynamic fighter had come only to buy guns, or maybe to woo a young woman, seemed unsatisfying. Surely a man like this must have more sinister motives. But apparently not.

(On May 11 Jefferson Davis would officially name Ben McCulloch a Confederate brigadier general, the first such appointment the Confederacy offered a civilian; at the time only a handful of Confederate officers outranked him. Not even Robert E. Lee then held a higher rank. A year later, in March 1862, McCulloch would die in the Battle of Pea Ridge [Elkhorn Tavern].)[101]

Was there anyone else who might have led a Southern army against Washington during these crucial few April days?

CHAPTER THIRTEEN

What if...?

To draw my sword.
—ROBERT E. LEE

Richmond, Sunday, April 21, 1861

Late Sunday morning the city's church doors opened and congregations stepped sedately outside. The sky was clear and
beautiful. Unexpectedly, the bells of St. Paul's—the city's primary alarm system—began pealing a warning, over and over.

During the previous night, as most citizens of Richmond already knew, Gosport, only a few hours by steamboat downriver, had fallen to Virginians. Now, as the alarm bells tolled,
frightened folks told one another that the federal warship
Pawnee had been spotted steaming up the James River, heading for Richmond's wharves, apparently to bombard the city.
Spectators raced to the roof of the capitol building to observe
the action. Militiamen scurried about like Keystone Kops. Some
raced home to don proper uniforms; others skipped such trivial concerns and instead grabbed weapons of every sort: knives,
pistols, blunderbusses, rusty fowling pieces. A group rushed
into the armory where they found two small bronze cannon,
often used during parades. As the would-be artillerymen pushed

these two popguns toward the river, the road's steep incline gave one of the cannon momentum, and it sped off on its own, jumped a gutter, and tumbled onto its side, where it lay for weeks.

This episode, it turned out, resulted from an inaccurate reading of a telegram sent from Norfolk. The *Pawnee* was nowhere near Richmond. But the incident convinced Governor Letcher that a calm military mind ought to take charge here. Individuals like Henry Wise and William Booth Taliaferro and Turner Ashby might be men of action, but this Sunday's exuberant nonsense showed Letcher that he needed the counsel of a professional soldier.[102] As it happened, the governor had been contemplating a possible solution.

Two days earlier the convention had passed a resolution authorizing Letcher to appoint someone to command Virginia's military — its "army" and its "navy." The resolution stipulated that the person, whoever he might be, would carry the state rank of major general. Letcher discussed prospective candidates with his advisory council. The person chosen, they agreed, must have several qualities. He needed to be a Virginian, of course, and mature enough to garner wide respect, yet not be too old or frail to take the field if necessary. Given the confusing nature of military matters, with their arcane French terms and the puzzling nature of things like "logistics," it seemed wise to choose a professional military man, probably one who had graduated from West Point. The person should be both intelligent and tactful, since he would be dealing with various political factions in the state, plus the sensitivities of volunteer soldiers.

What names did Letcher and his advisers consider? Did they discuss Philip St. George Cocke? He certainly fit the criteria. He was a West Point graduate (1832) who had resigned from the army after only two years but had maintained a relationship with the military, having served nine years on the Virginia Military Institute's board. He was extremely wealthy, extraordinarily bright, and well respected. At fifty-two he was hale and could be quite charming. Cocke might have been Letcher's first choice had it not been for three other men who fit the job description a trifle better.

The first, interestingly, was Winfield Scott, a native Virginian. Many in the state still hoped the distinguished old general would depart from benighted Republican Washington and come home to be with kith and kin. But there were rumors about the old soldier's shaky health, and a question about the level of his devotion to Virginia. Assuming he could not be persuaded to accept the assignment, two other candidates seemed almost as worthy: Joseph Eggleston Johnston and Robert E. Lee. Both were Virginians with long military experience. Both had served noticeably well in the Mexican War, the nation's most recent large-scale conflict. Either would seem acceptable. There was a difficulty: each remained a member of the United States Army, and neither had yet resigned his position, nor had given any indication he considered doing so. It seemed possible that one or both might refuse an offer from Letcher. After all, if they accepted command of Virginia's military, they would be making themselves fugitives from their homes (Johnston's being in Washington, and Lee's just across the Potomac in Arlington, within sight of the White House). Also, during their long careers both had taken countless solemn oaths of loyalty to the American flag and might find it unacceptable to break those promises and possibly be called traitors.

Both men came from distinguished families with excellent connections. Both had fathers who had served with distinction in the Revolutionary War. Neither was personally wealthy, but both had married well-to-do women. Both were admired for high integrity and much charm. In truth, either man would have been an excellent choice. (Presumably the governor's council did not realize that on March 15 the Confederate government in Montgomery had sent messages to both Johnston and Lee, offering each a Confederate commission as brigadier general. Whether either received the message is unknown, but since Virginia was still part of the Union in March, neither would have accepted such an offer.)

There is a famous story, often repeated, that Robert E. Lee was the first choice of both sides — Union and Confederate — to lead their armies. Most historians say, proffering little corroborative evidence, that Letcher and his council decided to offer the position to Robert E. Lee. On this topic historians usually accept, unblinkingly, the opinions of Lee's most devoted biographer, Douglas Southall Freeman; Freeman has stated clearly that the great General Lee was offered both jobs — federal military chief, and Virginia's — and that his sense of honor caused him to choose his home, Virginia, over the Union.

Yet logically Letcher and his council might have considered Joe Johnston a slightly better candidate. Since Johnston was already a brigadier general in Lincoln's army, he held a higher rank than Lee, who had only just accepted, three weeks earlier, a promotion to a colonelcy. Johnston was serving as the federal army's quartermaster general, and this expertise would be a plus considering Virginia's problems with her volunteers and matters of supply and distribution. Letcher's council of advisors would have been acquainted with both men. They might have recognized that Johnston had a slightly pricklier personality than Lee, but they might not have considered this entirely a drawback.

If in fact they really chose Lee, their decision might have been based on the fact that Johnston seemed more firmly wedded to the American army, while Lee's situation at the moment was a trifle anomalous. He had been stationed in Texas off and on for years. But in February 1861, after the army ordered him to Washington, he left Texas three days after Texas's convention voted to secede but just before Texas militiamen captured the American force there. Lee started toward Washington on February 13, having missed becoming one of McCulloch's prisoners by a whisker. Now, in mid-April, he was still without an official army assignment, and while awaiting one, was staying at his wife's family mansion in Arlington. Maybe Letcher's council considered him more available. (On the other hand it seems plausible that the council decided to feel out Johnston and Lee at the same time and make the offer to whichever was more willing. If this was the case, it would be interesting to know if they contacted Lee or Johnston first. All we know is that both soldiers spoke to Letcher's representative the same day.)

How about the Union army? Was Lee really the first choice? And if so, the choice to do what? To be what? Lee could hardly have been named the Union's top general. Scott already had that position, and there is no evidence from that period that Lincoln contemplated firing Scott, so what exactly would a top general do? As a sidelight, was it true that General Scott himself proposed Lee's name to Lincoln? If so, to take on what role? There was no plan in mid-April to have the weak American military take the field. The answers to these questions are less certain than most accounts suggest.

Take the matter of whether Lee was really Scott's choice. And, if so, whether Scott in turn influenced Lincoln. By early April President Lincoln was having doubts about some of the old general's judgments, thinking Scott's opinions too colored by political factors. Scott had made clear he thought a major assault ought not to be made against the Confederacy until autumn, and Lincoln therefore might have wondered about Scott's suggestions as to which officers ought to be appointed to higher ranks. Might his proposed nominees not mirror his cautious approach?

According to the later recollections of William Seward's son Frederick (who served as his father's personal secretary), on April 17 the senior Seward and Scott spoke about potential generals. The occasion was shortly after Fort Sumter fell, so the conversation would almost certainly have been in the context of staff, not field, positions. Men would be needed to administer the army of volunteers about to arrive — but such officers would be serving under Scott. A newly appointed general might have to take the field, but in a very restricted way.

Neither Scott nor Seward at that moment was contemplating extensive operations. According to Frederick Seward, General Scott said he would love to lead an army but knew he could not mount a horse in his present physical condition (involving, among other things, the "old soldier's disease" of diarrhea).

The two men spoke about several other officers, and Scott said, vaguely, that he knew of one possibility, an "excellent general [*sic*]" who lived not far away, whom he had asked to come see him. A day or so after this conversation, Seward and Scott talked again. Scott said he had learned that the man in question was going to go with his state and resign his army commission. Years later, when Frederick Seward wrote of this period, he was confident both conversations had been about Robert E. Lee, but he offers no proof for that contention. The two conversations mentioned in these memoirs do not state that Scott actually named the person he had in mind. Frederick Seward was writing long after the war, after Lee had proved himself a fine field officer, and after he had become a kind of American saint to people on both sides. In mid-April 1861, however, Lee would not have been that well known to civilians like William Seward; he might have seemed just another army officer. And although not critically important, if Scott really did say to Seward that he knew of an "excellent general," he may have meant Johnston, as Lee was only a colonel.[103]

The other evidence about General Scott's thinking is equally murky. Lincoln's secretaries, Nicolay and Hay, would assert, also many years later, that Scott had decided to choose Lee, seeing him "as the most capable and promising officer in the service." But neither Nicolay nor Hay liked General Scott or had been close to him, so their analysis of the old man's thinking seems undependable. As to Scott's private papers on this topic, they are not helpful.

How about Lee himself? Did he ever clear this matter up? Yes and no. Seven years later, three years after the end of the Civil War, Lee wrote the Maryland politician Reverdy Johnson. Lee said the only conversation he had on this topic was with Francis Preston Blair, Sr. The elder Blair, father of Lincoln's pugnacious postmaster general, Montgomery Blair, had been a prominent fixture in Washington since the days Blair, Sr., helped guide Andrew Jackson's Kitchen Cabinet. He had a fine home in Chevy Chase, Maryland, but frequently stayed at Montgomery's home (Blair House, as it is now called) diagonally across the street from the White House.

On the morning of April 18 Lee rode to Washington City from his wife's house in Arlington to chat with the senior Blair. According to Lee's note to Reverdy Johnson, Blair told Lee he was speaking "at the instance of President Lincoln," and made some sort of offer to "command" the United States Army. (This is curious because there was hardly any real army at that time, nor any immediate prospect of one. For days after this, Lincoln was still telling listeners that his military goals were minimal. Assuming Lee's recollections were accurate, was the elder Blair really representing the president? Assuming he was, was the offer as open and candid as Lee suggested? Within the confused thinking of those days, such clarity of intent seems doubtful.)

Another question might be raised: when Lee spoke to Blair, did the colonel know that Virginia's convention had voted to secede twenty-four hours earlier? The precise time when the two men spoke is unknown. A trip from Arlington would probably have taken Lee at least an hour, more likely two. By noon of this day, April 18, the *Washington Star* was openly discussing rumors coming from Virginia about the convention's action of the day before. Lee's letter to Reverdy Johnson did not clarify whether he had already heard anything about the convention; but when he declined Blair's suggestion (because he did not wish to invade the South) and we can rather confidently accept that he declined whatever "offer" was made — did he not at least suspect Virginia either was, or soon would be, part of that South?

Lee's note to the Marylander contained another nugget. He said that after talking to Blair he proceeded to General Scott's headquarters, where he told the old general about his conversation with Blair and how he had turned down the offer. Lee did not describe Scott's reaction. Only one witness to the Lee-Scott conversation of April 18 offers a clue. Edward D. Townsend was the old soldier's adjutant general and therefore privy to many of Scott's private thoughts and conversations. In 1881 Townsend published an assorted batch of reminiscences in a slender volume. According to it, when Lee entered the room that day, Townsend stood as if to leave, but Scott motioned that he should remain. Townsend listened to Lee describe to Scott his talk with Blair. Scott replied that these were times when each officer must check his conscience, and if Lee could not remain loyal he must resign. Scott stared at Lee, who said nothing. According to Townsend, Scott finally said — either with a wistful sigh or in disgust, it is not clear — "I suppose you will go with the rest. If you propose to resign, it is proper you should do so at once. Your present attitude is an equivocal one." Lee's reply, according to Townsend, was: He assumed his sons would go with Virginia, and, "I cannot raise my hand against my children." (Douglas Southall Freeman, is widely respected for his scholarship and literary ability, but he was an almost fawning admirer of Lee; Freeman's refusal to accept Townsend's account is unconvincing, especially because Freeman really offers nothing convincing to disprove it.)[104]

Whatever the exact words used by either Blair or Scott, and whatever Lee's responses to them, the Virginia colonel was obviously going with his conscience, though he himself would have applied the term "honor," a word he often used.

To strive for honor above all else can be an unfortunate quest: honor tends to involve what others think of you and can make one "other-directed," rather than self-motivated. It might seem incongruous to apply modern pop psychology to a man like Lee, but reading the letters he wrote during those days reveals a constant refrain.

On Saturday morning, April 20, less than forty-eight hours after talking to Scott, Lee sent his superior officer two notes.

One was a copy of his official resignation from the army, which he had formally directed to Secretary Cameron. The other was a discursive, more personal, and anguished explanation. He spoke of the emotional "struggle" this decision had caused him, of the friendships he had made in his more than thirty years of service, and the personal kindnesses he had received from others. And: "To no one, Genl, have I been as much indebted as to yourself for uniform kindness & consideration & it has always been my ardent desire to merit your approbation." As to his future, Lee added: "Save in the defense of my native State, I never desire again to draw my sword."

This same day he wrote his sister, living in Baltimore. He said to her what Townsend had heard him tell Scott: he could not imagine fighting his own family, his children. (No doubt his sons had recently told him they intended to stick with Virginia and fight for her.) He said to his sister, henceforth he would only "draw my sword...in defense of my native State."

He also, this day, wrote his brother who lived in Washington. Lee had chatted with him two days earlier, the day he spoke with both Blair and Scott. Lee now admitted to his brother that he had hoped to stall another month before making any definitive decision about resigning, to await the results of the May 23 referendum on secession. But with the successful attack against Harpers Ferry by Virginia militiamen and other military movements, "war seems to have commenced." He told his brother he would prefer now "to remain at home. Save in the defense of my native State, I have no desire to draw my sword."

So at least three times on this one day he used the exact same imagery about not wanting "to draw my sword," except to defend Virginia. But because he observed to his brother that war, for Virginia, "seems to have commenced," logically he must have expected he would be forced to fight. No doubt he felt reluctant to accept the reality of opposing the flag he had sworn so often to defend; but unconsciously he had accepted the inevitable. In his mind, Virginia was at war. This meant he would soon be using his sword against the United States. Part of him would have hated this reality, but another part had already embraced it, despite his protestations.[105]

That evening he received a note from Judge John Robertson, acting for Governor Letcher, asking whether they could meet the next day, Sunday, April 21. Since the next morning Lee intended to be sitting in his usual pew at Christ Church in Alexandria, he agreed to see Robertson then. As it turned out, Robertson was unable to make their meeting but he sent Lee a follow-up note, asking him to accompany Robertson the following morning to Richmond, where Lee would speak directly to the governor. Lee replied that he would, and started to pack...civilian clothes.

Monday, April 22, 1861

The two men boarded the morning train at the Alexandria station. Robert E. Lee was fifty-four years old. Dressed in a regular suit, he sported a black silk hat. He had a full mustache but was otherwise clean shaven. His hair had only just begun to turn gray. He made an excellent impression. Of middling height and muscular build, with a fine complexion and clear eyes, everyone agreed he was extraordinarily handsome. He was naturally courteous and sensitive to the feelings of others. Clearly intelligent, he had a well-organized mind.

The train reached Richmond in the early afternoon. Lee went to see Letcher right away, and the governor immediately offered him the position as leader of the state's army and navy, pending approval by the convention. Almost certainly Lee had known since at least the day before that this was coming. He accepted the offer. That evening, with little discussion, the convention officially confirmed the appointment.

This same day another man came to Richmond: Alexander H. Stephens, the vice president of the Confederacy.

Aleck Stephens was a small, wizened person, a mere raisin of a human being. Someone once said he looked like he had been "born out of season." He suffered some undiagnosed ailment that shriveled his body and made him feel constantly chilled. But his mind was sharp and his wit sardonic. Though usually genial, he could be feisty, and had challenged three men, all much larger than he, to duels. As a Georgia politician, he had served his state a long time. On most subjects he was moderate, and had, until recently, maintained a friendly correspondence with Lincoln. He recognized the three-dimensional complexities of issues. Not long ago he had given a speech in which he admitted that slavery was the Confederacy's cornerstone. He considered secession a mistake and had clearly said so, but when Georgia seceded he accepted her decision and represented this state in Montgomery. When the other delegates selected him as the Confederacy's vice president, he reluctantly accepted.

On April 19, after Virginia's convention voted to secede but when it became known she had not voted to join the Confederate States of America, rumors floated in Montgomery that Virginia might be considering making herself the core of a third American federation made up of the eight border states. Jefferson Davis thought that if Virginia could be induced to join the alliance of the Deep South, the states of the Upper South, including Maryland, Kentucky, and Missouri, might join, too. So, Stephens was sent to enlist Virginia in the Confederacy's cause. He was also told that in light of a probable invasion of the South by Lincoln's troops, it was imperative to persuade Virginia to join with the Confederacy in a military alliance, "offensive and defensive," and that this should be done right away rather than await the May 23 referendum.

Aleck Stephens arrived in Richmond on the morning of April 22, several hours before Lee. He held amicable discussions with Governor Letcher and was informed that excellent military materiel had just been grabbed at Harpers Ferry and Gosport. He was also advised that "Col. Robert E. Lee" was expected to appear soon and would be offered the command of Virginia's military.

That evening the city's mayor visited the Exchange Hotel where Stephens was staying and brought the little man outside. A large throng and band had gathered. Upon his appearance, everyone cheered mightily, and he, an accomplished politician, made a nice speech. He complimented Virginia's leadership qualities. He spoke of the coming war. "The conflict will be terrible," he said, "but the victory will be ours." The fight, he said, would be a crusade "for the preservation of your sacred rights," and to prevent Yankee hordes from desecrating the sacred tombs of Washington, Jefferson, and Madison. The states of Tennessee and North Carolina, he announced, would soon join them. So would Kentucky and Missouri, he said. And the good people of Maryland also stood alongside their friends in Virginia. It was a fine oration. The crowd yelled for him—and themselves—with gusto.[106]

In Washington City on this day, Brigadier General Joe Johnston sent Secretary Cameron his resignation. He and his wife Lydia packed some belongings, closed their fine home, and departed the next morning for Richmond—where Johnston would learn that Governor Letcher had already appointed his rival, Lee, to lead the state's forces.

Also on this day, an obscure schoolmaster from Lexington, Virginia, arrived in Richmond by train, stewarding 185 cadets from the Virginia Military Institute. His name was Thomas Jonathon Jackson. He and his students had come at Letcher's request, to help train Virginia's raw militiamen on how to drill properly, in an attempt to rein in some changes swirling around Richmond—changes making some citizens uneasy.

Into Richmond's delicate social mix was flowing a tidal wave of outsiders; some of these newcomers caused problems. Volunteers from elsewhere in Virginia arrived earliest, but troops from Georgia and South Carolina also began trickling in. The city's authorities sent these volunteers to the fairgrounds, where they could practice drilling, and where Richmond's fairer sex could demurely observe them. Soon soldiers seemed everywhere, the city a vast military camp. The noise of their drums and bugles grew incessant, and so was the tramp of their feet and the clatter of their horses. They wandered the streets in packs of two or four or ten, in search of interesting sights and activities. When off duty they frequented hotels, which soon were so jammed that three to a bed seemed not unreasonable. Their public rowdiness and drunkenness was disturbing. On April 23 two volunteers strolling through town espied a hitching post and decided to compare their shooting skills. One of their shots killed a horse and just missed two small children playing nearby.

The mayor of Richmond, Joseph Mayo, was a tolerant man, accustomed to misbehaving or obstreperous visitors, to rural politicians and commercial travelers clunking noisily around town; but even he grew disgruntled at the street violence. His city council supported his announcing an ordinance on April 23 banning the sale of intoxicants after ten o'clock in the evening. The rule affected all groggeries, whether saloons, hotels, even restaurants. The city council also told citizens to keep their eyes and ears open for individuals who might harbor unacceptable "sentiments." Mayo was authorized to detain such miscreants. A man named Earnest Noke was arrested as a suspicious person because he had been heard to suggest that Abraham Lincoln was president of all the United States. Female schoolteachers born in the North, in positions to influence Richmond's young daughters, were scrutinized with care. If they criticized slavery, the South's "peculiar institution," they were considered incendiaries, and the mayor was authorized to treat them accordingly. It soon became illegal in Richmond to sell Northern magazines like *Harper's Weekly, Frank Leslie's Illustrated Weekly,* and even *Godey's Lady's Book.*

There was also the matter of prostitution. Richmond had always had a few bawdy houses and blinked at their presence. Now a great many energetic young women arrived, fully prepared to satisfy the urgent loins of Southern heroes. Male prostitutes also appeared. Some whores lingered in hotels and saloons, some walked the streets, others owned their own places—like Clara Coleman's Cypriot's Retreat, not far from the capitol. The *Richmond Dispatch* complained about a "row of houses in rear of the Exchange Hotel," buildings, the paper said, which "contain many nests of vile and unclean birds." Police records show that Mary Wilson and Mary Walker were charged with keeping a disorderly house; so were Ann T. Hughes and Mary Gleason and Lizzie Hubbard. Usually such strumpets remained only names on police blotters. But sometimes, when the tarts were raped or fought publicly among themselves or shot pistols at drunken soldiers attacking them, their stories reached the surface.

What was not often spoken of was the rapid increase in the city's venereal disease. That problem rapidly grew to epidemic proportions. One Alabama regiment, only a few weeks after arriving in Richmond, reported sixty-two cases of gonorrhea and six of syphilis.

The new army attempted to bridle excesses. Officers transporting or marching troops through the city were ordered to enforce strict discipline on their soldiers—even to the point of keeping their men inside railroad cars if their trains were stopping only briefly in town before moving on to other posts. Such orders seemed insufficient to some Richmonders, affronted as they were by the unsavory changes wrought by the war and the arrival of such riffraff. These Richmond citizens were glacially polite but remained reserved and haughty withal. A South Carolinian found the city's upper class both rude and flippant, and even the city's African Americans impudent. "I am inclined," he admitted, "to dislike the people of Richmond."[107]

Tuesday, April 23, 1861

During the morning Robert E. Lee strode into the House of Delegates, where the convention awaited him. Aleck Stephens was already there. The Confederate vice president had a feeling his mission in Richmond would be successful. He quietly watched the convention's presiding officer officially welcome Lee. The brand new major general (of state troops only) was told that all Virginia wanted to be defended, "that no spot of her soil shall be polluted by the foot of an invader."

General Lee responded with a few graceful remarks. He thanked the convention. He said he was grateful they had picked him the night before. And he swore, "I will devote myself to the defense & service of my native State, in whose behalf alone would I have ever drawn my sword." There was that phrase again; Lee could not rid his mind of it.

When Lee departed the chamber, Aleck Stephens rose and addressed the members at length. Among other things, he said he was not in a position to guarantee anything, but he was confident that if Virginia joined the Confederacy, the city of Richmond would soon be the capital of the entire alliance.

That afternoon Stephens spoke privately with General Lee. The main thing they talked about was Lee's prospective rank in the Confederate army, which would definitely be lower than major general. Thus far the Confederacy's top men — like Beauregard in Charleston — were only brigadier generals. Lee said he understood.

Stephens later sent a message to Montgomery about the progress of his successes. He mentioned that a "Colonel" Lee had officially taken command of Virginia's forces, but other than that vague comment he was noncommittal. His instructions had emphasized the importance of putting Virginia's military under a Confederate commander, and Lee would be subordinate to that as-yet-unnamed person.

The next day Stephens and a committee of the convention signed a document making Virginia part of the Confederacy. In theory the agreement was legally dependent on the ratification vote of May 23, a month away, but the leaders of neither the Confederacy nor Virginia really paid any attention to that proviso. On April 27 the convention invited the Confederate government to transfer to Virginia. (The first South Carolina troops arrived in Richmond on April 24. Most were escorted to the fairgrounds, soon to be called Camp Lee, though their officers took digs at the Exchange Hotel, just down the hall from Aleck Stephens.)

The fate of Virginia and of the Confederacy were intertwined, long before Virginia's voters had their say in the matter.[108]

No one in Richmond or Washington seemed aware of it, but the decision as to whether Virginia ought to attack the District immediately — within the next few critical days — had just become Robert E. Lee's. For the next week, maybe longer, until Jefferson Davis and the Confederate Congress in Montgomery ratified the military alliance Stephens and the convention had tentatively signed, Lee was the person making Virginia's military judgments.

What was his plan?

Robert E. Lee was a professional soldier who knew that war demands far more than bluster. Surly drunks in Richmond saloons might be snorting confidently about taking Washington, but whiskey courage would not be enough. Assaulting the District would require tens of thousands of guns, hundreds of wagons, perhaps a thousand horses, plus tents, knapsacks, and cartridges of various sizes. And unless one assumed a mob could capture the American capital, the soldiers of the assault force would need plenty of what military men called "drilling." They would need discipline. This process would take time.

During the first hours after the convention confirmed his position, Lee showed his thinking on this matter. He wired Alexandria, a town he had left only the day before. Letcher had already named Philip St. George Cocke a brigadier general and assigned him to command Northern Virginia, where Alexandria was the most important city. Reportedly Virginians had been gathering nearby for days. Lee wanted to know their condition, their situation.

Cocke had already gone to Alexandria, investigated things, and was none too happy. On April 24 he telegrammed Lee his initial report. His troops, he said, only numbered about 300, at least those "fit for duty." He said he had no staff, no artillery, and no ammunition. Across the Potomac he estimated that he faced a force of between ten and twelve thousand well-equipped Union soldiers. He expected they might attack him "at any moment." (In this analysis Cocke fell into a pattern common throughout the war. He had mentally doubled or tripled the actual size of Lincoln's army in Washington, and he assumed it to be aggressive, when in fact Scott was going out of his way to be conservative.) When Cocke contemplated his own situation, his only hope was to remain "absolutely on the defensive." He was already withdrawing some things, like flour and railroad iron, to the interior, where they would be less vulnerable if or when the Yankees invaded. Cocke begged Lee for supplies and reinforcements. He added, "I would be glad to have your instructions or advice." Should he stay in Alexandria or should he withdraw? And, if so, to where?

Lee wired back. He said he was glad Cocke completely understood the need for caution. Lee said he hoped to send two cannon and a hundred artillery rounds immediately, but it was impossible just now to provide Cocke's troops with any provisions, especially pork. As to where Cocke ought to place his headquarters, that was up to him. Lee said he suspected Lincoln was not planning on invading Virginia right away. As to his own intentions, Lee said he planned "no attack."

General Lee sent a second and similar wire on this day. Another of Letcher's recent military appointees was Brigadier General Daniel Ruggles, stationed in the Fredericksburg area, halfway between Richmond and Alexandria. Ruggles had just wired Lee for advice. Lee replied promptly: "You will act on the defensive."

Why was Lee so cautious — even timid?

Four days after he took command, Lee wrote Governor Letcher that Virginia's volunteers lacked almost everything necessary to "take the field." Yes, they could move here and there by train, wherever there were rails; but real maneuvers would require things they did not now have: wagons, horses, tents. Had Virginia, he asked, begun raising money to purchase such items?

Lee felt discouraged. He wrote his wife Mary, still at their home in Arlington, and told her she had better move. As he saw it, the enemy might soon cross the Potomac. Their home — "the residence of one of the Rebel leaders," he termed it — would likely be irresistible to Yankee plunderers.[109]

Some Virginians grew impatient with General Lee. They believed he clearly lacked the proper audacity. He was no Napoleon, no Ben McCulloch. Leroy Walker, the Confederate secretary of war, had a spy in Richmond named D. G. Duncan. Sometime before April 20 Walker ordered Duncan to go to Washington, check things out, and report back with anything he, or any agents he could employ, might find. On April 26 Duncan sent two messages to Walker from Richmond. In one he said he had spoken to Lee and that the general "wishes to repress enthusiasm of our people." In a second, longer telegram Duncan said he had just learned that Aleck Stephens had admitted that Jefferson Davis would not be coming to Richmond, at least soon. This information, Duncan said, "causes dissatisfaction." The arrival of the heroic Davis would "inspire confidence." Virginia's soldiers, Duncan said, were "murmuring." In truth, Duncan went on, "they have not the confidence in Lee they have in Davis." General Lee, Duncan thought, seemed worried about Northern "aggression." "Is our cause," Duncan asked, "not in danger of demoralization?"[110]

In fact, Jefferson Davis was not feeling audacious himself. Although he had previously called for a Confederate army of 100,000, by April 25 he only had 40,000 troops available, and these men were spread from Texas and the Gulf Coast to Virginia. Most were only new recruits with no training and few weapons. If, or when, Britain joined their conflict, things would improve. After Davis received Stephens's report about the agreement with Virginia, he told the Confederate Congress in Montgomery that since Lincoln had declared war on them they needed to defend themselves. "We seek no conquest," he insisted, adding wistfully: "All we seek is to be let alone."[111]

These meek words were meant as much for Northern consumption as to stiffen Southern backbones. At the moment his line about not seeking conquest was relatively accurate, so long as one did not consider his desire to absorb states like Maryland as "conquest." But he was being disingenuous. In the long run Davis would have his eye on regions far outside the confines of his present Confederacy—from California to Kentucky, from Mexico to the Caribbean. Who could know the possibilities? At the moment Davis felt forced to remain as cautious as Lee. A few weeks later, however, he changed his mind. In mid-June, after arriving in Richmond, he concluded that the Virginians (Lee?) were still ill-organized. He was disappointed. If they had been more vigorous, he confided in a letter to his brother, "we might now have been contending for the bank of the Susquehanna [a metaphor for the southern border of Pennsylvania]."

Even back in mid-April, Davis wanted the Confederacy to acquire Maryland—by, among other things, supporting the secessionists there. A flurry of telegrams on April 22 highlight his inclinations. When the Pennsylvania militiamen were discovered at Cockeysville, Maryland's secessionist military leader, General Steuart, pleaded with Governor Letcher through a secret agent in Alexandria to send him arms. Steuart's request was forwarded to Montgomery. Jefferson Davis wired "Honest John" Letcher back: "Sustain Baltimore, if practicable. We re-enforce you." Letcher asked his own advisory council for their advice. They proposed that six thousand guns should be sent to Baltimore immediately, a thousand from Harpers Ferry and five thousand from a state arsenal in Lexington. (A few days later Steuart thanked Letcher: "God bless you, Governor, and your generous people, and may these bonds of friendship which have so long united your State and mine never be sundered.")[112]

Could the Confederacy, or even just Virginia, have captured Washington in late April 1861? The simplest answer is: probably not.

Many things stood in the way. The taking of Harpers Ferry and Gosport were dramatic events. In terms of the war about to be fought, they provided the Confederacy with important things it could use in the months and years to come: the dry dock, for instance; and the *Merrimack* (under its new name, *Virginia*); and the thousands of kegs of gunpowder; and the artillery that would be used so well to protect, among other things, the Southern coastline; and the machinery for making guns and ships and masts. But almost all these acquisitions only offered the Confederacy potential power, things that could be used during an extended war. Except for a few thousand muskets at Harpers Ferry, there was little that could be used immediately, perhaps, to win the war quickly.

But capturing Washington might possibly have changed everything, might have shortened the war to as little as a few months. Can a reasonable scenario be offered in which the District could have been taken in late April?

The window of opportunity was very narrow. Harpers Ferry fell in the early morning of April 19, but the flames at the arsenal were not entirely doused until late that afternoon. April 20, therefore, was the earliest date an attack on Washington could have been contemplated. (By chance that was also the day the railroad bridges north of Baltimore were burned and the telegraph lines cut.) But it would have taken Virginians at least twenty-four hours to move an assault force into position, so April 21 was really the first day an attack on the District might have been attempted. Yet Lee was not in organizational command until April 23. Washington was isolated and vulnerable now, but Northern troops would eventually—and, likely, soon—find a way to get to the capital in sufficient numbers to make any assault impossible. The crucial period, therefore, was this brief moment: a handful of days after April 23.

Might Robert E. Lee have ordered an immediate assault? Absolutely not. He had wrestled with his conscience and had resigned from the United States Army, promising many people, in his anguish, that he would only "draw his sword" to *protect* his native state, Virginia. As a man of honor, he could not have immediately thereafter led an army against Washington. His problem was not, as some Virginians thought, that his personality lacked sufficient brass. During the next four years he would reveal enormous willingness to gamble. But emotionally he had not yet reached that stage. Also, like Cocke, he recognized that Virginia's troops were completely unready to move in an organized, disciplined fashion. He had disdain for guerrilla forces, and would never come to accept or trust them.

So no reasoned analysis can presume Robert E. Lee would order an attack during this period. Was there anyone else who might have led an army of Virginians against Washington at this time? Three names come to mind.

The most likely was Beauregard, the Hero of Sumter. As soon as Fort Sumter fell, Davis could have ordered the Creole to Richmond. During the next few months Beauregard would prove — at least in his letters — that he could imagine assaulting Washington, though his plans always involved tens of thousands of men and many cannon. But had he arrived in Richmond as a representative of the Confederate army on, say, April 21, a week after Sumter fell, Jefferson Davis would almost certainly have restrained him from any dramatic adventures. Davis wanted to draw Maryland into the Confederacy, and did not want to bruise that state's ego.

This same reasoning would have even applied to Ben McCulloch. He was about to be named a Confederate general, and would therefore have had to accept Davis's orders.

A third possibility was Turner Ashby, who was in the Harpers Ferry area and certainly had sufficient boldness; but he was not a professional soldier, just a shopkeeper with a penchant for vigilante work. He could not have led a real army into Washington; he lacked sufficient understanding of logistics and complex maneuvers. But Letcher — or Henry Wise — might have encouraged Ashby to lead a raid against the District. Ashby would not have had many men, at most two or three thousand, and these, badly armed. But they could have crossed the Potomac on the B&O's railroad bridge, halted a train, and used it to move toward Lincoln's capital.

Winfield Scott had sufficient manpower and artillery in Washington to stop such a raid. Would it not, therefore, have inevitably failed? Two contrary possibilities exist. If a force of Virginians led by Ashby (or someone of his ilk) had started through Maryland, they would certainly have been joined by secessionist Marylanders who desperately wanted to take some action. And when this now bigger force approached the District, the many men inside Washington who secretly, or maybe unconsciously, supported secession, might have arisen. These combined three groups just possibly could have captured the capital. At least that is what Southern dreamers thought at that time, and later. Some later insisted a great opportunity had been missed because of the cowardliness or lack of vision of politicians like Letcher, along with the "treacherousness" of Hicks of Maryland. (They choose to ignore the apparent timidity of the heroic Robert E. Lee.)

A more likely reality was that if a sizeable force of Virginians crossed the Potomac during that week, most Marylanders would have felt their states' rights sensitivities had been affronted. They would have had the same grumpiness they felt when the Pennsylvanians came to Cockeysville. It seems implausible that many Marylanders would have welcomed Virginia raiders as liberators. The Maryland legislature that Hicks had just called into session would have almost certainly expressed outrage.

In any case the chance that such a raid would have succeeded is probably absurd. It would have had to fight its way into the District, and would have had to assault entrenched regulars who possessed good artillery. The attempt would have ratcheted Northern fury. A failure would have proved dispiriting to many in the Confederacy. What effects it might have had on Tennessee, North Carolina, and Arkansas, each of which was taking steps to secede and join the Confederacy, is impossible to guess.

Despite the likelihood of failure, would not a raid have been worth the gamble? Men like Jefferson Davis and Robert E. Lee were preparing for the worst: a long, drawn-out war. Perhaps a short one was at least possible. It is not implausible that someone (Turner Ashby?) might have decided to roll the dice if it became obvious that the federal capital was genuinely vulnerable.

The next few days constituted one of the most important periods in American history. At this moment Maryland was like a great beast's upper jaw, frozen in the air above Washington. The questions were: Would she clamp down and crush the capital? Would Union volunteers get through? No matter what Robert E. Lee's mood and feelings about honor, Virginians might insist on an assault. Much now depended on what happened inside Maryland.

CHAPTER FOURTEEN

The Contents of a Velvet Glove

Was Abraham Lincoln tough enough to handle this crisis? One of the great weaknesses with American democracy is that every few years the person elected to shepherd the nation is inexperienced. Each new president must go through a learning curve (though the arc of some would seem suspiciously close to flatlining). Sometimes the clumsiness of incoming presidents has led to disasters. John Kennedy's Bay of Pigs mistakes come to mind, as does Ronald Reagan's early economic stumbling. No president, however, has faced an immediate crisis as severe as Lincoln's. Yet in terms of preparation for the office, he was the rankest amateur of them all. His growth, his success, may well be the greatest miracle in the nation's history. But even his presidency contained some dark shadows.

Since his election the previous November, Abraham Lincoln had suffered unremitting tensions. A parade of visitors and an avalanche of correspondence had urged him to compromise on the issue of slavery; or alternatively, to hold firm his opposition to its expansion. He was told to take a stand against secession; he was told to say nothing about it; he was told to support strengthening the army; and to suggest no actions that might seem provocative.

As soon as Lincoln arrived in Washington, pressures increased. Voices grew louder, more insistent. To those meeting him for the first time, he seemed amiable enough, if a trifle rustic—the latest in a string of mediocre presidents. A few clucked at his countrified pronunciation of certain words, and some observers thought he seemed to lack the proper gravitas. Most however saw that he had a gift for charm and humor, for humanizing matters, sometimes in a homey phrase. All in all he appeared to possess a certain innate dignity, even a kind of calm: an important attribute inside a storm. Also, it was noted, he listened well; he did not preach or posture. (In fact Lincoln, during this period, and later, intentionally projected a certain ambiguity. It was during this time that he was heard to admit, "My policy is to have no policy.")

Abraham Lincoln had his flaws. Among other failings he was capable of making dangerous errors about small details and misjudgments about people. James S. Wadsworth, an extremely canny lawyer arriving in Washington from New York, had a chance to speak to members of the new administration. Wadsworth was distinctly unimpressed, particularly with the president. "The truth is," he privately wrote New York's governor Edwin D. Morgan, "the Government is weak, miserably weak at the head. The President gets into at least one serious scrape per diem by hasty, inconsiderate action." Later Wadsworth would revise his verdict, but he had a point. At this stage of Lincoln's administration, the president's decisions, small and large, were often awkward, even foolish. Many men died because of his mistakes. His education in governing would take time. Luckily for America, he was an excellent student. For example, he shrewdly observed that Buchanan begat vexations by appearing to waffle, and Lincoln wanted to avoid such land mines, though it would turn out he himself did not yet recognize the best roads to tread.[113]

In time he would prove himself a person of great sensitivity, as well as a poetic wordsmith capable of penning the astonishing Gettysburg Address. His most important trait, however, often went unnoticed: he had a vast reservoir of strength. His remarkable willpower was not simply part of his character; it also derived from his firm belief in a couple of simple ideas.

As Lincoln would say on several occasions, he genuinely considered the United States the world's model of democracy. Other nations, he thought, were watching her direction. If she did well they might follow her path, and democracy would spread. But if she failed, the very system itself would be in doubt. If secession succeeded, he thought, then the American Experiment had expired. He believed it was his personal responsibility — to the world, to the future — to prevent such a disaster.

In his mind, therefore, the issue he must confront was secession, the right of any dissatisfied state to leave the Union. Acutely conscious of the solemn oath he had taken on March 4, 1861, to defend the "United States," secession was unacceptable. According to his analysis of the law, any state that declared itself no longer part of the United States was proposing something legally impossible. Just before the attack on Fort Sumter, Lincoln's young assistant secretary John Hay was chatting with an acquaintance. They talked of the parlous situation. "The Tycoon," Hay said, speaking in his impish way about the president, "thinks the slavery question of inferior importance." The main issue in Lincoln's mind, said Hay, was whether a state like South Carolina "has the right to break up the government.... If it has, then popular government is impossible."

To put it another way, using part of Lincoln's Gettysburg Address: the question about the constitutional right of secession involved whether America, as virtually the only truly representative democracy in history — "or any nation, so conceived and so dedicated, can long endure." To Lincoln, even in these early weeks, he was not just defending his party's platform — though doing that was important to him. He was trying to preserve the very concept of representative democracy.

Lincoln did not read most of his mail, leaving that onerous duty to his secretaries. One day in early May, John Hay was explaining to him how many letters the White House had been receiving that pressed the president to use this opportunity to end slavery. Lincoln did not agree. And it can be argued that he never came to see the Civil War that way; that eliminating slavery, when he did finally come to accept that idea, was a mere by-product of what he believed was his more important goal. "For my part," he told Hay, "I consider the central idea pervading this struggle is the necessity that is upon us, of proving that popular government is not an absurdity. We must settle this question now, whether in a free government the minority have the right to break up the government whenever they choose." As he saw it, the Union cause must prevail. "If we fail, it will go far to prove the incapability of the people to govern themselves." After this conversation Hay wrote in his diary that the Tycoon was already contemplating what he should tell Congress in July about the meaning of this war — and that this concept would likely be the essence of that message. In fact that turned out to be essentially just what Lincoln did say to Congress when it finally met.[114]

Because of his conviction, it can be argued that Lincoln almost saw himself as a servant of Destiny, and was therefore willing to do virtually anything to succeed. Ironically, his reputation among later generations would be as a kindly, even gentle person of intense humanity, a man who eliminated slavery because he saw the institution as a moral evil: the Lincoln Memorial persona — a wise and even biblical personage settled into his massive throne. To be sure, Abe Lincoln had long considered slavery loathsome, but the engine that really drove him was neither humanity nor morality — though he certainly possessed both. It was politics, in its broadest or highest sense. He had a dream, and that dream was democracy. In his mind, every thing else remained secondary — including legal rights, civil rights, even human rights. John Hay would affectionately call Lincoln an "opportunist," because the president was willing to use whatever or whoever came to hand to accomplish his goals. As it would turn out, the main tool he had available would be his soldiers, and he could be astonishingly callous in their use.

He would weep uncontrollably when friends perished, but after the war's first great battle at Bull Run, with all its shocking losses, he was heard to say, "There is nothing in this except the lives lost and the lives which must be lost to make it good." One of his secretaries later claimed, after the horrific disaster at Fredericksburg, that Lincoln said such terrible Union losses could be accepted because General Lee had also lost many men there; and if the two sides fought like that every day, Lee and the Confederacy would eventually run out of manpower, while Lincoln's army would still remain sizeable.[115]

To understand the president's mood during this period, we are primarily dependent on those two young secretaries, already frequently quoted: John George Nicolay, twenty-nine; and John Hay, twenty-two. Nicolay officially began working for Lincoln after the nomination in 1860; Hay, a boyhood chum of Nicolay's, climbed aboard in November after the election, mostly as a temporary favor to his pal. Nicolay was scrawny and irascible, methodical and hard working. He admired his boss, whose schedule he tried to control, whose mail he attempted to stay ahead of. Hay, the favored son of well-to-do parents, at first found the president pleasant, but nothing special; it took Hay awhile to recognize the Tycoon's depths. After the Civil War these two ex-clerks put together a ten-volume history — in some ways still the best single source on Lincoln. It is from their efforts, along with a few nuggets from assorted sources, that we learn about the president's spasms of insecurity during the war's first weeks.

Frightening rumors flowed through Washington after Fort Sumter. Did Lincoln hear them? If so, did he believe any? If he did, how did he react?

In late March he wrote a note to General Scott, asking for "short, comprehensive, daily reports to me on what occurs in [your] department." Scott did so, starting the first day of April, thus beginning a practice that many modern presidents have had to endure: the daily, often terrifying report. Abraham

Lincoln tried to present an unperturbed demeanor, but at night he often slept badly. Scott's intelligence reports would hardly have made for relaxing reading. On April 5, for example, a week before Fort Sumter, the general wrote: "The machinations against the Government and this capital are secretly going on all around us—in Virginia, in Maryland, and here." Three days later, the general reported: "There is growing apprehension of danger here."

By mid-April the skin beneath Lincoln's eyes had turned into reddish blue bags; his complexion, normally the color of yellow parchment from years behind a plow or on a horse, now seemed as pale as old clay. On Monday, April 15, after releasing his proclamation, he doubtless assumed he would quite soon be hip-deep in volunteers. After all, governors like Curtin of Pennsylvania had been urging him for weeks to call on them for assistance. Now he had. Scott's morning update stated, "little of special interest to report today." The general added that the capital ought to remain secure with enough proper "vigilance"—or "till reinforcements arrive." The next day Scott reported that if enough District militiamen were called up, and marines were sent from the naval bases in Philadelphia, Brooklyn, and Boston to Gosport, these actions ought to keep "the capital a little ahead of impending dangers."

By Friday morning Lincoln knew that Virginia had seceded and taken Harpers Ferry. He had also learned that Virginia was threatening to seize the Gosport Navy Yard. He had heard rumors about rebel mortars being readied for placement on Arlington Heights, on the far side of the Potomac, almost directly across from the White House. If that happened, insurgent artillerists could easily blast the Executive Mansion, just as they had Fort Sumter. Virginia had already raised thousands of troops. Winfield Scott had on hand several hundred regulars he might use, and a few thousand District militiamen of dubious loyalty or military quality.

With armed bands of hornet-angry Marylanders swirling north of the District, perhaps thousands strong, the threats to the capital felt disturbingly near. Until Baltimore cut the tele-graph lines, wires from New York, Rhode Island, Massachu-setts, Pennsylvania, and other states announced that troops were on the way. But such messages were only words. Where were the promised troops?

On Monday evening, April 22, the White House received a report that Northern troops had been seen in the waters off Annapolis. But when none of these soldiers arrived in Wash-ington, such optimistic sightings had a tendency to wear the president down emotionally. As the days rolled by and only a few hundred ragged troops from Pennsylvania, then the Sixth Massachusetts, stumbled into Washington, Lincoln began to unravel. Frustration was making him itchy. Despite all the talk about waves of volunteers coming, where were they? He had heard that the Seventh Regiment was coming from New York, that Rhode Island was sending troops. And so on. A few of the Sixth's wounded troops visited the White House. Lincoln spoke to them. He told them that the only Union volunteers he had seen were them. "I don't believe there is any North," he said. "The Seventh Regiment is a myth. Rhode Island is not known in our geography any longer. You are the only North-ern realities."[116]

That day another guest at the Executive Mansion, sent by Governor William A. Buckingham of Connecticut to assure Lincoln of his state's full support, found the president staring intently across the Potomac toward the heights across the way. Near him was a spyglass. Lincoln listened to the Connecticut governor's message, but remained patently depressed. The ab-sence of incoming volunteers was acting on his psyche. "What is the North about?" he burst out. "Do they know our condition?"

On April 22, Scott's morning report mentioned several ru-mors the old general considered plausible. First, between 1,500 and 2,000 armed Virginians might be building a battery on the Potomac, about fifteen miles below the capital. Those guns, once installed, could prevent reinforcements from using the river to get to Washington. Second, an additional enemy force possibly was preparing to assault tiny Fort Washington, that small federal bastion on the Maryland side of the river, several miles closer to the capital (with the thirsty sergeant now its sole occupant). Third, a train had reportedly just halted at Harpers Ferry to pick up two thousand Virginia troops that were on their way to attack Washington. Despite all this, the general added, he still felt relatively confident his men could defend the District's major "executive buildings."

Scott knew that Beauregard's army in Charleston, by itself, outnumbered the entire military force in the District. The general certainly shared this knowledge with the president. Reportedly Lincoln told Scott: "It does seem to me, General, that if I were Beauregard, I would take Washington."

A New York journalist, Henry Villard, saw the president during this period and spoke to him several times. Villard later said that Lincoln "fairly groaned at the inexplicable delay in the advent of help from the loyal States." It was during these days of unrelieved tension that John Hay observed Lincoln in his office, pacing back and forth for half an hour. Every so often he'd stare out the window, eastward, down the Potomac, past Alexandria, to the outside world. "Why don't they come?" he muttered to himself. "Why don't they come?"

The president grew fixated by what his own eyes could observe. One day he asked Hay to accompany him upstairs to the highest spot in the White House, where "the Ancient took a long look down the bay." A few days later Lincoln admitted to Hay he had "imagined he had [just] seen something significant steaming up the River." He ordered the young man to go to the navy yard and get whatever information he could. The boat Lincoln had observed turned out to be a small commercial steamer traveling its usual route up the Potomac, but it is telling that once again the president was down at the river.

Although at least one Washington insider considered Lincoln "imperturbable," it was becoming obvious that the president's nerves were growing ragged. Nicolay and Hay would

262 / David Detzer

later admit their employer was now in "a state of nervous tension." Lincoln later admitted to Carl Schurz, the writer and diplomat, that one day during these few weeks he was sitting in his office, despondent, convinced that even a middle-sized enemy force could force its way into the District and capture him and his entire cabinet. He told Schurz that he had suddenly become sure he heard a cannon going off somewhere outside. He immediately thought to himself, "There they are!" But when he rushed from his office, those he asked said they had heard nothing. He decided to check further. He left the White House and started to walk. Everything seemed normal, all being quite still. He stopped passersby and probed: Had they not heard something? No, they replied. He kept striding along. Eventually he reached the Arsenal, three miles away, near the Potomac. Its doors sagged open, not a soul within. This seemed curious, but certainly suggested no enemy was attacking. Finally he wandered back to the White House. He decided, he told Schurz, that the explosion had been his imagination. (Years later a Washington resident, writing about these weeks, said that District citizens had been advised that a particular cannon was designated to announce any attack on the capital. One afternoon, he recalled, that gun was fired at two o'clock. Many people, he said, panicked until they learned the cannon was only being tested. Almost certainly this was the booming sound Lincoln had heard, and during his stroll he simply did not encounter anyone who happened to catch it.)[117]

The president's tensions derived from a feeling that the District lay beneath a kind of siege, with Virginia active just across the Potomac, and Maryland teetering to the north. Nothing, it seemed, could be done to persuade Virginia to change her course; Lincoln's appeasement policy had failed. But Maryland was a different story.

That state was about to feel the iron of Lincoln's hand that lay within his velvet glove.

———

Just prior to Fort Sumter, Governor Hicks spoke to the president in Washington. Lincoln offered Hicks little concrete information about his plans for Fort Sumter, even though reports about Lincoln's message to Governor Pickens of South Carolina were in the newspapers, and no doubt Hicks understood the tenor of events. The two men discussed the shaky situation in the nation as a whole, and especially the mood in Maryland. They talked about the prospect of Maryland seceding. Hicks said that he suspected his state might vote to leave the Union if Virginia went out first, because of the symbiotic relationship between those two states. At that juncture Lincoln was still working hard to keep Virginia in the United States, so he may have felt reasonably confident, despite Hicks's warning. After all, only a week earlier Virginia's convention had overwhelmingly voted against secession.

Then things deteriorated, fast. When the first Pennsylvania companies passing through Baltimore were almost blocked by the mob on April 18, Hicks sent a secret message to Scott, asking him to send federal troops to Maryland if the situation grew worse. Cameron replied with a promise that this could be done. But after the Baltimore riot the next day, and Hicks's return to Annapolis under the guise of illness, the governor wrote Washington that he thought it would not be "prudent" for troops to travel anywhere within his state. In fact, he even ordered a federal recruiting agent in Frederick to leave.

Hicks was continuing to wriggle nervously through dangerous reefs. Mayor Brown was more active. As part of his feverish activities on the evening of April 19, as we have seen, he had sent three emissaries to Washington with his personal plea to Lincoln. Though the emissaries arrived too late to speak to the president, they did go to the White House first thing in the morning. When they appeared, Lincoln had just stepped outside to confer with General Scott, sitting in a carriage. The old man was semicrippled with an attack of gout, and Lincoln was hoping to save the poor fellow the pain and indignity of stomping pathetically inside. The three messengers

quickly told the president the purpose of their visit: to persuade the government to avoid Baltimore.

In a sense they were making a logical request. Lincoln
wanted troops in the District as soon as possible, but if the
transfer could be done delicately, without rousing Baltimore
(and Maryland) unduly, he was perfectly willing to consider
alternatives. The president turned to the general, still in his
carriage, and asked him for his expert opinion. Scott had advised Lincoln a day earlier, when they first heard of the problems of the Sixth, that Maryland's authorities had no legal
right to stop federal troops from passing through Baltimore;
but now the old general said that avoiding Baltimore was possible. Infantrymen, coming by train, could halt just north of
that city, get off their cars, march about five miles around the
city, and be picked up by another train south of town. The
process would be cumbersome but not impossible.

Scott did not raise one logistical problem, or at least Lincoln did not mention it in his reply to Brown: men could walk
five miles from one train to another, but moving heavy equipment, like artillery and provisions, was another matter. Any
promise that federal volunteers would avoid Baltimore was, at
best, temporary. Eventually, and sooner rather than later, Lincoln's army must pass through that city—which would mean
controlling its major thoroughfares. If the president was aware
of this prospect, his note to Brown (and Hicks) was neutrally
lawyerlike. At any rate he also sent a follow-up telegram later
in the day, asking those two officials to consult with him immediately about "preserving the peace of Maryland."

The mayor did not receive this message until three o'clock.
He wired back right away that Governor Hicks had already
departed for Annapolis, and asked whether he should come
without the governor. Lincoln, anxious to deal with the issue
of Baltimore, Hicks or no Hicks, assented to this arrangement,
and Nicolay crisply wired the mayor: "Come."[118] Brown, accompanied by three prominent Baltimore citizens, took a special evening train and arrived at the White House about eleven
o'clock the next morning, none of the four (including Mayor

Brown, who had been on the go for days) having had much opportunity to rest.

Lincoln had informed Brown's previous emissaries that he would not allow volunteers to press through Baltimore, but had added, "half playfully" according to Nicolay's private memorandum, that he was sure Baltimore's officials would soon be back, demanding that federal troops must not even walk around their city.

At this second meeting with Baltimore representatives, Brown and his cohorts (two of whom had attended the previous day's session) claimed that Marylanders all across the state were outraged at the thought of Lincoln's soldiers clomping across their soil, off somewhere to "subjugate" fellow Southerners. General Scott was in the room, along with members of the cabinet. Lincoln turned to the old soldier and asked whether there was a way troops could get to Washington without passing near Baltimore. Scott said yes, there was an alternative route. He described it at length. Volunteers from the North could travel by train to Philadelphia, then continue by rail (taking Felton's Philadelphia, Wilmington and Baltimore Railroad) to Perryville (on the northern bank of the Susquehanna River, in the upper quadrant of Maryland, directly across the river from Havre de Grace). At Perryville, which had docks, they could board a ship that could steam all the way down the Bay to the Potomac, then on to the capital. Or perhaps better (since the administration had just learned of the fall of Gosport), the oncoming troops could stop at Annapolis. The general noted that the soldiers might, of course, march from Annapolis to Washington; the road connecting the two cities was good and only about thirty miles long. Or they could hop a short-line railroad there that would carry them west a few miles to a tiny hamlet named Annapolis Junction, where they would link up with the B&O tracks stretching between Baltimore and the federal capital.

Scott could be long-winded when discussing details, but this much was clear: by taking any of these three routes, volunteers would be avoiding Baltimore altogether; but each one would require them to cross a section of northern Maryland (from the Pennsylvania border to Perryville), though from there they would not need to push through the volatile midsection of the state. (When Secretary of War Cameron mentioned the burned bridges in the northern counties of Maryland, Mayor Brown openly admitted that he and other authorities had ordered it done, solely to prevent further bloodshed in Baltimore, not as an act of hostility against the federal government.)

The mayor and his companions did not seem pleased with any of Scott's proposed itineraries, but they were in no position to raise major objections, because, after all, they only represented Baltimore and its environs.

They prepared to leave. Before departing, several would later claim they heard the president exclaim, with some emotion, "Mr. Brown, I am not a learned man! I am not a learned man!" This remark seemed curious. The Marylanders thought Lincoln meant he was not a polished communicator; that the only purpose he had in mind for the volunteers coming to Washington was to have them protect the capital; nothing else.

It is true that Lincoln suggested exactly this point to several listeners about this time, but on this particularly tricky occasion it seems unlikely he would have so misled the Baltimoreans. His proclamation of a week earlier had been clear; he was planning more than a purely defensive posture. He intended to use the volunteers to retake federal properties snatched by the rebels. Assuming he did use that odd phrase about not being a learned man, he could only have meant his abysmal ignorance of military logistics and transportation, General Scott's specialty, so he was forced to depend on military advisers on that matter.[119]

Brown and his delegation left the White House far from satisfied, but constrained from saying more. They had reached the train station when they learned that Garrett, president of the B&O, had just wired them. His telegram held the news (which had so stirred the church-going population of Baltimore two hours earlier) that thousands of federal troops had poured into Cockeysville. Garrett's message emphasized that the city was in a tizzy, frantically arming itself. Brown wired back, "Be calm and do nothing until you hear from me again." His delegation hustled back to the White House to confront the president. They had a question, they angrily said to Lincoln. Had he not just assured them that his volunteers were going to avoid going anywhere near Baltimore? Had that promise been a ruse? Even a direct lie?

They showed him Garrett's telegram and demanded an explanation. Lincoln admitted to being astonished. He immediately ordered both Scott and Cameron to return to the White House. They came, read Garrett's wire, and said that the troops in Cockeysville were supposed to have marched *around* Baltimore—a route, Cameron and Scott had been led to believe, that was satisfactory. Lincoln listened to the exchange and decided on the spot on a more conciliatory action. He had tried appeasement unsuccessfully with Virginia; maybe it would work with Maryland. He told the Baltimore emissaries he had had no idea that troops were being sent that way, and to prove to Mayor Brown his good faith, he would, right now, order them home.

Nicolay's diary states that the president's two chief military advisers expressed instant disagreement: "Gen. Scott & Sec. War [Cameron] dissent." Obviously they considered this approach far too timid, and that perhaps it would encourage disloyal Marylanders to take more assertive steps. Seward and Welles wandered in during this confab. They too did not concur with Lincoln's renewed attempt to placate Baltimore. Welles, for one, was outraged. One of his aides would later say the naval secretary was so disturbed that he leaped to his feet, shoved his hat under his arm, and strode out, saying he refused to participate in any such policies. Seward may have appeared more controlled, but a few days later John Hay heard him curse Baltimore, saying "*delenda est*" (a well-known Latin phrase once uttered by Cato the Elder, meaning, "It must be destroyed"). The disaster at Gosport probably suggested to these men that appeasement was no longer a proper approach. This would explain their strong reactions. Also, it should be remembered, Cameron had just learned that bridges owned by his own railroad had been burned at the orders of Mayor Brown; he could hardly have felt generous.

The president, however, had made up his mind. Cameron instantly penned a message addressed to "the officer" in command of those troops in Cockeysville. (This vagueness resulted from the telegraph lines being cut; Cameron had no idea who was in charge there.) The message said: in order to "gratify the mayor of Baltimore," the president hereby orders the troops in Cockeysville to return to Pennsylvania. (Cameron did add a closing sentence, saying that some volunteers must remain stationed along the railroad line to prevent further depredations.)

Winfield Scott wrote a separate order clarifying Cameron's note, telling the volunteers at Cockeysville not merely to return to Pennsylvania, but to continue their passage to the federal capital by way of the Annapolis route. The general's message showed that Lincoln had not, after all, really retreated. Brown would later recall the old general as having said, "Mr. President, I thank you for this, and God will bless you for it."

Lincoln's patience was wearing thin. A few hours later he was talking to Major Hunter, who was still patrolling the White House. That officer had heard about the Cockeysville discussions and forthrightly told Lincoln that the president ought to have ordered those troops to crash through Baltimore, no matter what, leveling that city if it resisted. Lincoln took no offense at the major's bluntness. He told Hunter his conciliation of Maryland had reached an end. He had made this last gesture to try and calm the hysteria there. But if this approach didn't work, he would no longer stop his troops from applying alternative methods.[120]

The next day, Monday, April 22, Lincoln's exasperation became clearer. A delegation of about thirty members of the Bal-

timore YMCA, led by a Dr. Richard Fuller, minister at Baltimore's largest Baptist church, called at the White House. Dr.
Fuller was deeply devout, a prominent leader of the Southern
Baptist Convention. He loved sermonizing from his pulpit and
was more than a bit full of himself, pompously confident that
he represented the Word of God. He spoke often about sin and
the importance of being a "true Christian." He was the sort of
stuffed shirt Lincoln found insufferable.

Their meeting did not start auspiciously. Dr. Fuller offered
a solution to the present crisis: Lincoln must immediately recognize the Confederacy, no more, no less. The situation, Fuller
said, was obvious: the Confederacy was a fact, a fait accompli.
The president, if he did not want to enter the sticky thicket of
secession, would not even have to mention the word. Lincoln
snorted: such a policy would be craven. "There is no [George]
Washington in that, no [Andrew] Jackson in that, no spunk in
that!"

Dr. Fuller did not care for the emphasis on machismo, on
Lincoln's use of that vulgar term "spunk." Fuller said he hoped
the president's need to show his manhood would not cause him
to ignore the higher quality of true patriotism.

At this moment, according to a member of the delegation,
Lincoln asked a lawyer's question: where would the government find revenue? The reverend had the answer to that problem: take it from the rest of the states. Lincoln replied that
neither he nor Congress would recognize the Confederacy. As
for himself, Lincoln planned to "run the machine as I found it."

Then the conversation turned to the matter of federal
troops crossing through Maryland. Fuller of course said he
was utterly opposed to it. To which the president expostulated,
he had to have troops to defend Washington. Their natural
pathway to the capital would, of necessity, take them through
Maryland. "Our men are not moles, and can't dig under the
earth; they are not birds, and can't fly through the air." He also
said he noticed that these good Christians of the YMCA who
spoke so strongly against the "great horror of bloodshed" said
nothing against the willingness of Southern insurgents to

"make war on us," or the preparations in Virginia to attack and capture Washington.

To bring this painful session to a close, Lincoln attempted one final tack. In reference to his troops crossing Maryland, which they would be doing: "Now, sir, if you won't hit me, I won't hit you."

As the delegation was leaving, one of its members was heard to mutter in disgust: "God have mercy on us, when the government is placed in the hands of a man like this!"[121]

A few days later Lincoln finally loosened his velvet glove, revealing the metallic nature of his resolve. The actions he finally embraced, he believed, were legitimately drawn on a concept called "presidential powers."

The Constitution is a remarkable document. In a sense it was originally a committee report, even though we are referring to mostly intelligent and dedicated men who deserve kudos for having been willing to sit and drone through the stifling heat of Philadelphia in 1787. Portions of the Constitution are quite precise, particularly those enumerating the powers of Congress. But the powers of the president were left indistinct. Maybe these men in Philadelphia were ultra-sensitive because of the recent war they had fought against George III, or perhaps they were simply being shrewd. Mostly, regarding the Executive, they discussed how a president would be chosen. And even here they were so imprecise that it has required several amendments to try to correct their clumsiness. In terms of the president's power, their main point was this: the executive power shall be vested in a president (as though saying such cleared everything up). That official would have the power to command the nation's military and to receive ambassadors and make treaties (with the advice and consent of two-thirds of the senators). America's army during the summer of 1787 was almost nonexistent, so one wonders if the Founding Fathers grasped where those brief phrases might lead. It would seem they intended the key constitutional phrase about the presidency would be this: "He shall take Care that the Laws be faithfully executed." It is probable most of the men who worked on the Constitution thought that the president would remain a servant of Congress, much as a sheriff is usually a subordinate of county administrators. (A "president" is, after all, merely the person who "presides" within the government.)

The decades after 1787 fleshed out, somewhat, a few of the potential powers of the presidency. In fact, George Washington would define the office almost as he saw fit. As an old soldier he had no hesitation acting as commander in chief when, for example, some whiskey rebels announced they would not pay federal taxes. The 1790s also constituted the decade of an ongoing war between revolutionary France and its opponents, a war that almost sucked in the United States like a whirlpool. George Washington and John Adams, his successor, had to focus much of their attentions on military and diplomatic affairs. Beginning four decades later, however, after Andrew Jackson left office in 1837, the office of the presidency tended to drift. The position never quite transmogrified into that of a figurehead, but the assumption of most knowledgeable people was that the real power resided in Congress, not the White House. And the eight presidents who followed Jackson seemed to accept this tenet.

One cannot know what Lincoln might have done with the office had a war not intervened. Presumably not very much. He would likely have been only the latest in a string of inactive presidents. The crisis during his first weeks in office changed everything. In four months Lincoln went from being a country lawyer with a fund of charming rural tales to the status of a dictator. The office of president, and the country, would never be the same. After him there would be many weak presidents, but Lincoln had created precedents that other men, some far less scrupulous than he, have found useful.

It really started with the Confederate assault on Sumter.

On Wednesday, April 17, Jefferson Davis announced that the Confederacy would issue letters of marque (licenses to civilian ship captains to legally prey on merchant ships flying the

American flag). Lincoln's cabinet discussed this development
and agreed on the administration's second war proclamation
(again, without congressional approval): a naval blockade of
Confederate ports. This proclamation included a statement
that any sailors found using such letters of marque would be
considered pirates and would receive the traditional punishment: hanging. (That is, such seamen would not be treated as
prisoners of war.)

During these days, Lincoln began acting with growing confidence about his presidential powers. He still consulted experts,
but he was less hesitant to make strong decisions. On Saturday,
April 20, he personally authorized a raid on all important telegraph offices in the North. The marshals seized and, in time,
scanned every wire sent during the previous year. The next day
the administration, meeting secretly in the Navy Department,
away from inquisitive eyes, removed vast funds from the Treasury. Then with little historical precedent, Lincoln's government
offered certain New York merchants carte blanche to purchase
items for the federal government.

Lincoln would later attempt to justify such actions, saying
he was only fulfilling his constitutional duty to suppress insurrection, and hoped, or assumed, that Congress, when it met,
would sanction his decisions. His July message to Congress
would include this sentence: "These measures, whether strictly
legal or not, were ventured upon under what appeared to be a
popular demand and a public necessity, trusting then, as now,
that Congress would readily ratify them." He was saying that
he had been forced to act, and act alone, because Congress was
not in session and "existing exigencies" and "popular demand"
insisted on it. His logic was amusingly twisted, since it had been
his decision not to convene Congress immediately. (In August
Congress voted to legalize all actions Lincoln had taken since
April, but later, federal courts would question some of them.)

Among the decisions Lincoln made were: the suspension of
habeas corpus; the arrest of individuals (eventually thousands

of them) with no judicial warrant and little attempt to provide rationales for each arrest; the seizure of private property; and the suppression of free speech and a free press.

Lincoln profoundly believed in what has since been called The American Dream. To save that ideal, he allowed, even encouraged, arbitrary arrests, the silencing of free speech and free press, the quashing of the right of assembly. Some — perhaps all — of these dictatorial actions may have been constitutional "in cases of rebellion," but they leave a feeling of queasiness. Lincoln was creating dangerous precedents. The Bill of Rights is America's greatest treasure. Those few sentences, appended to the original Constitution, were intended to guarantee that the government would never fall into patterns far too common elsewhere in the world. To some extent Lincoln was ignoring them.

Maryland bore the brunt of Lincoln's "dictatorship." As the mood of crisis inside the federal capital rose to fever pitch between April 23 and 25, the White House learned that Governor Hicks had just asked his legislature to convene. This seemed an ominous development. Such a gathering might pass a secession measure. If it did, and Maryland immediately joined Virginia, Washington would be in desperate peril.

The handful of Northern newspapers that had been furtively carried into Washington described a North that quivered in fury at the Confederacy. The only criticism of the administration's position seemed to be that it was apparently acting too cautiously. There was much talk of hanging traitors, particularly Jefferson Davis. There seemed no concern about the Bill of Rights. For months, throughout the South, strangers who looked like spies or even seemed suspicious had suffered threats, beatings, or death. Northerners were now acting with equal brutality. From New Haven to Harrisburg, and far beyond, those who refused to show enough patriotism were in danger. One example: On April 19 a telegram arrived in Beloit, Wisconsin, describing what had happened to the volunteers of the Sixth Massachusetts a few hours earlier in the streets of Baltimore. A militia officer read this news aloud to his militiamen. "Kill them," one soldier shouted. "Kill every mother's son of them."[122]

Several members of Lincoln's cabinet pressed the president to take stronger measures in Maryland. Postmaster General Montgomery Blair, a West Point graduate, had been during these weeks the administration's most pugnacious official. Now he raised his decibel level. Even the determinedly sedate Christian Salmon P. Chase, secretary of the treasury, was ready to fight. He received a message from a subordinate at the New York Custom House stating that "the administration is much blamed by its friends for its inaction. They find themselves unable to justify its moderation." Unless Washington sent troops clawing their way through Maryland "at whatever cost," Lincoln and his administration would be severely censured. Perhaps Chase was thinking of these bellicose sentiments when he jotted a note to the president on April 25. The rebels, he said, were active and ahead of them, and the administration had thus far "accomplished nothing." Chase warned Lincoln that if Maryland's legislature passed a secession ordinance, that state's insurgents would likely attack, almost immediately, the Baltimore Custom House (part of Chase's bailiwick), and even Fort Henry. "What next?" Chase asked.

This very day, perhaps after receiving Chase's advice, the president wrote Winfield Scott. Lincoln was not quite ready to leap to martial law. His letter to Scott hints of the president's uncertainty. He told Scott that the Maryland legislature was about to assemble. "The question has been submitted to, and considered by me, whether it would not be justifiable, upon the ground of necessary defense, for you, as commander in Chief of the United States Army, to arrest or disperse the members of that body." Lincoln said he considered "it would *not* be justifiable," or at least, that doing so might not accomplish "the desired object." He went on to explain his concerns. The Marylanders had a "legal right" to meet. More importantly, it was not yet clear what action they might take when they did gather. There was, Lincoln went on, an additional practical matter. The legislators, he thought, could not be held under arrest indefinitely. (As it turned out they could, should the president so decide, but he had not yet reached that slippery, fascistic place.) And if arrested, he said, once they were released they would merely go ahead with what they had already planned, probably even more determined now.

Given these factors, Lincoln instructed Scott to: "Watch, and await their action." If the legislature drifted in the direction of secession, he authorized Scott "to adopt the most prompt, and efficient means to counteract" that possibility. If necessary, Lincoln added, Scott could even bombard their cities (meaning, primarily, Baltimore). And in the "extremist necessity," he authorized General Scott to suspend habeas corpus. (It is telling that Lincoln, a lawyer, considered the suspension of that writ more extreme than blasting largely defenseless civilian cities.)

Despite Lincoln's use of the phrase "extremist necessity," only two days later he was ready to take a more drastic step, though almost nothing had really changed. He admitted he was worried about the volunteers going from Annapolis to Washington. He wrote Scott again, opening with a justification drawn from the Constitution: "You are engaged in repressing an insurrection against the laws of the United States." He told the old general that if any resistance occurred along that line, Scott, or *any* officer who happened to command "that point where the resistance occurs" was hereby authorized to suspend habeas corpus, an action Lincoln himself had described only forty-eight hours earlier as "extremist."

So there it lay, bare. With this presidential approval as a basis, military law could replace civilian law. To be sure this moment was a genuine crisis. The geographical region Lincoln specified was narrow. But the Civil War had just changed. A man as decent and sensitive as Abraham Lincoln had turned immense military power over to unspecified officers. Moreover, the sector where martial law could be imposed could easily be expanded, like the spread of some dread epidemic, under orders from the White House.[123]

When the Maryland legislature did open its session, it immediately voted against secession. But even that did not satisfy the administration. Between late April and early September, Maryland came beneath increasing military pressure. Hundreds of individuals were imprisoned on suspicion of having secessionist sympathies. The inviolable sanctity of freedom of thought had gone by the wayside. During the Civil War federal authorities would eventually jail 2,094 Marylanders — including seventeen owners of newspapers, twenty-nine elected members of the state legislature, countless bankers, merchants, and manufacturers — for such political reasons. A grandson of Francis Scott Key was jailed, as was Wallis Simpson's grandfather, the lawyer Severn Teackle Wallis, whose mistake had been to serve as legal adviser to Baltimore's police board.

Marshal Kane was arrested and flung into prison, even though his activities on April 19 had saved the lives of hundreds of Union volunteers. The telegram Kane had sent after that incident, saying he was now prepared to fight and "whip" incoming Union volunteers, was the rationale. Kane would be jailed for fourteen months — charged with helping incite the riot of April 19. This charge was a travesty, of course, but Abraham Lincoln was determined that Maryland would remain in the Union, and matters like justice became secondary.

Mayor Brown was also arrested. When a special envoy came and begged Lincoln to intervene, the president snippily refused. Many of those imprisoned were tossed into Fort McHenry. Few were tried for any crime. (One member of Baltimore's police board, Charles D. Hinks — an elderly fellow in fragile health — had not even been in the city during the April 19–20 riot. On July 1, 1861, when the other members of the police board were arrested under orders of Lincoln's administration, Hinks was among those swept up. His arrest hardly represents Lincoln and his government at their best.) Some of those imprisoned would be released in several months; the jail time of others lasted much longer.

People who considered Honest Abe weak would learn, at their cost, to recognize his steely resolve.

The state of Maryland was essential to the president for two reasons, one obvious, the other less so. Its geography screamed its importance. Lincoln was advised by military experts like Winfield Scott to maintain a clear highway from the North, that such a route was necessary for the safety of the federal capital. Lincoln also thought that if Maryland, a slave state, could be "persuaded" to remain in the Union, this might have a salutary effect on other slave states like Kentucky and Missouri.

On May 1 John Hay wrote in his diary that the Tycoon might be "considered the first of the redeemed."[124] This judgment seems kind.

CHAPTER FIFTEEN

On the Road

We are making our history, hand over hand.
—THEODORE WINTHROP, 1861

He mirrored some of the best traits of the America each side claimed to be defending: courage and generosity of spirit. When, in June of 1861, Theodore Winthrop would be killed in Virginia at an obscure place called Big Bethel, he was literally leading men, facing the enemy, climbing a fence, shouting encouragement to comrades behind. The war was still young then, and the death of this worthy man pained people on both sides. And yet Winthrop was an odd duck: a lawyer who hardly practiced law, a writer who published almost nothing, a peripatetic hiker who thought nothing of walking fifty miles for fun, a genuinely heroic figure in battle whose writings suggest a sexual ambiguity.

In 1861 Theodore Winthrop was thirty-two and handsome in a pensive, poetic way. Slender and wiry, he had a straight nose, a thick mustache, and deep-set, sad gray eyes. As a boy he had often suffered bouts of ill health, but he strengthened himself by tramping extraordinary distances. He possessed old New England roots. His father was a New Haven lawyer, descended from the two John Winthrops who had served as governors —

one, of Massachusetts; the other, of Connecticut. His mother, a descendant of Jonathon Edwards, was related to seven presidents of Yale. Both parents were devoted readers, and Mrs. Winthrop wrote poetry. In his midteens the young man started taking classes at Yale, a few blocks from his home. After a boyish scrape during his sophomore year involving snowballs and the fragility of window panes, he knuckled down, studied hard, and performed well academically. After graduation, using inheritance money, he took an extended sojourn in Europe. For a year-and-a-half he hiked across much of England and Scotland, then France and Germany, then Switzerland and Italy. He examined famous buildings and checked out well-known works of art. At first he was completely smitten. "Since I have been in England," he wrote home, "I have had either a smile on my face or tears in my eyes almost the whole time." Previously he had read so much about this land, the home of his Puritan ancestors, that he found himself deeply moved by a trip to Westminster Abbey. And after visiting a chamber where Queen Elizabeth once slept, he looked at the mirror on its wall and recognized he was seeing "a looking glass which has reflected the charms of the Maiden Queen and Mr. Theodore Winthrop, a young gentleman quite ready to spoil his cloak for a lady's sake." But this was also the England of Charles Dickens and "Oliver Twist," and soon he felt offended by its poverty and rigid caste system. (Such injustices distressed him throughout his life, especially when he found them at home. As to the South's peculiar institution, he would decide: "We must put our heel on slavery forever.")

After returning to America he contemplated becoming a professor but finally rejected the notion of a scholarly existence. "I would not choose the life even if I could, my wishes are for action perpetual and violent, even, for if I am not severely taxed and in constant motion I stagnate." But what? Winthrop lacked focus or ambition. His mind, he admitted, was a "tangled, rag-bag of a thing." For a while he tutored the son of William H. Aspinwall, a wealthy New York merchant;

he then clerked a couple of years in Panama for one of Aspinwall's ventures; later he studied law, and practiced it briefly, with little enthusiasm, in St. Louis. Finally he settled in with his sister Laura at her house on Staten Island, when that out-of-the-way spot was a pleasant settlement for New York's artistic crowd. He continued to dabble in law, but spent much of his time now scribbling. He wrote three novels and two books about his travels, none of which was published during his lifetime, and which only came to light after his death, when Laura discovered the manuscripts in dusty piles on his desk. She sent them to one of America's most prestigious publishers, Ticknor & Fields of Boston. The books became an instant literary phenomenon, printed in scores of editions. His novels are justly forgotten now, but his two travel accounts are quite good — especially *The Canoe and the Saddle,* about his trekking through the wilderness that was northwest America at mid-century. He was a lively observer of things and people. He had the opportunity to shake the hand of William Seward, of Brigham Young, and of Abe Lincoln. He would tell a friend: "I have fun. I get experience. I see much." His writing tended to be arty and contrived, but he was also capable of describing his world with vivid force. "An aspen under the window," he once wrote, "whispers to me in a chorus of all its leaves."

Yet he felt melancholy during his time on Staten Island. Much had been expected of him. What had he accomplished? He was a disinterested lawyer, an unpublished writer, and a bachelor, unlikely to marry. Friends noticed he seldom laughed, and that he often fell into morbid moodiness. He wanted to be of some service to the world but was too rootless, too scattered. "The great want in my character," he once wrote, "is earnestness, passion, intensity, or whatever you choose to call it; so that I almost fear I shall never 'do anything in life.'"

Then came Fort Sumter.

On the Sunday after the Confederate attack, he pondered its implications. He spent the day talking to his friend, George William Curtis, an avid Republican and a journalist with

Harper's and the *Atlantic Monthly*. Winthrop felt compelled to enter the coming war. The next day he volunteered as a private in America's most famous militia regiment, the Seventh New York. His military specialty was to be artillery, though he had never fired a cannon. He seemed focused now and very happy. He promised Curtis to write about his experiences, and he did, sending three splendid descriptive essays to the *Atlantic Monthly*. These articles made his name known to people across the Union. It turned out that his life, up to this moment, had been a preparation for the next two months.

Theodore Winthrop and the rest of the Seventh were about to try breaking the siege of the national capital, in a desperate gamble to save Washington, and America.[125]

The Seventh Regiment was famous for several reasons. Most of its members came from middle-class or wealthy backgrounds. This meant they generally could afford to purchase and maintain their own accoutrements and fancy gray uniforms with flattering white crossbelts. (Those who could not produce the necessary funds received assistance from wealthy New Yorkers who subscribed to the Seventh's general fund.) Sometimes rivals sneeringly called the Seventh the Silk Stocking Regiment, but its members considered such carping the result of jealousy or envy. Money did not fully explain their reputation. Many communities had militia units drawn from their town's young elite. Philadelphia, Richmond, and New Orleans all bragged of their high-toned militia companies. But no other city had been able to maintain a full regiment of such glitter, at least one whose history spanned several generations. A mere company of stylish gentlemen in snappy uniforms, numbering about forty, could be eye-catching in a parade, but would not be nearly as impressive as hundreds and hundreds of such youths. Because of this factor, the Seventh was called on to act as an honor guard for exceptional occasions, such as those times when foreign dignitaries like the Prince of Wales came to visit the United States. The Seventh was written about and emulated across the land. (An interesting sidelight of their history involved their nickname. In the 1820s they started calling themselves the National Guard, and were the only American unit to refer to themselves by that name. In 1862 Congress adopted that famous moniker as the official label for all state militia.)[126]

In January 1861 the officers of the Seventh held a meeting. In light of the growing secession crisis and problems in South Carolina, they agreed to offer the services of their regiment to Winfield Scott. The general thanked them and said he hoped things would not get that bad, but he would keep their offer in mind. He knew the Seventh well. Since he had maintained his headquarters in Manhattan for most of the past decade, he had often socialized with its leaders. He knew they possessed most of the necessary equipment — blankets, muskets, knapsacks, and so on — and would not need to be supplied by the federal government, unlike, for example, regiments from Pennsylvania. Besides, he knew they frequently drilled as a group. The regular army was so small and its duties so geographically widespread that its troops normally operated only as truncated companies, at most, sometimes only in squads. Hardly a single regiment of regulars had worked as an integrated unit since the Mexican War. The Seventh, therefore, was highly unusual.

Scott almost decided to use them in February, when the electoral votes were counted in Washington, but finally concluded that rumors of an attempt to disrupt that process were not serious. On the other hand, when Lincoln issued his mid-April call for volunteers, Scott immediately wired Governor Morgan of New York. He asked for the Seventh; and wanted them quickly.

This same day, the Monday, April 15 when Winthrop joined them, the men of the Seventh were already organizing. In less than twenty-four hours the officers told the governor they were ready, saying they could leave in three days. They needed, they said, that much time to fill out their ranks, as a few of their members thought that their family's immediate needs or job pressures made it impossible for them at this moment to drop everything. The resulting vacancies needed to be filled to achieve a full regimental complement. There would be no difficulty finding replacements since the regiment was being inundated by applicants.

On Thursday, while the Seventh was finalizing arrangements to leave the next day, two events stirred New York to a frenzy. The Sixth Massachusetts came through town, on their way to Washington, and Major Robert Anderson and his handful of Fort Sumter heroes arrived by ship, exhausted and subdued. The volunteers of the Seventh redoubled their efforts to get going.

Friday morning they bustled about. Carriages, jammed with uniformed young men and their families, arrived at the armory (not far from Cooper Union, where a year earlier a speech by an obscure Abraham Lincoln had captured the interest of prominent Republicans). The Seventh learned that a second Massachusetts regiment, the Eighth, had just passed through the city during the morning, led by Ben Butler. The Seventh sped up; they did not want to miss the fun. They made arrangements to board a ship at five o'clock; it would ferry them across to New Jersey, where they would catch a train which would take them to Philadelphia. From there they planned to go through Baltimore, and on to the capital. When they started marching toward the pier that afternoon, they knew nothing about the Baltimore riot, which had taken place a few hours earlier. They numbered 991 men — a real regiment, unlike the partial units in motion from states like Pennsylvania and Massachusetts.

New York's morning newspapers had prominent stories about their planned departure, specifying when they would leave their armory and the route they would take. By midafternoon, sidewalks were jammed as the regiment began its march across town. Their fine, large band banged and tootled enthusiastically, but the yelling from either side was so deafening it drowned out the music and the tramping of their feet. "Bully for you!" the crowds shouted. Strangers jumped from the side-walks to clap them on their knapsacks.

The Seventh passed the hotel where Major Anderson was staying, and he honored them by appearing and standing militarily erect above them on a balcony, nodding wearily to them as they grinned and cheered his name and twirled their hats in the air, trying to maintain a perfect step.

"It was worth a life, that march," Winthrop would write. "Only one who passed, as we did, through that tempest of cheers, two miles long, can know the terrible enthusiasm of the occasion." Girls threw handkerchiefs and scented gloves from the upper windows, and these delicate things drifted down like thick snowflakes, to land gently on the shoulders of the marchers.[127]

Their boat drew away from the dock as scheduled. In Jersey City, before their train jolted into activity, a few of the Seventh purchased local evening newspapers, which contained accounts of events in Baltimore. Reading these stories, the Seventh's volunteers were angry; they spoke to one another of vengeance.

They arrived in Philadelphia about two o'clock in the morning. While most of the men continued to doze inside their stuffy cars, Colonel Marshall Lefferts went to see if he could get an update about the next stage of their trip. A messenger informed him that Mr. Felton, president of the Philadelphia, Wilmington, and Baltimore Railroad, which was slated to take them on their next leg, wanted to speak to him right away. Felton told Lefferts that problems south of Philadelphia were serious. The railroad man showed him telegrams that had arrived during the past dozen hours. Among other things, Governor Hicks and Mayor Brown were requesting that Felton not send any more troops through Baltimore. (The bridges had not yet been torched, but Felton had been hearing stories that gangs of Baltimoreans might soon leave their city, bent on some violent errand.)

Colonel Lefferts was a civil engineer by training and a merchant. Forty years old, he had become wealthy in the telegraph business. He had joined the Seventh as a private ten years earlier and been named its colonel in 1859. Still slender, handsome, and youthful-looking, he had an excellent, well-organized mind. He knew nothing about war, really, but he had gumption. He told Felton he cared not a fig about Maryland politicians, he was only concerned about getting to Washington, and soon. What, he asked, was the likelihood that the Seventh would get stopped on the way? Felton replied that he feared the worst. He calculated his trains could only take them as far as Perryville. The normal practice for anyone going from Philadelphia to Baltimore by train was to stop at that town, where their cars would be slid, one at a time, onto rails nailed against the deck of a large steamboat, the *Maryland*, owned by Felton's railroad. That ship would ferry them across the wide mouth of the Susquehanna to Havre de Grace, where their cars would be hooked together again, and from there they would chuff to Baltimore. (This is how the Sixth Massachusetts had traveled only the day before.) But under these new circumstances since the riot it seemed possible the Seventh might not get farther than Perryville. They could march from there to the capital, south across Maryland, but it would be eighty miles.

Lefferts did not consider such a march realistic. The majority of his men had done a fair amount of drilling, but an eighty-mile march would be punishing, especially if they had to fight a foe along the way. Another problem derived from a deficiency of wagons. They would be unable to take enough provisions, to say nothing of ammunition, medical supplies, heavy iron cookware, and the trunks each officer had been permitted to bring.

Lefferts wired Secretary Cameron for advice, but the wires had been cut by this time and his query never reached Washington. He discussed the precarious situation with his officers. This war council concluded that getting to Washington as quickly as possible was so critical they should not gamble.

They agreed they would not even bother taking Felton's train to Perryville. If the insurgents in Maryland had reached Havre de Grace, as seemed probable, they almost certainly would have grabbed or burned the *Maryland*, docked there. The Seventh could find themselves stuck indefinitely in northern Maryland, far from the national capital. Lefferts and his officers decided a more rational approach would be to rent a civilian steamship right here in Philadelphia, and that, no doubt, several ships would be available. They could steam down the Delaware River to the Atlantic, then head southward along the outer coastline of the Delmarva Peninsula until they reached the mouth of Chesapeake Bay. This involved a more roundabout route, to be sure, but it guaranteed them access to the crucial region. Once inside the Chesapeake, they would steam northward until they reached the Potomac. They assumed Virginians might have, by now, blocked passage on the Potomac with artillery. If not, the Seventh could enter that river and steam directly to the docks of the District. If the Potomac was indeed blocked, they would skirt it entirely and continue north until they reached Annapolis. From there, it should be easy to get to Washington. (When the District had originally been on the drawing boards more than sixty years earlier, its planners assumed that nearby Annapolis could serve as the port for the American capital, just as Le Havre was the primary Atlantic port for Paris.)

At eight fifteen that morning, April 20, Lefferts telegraphed his brother-in-law in New York that the Seventh would probably be traveling to Washington by way of Annapolis, and that supplies should be forwarded there. He left to find a vessel roomy enough to carry his large regiment. Using funds from his own firm, he rented the *Boston*. This ship was already loaded with cargo slated to be taken to New York, and these things needed to be removed before the vessel would be ready to take on the Seventh and leave. While this process was going on, Lefferts purchased provisions in the city and had them stored aboard. The *Boston* was ready at 4:20.

———

While all this was transpiring, Ben Butler was in a similar predicament. He and the Eighth Massachusetts had arrived at the Philadelphia station the night before. He had wired Governor Andrew he intended to depart immediately for Washington. But an hour later he sent Andrew a second message: "I will telegraph again, but shall not be able to get ready as soon as I had hoped." He went to a hotel and took a room. He was aware that Lefferts and the Seventh were due to arrive in an hour or so; Butler seems to have decided to link his men with the Seventh and press through Maryland to Washington, using their combined force as a ramrod.

About one o'clock in the morning, an hour before the Seventh arrived, Felton went to Butler's hotel and showed the Massachusetts officer the telegrams from Hicks and Brown, and perhaps other messages about the exploding situation in Baltimore. Butler asked for advice. The railroad man said he had been discussing options with, among other people, General Robert Patterson, whom Winfield Scott had just named commander of federal troops in this region. Patterson, a wealthy Philadelphia businessman and an old comrade of Scott's from the Mexican War days, was one of Pennsylvania's leading figures. Patterson had told Felton he was in an awkward position, since, by law, he could not give orders to volunteers until they had been mustered into federal service. Until then, they remained militiamen, meaning they could only be commanded by their governors, or officers like Butler acting as official representatives of the governors. General Patterson believed he could only *suggest* that Butler take his Eighth Massachusetts to Washington by way of Annapolis. As to how, specifically, he might get there, Felton proposed the same thing he would later say to Lefferts: take the train to Perryville, board the *Maryland*, and use it to carry him on to Annapolis. (Felton had just wired Captain M. Galloway, commander of that steamship, to load on plenty of coal so as to be ready to take incoming volunteers as far as Annapolis.)

Exactly what then happened is unclear, but perhaps Butler simply fell asleep. A few hours later one of his officers went to the railroad station to seek out Colonel Lefferts. The aide asked the New York colonel to come to the hotel to confer with Butler. Lefferts asked: who is this fellow Butler? The aide explained that Brigadier General Butler was in charge of all of Massachusetts's first wave of volunteers. Okay, said Lefferts, he would see him, but first he had to await replies he was expecting from telegrams he had sent to New York.

At ten o'clock that morning Butler bustled into the station to confront Lefferts. Would not the Seventh, Butler asked, join their brethren from Massachusetts? The two groups could go to Perryville together, and there, board the *Maryland*, which would steam them to Annapolis as a single unit. (In addition to the possibility that the *Maryland* might already have been destroyed by insurgents, Butler failed to consider two problems that made his proposal to Lefferts impossible. Felton had insufficient trains on hand to take both regiments, along with their equipment. Worse, the *Maryland* was too small. It would have required three trips to carry all the volunteers on hand between Perryville and Annapolis. In any case, Lefferts had already made arrangements to take the *Boston* and go via a different route. His trip would be longer in distance — about 350 miles, as opposed to 100 — but it was far more certain.)

Butler stomped off. At eleven o'clock he grumpily wired Governor Andrew that Lefferts "refused to march with me." Soon after that he gathered his troops, boarded Felton's train, and started southward. He saw himself as a solitary hero, valiantly embracing Destiny on his own. "If I succeed," he told Andrew, "success will justify me; if I fail, purity of intention will excuse want of judgment or rashness."

Butler and the Eighth left Philadelphia just before three o'clock that afternoon, giving them an hour or so head start on the Seventh. The two regiments were both heading for Annapolis, then Washington, but taking two very different routes. Butler's Eighth had the advantage of going a shorter distance, though the Massachusetts men had a problem that was bound to get worse: Butler had failed to think through the matter of provisions. His troops were already running out of food. If they needed several days to reach Washington, they would grow weak with hunger.

The enlisted men from the two states encountered one another at the railroad station and out in the streets of Philadelphia as they wandered in search of nourishment. One member of the Seventh remarked on the differences between them. The men of his regiment looked better, of course, far snappier. And they carried themselves with panache; they were "gay and careless." The New Englanders, he thought, were "earnest grim, determined," and unlike the Seventh, they were "badly equipped, haggard, unshorn." Yet, he observed, they retained "a manhood in their look." As he considered the regiments, "the one was courage in the rough; the other was courage burnished. The steel was the same in both."[128]

The town of Annapolis, perched on the southern side of the Severn River where that short waterway flowed into the Chesapeake, had a population of about 5,000, a fairly large proportion of whom were African Americans, most of them slaves. The city, a child of the seventeenth century, was attractive in its brick-clad way. The town's first colonists had arrived in 1649, making it almost as old as Boston. Chosen as the capital of the colony in 1695, Maryland's State House now sat atop a hill, a nice domed structure overlooking the Bay. When in session, Maryland's Senate and its House of Delegates debated within, and the governor and other state officials maintained their offices upstairs. At the moment only Hicks and a few officials were in town. Not far away, on another hill, was St. John's College, a hundred-and-fifty-year-old school occupying a four-story building. Closer to the river, on a small spit of land, perched the United States Naval Academy, surrounded on three sides by a brick wall. It had only been at this spot sixteen years. About a score of its midshipmen and some of its faculty had already departed to throw in their lots with the South.

Since the town was equidistant between Baltimore and Washington, Annapolis was a convenient stopping place. People coming here often arrived by water, their boats tying up at one of the many docks. When weather permitted one could travel from here by carriage or wagon to either Baltimore or the federal capital, though the roads hereabouts were mostly dirt and not well maintained. A railroad station stood on the far edge of town, a depot of the minuscule Annapolis & Elk Ridge Railroad, only about fourteen miles long. This railroad consisted primarily of a single engine, two or three baggage cars, and two passenger cars. Its rusty tracks and worm-filled wooden ties were tired and out of date. Its rails stretched west to the hamlet of Annapolis Junction, really only a watering station. Trains of the B&O carrying travelers between Baltimore and the national capital stopped at Annapolis Junction to take on water and wood for their engines. Passengers on the B&O generally stepped out to stretch and grab a sandwich and a drink or two at the Annapolis Junction Hotel, a few dusty feet away. The only significance of this small cluster of undistinguished buildings was that they constituted a critical link between the Northeast and Washington, D.C.

Ben Butler and the Eighth Massachusetts rumbled southward toward Perryville on Felton's rail line. Their passage was slow. Several times their train stopped to take on fuel, and at each place they were informed that more than 1,800 armed Baltimoreans awaited them somewhere south. Most of the Eighth were armed with good Springfield rifles, and these men were given ten cartridges each. But Butler had been so eager to hurry out of Boston that one of his companies had not received guns, and they — seamen from Marblehead, most of them — only carried axes. On the train ride to Perryville these axe-carriers were told their assignment. If the regiment encountered enemy wooden emplacements, the axe-wielding troops were expected to chop through the barrier, while being shot at by outraged Baltimoreans, as their rifle-bearing comrades returned fire.

The rumors turned out to be false. Perryville was quiet when the Eighth arrived, and Felton's ferry sat waiting for them. They boarded her, squeezed together like coal-dust-coated sausages on her deck, and began their journey again. It was dusk.

A few minutes before midnight their ship arrived outside Annapolis. They hoped to slip into the harbor before being discovered, but somebody on shore spotted their approach and fired off signal rockets. The captain of the *Maryland* halted immediately. His vessel was unarmed; he did not want to hazard going in until daylight. For all he knew, rebels in the town had taken over the Naval Academy and were, at this moment, aiming naval guns at them.

The *Maryland* anchored two miles out. Butler sent a boat to Annapolis bearing a young officer to check out the town's status. At some point during that night a rowboat came to the *Maryland* with a note from Governor Hicks addressed "to the Commander of the Volunteer Troops on board the steamer." (Obviously Hicks did not know the identity of the vessel, but he was aware that on it were Northern troops. Their presence made him nervous.) "Sir," he pleaded, "I would most earnestly advise that you do not land your men at Annapolis. The excitement here is very great, and I think that you should take your men elsewhere."[129]

Hicks was not being hysterical. He was correct. The white folks of Annapolis were indeed agitated. In addition to feeling a certain pro-Confederate bias, most felt uneasy about armed Yankees entering their town. If the troops had come from Massachusetts, as some rumors had it, perhaps they would attempt to free the slaves. Would the seemingly placid black servants of Annapolis suddenly rise and commit heinous acts of racial violence? Was the Civil War, hardly begun, about to become a revolution?

Annapolis, Monday, April 22, 1861

The men of the Seventh New York no longer looked quite so spiffy. The *Boston* was a small steamship, heavily overloaded.

On the Atlantic leg of their voyage she had rocked noticeably, and some New Yorkers became violently ill. But the sky had remained clear and the setting April sun had warmed the faces of the men lying on the deck. "A glorious, cloudless day," one of them called it. Loons and ducks, in formation, had floated gracefully overhead. During the evening, as their ship churned upwards through the quieter waters of the Bay, the cool breeze made the men, lying against bags of coal, glad they were wearing overcoats. It was a Sabbath evening. A handful of the regiment's best choristers assembled to sing hymns. Around them, their comrades sat and listened to the old, well-known tunes.

When they approached Chesapeake Bay, the New Yorkers learned from the captain of a passing vessel that Gosport had fallen, and this news seemed to mean that all Virginia had become dangerous ground, so even attempting the Potomac was out. The *Boston*, therefore, headed straight for Annapolis and halted during the wee hours, well outside the harbor, to await daylight. No one aboard noticed the *Maryland*, anchored in front of them in the murk.[130]

At dawn, when the sun peeked above the horizon, the men of the Seventh stared toward Annapolis. In the distance they saw a large, old-fashioned sailing vessel. This was the *Constitution*, the famous Old Ironsides, 204-feet long, her great masts swaying gracefully high above her. Once manned by 450 men, she had passed her prime, but she was still a beautiful old girl. The navy had given her to the Academy to use as a training vessel for midshipmen. What most struck the Seventh as they gazed at her was the fact that the American flag flapped above her. That could only mean Annapolis was still part of the Union. They felt relieved.

The fate of the *Constitution* had in fact been decided only a few hours earlier. The aide whom Butler had sent to look at the town had encountered the superintendent of the Naval Academy, Captain George Smith Blake, a balding, portly old gentleman. Captain Blake insisted he must immediately speak to the officer commanding the Massachusetts troops, and he was rowed to the *Maryland*. There, with tears in his eyes, he explained that local rebels planned to seize Old Ironsides. She might be something of a fossil, he said, but she and her guns could be a handsome addition to the Confederate cause. Besides, snatching this famous ship would be another coup for the Southerners. Blake said he lacked the manpower to move her out of harm's way and asked Butler for assistance. The Massachusetts lawyer volunteered his axe-carrying company from Marblehead. These fellows were seamen, he said, sailors and lobstermen; they could do it. And they did. They climbed into Old Ironsides and pulled up her anchors, embedded deep in the mud of the Severn. They muscled her guns onto the steamship *Maryland* which then hauled the distinguished old warship into deeper waters, where she was safe from capture.[131]

Unfortunately, as the heavily overloaded *Maryland* headed back toward Annapolis, she ran aground. Embarrassingly she was still stuck there on a mud bank when the *Boston,* with the Seventh aboard, entered the Severn. The New Yorkers observed the men of the Eighth throwing things over the *Maryland*'s side, and rushing like a herd of water buffalo from port to starboard to rock their ship loose. The captain of the *Boston* offered to help. A hawser was thrown across, and the *Boston* struggled, without success, to pull the *Maryland* free. Finally, the *Boston* moved on, heading toward the Academy, leaving the sweating men of the Eighth to gaze forlornly at her retreating stern.

The Seventh disembarked and stepped onto the grounds of the naval school. The mayor of Annapolis awaited them. He vigorously protested to Lefferts, to no avail. Lefferts jotted down a short message to his superiors in New York, telling them his regiment had arrived at Annapolis. "There is," he said, "considerable excitement."

Private Theodore Winthrop looked around and decided the town was "a picturesque old place." A midshipman pointed across the Severn at a white farmhouse, which he declared was the headquarters of locals who had plotted to seize the

Academy this very day, as well as the *Constitution*. That evening the gray-clad Seventh marched into the school's several buildings and settled down for the night.

After dark the Eighth transferred themselves onto the now-empty *Boston*, which deposited them also at the Academy. Butler's Massachusetts men were tired, thirsty, filthy, and hungry. They were forced to bivouac on the Academy's grounds, and they had not brought tents with them. Fortunately, although the air held a hint of coolness, it did not rain that night.[132]

While the enlisted men of the two regiments rested, their officers conferred about their next step. Immediately disputes arose. The problem stemmed from Butler's personality. A politician and a superb courtroom lawyer, he had a flair for the dramatic and liked to be the center of things, the star of the show with the spotlight shining squarely on his balding pate. Governor Andrew had placed him in command of Massachusetts's first volunteers — four regiments — but Scott had sidetracked two of these to Fort Monroe, and the Sixth Regiment, which had departed before the others, had already passed through Baltimore and reached the capital. So here was Butler, expecting to lead a large brigade, one that would save America, but it now turned out he only commanded a partially armed crew of Massachusetts militiamen. The arrival of the Seventh New York seemed to give him an opening — and Butler was an opportunist by nature. He believed — or at least convinced himself — that the Articles of War stipulated that he commanded both regiments. He would later quote a 1795 federal statute, which stated that militiamen suppressing a rebellion had to follow the same rules as regular troops. He was aware that whenever units of regulars marched together, the officer with the highest rank was in charge. He bore the title of brigadier general, whereas Lefferts was only a colonel, so it seemed obvious he had the right to give orders.

Butler was ignoring the reality that both he and Lefferts had been granted their military ranks by their respective governors, and that neither regiment had yet been officially mustered into federal service, so each unit still remained legally in the service of their individual states. A simple proof of this was their pay. Until they took the federal oath, their home states were required to provide them with wages. Yet to Butler, such matters amounted to mere quibbling. He wanted to command, and insisted on it. Lefferts disagreed. Several scenes ensued.

The first incident occurred even before the Eighth limped off the stranded *Maryland*. While those poor fellows were heaving boxes into the Severn and running from one side of the ship to the other, Butler had himself rowed to the Academy. There he spoke to Lefferts. Or as he worded it in his later recollections: "Colonel Lefferts reported to me at my headquarters on the grounds of the academy." At first the conversation seemed to go all right, despite their differences back in Philadelphia, thirty hours earlier. Butler said he would like to use the *Boston* to bring his regiment ashore once Lefferts's men had disembarked. Lefferts agreed. Although he had personally paid the rental fee for the vessel, permitting the Eighth to use it would not only be considerate, but reasonable (and, as we have seen, this was accomplished).

The two commanders then talked about what should be done next. As Butler would recall it, he urged Lefferts to press on toward Washington "at once" (presumably the next morning), but that Lefferts resisted because of an innate overcautiousness. In fact, their disagreement was a replay of their Philadelphia dispute: each wished to proceed by a different route. Lefferts wanted to march straight toward the capital following the wagon road. It seemed, to him, absurd to go west along the railroad line. If the train was working, that idea would have seemed logical, but local men — including Governor Hicks — had just informed them that Maryland insurgents had recently destroyed the tracks. Utilizing a train, therefore, appeared impossible, and there would be no advantage to marching westward toward Annapolis Junction, then south to Washington. Proceeding by that route, the distance would be much greater than taking the hypotenuse which the wagon road represented. Also, Lefferts had heard that bushwhackers were awaiting them at Annapolis Junction. (This rumor was not entirely false. Although Lefferts's informants, intentionally or unintentionally, exaggerated the tally, three companies of Maryland horsemen had been lingering at the Junction or near it — maybe fifty to a hundred men. The *Baltimore Sun* had been openly reporting that they were there, that they were "determined to give the Northern troops a fight in their march to the capital," though the newspaper did admit the number of horsemen at Annapolis Junction was dwindling after "exhausting service.")

Whichever route he took, Lefferts was concerned about one problem: he had neither wagons nor horses. Carrying their provisions and personal belongings would be hard enough, but the real problem involved two howitzers they had brought with them, and the ammunition and equipment that, of necessity, accompanied artillery. If nothing else, given the rumored bands of guerrillas, these guns might enable the Seventh to break through to the capital. One of his officers wrote a note home that the regiment would be leaving soon, but they had no horses and would have to go by forced marches. "We expect to have fighting by the way to Washington." He added: "Men in good spirits."[133]

Although Butler would later insist he himself planned from the beginning to follow the tracks of the Annapolis & Elk Ridge Railroad, the claim is dubious. He too had been told the train was unusable. His real disagreement with Lefferts was over his right to command the New Yorkers.

By nature Butler was disputatious; he hated to compromise. He pressed the New York colonel. Lefferts gave the Massachusetts lawyer permission to address the other officers of the Seventh, but when Butler did so, they also refused to be compliant. "Colonel Lefferts," Butler finally blurted out, virtually stamping his foot, "by the Articles of War, I am in command." He threatened to spread word that the men of the Seventh Regiment were just a bunch of overdressed sissies. "And that," Butler recalled, "was the last communication that I had in person with Colonel Lefferts."[134] (Actually this latter statement was not completely true. Late in the evening Lefferts sent a note to Butler, whom Lefferts dryly addressed as the person "Commanding Mass. Volunteers." It read: "I do not deem it proper, under the circumstances, to cooperate with the proposed march by railroad." Then the next morning, either by note or in person, Butler chastised Lefferts for not seizing the railroad station, as Butler had "ordered." Lefferts calmly replied he had checked out the depot and found it empty. For this "insubordination," Butler "threatened arrests and court-martials"[*sic*].[135])

Annapolis, Tuesday, April 23, 1861

All at once, Lefferts altered his plans. A messenger arrived from Washington, one of eight men who had been sent to Annapolis by Winfield Scott. Six of the messengers had been either captured along the way or forced to turn around. An eighth actually arrived a bit later and reinforced the communication, which was, in substance: Washington City is at this moment still free, but she is in danger. Hurry! And, if possible, come by train. (General Scott was obviously concerned about the federal capital receiving regular supplies. He could not be sure how long the siege would last. Not only would incoming troops need provisions, but eventually the civilian population would, as well. If goods could not be brought up the Potomac—and given the recent fall of Gosport, he could hardly be confident about free passage on that river—he wanted the use of a railroad, if possible. If not, he still wanted the troops as expeditiously as possible.) These orders from Scott were enough for Lefferts.

Meanwhile Ben Butler, accompanied by two companies of his men, had gone to seize the railroad depot. (It is not clear whether he did this before or after Scott's message got through, whether he took this action out of aggressiveness or because of Scott's entreaty. Butler would later claim that during these days he acted completely on his own.) The railroad station consisted of several buildings — sheds, mostly. After examining a few, Butler pointed to another and asked the station master what was in it. "Nothing," the man replied. Besides, the station master added, he had no key for that particular storeroom. This seemed suspicious and Butler ordered the building's door broken. Inside sat an engine. She was rusty and ancient, and she had quite recently been partially dismantled, obviously to make her unusable. Butler turned to his troops and asked if they knew anything about trains. Serendipity! A private stepped forward: Charles S. Homans, twenty-six, of Beverly, Massachusetts, a coastal town about fifteen miles north of Boston. "That engine was made in our shop," he announced. "I guess I can fix her up, and run her."

And so he did. Parts that had been taken from the engine were found nearby. Private Homans clanked them into place. (A few accounts even insist that Homans had long ago scratched his name on the engine and now proudly showed off his foresight.) In a few hours he had the machine fired up and running. During the next two days, acting as engineer, he would drive this train. Doing so, this obscure enlisted man served his country well.

While Homans was hammering and bolting the J. H. Nicholson (as the engine was called) back together, Butler checked to see whether any members of his Eighth Massachusetts had ever laid railroad tracks. Twenty of them had, and they appeared. He ordered the two companies of infantrymen at the depot to accompany these twenty men and head down the tracks, checking them for damage, repairing any breaks in the line they encountered if they could. (The second messenger from Washington, who had just arrived, told them he had seen groups of bushwhackers riding the roads — so the federal troops should be watchful.)

Late that second evening in Annapolis, having learned that Lefferts and the Seventh would now be willing to accompany the Massachusetts regiment after all, Butler penned "general orders," as though he truly were in command. These declared that the Eighth's two advance companies would halt a few miles out of Annapolis and await a forward battalion of the Seventh, which would come with the train. Once the front companies of the two regiments were melded, the train would return and pick up more of the Eighth, drop these men off, and go back for more. And so on. The last troops to leave Annapolis, according to Butler's note, would be a portion of the Seventh. Lefferts was ordered to "cooperate."[136]

As for himself, Butler decided he would remain in Annapolis. Several hours earlier, ships carrying four more regiments of volunteers had sailed into the harbor. Three of these were from New York, the other had been sent by Rhode Island. The Rhode Islanders were well supplied by a civilian accompanying them, Governor William Sprague, but the New Yorkers suffered from the haste of their departure. (The men of the Seventy-first Regiment, for example, had no knapsacks; most had to carry their personal stuff in valises or roped-up bundles, which they gripped tightly in their hands, and which swung awkwardly against their legs as they walked.) Butler planned to oversee the disembarkation of these four new regiments and their organization. Once he had hurried them toward the capital, which ought to take at least a day or two, he would await the arrival of others. He would act as an expediter. The task would be important, one likely to increase his profile. Here in Annapolis he could claim to be the highest-ranking officer, but if he continued on to Washington, he would be outranked by many others.

As an exceedingly ambitious man, Ben Butler always liked to keep his options open. Before going to sleep that night he wrote his wife, Sarah. "I have worked like a horse," he told her, "slept not two hours a night." He described some of his successes, like saving Old Ironsides and seizing Annapolis. "I think," he said, "no man has won more in ten days that I have." (Officials in Washington saw an advantage in using this rather prominent Democrat. As in the case of getting the support of Stephen Douglas, Butler's participation would prevent political opponents from claiming that this war, just under way, was merely a "Republican crusade." Four days later, Scott officially created the Department of Annapolis, comprising that town and the pathway to Washington, and put General Butler in charge.)[137]

A kind of footrace was about to develop out beyond Annapolis. On one side would be the men of the Seventh New York plus a portion of the Eighth Massachusetts, stumbling along the wormy ties of the Annapolis & Elk Ridge Railroad. On the other was a shadowy force. The contest between these opponents involved the future of the nation. If reinforcements (like the Seventh and Eighth) did not arrive in Washington soon, the lure of capturing the capital would almost certainly prove too enticing to audacious, opportunistic men in Virginia and Maryland. A bundle of cash lying on a sidewalk will stay ungrabbed for only so long. Lincoln was worried; so was Scott.

Maryland's insurgents had done a fairly good job of dismantling the tracks that stretched out of Annapolis, given the fact they had only started the task just before the Yankee troops began their march. These unnamed guerrillas performed three types of demolition.

Their least effective activity consisted of prying up rails and ties and flinging them aside into nearby bushes. Doing this might have seemed a good idea, but in fact served only as a nuisance. The oncoming Yankees quickly recognized the pattern. Their own skirmishers, walking ahead on either side, would discover gaps in the rails, search for the lost pieces, find them, and toss them back in the direction of the track, then move on. Behind them, men worked speedily to hammer the ties back into place.

The guerrillas had a second method that worked better; they carried the ripped-up materials off with them. It is likely these guerrillas had wagons, and it is therefore probable that at least two different bands of insurgents were at work. Yet it turned out that even this method did not stop their oncoming foes. The railroad company had built a few sidings so its trains could travel simultaneously from both directions. The Yankees found these sidings, yanked up their rails and sleepers, and carried the materials with them as handy spares.

The third method of destruction worked best: burning a wooden trestle. Unfortunately for the cause of the guerrillas, the Annapolis & Elk Ridge line passed across a flat topography. The railroad had only one relatively important span, and even it was little more than sixteen feet across. The skill and muscles of the Yankees would be tested by its destruction.

The main thing the guerrillas accomplished was to slow down the inexorable movement of the Yankees. But would that prove enough?

Along the tracks, Wednesday, April 24, 1861

When the federal troops left Annapolis, they did not know what to expect. It was early morning as the Seventh marched out of town. Early-rising locals stared at them, their hooded eyes hiding emotions. As Theodore Winthrop said, "We really knew little more of the country before us than Cortes knew of Mexico." Winthrop, the inveterate tramper, was entranced, his senses in tune with nature's wonders. "The air sings with birds," he mused. "The chestnut-leaves sparkle. Frogs whistle in the warm spring morning."[138] Soon he and his companions heard a train rattling toward them from back at the depot. Private Homans was driving it, an armed sentry on either side of him watching for bushwhackers. His engine pulled two passenger cars crammed with two of the Seventh's companies. Pushed along in front of Homans's engine were two flatcars (which had been freight cars until the day before, when their walls had been sawn off). The howitzers, the ammunition, and certain equipment like medical supplies sat on these flatcars. Gunners had loaded a howitzer with canister and placed it on the front car so it aimed in the direction of any approaching attack force. Sixteen artillerists stood by it, ready to open fire.

The Seventh with the train now just behind them continued down the line. They had not gone far when they came to the two companies of the Eighth assigned by Butler to guard the first few miles of track. The Massachusetts men were glad to see the New Yorkers. This region was unpopulated and barren, not even a schoolhouse or rustic church to punctuate the monotonous landscape, and breaks in the tracks had shown that enemy guerrillas were nearby. The New Englanders mentioned that they were hungry and thirsty, that Butler had not thought to provide them with provisions. The dandies of the Seventh generously reached into their bags and shared food and drink with their new friends.

Together they started off. In a few minutes they spotted insurgents in the distance trying to jimmy up a few rails. The rebels scurried away before they could be captured. The men of the Eighth and Seventh repaired the damaged track and began marching again. The sun, high in the skies now, beat fiercely on their shoulders, and a few, then a few more, faltered. It turned out to have been far easier to stride down a few city blocks under the admiring gazes of fashionable ladies and shopgirls than to stumble along railroad ties or through the soft, clinging, six-inch-deep sandy Maryland soil. Their feet hurt. Shoulders ached. Faces used to softer indoor lighting dripped with sweat and reddened—sometimes turning unhealthily ruby. The sickest men were laid on the train. Some of these overheated unfortunates were New Yorkers, others from Massachusetts. Status and geography seemed to have little to do with it.

Private Winthrop was having a grand time. Although previously unsuccessful at the practice of law or writing, his legs were sturdy, his back strong. He felt something inside himself soar. For the first time in his life, this lonely man found that he enjoyed the companionship of his fellows. This hike was a fine adventure, and the mission important. But it was more than that. Up to this moment, as he wryly put it, his motto had always been one of individualism: not *e pluribus unum* (out of many, one), but *in pluribus unum* (in the midst of many, one). Now he felt a glow: he had a sense of belonging.[139]

Private Homans braked the train; he intended to head back to Annapolis to pick up more volunteers. Those in the Seventh who had been sitting inside the passenger cars stepped down. The two platform cars were unhitched from the front of the engine, and ropes were attached to the now-stationary flatcars. Men of the Seventh, stepping forward, grasped the lines and began pulling. If necessary they would drag these cars and their contents all the way to Annapolis Junction, then, maybe, to Washington. The salty odor of their perspiration mixed with the sweet aroma of spring blossoms and marsh grass.

Their skirmishers crept forward, simultaneously checking along the sides, especially whenever they passed through thickets. Now and then they could espy men in the distance, riding away. The New Yorkers often chased after them, without success. The marchers passed a few hovels. Most were empty, though one farmer who had remained at his place reluctantly sold them eggs, at an exorbitant price.

About eight miles or so out of Annapolis they found the burned trestle. It had crossed a gulch twenty feet deep. Unless they could fix it they would be stymied. They could walk from here to the Junction, but they would have to leave the howitzers. Since they had heard that a large force of insurgents awaited them at Annapolis Junction, the guns seemed important. A member of the Seventh stepped forward. He said he was an engineer and thought he knew how to repair the bridge. The men cut some trees down, shaped them into approximate timbers, and rammed them into place. It took the crew three hours, but the jerry-built span seemed as though it just might hold. They tried dragging the platform cars across it, pronounced themselves satisfied, and continued on.

Late in the afternoon a fierce storm hammered them. It reduced the heat of the air, but their damp clothing now chafed and made them more miserable. With nightfall came other problems.

The first moonlight provided enough light to march without slowing down much. Then cloud cover obscured the moon, and the night grew black. Men tumbled down the embankments on either side. The pace of the entire column slowed. Whenever they discovered gaps in the track now, they had more trouble finding the missing rails. About midnight the temperature dropped, a lot. A chilling dampness oozed from the swamps on either side. One man would recall: "Most of us had not slept for four nights, and as the night advanced our march was almost a stagger." He became so exhausted he fell asleep while walking.[140]

In Washington, Winfield Scott wondered where the capital's alleged saviors were. Several of the messengers he had sent northward returned and said they had been unable to get through to Annapolis. The general had enough foresight to have ordered the seizure of the railroad station in the capital, just in case its owners or workmen thought about hindering things. Charles Stone and some of his District militiamen carried out the order. They were able to capture two engines at the depot and a bunch of cars.

On Wednesday one of these two trains filled with District militiamen headed toward Annapolis Junction. Here and there, some of these men dropped from the cars to guard vulnerable bridges. The train went as far as the Junction, but finding no one there, returned to the District. Stone's volunteers intended to return each day until troops from the North finally arrived.[141]

Thursday, April 25, 1861

In Washington this morning, General Scott's orders were extraordinarily ominous: "From the known assemblage near this city of numerous hostile bodies of troops, it is evident that an attack upon it may be expected at any moment."[142]

At Annapolis Junction, the time was between three and four o'clock in the morning when exhausted members of the Seventh, skirmishing in front, spilled out of some woods and realized they were but a mile or two from their immediate goal, the railroad station. About 150 of the Seventh, led by Colonel Lefferts, crept ahead to check out the hamlet. The rest of the tired troops dropped to the ground and lay there, half-wondering if they would soon be hearing shots.

Nothing. Most of the men fell asleep. Perhaps an hour later Lefferts returned. Everything at the Junction was quiet. Until daylight, the Seventh would remain there. If they wanted to, he said, his men could light fires. A few did to keep warm, others to brew coffee. Some men foraged. In the next few hours the hotel at the Junction did a fine business selling sandwiches and booze. Local inhabitants realized the Yankees had not come to pillage. Portions of the populace came to chat and peddle edibles.[143]

About nine o'clock that morning, a train from Washington, coming up on its second run, arrived at the station. The train turned out to be not large enough to carry both the Seventh and those members of the Eighth who had arrived here with them, so the Eighth stayed behind, awaiting their comrades. The cars, crammed with tired New Yorkers, started southward, toward the capital.

Lucius Chittenden, a high-ranking clerk at the Treasury Department, had been keeping a diary. Sometime that morning he jotted an angry note: no mail had come, again. Everything was still quiet. He found himself in a paroxysm of rage. "Shame!" he wrote furiously. "That this should be in the capital of the United States."

About two miles from Chittenden, up the hill from the empty corridors of the Treasury, the men of the Sixth Massachusetts who had fought their way through Baltimore six days earlier were drilling outside the Capitol when they heard a train whistle and turned to stare toward the empty station a couple of blocks away.

Inside the stuffy passenger cars, many of the Seventh were still uncertain about the status of Washington. Maybe it had fallen, even in the last few hours. When their train slowed and blew its whistle, they peered out its windows. And there, high above the Capitol, fluttered the American flag. The volunteers inside the cars started cheering. Through the open windows, their voices carried.

The Sixth Massachusetts heard the shouts and saw the waving arms. They themselves burst out with a great yell. This bellow of happiness could be heard a mile away. Citizens came running from all directions. They felt they had just been saved. Pell-mell, they ran. Many folks had been lingering near the station the previous two days, only to drift away forlornly each evening, then returning to the depot again each morning. They, too, yelped their delight. And the sounds of joy flowed in waves, backward, down toward Executive Square. At the White House, Abraham Lincoln heard it. And, in his office, so did Winfield Scott.

It took the Seventh an hour to assemble properly at the depot. As they brushed themselves off, yanked at their no-longer-really-white crossbelts, and stepped into rumpled rows, citizens around them beamed. Finally the Seventh was ready. So was their forty-four-man band, which led off down the hill toward Executive Square. The men of the Seventh straightened their spines as best they could, and started. All things considered, they looked fairly well pulled-together.

They still had a two-mile march. But the sky was clear, the temperature not too warm. Along their route down Pennsylvania Avenue, people stood at windows, waving. Crowds thronged rooftops and sidewalks, swinging handkerchiefs, screaming their elation, their thanks. Across the District, church bells pealed. The Seventh marched past Willard's and onto the grounds of the White House, and passed beneath its very eaves, saluting the president of the United States, who stood at his doorway wigwagging his large hand in the air, again and again. A reporter, observing Lincoln, said the president "smiled all over."[144]

Colonel Lefferts dismissed his men, then entered the White House to share with the president his observations about Annapolis, and about Maryland in general.

The volunteers of the Seventh, young men like Private Theodore Winthrop, drifted off, most of them to hotels like Willard's or Brown's or the National. They were in the mood for something savory to eat, something to quench their thirst. A few of the more fastidious went in search of clean linen. Others looked for barbers.

At the Treasury, Lucius Chittenden was immensely glad. He had watched as the Seventh marched right past his office in the Treasury. He could still hear the music of their band and the manly warmth of some of their voices. He wanted to jot down his reactions immediately. Sitting at his desk, he wrote: "Thank God for this hour! A thousand cheers for New York!!" He tried to find the proper words. "How they came, we know not, nor do we care. It is enough to know that they are here and the Capital of the Nation is safe! There were many wet faces as this noble regiment marched up Pennsylvania Avenue, and I do not deny that mine was one."[145]

CHAPTER SIXTEEN

The Best Defense

Once the Seventh had ingested the necessary ablutions and satisfied certain prandial (and other) needs, they wandered up to the Capitol. They had been assigned the chamber of the House. Like the volunteers of the Sixth Massachusetts, still ensconced in the Senate, they found their temporary digs quite fun. Sitting at dignified desks, they, too, held burlesque debates. Good orators were cheered, bad ones taunted. The Eighth Massachusetts finally appeared the next day, somewhat the worse for wear, and took quarters in the Rotunda.

The next morning, Saturday, a commercial ship from New York, the *Daylight,* arrived at Washington's docks. She symbolized an important change. She was the first privately chartered, unarmed vessel to steam up the Potomac since the crisis came to a head a week earlier. Clearly the Virginians had not — at least not yet — planted guns along the river to impede traffic. At the very least, the Potomac could become as valuable an artery as the Annapolis route.

Among the items the *Daylight* brought were foodstuffs for the Seventh. The telegram Lefferts had sent to New York from Philadelphia had just paid off, handsomely. The men of the Seventh refused to hoard these treasures; they invited their hungry friends of the Eighth to join them in a fine feast. These two regiments — true comrades-in-arms from the hours of their exhausting trek to the Junction, the clerks and dandies from New York, the farmers and fishermen and mechanics from Massachusetts — assembled beneath the partially completed dome of the Rotunda. The Seventh rolled out fifteen or twenty kegs of lager, brought in boxes of citrus fruits, beef, wheels of cheese, bread and biscuits, and good cigars. For hours the air was redolent with smoke and good cheer. That evening, before returning to their sleeping quarters in the House, the Seventh even handled $500 to the Eighth, money they had individually raised for an unfortunate fellow from Beverly, Massachusetts, whose foot had been crushed in an accident on the way to Washington. (The men of the Eighth soon passed a resolution of thanks for all the generosity and the bonhomie: "No words can do it justice or do justice to our gratitude." The notion about states' rights seemed, at this moment, a puny thing compared to the embrace of nationalism, or at least interstate hospitality.)[146]

The Seventh soon moved from the Capitol. When their tents and cooking gear arrived, they took up residence on the grounds of a lovely estate a couple of miles back from the Potomac. James Madison had first lived at this place; other presidents had visited it. If one had to endure camping out, this spot was really quite pleasant. Its oak-lined driveway entered from Fourteenth Street, and it stood serenely on a hill, providing a fine view of the river. The Seventh's band gave evening concerts, and folks, including the president and his wife and boys, often came by, listened to the music, and watched the regiment spin through its elaborate drills. Citizens, male and female, cheerfully drifted about the encampment, selling treats, shooting the breeze, flirting. The "war" seemed far away, almost nonexistent.

In the next few weeks additional regiments found their way to Washington. At first the War Department was overwhelmed. With a lack of housing, it placed volunteers in assorted government buildings, in warehouses, and even the Palace of Aladdin just behind City Hall. Like the wizard's assistant in *Fantasia*, Secretary Cameron felt inundated by far too much of a good thing. The government, having asked for volunteers, had to come to grips with insufficient housing and provisions, to say nothing of arms and ammunition. Cameron asked the governors to stop sending so many men, to keep them at home until called for. But thousands of volunteers still poured into the capital.

It was partly a matter of state pride. William Sprague, the governor of Rhode Island, had wired Cameron back on April 17: "We are using every exertion to be first in the field." Three days later, even though Rhode Island was only able to assemble half a regiment, Sprague led those 544 volunteers onto a ship, and they steamed off. They landed in Annapolis and followed the path the Seventh had taken. They, too, repaired tracks along the way, because guerrillas had once again yanked up rails, but all in all, their trek was rather uneventful. When they arrived in Washington they were quartered in the Patent Office. As one of them would later recall, they found this aspect of their stay in the federal capital quite captivating. "Here were models of all kinds of machines, which our mechanics viewed with perpetual interest. Here were articles of value from beyond the sea, the gifts of foreign princes to our own rulers. Here, also, were the relics of heroic times — the original Declaration of Independence; the staff of Franklin; the sword, the uniform, and the camp chest of Washington."

After a while, they marched to a spot on a hill not far from the Seventh's encampment. The Rhode Islanders proved themselves an inventive, energetic crew. They had few tents, but they built themselves a little village of board huts. Each structure housed eighteen men, who decorated their residences to fit their tastes: flowers, curtains, flags, musical instruments. The regiment also built brick cooking facilities, and they were soon able to brew 960 gallons of coffee, grill 1,300 pounds of meat, and bake hundreds of loaves of bread, even gingerbread, each day. They gave names to their regimental "streets," and called the place Camp Sprague. Their indulgent millionaire governor fussed over them, and their encampment was recognized as the best organized and most hygienic in Washington.[147]

———

Soon scores of other camps checkerboarded the District. Some volunteers slept in tents, which the Army had found somewhere, or in temporary wooden sheds of dubious quality, hammered together. Within a few weeks the previously terrified capital contained tens of thousands of troops tramping up and down its broad avenues.

The impact of their arrival spread beyond Washington. Maryland altered its posture. If it had been drifting toward secession — or even neutrality — much of its population soon embraced the Union. Perhaps its new stance was inevitable. Baltimore, by far the state's most important city, actually contained more unionists than secessionists, though the unionists had remained rather muted during the crisis. The collapse of Baltimore's economy resulting from cutting itself off from most of the rest of the nation hurt too many pocketbooks. Soon, Baltimore appeared chastened. Sometimes economic deprivation cows a population faster than bullets.

Annapolis was the first state capital during the Civil War taken by an outside military force. If nothing else, this fact was an important symbol and should have suggested to Confederates and would-be Confederates the fierce determination of Lincoln. A few days later a ship bedecked with American flags sailed into Baltimore's harbor. As the boat passed Fort McHenry, the men aboard her saw the fort's United States banner floating o'er her ramparts, and started to shout happily. The fort showed her appreciation by dipping its flag, like a girl curtseying "thank you."

Winfield Scott remained concerned. He still received reports that Virginians were massing across the Potomac. If they brought batteries to Arlington Heights, within artillery range of the White House, they could destroy it, as well as the War Department, the Treasury, and other federal buildings. If that occurred the United States government would seem too weak to defend itself. The British might decide, after all, to recognize the Confederacy or offer it military aid.

General Scott also worried about Alexandria, the linchpin to Northern Virginia. Ships flying the United States flag were steaming watchfully past Alexandria, but Scott knew the rebels on the Virginia side could at any time erect gun emplacements somewhere along the Potomac to interdict river traffic. A battalion of rebel troops was known to be stationed in Alexandria, and he was aware they had at least one battery of artillery of their own, plus more guns available to them. The *Baltimore Sun* had a report in its April 23 issue: "At Alexandria the citizens are preparing an iron battery, similar to that used at Charleston [in the attack on Fort Sumter], for the purpose no doubt of preventing government vessels from passing up or down river." The old general shared his concerns with the president.

Lincoln continued to focus his spyglass on the Potomac. He watched the masts of sailboats gliding silently past and saw puffs of black smoke rising from steamboat engines, and he wondered if all those ships were loyal. On May 7 John Hay went to speak to him and observed Lincoln "calmly looking out of the window at the smoke of two Navy steamers puffing up the way, resting the end of the telescope on his toes sublime."[148]

Was Virginia, in fact, subtly becoming more aggressive? The question really might be worded: was Robert E. Lee having second thoughts about his own cautiousness? The answer is not simple. Lee remained uneasy about Virginia's limited supply of military necessities. On May 10 he chided Colonel Jackson, now in charge of the forces in Harpers Ferry, when Lee learned the colonel had sent a portion of his troops across the bridge into Maryland to occupy high ground there. Lee considered this action militarily imprudent, yet one of his scolding words offers a fascinating window into his thinking: "The true policy is to act on the defensive," he began, which certainly sounds like Lee had not altered his stance. But he added this line: "I fear you may have been *premature* in occupying the heights of Maryland with so strong a force near you [emphasis added]."

Changes were at work in Virginia. The referendum on ratification would take place on May 23, and the capital of the Confederacy would shortly transfer itself to Richmond.[149]

A hidden issue in the push-pull of General Scott's planning
was politics. Prominent Northerners were growing dissatisfied
with Lincoln's apparent inaction. States had been sending
thousands of enthusiastic volunteers to Washington, along
with mountains of supplies and guns. Why was there not more
movement? On April 23 a New York attorney, Hiram Barney,
who had many powerful friends, wrote Secretary Chase that
New York's merchants wanted the "instant reopening" of all
rail lines between Philadelphia and Washington, "at whatever
cost." And he warned, in a strong sentence that he boldly underlined: *"Unless that is done, the administration will be severely censured and its moral hold on the community will be lost."*

On May 7 a gaggle of politicians came to the White House
to confront Lincoln. These men constituted a committee representing the governors of six Northern states: Ohio, Pennsylvania, Illinois, Wisconsin, Indiana, and Michigan. The committee
wanted the president to know that their governors pledged the
full resources of their states to the war, but they insisted on
more vigor.[150]

The truth was, though Lincoln probably did not clarify this
to the committee, plans were already bubbling.

During the previous half year, first under Buchanan, then Lincoln, Winfield Scott had given much thought to the situation.
His analysis was based on certain precepts.

First, he hated useless killing. He declared that "no Christian nation can be justified in waging war in such a way as shall
destroy 501 lives, when the object of the war can be attained at
a cost of 500. Every man killed beyond the number absolutely
required, is murdered." The whole point of war, in his opinion,
was to compel the enemy to accept your will, nothing more.
Any loss of life beyond the barest minimum was "unjustifiable
homicide." During the Mexican War he had strained to avoid

unnecessary losses—of his own soldiers, or Mexicans. His movements there had been daring but never bloodthirsty.

Second, he had little respect for civilian soldiers, the very kind of volunteers now rushing to Washington to join the colors. They might be fervent patriots, he thought, but their ignorance of military facts would cause problems. They resisted discipline—in camp and out. Once in motion they too often plundered and raped their way across a ravaged landscape. In battle they were, at best, shaky. He had seen it before, far too often. Their behavior in Mexico had bothered him as a soldier and as a devout Christian.

Third, he knew the South and Southerners. He was positive they would be an obstinate foe, fighting ferociously for what they considered their own soil. Moreover, as a Virginian, he knew that if the Union flung an army in the direction of Richmond, geography would be on the side of the rebels. Most rivers in Virginia flowed eastward from the Appalachians toward the sea, creating a series of moats, behind which Confederate armies could stand and wait. He also suspected that the heat of a Southern summer might weaken the stamina of Northern soldiers.

Finally, he was suspicious of emotionalism. Actions based on the childish fervor of rage or patriotism were often foolhardy. "I have lived long enough to know," he said, "that human resentment is a very bad foundation for a public policy." He of course heard the voices beginning to squeal for an immediate all-out attack on the South, but he resisted their chorus.

He had a master plan that would take time, and patience. He openly and often spoke of it. Word about it spread. Disdainful newspapers called it his Anaconda Plan. He proposed that the United States significantly expand its naval power and use that force to create a blockade that would squeeze off the South's sea trade. Simultaneously he would *threaten* Virginia with a large and menacing army stationed in Washington, pinning Confederate troops there into a defensive posture. He would meanwhile create a second massive army in the West.

When autumn and cooler weather arrived, he would roll that Western force down the Mississippi River toward New Orleans. As in his campaign against the Mexicans, this army would be rumbling through less-inhabited sectors, thereby reducing bloodshed. He believed this would display to Southerners both the military might of the federal government and its determination. The South would come to its senses before too many deaths pressed it into an implacable mood.[151]

He recognized that his Anaconda Plan was long range, and that it would not solve the immediate problem of Washington's vulnerability. He told Lincoln that although he opposed striking *deeply* into Virginia at the moment, Union troops ought to cross the Potomac and station themselves on Arlington Heights as soon as possible, simply as a precautionary measure.

As a young man Lincoln had served a few months as a volunteer soldier in Illinois, but he knew he had much to learn about war. When General Scott spoke about military matters, Lincoln listened. He agreed to send troops across the river. The only questions involved the precise date they would cross, and exactly where they would then head.

Toward the end of April, young John Hay dropped into Nicolay's office. Two visitors were already there: Carl Schurz and Jim Lane. As Hay entered, he noticed Lane intently using a telescope to stare across the Potomac at Alexandria. The fiery Lane was outraged by what he was observing. High above the roofs of that Virginia town was a large Confederate flag. He did not like it. "Let me tell you," he muttered, "we have got to whip these scoundrels like hell, Carl Schurz. They did a good thing stoning our men at Baltimore and shooting away the flag at Sumter. It has set the great North a-howling for blood, and they'll have it."

On May 16, a week before Virginia's referendum on secession, the *Alexandria Gazette* reprinted an article that had originally appeared in a New York newspaper. According to the item, Senator Benjamin F. Wade of Ohio had recently visited the White House, where President Lincoln showed him a telescope he had been using to watch things. Ben Wade peered through the glass, and he too turned his attention to Alexandria, several miles away. The telescope was powerful enough that he could make out details. He noticed a secession flag (presumably the same one), and it offended him. Wade, as pugnacious as Lane, asked the president how long such an obnoxious rag in plain sight would be tolerated. According to the article, now being read in Alexandria, Mr. Lincoln mildly replied that "he did not think it would wave there long."[152]

Winfield Scott had assigned Brigadier General Joseph K. F. Mansfield to command what was termed the military district of Washington. Mansfield had reviewed his available manpower (mostly the incoming volunteer regiments). Scott asked for his opinion about the situation. The District of Columbia, Mansfield was confident, was now relatively safe, but he was concerned about Arlington Heights across the way. "It is clear to my mind," he said, "that the city is liable to be bombarded at the will of the enemy, unless we occupy the ground." Mansfield recognized that crossing to Virginia "would create much excitement," but considered it necessary.

A month earlier, as we have seen, Lincoln had told several concerned citizens of Maryland he had no intention of using the troops he had called to Washington for anything other than the defense of Washington. On April 24, in the midst of that week's crisis atmosphere, he had written Reverdy Johnson, the prominent Marylander, emphatically underlining certain words: "I *do* say the sole purpose of bringing troops *here* is to defend this capital. I *do* say I have no purpose to *invade* Virginia, with them or any other troops." But he appended a lawyerly, weasel-phrase: "as I understand *invasion*." In what seemed a casual aside, he mentioned he *might* choose to send volunteers across the Potomac, if Virginians (or Confederate troops) threatened to "assail" the capital. He might opt, he said, to move aggressively if Virginia or others built batteries that could bombard the District.

A couple of weeks later, Lincoln and his cabinet secretly agreed on a thrust into Virginia. They told Scott he must wait until after Virginia held her referendum on May 23 — but no longer.[153]

The Plan

At least one member of the administration was looking beyond Arlington Heights. On May 16 Major Irvin McDowell wrote Secretary Chase. McDowell was a native of Ohio, Chase's home state. Chase appreciated the officer, who like himself was both intelligent and a teetotaler. In the past two or three weeks Lincoln had handed over a surprising number of military details to the Treasury chief, to relieve the overburdened Cameron of some onerous tasks. Since then Chase had sought out McDowell and asked his opinion of military steps the administration ought to consider. As it turned out, McDowell had been mulling over an ambitious lunge into Virginia. He mentioned a few highlights of his thinking. Chase asked him to jot down these ideas in an organized fashion. McDowell had a well-disciplined mind and accepted the assignment with pleasure. The note he sent Chase described an operation that would push the enemy away from the banks of the Potomac. Moreover, he proposed a drive well inland into northern Virginia, all the way to a railroad depot called Manassas Junction. Secretary Chase was intrigued, but the secretary learned General Scott had in mind a more measured plan, one meant simply to take and hold Arlington Heights. Chase filed McDowell's plan, and sat back to see how Scott's ideas would work out.[154]

When Scott and Mansfield sat down to design a thrust into Virginia, they had to consider many factors. The Potomac was over a mile wide at Washington City, and only one major bridge crossed it, the Long Bridge, an antique structure. This span, three carriages in width, had been designed not only to allow traffic to cross the river, but to permit boats to sail or steam past the District. Its builders had erected a quarter-mile masonry foundation in the middle of the river, then linked it to the banks on either side with long wooden sections. Both timbered portions had drawbridges that could be raised or lowered as ships required. Over the years the wooden portions of the bridge had decayed. Structural timbers rotted. It was not only rickety; entire sections of its planking were missing.

Scott and Mansfield worked on their plans in intense secrecy. Washington was still filled with spies. If a single clerk in a critical position was disloyal, the Confederates could disrupt the advance. They could place a battery or two at the Virginia end of the Long Bridge and rake Union troops trying to cross with canister. For that matter they could mine their end of the span and blow it up it at the first sign of a Union thrust. The military movement could turn into a bloodbath.

According to Scott and Mansfield's blueprints, troops would start to get into position on the evening of May 23, the day of Virginia's referendum. These volunteers were camped all over the District. It would take time, certainly hours, for the regiments to rouse themselves, get organized, and march to their assigned jumping-off places.

The two generals assumed their main force would not reach the far side of the Long Bridge until the morning of May 24. If the referendum went as almost everyone claimed it would, Union soldiers would be stepping onto the soil of a state that had just officially seceded and was now therefore part of the Confederacy. Lincoln was taking an aggressive step.

Scott insisted that enlisted men must be told nothing in advance, and even the highest-ranking officers would only learn of their particular assignments a few hours before they were to start getting their men ready. As an example of Scott's desire to maintain caution, it was not until the afternoon of May 23 that Mansfield got around to telling his own inspector-general, Colonel Samuel Heintzelman, to accompany him while he spoke to some army engineers. This was the first time Heintzelman heard about the plan, yet his position as the District's inspector-general would normally have made him an early participant in the discussions. Scott and Mansfield expected Heintzelman to supervise the entire operation, so his being out of the loop until the last minute proves how circumspect the two generals had been.

Scott, however, was keenly aware how unlikely was the prospect of a successful surprise. The operation required much military chutzpah. The old general would be sending about twelve thousand troops — almost all of them civilians in everything but name — at night, against an enemy that must suspect they were coming. In a way Winfield Scott was Ike Eisenhower sketching out D-Day. His table was smaller, to be sure, but the stakes were high.[155]

The Confederates did think an attack was brewing. Montgomery, Alabama had been hearing things. On May 3 — the day Scott originally planned to cross the Potomac — the Confederate secretary of war, Leroy P. Walker, read a worrisome telegram from his agent, Duncan, in Richmond: "Great excitement here. Troops expected from Washington.... Alexandria unprepared to oppose attack."

Two days later Walker received another secret note from Duncan. "Chaos and confusion reign here." Duncan told Walker that Virginia troops, "dissatisfied, threaten to go home." Also: "On the part of some, there is a want of confidence in Governor Letcher and General Lee." And: "It is intimated by good authority Scott will attempt to retake Harpers Ferry, Alexandria, Norfolk.... Dispatch just received (9:30 P.M.) from Alexandria says it is expected that city will be occupied by Federal troops tomorrow." (It was about this time that a person named J. D. Hutton, who had recently been employed by the War Department, somehow got a copy of Scott's original order to cross the Potomac and passed it to Virginia's military leaders in Alexandria. This was probably the origin of the dispatch mentioned by Duncan.)[156]

Cocke issued a proclamation, promising retribution against any Union troops who invaded his state. If "Virginia soil or the grave of Washington be polluted by the tread of a single man in arms from the North of the Potomac, it will cause open war. Men of the Potomac border! Men of the Potomac Military Department; to arms! Your country calls you to her defense!" Everyone, Cocke announced, must become involved. "Women of Virginia, cast from your arms all cowards; and breathe the pure and holy, the high and glowing inspirations of your nature, into the hearts and souls of lover, husband, brother, father, friend!"

May 23, 1861

In Lexington, Kentucky, the state legislature had been in session almost continuously since January. It had spent exhausting hours debating secession. Kentucky was a slave state, but the legislature's mood was at least as divided as Maryland's or Missouri's. Part of the population felt kinship or emotional ties with brethren farther south, but just as many Kentuckians felt drawn to friends and family to the north, especially just across the Ohio River in the lower counties of Ohio, Indiana, and Illinois.

On this day the legislators decided the matter was too divisive. They proclaimed their state's neutrality and adjourned.

Lincoln was greatly relieved. He would be quoted as saying he would like to have God on his side, but he must have the allegiance of Kentucky. Now, at least, he could assume his native state would not jump into the arms of the Confederacy.

All across Virginia on this day average voters had their own say on secession. The results of the referendum were: 96,750 in favor of secession, 32,134 against.

In reality these numbers constituted a sham. Virginia already housed thousands of out-of-state Confederate soldiers on its soil.

Like most states, Virginia was a loosely sewn garment. Her southeastern counties, where men like Henry Wise and Edmund Ruffin lived, were avidly secessionist; but along the Potomac a goodly portion of the population retained mixed feelings. Many in that region had either been born in the North or had relatives there. The western counties of the state were firm in their unionism. Troops were sent to polling places near Harpers Ferry to overawe those who might contemplate voting against the resolution. In Jefferson County (where Harpers Ferry was) this tactic worked; many frightened voters stayed home on the day of the referendum; but in Berkeley County, just to the west, the troops faced such a strong and violent opposition they quietly returned to their barracks. Farther west, in Morgan County, the vote *against* secession was six-to-one. Such counties, and their neighbors, would soon make up the state of West Virginia.[157]

Washington, May 23, 1861, evening

Lucius E. Chittenden could not sleep. Although a rather high-ranking official in the Treasury Department, he had not been privy to cabinet discussions. Yet he had a sensation something of great import was about to occur. The small hotel he used as his residence was near the camps of several regiments. He lay abed, restless in the darkness. He would later write in his diary, "I heard a clock in a distant room faintly strike the hour of midnight. Very soon a single horseman galloped past." He detected, above the clatter of the hooves, the clanking of the man's saber. "Soon there were two light taps of the drum at the camp of the N. Y. 12th encamped on the square opposite. What did this mean?" Time passed; he heard nothing else. He gave up trying to sleep and decided to use this late hour more fruitfully. He turned on his light, picked up his Bible, and started to read. Then, "I heard a faint noise in the distance. I went to the window and threw it open. The night was exquisitely lovely. The full moon shone serenely and soft out of an unclouded sky upon the quiet city. The silence was unbroken save by the barking of a dog in the distance — and — the regular measured sound which first arrested my attention — growing clearer now as if approaching, and regular as the beating of a clock. It comes nearer now, and I am no longer in doubt." He was struck by the metronomic quality of all those marching feet. "There was neither music nor conversation, nothing save the regular *solemn* sound which I shall never forget — the tread of armed men."

A New York volunteer would recall: "We formed platoons and marched down Fourteenth Street, directly to the Long Bridge, scarcely meeting an individual on our route, so quietly was the whole thing conducted." Near the Potomac he and his comrades stopped and loaded their guns, the click-click of their ramrods breaking the stillness, then started marching again. They noticed that other regiments already stood waiting near the bridge, thousands of uniformed men, "as far as the eye could reach." He and his fellows picked up their pace and crossed the river, only slowing a bit on the two wooden portions of the bridge "for fear of breaking it down at those places by the steady tread of 1000 men." Another soldier would remember that their passage across the bridge was so quiet he could hear the river's bullfrogs sing "their monotonous songs."

"This night," Private Theodore would later write, "was full moon at its fullest — a night more perfect than all perfection, mild, dewy, refulgent." As they marched past Willard's he noticed "a hag in a nightcap" at an upper window. In his mind she seemed to be reviewing them as they tramped past. As with most of the regiments, the movements of the Seventh passed without incident. The next day these self-styled New York "dandies" devoted many hours to digging entrenchments. One of their wags would later say, "I have not bled for my country exactly, but I can say, with solemn, heartfelt pride, that I have raised blisters for her."

As Lincoln's soldiers headed toward Virginia, several prominent officials stood on the Washington side of the Potomac, watching the procession pass. The moon's rays caught the glistening bayonets, transmuting them into Death's icicles. Winfield Scott was there with Secretary of State William Seward and a sprinkling of politicians who had learned of the move. Earlier in the evening, before Seward slipped out to observe the proceedings, he advised his family not to go to bed early. He suggested they ought to open the windows, sit near them, and listen. About midnight, according to Frederick Seward's later recollections, they easily heard the "tramp, tramp, tramp of the unseen column."

Everything appeared to be working smoothly. The Confederacy had just been invaded; the war had changed.[158]

POSTSCRIPT

Luke's Question:
The Beginning of an End

Americans will always do the right thing—
after they've exhausted all the alternatives.
—WINSTON CHURCHILL

On May 24, in Charlottesville, Virginia, where Elizabeth Lomax, émigré from Washington City had brought her daughters, she learned the results of the referendum vote of the previous day. She was disconsolate. "Sad day," she wrote in her journal. "Virginia goes out of the Union today." She also learned that Lincoln's soldiers had crossed the Potomac, and that there had been some bloodshed. "Truly these are dreadful times," she wrote. For many Americans these were indeed dreadful times. But for some people, things were looking up. The night Lincoln's army marched into Virginia, an incident took place hundreds of miles away, connecting two men, General Ben Butler and a slave named Luke.[159]

Butler had only been in Annapolis, Maryland, a few days when Scott officially put him in full command there. According to his orders he was to secure the town as well as the railroad line to Annapolis Junction. With this glossy new authority in hand, Butler could act with even greater confidence. He was far from bumptious and his mind was obviously keen, but he had what a later generation would have termed "authority issues." He had never cheerfully taken orders, and he hungered to give them — no doubt the residue of his arid childhood. But he lacked tact — a quality he considered overvalued. Inevitably he would tread on toes, sometimes painfully hard.

Given the limitations of his military expertise, Butler actually did surprisingly well in Annapolis fulfilling Scott's assignment. He sent troops to man two or three nearby elevations, which might otherwise have been used by insurgents to interfere with the Union tide coming into Annapolis. He not only oversaw the protection of the Annapolis & Elk Ridge Railroad, he had engineers and railroad workers completely repair its tracks and rebuild its bridges. Soon he decided to do far more — something dramatic.

He would later claim he heard reports of nefarious doings in nearby Baltimore. On May 14 he led about a thousand soldiers through a downpour into that city. They arrived, scrambled from their train, and Butler marched them, along with some artillery, on to Federal Hill, a high point near the middle of town, from where he could stare down on most of the city.

Given the ongoing delicacy of relations between the federal government and Maryland, Lincoln was aghast. General Scott was outraged because Butler had overstepped his orders, something subordinates were not supposed to do. The old general wanted to court-martial the lawyer, but Lincoln — perhaps noting the wave of popular support for Butler's Baltimore coup — told Scott simply to chide the offender in an official message.

When Butler received Scott's note he recognized he had just been spanked. He hurried to Washington to complain personally to Lincoln. To placate him the president took the remarkable step of promoting him to major general, making Butler one of the highest-ranking officers in American history up to that moment. Lincoln also suggested that Scott assign Butler to Fort Monroe, where, it was assumed, he would create fewer waves.

Scott chatted with Ben Butler about this new assignment. The old general, ever the gourmet, advised the pudgy Massachusetts man that he was lucky. "It is just the season for soft-shelled crabs," Scott said, "and hog fish have just come in, and they are the most delicious pan fish you ever ate."[160]

It would be at Fort Monroe, a few days later, that Benjamin F. Butler would perform the most important act of his life. Partly by chance, what was about to occur would begin on May 23–24, precisely as Lincoln's army was rising from camps in the District and marching into Virginia.

Fort Monroe sat on a rocky island a bit over 120 acres in size. A wide moat and fifty-foot walls protected the fortress, and inside it was a virtual city, with barns and storehouses and gardens, a hospital, a chapel, an imposing home for its commander, and enough barracks to house a 6,000-man garrison. But when the war began, the garrison only numbered 415, commanded by Brevet Colonel Justin Dimick, a slender, gray-eyed professional soldier in his midsixties.

The fort, atop its island, sitting a bit off the mainland, was connected to the rest of Virginia by two causeways, each more than a mile in length, one of which led northwest to the nearest town: Hampton, Virginia.

Fort Monroe was federal property. On May 23, 1861, with the referendum on secession about to pass, the village of Hampton, a mile away, was about to be part of the Confederate States of America. Therein lay the seeds of History.

Ben Butler arrived at Fort Monroe on May 22. Two Massachusetts regiments and another from Vermont were already there, along with Dimick's few hundred regulars. Butler's new command numbered about 3,000, with more men expected shortly.

He investigated conditions at the fort and concluded that its only immediate problem was a lack of fresh water. When his command began growing, this factor could become serious.

An obvious solution would be to transfer men away from the fort — toward Hampton — as long as that village was not occupied by rebel troops. The day after his arrival, Butler ordered Colonel J. Walcott Phelps, head of the First Vermont Regiment, to take his regiment and check out the town of Hampton and the area around it, to see whether reports were accurate about the presence there of rebels.

That afternoon, May 23 — while Virginians across the state were still voting on their referendum — 779 Green Mountain Boys, as they called themselves, who had left Vermont two weeks earlier with sprigs of evergreen pinned to their caps, marched toward Hampton. (Scott and Mansfield's plans would not go into effect for several hours, so although they could not know it, these New Englanders constituted the very first Union regiment to enter the Confederacy during the Civil War.)

They had walked only a few hundred yards when they saw a farmer in the distance plowing his field, watching them. Suddenly the man unharnessed his horse from the plow and rode rapidly away. A few minutes later a uniformed young man, Lieutenant Cutshaw, galloped up astride a white steed. He was obviously much agitated. Why, he demanded to know, were these Yankee troops "invading" Virginia?

Colonel Phelps, a soft-spoken man with a high, reedy voice, told the lieutenant their intentions were peaceful. Cutshaw asked if the invaders would permit the Virginians of Hampton time to "remove the women and children."

"Oh, let them stay," Phelps said, "we want to see them, too." The young Virginian sped off, and the Vermonters began marching again. When they arrived in the village of Hampton, less than an hour's walk from the fort, they found its white population in a state of near hysteria. Some days earlier, those who could afford to leave had departed. The whites left behind were terrified, convinced that all Yankee soldiers were barbarians, and that rapine and butchery was about to begin. Much of the visible population, however, was black — slaves left behind by their departed masters to look after the houses. These blacks watched the passing Union troops with equanimity. A few smiled and said howdy.

The Vermonters, having accomplished their mission, and discovering no camp of rebel soldiers, returned to Fort Monroe. It was getting dark.[161]

A few minutes later a slave named Luke, accompanied by two male companions, also slaves, arrived at Fort Monroe's outer picket line. They asked for asylum. They said they were field hands at a nearby plantation, from which they had slipped away that afternoon. They had hidden until nightfall. Now, here they were.

The officer of the guard was uncertain what to do. It seemed too late to bother General Butler, so he told the three runaways to stay until morning, when their fate could be determined.

Luke's request was about to change this war, and America.

Slavery arrived in America within the mental baggage of the first European settlers who came with a vague concept about a system of bondage that might be a useful solution for labor shortages. To them, slavery did not involve race. Elizabethan law permitted the enslavement of British citizens for certain infractions — punishments seldom applied but on the books. In the mid-seventeenth century Oliver Cromwell sent boatloads of captured Irishmen as slaves to the West Indies.

The first permanent English settlement at Jamestown had an abiding need for extra workers. Many of its original settlers soon sickened and died. Even if everyone at the settlement had remained healthy, the amount of work required simply to survive was enormous. In 1619 a Dutch vessel arrived from Africa. According to John Rolfe's account, the ship deposited — for a price — "twenty negars."

In time, every British settlement in North America adopted the system of utilizing blacks as slave laborers. In 1775 all thirteen colonies contained slaves. The system seemed as American as apple pie. Then in 1780, representatives of the newly self-declared state of Massachusetts rejected its status as a colony and wrote a constitution. Among other things, this document announced that everyone inside its borders was free.

Ten years later the new nation recorded its first census. It listed the numbers of slaves and free blacks in each state. New Hampshire had 158 slaves, New York had 21,324, Pennsylvania had 3,737, and so on. But slavery was gradually ending in what was already beginning to be called "the North," eliminated by state legislatures using a principle called *post nati*, whereby children born to slave parents after a specific date would be free. This system of emancipation was adopted to reduce the social and economic consequences of immediate abolition, dampening its effects on both whites and blacks, but also serving as a kind of social security for elderly slaves, to prevent white owners from freeing them when their bodies wore out. By the 1850 census, only New Jersey among the Northern states still had slaves—222 to be exact. Meanwhile the numbers of free African Americans inside the North had risen dramatically. Partly it was their presence, acting as a living symbol of freedom, magnets for the imagination, that induced slaves in the Upper South—the border states—to attempt to flee northward. Some runaways made it. The federal and state laws labeled them "fugitive slaves." Issues revolving around them may have been the single most important cause of secession—and therefore of the Civil War.

In essence, slavery is not simply enslavement. Any monster can enslave another person, chaining him or her to a radiator or piano leg (or, if one chooses to be cynical, to a variety of social arrangements based on threats). But for a system of slavery to exist in a society, it must be enforceable by law—like the ownership of any possession—a horse, for example. Once the necessary laws are in place, a police force is involved: the executive branch of government.

As soon as America had even a single state *without* slavery (that is, with laws prohibiting the institution), the subject—from a legal point of view—grew unstable. If a runaway escaped from a slave state to a state without slave laws, did that person become free? Were law-abiding citizens of a free state obligated to return this human being to his or her "owner" far away — much as they might return a stolen carriage (especially since the out-of-state "owner" could not legally own anyone in a free state)?

The men who wrote the Constitution in 1787 agreed that a slaveowner had the right to get back his or her property (Article IV, section 2). In 1793 Congress passed legislation refining this matter further. Later, other national statutes were passed, the most important coming in 1850, when an especially stringent law was pushed through Congress. This statute required the punishment of anyone who even interfered with officials seeking fugitive slaves. Many Northerners were appalled. One result was the huge popularity of Harriet Beecher Stowe's *Uncle Tom's Cabin*, humanizing the topic.

All this, and much more, heightened emotions, particularly in the South. White Southerners, whether they owned slaves or not, felt insulted at what they perceived as abolitionist snickering about the low level of Southern morality. A relatively pejorative term for New Englanders, "Yankees," began to be applied to all Northerners. It galled Southerners that during the 1850s the legislatures of almost every Northern state passed resolutions against the federal Fugitive Slave Law. To be sure, such state resolutions were not legally binding, but each was a slap at the South's peculiar institution — and therefore at white Southerners. These resolutions, coming in waves, year after year, capped off by John Brown's raid in 1859, made those Southerners feel defensive.

Abraham Lincoln understood that Southern sensibilities were delicate about this question. In his inaugural address of March 1861 he specified how he stood on the matter. He said he had just sworn a solemn oath to enforce *all* the laws of the United States. This meant, he said, he would not interfere with slavery in any slave state. It also meant, he went on, that he would enforce the 1850 Fugitive Slave Law. In order that there would linger no question, he even quoted that law, and added: "I take the official oath today, with no mental reservations."

Now, on May 23, 1861, here at Fort Monroe, stood the man Luke.

If President Lincoln was duty-bound to return this person to his owner, so was every representative of the executive branch, including — perhaps especially — all soldiers in the Union army. Earlier in the year even the pitiful garrison at Fort Sumter, under siege for months, had handed over a slave to South Carolina's authorities and turned away another who begged for asylum. It must also be recalled that four states still within the Union — Kentucky, Maryland, Missouri, and Delaware — as well as the District of Columbia — retained slave laws. On May 23, of these five places, only Delaware and the District seemed certain to remain part of the Union.

Ben Butler's own previous record on the issue of slavery had been clear: the institution was a matter involving property, and being a successful lawyer and wealthy factory owner, he enthusiastically embraced the concept of property. As a Democratic politician, he was a member of a party with a long tradition of supporting slavery.

A month earlier, on the morning he arrived in Annapolis, Butler had sent Governor Hicks a note. "I have understood," he said, "that some apprehensions were retained of an insurrection of the negro population of this neighborhood." Butler wanted to convince the good citizens of Maryland that his troops were not rabid abolitionists. To do so, he said, "I am therefore ready to cooperate with your excellency in suppressing most promptly and effectively, any insurrection against the laws of Maryland."

Hicks was determined to show that Maryland's white citizens were quite able to control their slaves without assistance from a bunch of armed Yankees, so he responded immediately:

332 / David Detzer

"I thank you most sincerely for the tender of your men, but I had, before the receipt of your letter, directed the sheriff of the county to act in the matter, and am confident that the citizens of the county are fully able to suppress any insurrection of our slave population."[162]

Soon after this exchange Butler did see to it that one runaway was returned to his master. Later he openly congratulated his troops, who were guarding the rail line to Annapolis Junction, whenever they sent runaways back.

Butler's notes to Hicks were reprinted widely in Northern newspapers and elicited much comment, pro and con. Governor Andrew decided he must step in. The Massachusetts militiamen, after all, had not yet taken a federal oath, so they were still entirely subject to the governor's orders. He sent a message to Butler saying a few complimentary things in passing, then chiding him mildly for Butler's offer to use Massachusetts volunteers to suppress Maryland's slaves. Andrew said he thought that offer "unnecessary." Andrew considered many of Maryland's whites were rebels. (Recall that the Sixth Massachusetts had been attacked in the streets of Baltimore only a week earlier, and the bodies of the men murdered there had just been returned to their home.) Andrew stated that he considered assisting rebels in any way counterproductive. A "servile insurrection," he said, could in fact weaken the enemy.

Butler's reply was revealing. "Would your excellency," Butler asked, "advise the troops under my command to make war upon the defenseless women and children of any part of the Union, accompanied with brutalities too horrible to be named?"

There it was. Slavery and racism in America had long been one intertwined fabric. Most American whites were, at the very least, uneasy about a long list of things that might tip what they perceived as a delicate balance: the mood of the slaves. Despite the decades of confident talk about the loyalty of their "servants" (the term often applied to slaves who worked closely with whites), there remained a fear that the four million slaves were not as docile as they seemed. It can be argued that secession (and therefore the Civil War) grew out of this fear. Lincoln the man was an unknown quantity, but to most white Southerners he represented the possibility of change — and thus was something dangerous. Butler understood this. Here he was, telling Andrew he had only acted to preserve the safety of innocent women and children. He felt no need to specify he was concerned here about *white* women and children. Nor did he stop there. He went on to describe the slave population of the South as "worse than savages" — men, women, and children who might start a maddened spree of "rapine, arson, and murder" once they have "tasted blood." Encouraging such a nightmare, he reminded Andrew, would be downright un-Christian.[163]

But Butler's attitudes were about to change. A few weeks later John Hay had a conversation at the White House with Carl Schurz, a prominent Republican. Schurz loathed the Fugitive Slave Law and had given numerous speeches against it. Hay wrote in his diary that "Carl Schurz loafed into my room this morning," May 10. Schurz told Hay he was unhappy that the commandant at Fort Monroe (Colonel Dimick), to say nothing of other military leaders, had been returning runaways to their masters. Schulz thought the administration should order soldiers to cease doing so — if nothing else, to remind slaveowners "that they are dependent on the good-will of the Government for the security of their lives and property."

Perhaps Butler now heard about Schurz's notion. Butler had been in correspondence with Postmaster General Francis Blair, who may have mentioned the subject.[164]

On the morning of May 24 the officer who commanded Fort Monroe's picket line when Luke arrived the night before spoke to General Butler about his encounter with the slaves. The three African Americans then entered the room. General Butler interviewed each of them, one by one. Two had wives in Hampton, and children. Their owner, Colonel Mallory of the

Virginia volunteers, a Hampton lawyer and well-to-do plantation owner, intended to send them to North Carolina to work on fortifications being built there.

Shortly thereafter, Major J. B. Cary, of the Virginia volunteers, appeared at Fort Monroe's outer lines, claiming to represent Charles Mallory, who wanted his three field hands back. Cary demanded that Butler enforce the appropriate clauses in the Fugitive Slave Act.

Ben Butler was acquainted with Major Cary; both had attended the previous year's Democratic Convention in Charleston. Butler told Cary his intentions in this matter: Fort Monroe could use laborers, and he would utilize the services of the three runaways. "I would send a receipt to Colonel Mallory," Butler said, "as I would for any other property [*sic*] of a private citizen which the exigencies of the service seemed to require." Cary vigorously complained. (Butler wrote Scott the next day, "I replied that the fugitive-slave act did not affect a foreign country, which Virginia claimed to be, ... that in Maryland, a loyal State, fugitives from service had been returned.") But if Colonel Mallory, Butler told Cary, would merely come to Fort Monroe and take an oath of allegiance to the United States, he could get back his slaves. Cary muttered that Mallory was not nearby at the moment, and departed.

Butler realized that Mallory intended to use these slaves — his property — to assist the cause of the Confederacy. As a lawyer, Butler knew that property used in a crime — and rebellion, under the law, was certainly illegal — can be confiscated as "contraband" by legal authorities. But Butler did not use the word "contraband" at this time, though he had previously applied that term in the Annapolis region after confiscating items that pro-Confederate Marylanders were trying to send southward. Apparently the first time "contraband" was used to apply to individuals like Luke was in a letter to the *New York Tribune*. This letter, written shortly after Butler's conversation with Cary, was penned by an unnamed contributor stationed at Fort Monroe. The item's author was almost certainly Edward

Lillie Pierce, thirty-two, an abolitionist attorney who was a private in one of the Massachusetts regiments at the fort. Pierce was a person of note, a friend of both Senator Charles Sumner and Secretary of the Treasury Salmon Chase, and an extraordinarily nimble lawyer. He understood the nuances of legal language. Whether the original use of this term as applied to slaves was Pierce's or Butler's (and Butler was certainly a canny lawyer himself), or the creation of other subtle minds in Butler's entourage, will likely remain a mystery. But the term turned out to be a brilliant coup.

Butler soon wrote General Scott about another problem: "Since I wrote my last dispatch, the question in regard to slave property is becoming one of very serious magnitude. The inhabitants of Virginia are using their negroes in the batteries and are preparing to send the women and children south." More runaways, he said, had just appeared at his picket lines, some accompanied by their families. Since he could not, he said, employ young children as workers at the fort, "I am in the utmost doubt what to do with this species of property." His plan, he said, was to feed them all and to employ those who were physically able. "As a political question and a question of humanity, can I receive the services of a father and mother and not take the children? Of the humanitarian aspect I have no doubt; of the political one I have no right to judge."

By this day, May 27, fifty-nine fugitives were at the fort, ranging in age from three months to eighty-five years. Inevitably more would be arriving—hundreds, maybe thousands. Butler had put Luke and his two companions to the task of building a bakery—an inoffensive, nonmilitary assignment. Some, but certainly not all of the incoming runaways might work as servants of officers. With new regiments arriving at the fort almost daily, Butler intended to station some volunteers outside the walls. Entrenchments would have to be dug. This meant the "contrabands" would be performing a military activity, assisting the Union's war effort. Logically, Butler could trade them food, and perhaps lodging, for their labor.

But how about their families, those who performed no useful work at all? How could he justify feeding them? Was he obligated to return them to their masters?

Winfield Scott read Butler's two reports. The general jotted some words on Butler's first message: "There is much to praise in this report, and nothing to condemn." He forwarded the note, and his own comment in its margins, to Cameron, who, on May 29, scribbled across it that he agreed with Scott's approval.

The next day Lincoln met with his cabinet. Secretary Cameron was there, and raised the question that Butler had asked: Had the Massachusetts general acted properly in not enforcing the fugitive slave law? Had he done the correct thing in expropriating this two-legged property of the rebels? It must be emphasized, Butler had not freed the slaves — men like Luke. By using their labor at the fort, he was not directly challenging the institution of slavery, he was in a sense adopting it. These contrabands, as they were being called, officially remained slaves. That is, by law they remained property. They simply belonged to the army at Fort Monroe. Slaveowners — in Maryland or Kentucky, for example — would be hard-pressed to find fault with Butler's policies. As Cameron described Butler's actions and rationale to the men at the cabinet meeting, Lincoln began to laugh. His own lawyer's mind appreciated the delicious, clever irony. He called it, "Butler's fugitive slave law."

But the president and his cabinet recognized the complexity of the matter, and they decided to proceed cautiously. They agreed that Secretary Cameron must officially tell General Butler the administration approved his actions, yet warn him he had to keep very careful records of all monies spent, of all labor performed, and so on.

This maneuvering in Washington was exceedingly legalistic. But Luke and his fellow runaways understood something that neither Lincoln nor Congress would yet admit. Once the genie was out of the bottle, it could never be stuffed back in.

One might argue that Luke had not arrived at Fort Monroe for some abstract concept of freedom. He and his companions appeared at the picket line because they wanted to remain in their home region of Hampton, where their friends and families lived, rather than be sent to far-off North Carolina. They wanted to decide for themselves where they lived—and this, of course, is the essence of freedom.

Once slaves, wherever they resided, began slipping past the pickets of the Union army and were accepted as contraband, their status changed. They might not exactly be legally free, but they were no longer precisely slaves. By their own choice, their own actions, with their own feet, they had altered their existence. So long as Lincoln's army did not force them back to their previous owners, these people had taken a giant leap forward.

And this did not involve something granted to them. They had reached out and grasped—freedom.

On July 9, 1861, the House of Representatives passed a resolution—a statement of mere opinion, not a law: henceforth, Union soldiers were no longer required to capture and return fugitive slaves. In months to come, Union commanders adopted Butler's policy about contrabands. Long before the Emancipation Proclamation, throughout the Confederacy, whenever possible, slaves ran into Union encampments, and ceased to be slaves.[165]

For a six-week period after the assault on Fort Sumter—from April 12 to May 24—the war had centered on the right of a state to secede.

During the previous two generations, the concept of Union had been fashioned by men like Senator Daniel Webster of Massachusetts, to refute the notion of states' rights. Men like Webster had declared that Union—this abstraction—was really the country. They had said there was something more than, greater than, all these little feuding states: there was a people, a nation.

In May 1861 Lincoln was still insisting that the dispute of the past few months only involved Senator Webster's definition of "Union." Lincoln would occasionally play with some of the implications of that word, but it would be a while before he fully embraced the fact that the Civil War was about more than just a disagreement over political terms (and the allegiances that had grown out of them). Lincoln continued to think the war was about democracy, a struggle over the concept of "a government of the people, by the people, for the people"—and not a conflict about the very soul of his nation.

Long before Lincoln changed his mind, the man Luke had come to Fort Monroe—a person so obscure that that single syllable is the only name we know him by. It was Luke who was the real issue in this war. And in their deepest hearts, most Southerners knew it.[166]

The war had been "caused" by the Confederate attack on Fort Sumter. In turn, that gunfire had been initiated by Jefferson Davis's felt-need to defend the new and uncertain Confederacy, itself the child of the process called "secession." Going further back, the cause of secession had been the November election of Abraham Lincoln, perceived to be a threat to the South's control of folks like Luke.

In other words, in essence it was really Luke and his status that caused this war: at the most basic level, the Civil War was about Luke's right to decide whether he was willing to abandon his home and friends near Hampton and go to North Carolina with a man claiming to be his "master."

On the night of May 23, 1861, at Fort Monroe, Luke and his companions changed the nature of the Civil War. And they performed this miracle before the two sides had even engaged in the first great battle—one that would soon take place near a stream called Bull Run.

The real war—civil in name only—was a revolution. It had just begun.

Acknowledgments

I cannot thank every person who assisted me along the way as I pored through so many thousands and thousands of books and letters and diaries. Since I began this project, the Web has altered research. Countless unnamed men and women have generously chosen to assist research by making primary materials accessible to every person with a computer. I would like to hug most of them. Dozens of other individuals have offered me welcome suggestions and critiques along the way that have steered me away from some egregious errors; I only wish I had been able to eliminate every mistake (like a few embarrassing misspellings that have tiptoed in, unannounced). As always, I am totally beholden to Joanne Elpern for her cheery assistance in tracking down materials. I also wish to thank again my friend George Combs, of Alexandria, for sardonically guiding me through some of that city's, and Washington's, briar patches.

Notes

Throughout this book I have occasionally altered quotations in slight matters involving punctuation and spelling, but only to modernize nineteenth century usage.

For the sake of brevity, I have used the following shorthand notations in the footnotes:

AL   *The Collected Works of Abraham Lincoln*, 9 vols., New
            Brunswick, NJ: Rutgers University Press, 1953–55.
B&L   *Battles and Leaders of the Civil War*, 4 vols.
CV   *Confederate Veteran.*
CWTI   *Civil War Times Illustrated.*
ER   Edmund Ruffin, *The Diary of Edmund Ruffin*, edited by
            William Kauffman Scarborough, 3 vols., Baton Rouge,
            LA: Louisiana State University Press, 1972–1980.
JD   Jefferson Davis, *The Papers of Jefferson Davis*, eds. Lynda
            Lasswell Crist *et al.*, Baton Rouge, LA: Louisiana State
            University Press, 1971–.
LSUP   Louisiana State University Press (Baton Rouge,
            Louisiana).
MHS   Maryland Historical Society (Baltimore).
MOLLUS   Military Order of the Loyal Legion of the United States.
OR   *The War of the Rebellion: A Compilation of the Official Records
            of the Union and Confederate Armies*, 1880–1901.
ORN   *Official Records of the Union and Confederate Navies in the War
            of Rebellion, 1897–1927.*
SHSP   Southern Historical Society Papers.
SOR   *Supplement of the Official Records of the Union and Confederate
            Armies* (Wilmington, North Carolina, 1994–)
UNC   Archives, University of North Carolina.
UNCP   University of North Carolina Press (Chapel Hill).

USC   University of South Carolina, Columbia, SC.
UVA   University of Virginia.
VHS   Virginia Historical Society (Richmond).

Introduction

1. The journals of Elizabeth Lindsay Lomax are part of the large collection of Lomax papers, VHS; most of the quotations here are drawn from the published version of a portion of her journals: *Leaves From an Old Washington Diary, 1854–1863* (New York, 1943), pp. 30 and 102–155, *passim*. A recent book on the capital during the era is Ernest B. Furgurson, *Freedom Rising: Washington in the Civil War* (New York, 2004).

Chapter One: City of Magnificent Intentions

2. "armed sentinels": William D'Arcy Haley, ed., *Philp's Washington Described* (Washington, 1861), p. 70.

3. The best book on the subject of slavery in the District is still Mary Tremain, *Slavery in the District of Columbia* (New York, 1892).

4. "the most filthy city": "L" to the Editor, *Lowell* [Massachusetts] *Daily Courier*, May 5, 1861. A potpourri of contemporary descriptions would include, in addition to Philp's guide, mentioned above: the city's newspapers, especially the *Evening Star*; "Social Aspects of Washington before the Disunion," *Once-a-Week* (December 6, 1862); J. G. Kohl, "The Federal City of Washington," *Bentley's Miscellany* (Washington, 1861); George William Bagby, "Washington City," *The Atlantic Monthly*, VII (January 1861), 1–8; and *Morrisons' Strangers' Guide and Etiquette for Washington City and Its Vicinity*, 5th ed. (Washington, 1862) — which notes, p. 58, that visitors to the city ought to remember: "It is highly disgusting to spit or blow the nose with a loud explosive noise at table. The knife is never used to convey food to the mouth; the fork being generally sufficient for the purpose."

5. The best books on Winfield Scott are: Charles Winslow Elliot, *Winfield Scott: The Soldier and the Man* (New York, 1937), and Timothy D. Johnson, *Winfield Scott* (Lawrence, Kansas: University Press of Kansas, 1998).

6. Charles P. Stone, "Washington on the Eve of the War," B&L, I, 7–25; Stone, "Washington In March and April, 1861," *Magazine of American History*, XIV (July 1885), 1–24; James H. Whyte, "Divided Loyalties in Washington during the Civil War," *Records of the Columbia Historical Society of Washington, D.C., 1960–1962* (Washington, 1963), pp. 103–22; OR, CVII, 321–24.

7. John Nicolay to Therena Bates, April 7, 1861, *With Lincoln in the*

White House, edited by Michael Burlingame (Carbondale, Illinois, 2000), p. 33.

8. OR, CVII, 109.

9. Gustavus Vasa Fox, *Confidential Correspondence* (New York, 1918), pp. 26, 31–32.

10. Baldwin to Lincoln: John M. Botts, *The Great Rebellion* (New York, 1866), p. 198. AL, IV, 324; *Richmond Enquirer*, April 15, 1861.

11. OR, CXI, 143–44.

12. Edward Bates, *The Diary of Edward Bates, 1859–1866* (New York, 1933), pp. 17–18.

13. Frederick W. Seward, *Seward at Washington* (New York, 1891), II, 544. Among the hundreds of works that touch on "presidential war powers," see, especially, Clarence A. Berdahl, *War Powers of the Executive in the United States* (Urbana, Illinois, 1920); James G. Randall, *Constitutional Problems Under Lincoln*, 2d ed. (Urbana, Illinois, 1951). Both are excellent, but each reflects a postwar mood, the time when each was written.

14. David Detzer, *Thunder of the Captains* (New York, 1977), p. 120.

15. For the proclamation and Lincoln's reply to the commissioners: AL, IV, 329–33. On April 12 one of the *Baltimore Sun*'s regular correspondents, "Ion," informed the newspaper that Attorney General Edward Bates had recently reviewed the laws and precedents and gave Lincoln the information that he had authority to call up volunteers: *Sun*, April 13, 1861. Cabinet meeting and writing of proclamation: John G. Nicolay, *The Outbreak of Rebellion* (New York, 1881), p. 73; Nicolay, *With Lincoln*, pp. 33–34.

16. "Reminiscences of Stephen A. Douglas," *Atlantic Monthly*, VIII (May 1861), 212; "Statement," April 14, 1861, *The Letters of Stephen A. Douglas*, edited by Robert W. Johannsen (Urbana, 1961), 509–10, John W. Forney, *Anecdotes of Public Men* (New York 1881), I, 224–25.

17. Ramsey's offer: Richard Moe, *The Last Full Measure: The Life and Death of the First Minnesota Volunteers* (New York, 1993), pp. 7–8. OR, I, 486, 666–67; CX, 49; CXXII, 77–83, 122.

Chapter Two: The Firebrand

18. The city: Ernest B. Furgurson, *Ashes of Glory: Richmond at War* (New York: Alfred A. Knopf, 1996); Thomas M. Emory, *The Confederate State of Richmond* (LSUP, 1971); Barbara Lawrence Bellows, "Tempering the Wind: The Southern Response to Urban Poverty, 1850–1865," PhD dissertation (USC, 1983); Thomas Cooper DeLeon, *Four Years in Rebel Capitals* (Mobile, 1870). Slavery and racism: drawn from the Richmond *Dispatch*, the Richmond *Examiner*, and the Richmond *Enquirer*. Story of drowning: *Dispatch*, April 18, 1861.

19. Elizabeth Lomax, *Leaves From an Old Washington Diary, 1854–1863* (New York, 1943), pp. 68–69; ER, I, 119, 385, 398, 404–05, 416, 491–92, 605.

20. On the two Wises and their attitudes, see Craig M. Simpson, *A Good Southerner: The Life of Henry A. Wise of Virginia* (UNCP, 1985), especially pp. 219–45; John Coles Rutherfoord, Diary, January 1, 1861, VHS; Henry Wilson, *History of the Rise and Fall of the Slave Power* (New York, 1969), pp. 3, 164–65.

21. "grimly dirty": DeLeon, p. 88. "howling mobs": Daniel H. Strother, "Personal Reflections of the War," *Harper's New Monthly Magazine*, XXXIII (June 1866), 4. Unionism in Virginia: *Washington Evening Star*, April 2, 8; *Richmond Dispatch*, March 28 to April 8, 1861. Circular: *Washington Star*, April 2 and 3; Simpson, p. 245; Daniel W. Crofts, *Reluctant Confederates: Upper South Unionists in the Secession Crisis* (UNCP, 1989), pp. 308–14.

22. Plots and plotters: *Baltimore Sun*, April 19, 1861; ER, II, 568–71; Letter, J. D. Imboden to John McCue, February 24, 1861, on "The Valley of the Shadow" website; Imboden, "Jackson at Harper's Ferry in 1861," B&L, I, 111–12; OR, CXXII, 76; Crofts, p. 318; Simpson, pp. 248–51; Harold R. Woodward, Jr., *Defender of the Valley: Brigadier General John Daniel Imboden, C.S.A.* (Berryville, Virginia, 1996), pp. 19–21; John Marshall Hagans, *Brief Sketch of the Erection and Formation of the State of West Virginia* (Charleston, West Virginia, 1891), p. 28; Furgurson, pp. 35–36. Reactions to Virginia's secession: See, e.g., *Philadelphia Public Ledger*, April 19, 1861.

Chapter Three: Cliffhanger

23. Jefferson, *Notes on the State of Virginia* (UNCP, 1955), p. 19.

24. OR, II, 6.

25. Rising of Virginia's militia: see, e.g., the letters to *Richmond Dispatch*, April 19–20, 1861; Daniel W. Crofts, *Reluctant Confederates: Upper South Unionists in the Secession Crisis* (UNCP, 1989), p. 336; James M. Garnett, "Harpers Ferry and First Manassas: Diary," SHSP XXVIII (1900), 58–59; John Imboden, "Jackson at Harpers Ferry in 1861," B&L, I, 112–14.

26. The best biography of Ashby is: Paul Christopher Anderson, *Blood Image: Turner Ashby in the Civil War and the Southern Mind* (LSUP, 2002).

27. The takeover of Harpers Ferry: In addition to works already cited, see Jones's reports: OR, II, 3–6; SOR, I, 101–03; Joseph Barry, *The Annals of Harper's Ferry* (Hagerstown, Maryland, 1869), pp. 5–43; Daniel H. Strother, "Personal Recollections of the War," *Harper's New Monthly Magazine*, XXX (June 1866), 1–25; Donald B. Webster, Jr.,

"The Last Days of the Harpers Ferry Armory," *Civil War History,* V (March 1959), 30–44; Letter, A Laroy Bigelow to Mother, April 21, 1861, *Southbridge* (Massachusetts) *Journal,* May 3, 1861. Lieutenant Jones was aided during his final hours at the arsenal by the unexpected arrival of Captain Charles P. Kingsbury, an accomplished ordnance officer with over twenty years of service at that time and a veteran of the Mexican War. His chief contributions during the twenty-four hours he was there mainly involved dealing with the civilian workmen, and giving Jones advice about ordnance. I have not included his activities because they remain murky.

28. Drunkenness: Strother, p. 14. "duties are new": Frank Jones to Susan Clark Jones, April 23, 1861, Margaretta Barton Colt, *Defend the Valley: A Shenandoah Family in the Civil War* (New York, 1994), p. 61. Sheriff's note and Harper's: OR, II, 589, 772.

Chapter Four: ten-HUT!

29. Abner R. Small, *The Road to Richmond* (Berkeley, 1939), p. 4; William W. Blackford, *War Years with Jeb Stuart* (LSUP reprint, 1993), p. 15.

30. "public nuisance": John M. Gould, *History of the First-Tenth-Twenty-ninth Maine Regiment* (Portland, 1871), p. 17. "lessons of today" and "no studying": Quoted in James M. McPherson, *For Cause and Comrades: Why Men Fought in the Civil War* (New York, 1997), pp. 16, 17. "every cart horse": George Templeton Strong, *Diary of the Civil War, 1860–1865* (New York, 1962), I, 124. "drum & fife": Letter, Herbert Henry Hawes to Samuel Horace Hawes, April 27, 1861, Hawes Papers, VHS.

31. Blackford, p. 14. Upper New York: Newton Martin Curtis, *From Bull Run to Chancellorsville: The Story of the Sixteenth New York Infantry* (New York, 1906), pp. 3–17.

32. *Baltimore Sun,* April 13, 1861.

33. Edmund McDonald, "The First Defenders," *Philadelphia Weekly Press,* March 24, 1886; William F. McKay, "Early Volunteers," *Philadelphia Weekly Times,* April 16, 1861; Margaret Leech, *Reveille in Washington, 1860–1865* (New York, 1941), pp. 58–59; Frederic Emory, "The Baltimore Riots," *The Annals of the Civil War* (reprint, New York, 1994), pp. 777–80. McKay claimed that they numbered 530, but a note to Cameron from Harrisburg said 460: OR, CVII, 328.

Chapter Five: The Sixth Massachusetts

34. In addition to Ben Butler's *Autobiography and Personal Reminiscences* [often referred to as *Butler's Book*] (Boston, 1892), see Hans Louis Trefousse, *Ben Butler: The South called him Beast* (New York, 1957),

Robert Werlich, *Beast Butler* (Washington, 1962), Robert S. Holzman, *Stormy Ben Butler* (New York, 1954), Howard P. Nash, Jr., *Stormy Petrel* (Rutherford, New Jersey, 1969), Richard S. West, Jr., *Lincoln's Scapegoat General* (Boston, 1965); and Chester G. Hearn, *When the Devil Came Down to Dixie: Ben Butler in New Orleans* (LSUP, 1997).

35. Butler, *Autobiography*, pp. 150–74; Butler, *Private and Official Correspondence of Gen. Benjamin F. Butler during the Period of the Civil War* (Norwood, Massachusetts, 1917), pp. 5–15. Horseshoes: OR, CVII, 357. Andrew's request for muskets: *Ibid.*, CXXII, 66–67.

36. *Ibid.*, CX, 49; CXXII, 79, 86.

Chapter Six: Mobtown

37. Among many useful general works on the rich history of Baltimore, I have here leaned especially on David C. Holly, *Tidewater by Steamboat: A Saga of the Chesapeake* (Baltimore, 1991); Francis F. Beirne, *The Amiable Baltimoreans* (New York, 1951); and Frederic Emory, "The Baltimore Riots," reprinted in *The Annals of the Civil War* (New York, 1994).

38. An eyewitness account of the incident at the Baltimore station: John C. Robinson, "Baltimore in 1861," *Magazine of American History*, XIV (1885), 259. Among the better descriptions of the entire affair are: James D. Horan, *The Pinkertons* (New York, 1967), pp. 52–67; Richard Betterly, "Seize Mr. Lincoln: The 1861 Baltimore Plot," CWTI, XXV (February, 1987), 14–21.

39. Maryland politics: William J. Evitts, *A Matter of Allegiances: Maryland from 1850 to 1861* (Baltimore, 1974), a solid work, claims that unionism in the state was "fragile"; less convincing is Lawrence M. Denton, *A Southern Star for Maryland: Maryland and the Secession Crisis, 1860–1861* (Baltimore, 1995), who thinks that Maryland was essentially pro-South. Professor Frank Towers kindly allowed me to read his informative unpublished essay, "Secession in an Urban Context: Municipal Reform and the Coming of the Civil War in Baltimore," (2001). See, also, his "'A Vociferous Army of Howling Wolves': Baltimore's Civil War Riot of April 19, 1861," *The Maryland Historian*, XXIII (1992), 19–20. Hicks's serenade: *Baltimore Sun*, April 17, 1861; a good general work about the governor: see George L. P. Radcliffe, *Governor Thomas H. Hicks of Maryland and the Civil War* (Baltimore, 1901). Resolution of the States Rights Convention: George William Brown, *Baltimore and the Nineteenth of April 1861* (Baltimore, 1887), p. 38.

40. Sumner's night in town: *New York Tribune*, April 27, 1861.

41. Sixth's trip to Philadelphia: John B. Dennis, "March of the Old 6th Massachusetts Through Baltimore, April 19, 1861," MOLLUS (Omaha, Nebraska, 1888), pp. 12–19. "My Dear Wife": April 17, 1861,

www.letterscivilwar.com. "grass was as high": Lyman Van Buren Furber to Louisa, April 27, 1861, Furber Papers, Maryland Historical Society. "marched down Broadway," "we feel confident," and being given cartridges: Letter, "W.L.S." to "H", written late on April 18, 1861, printed in *Boston Herald,* April 20, 1861. See, also, Letter, R. C. Bailey to Anonymous, April 20, 1861, printed in *Lawrence* (Massachusetts) *Daily Journal,* April 26, 1861; Letter, F. M. Sweetser to Anonymous, April 20, 1861, printed in *Woburn* (Massachusetts) *Journal,* April 27, 1861; Letter, Jim Whittaker to Charles, April 20, 1861, printed in *ibid.* The fate of John Brady: After-action Report, Colonel Edward Jones, OR, II, 7.

Chapter Seven: Patriotic Gore

42. Baltimore newspapers, April 20, 1861.

43. Jones's report: OR, II, 7. See, also, John B. Dennis, "March of the Old 6th Massachusetts Through Baltimore, April 19, 1861," MOLLUS (Omaha, Nebraska, 1888), pp. 20–21; Matthew Ellenberger, "Whigs in the Streets? Baltimore Republicanism in the Spring of 1861," *Maryland Historical Magazine,* LXXXVI (Spring 1991), 27. Jones and the band: John W. Hanson, *Historical Sketch of the Old Sixth Massachusetts Volunteers* (Boston, 1866), p. 24.

44. Ernest Wardwell: Recollections, 1907, on the Web; also in "Military Waif: A Sidelight on the Baltimore Riot of 19 April 1861," edited by Frank Towers, *Maryland Historical Magazine,* LXXXIX (Winter 1994), 429.

45. The best source for this phase of the day is the account by Benjamin F. Watson, "The Passage of Company K Through Baltimore, the Baltimore Riots," *Lowell Weekly Sun,* April 24, 1886. "wild terrible, and venomous": Letter to the Editor, "W.D.G.," *Cambridge Chronicle,* April 27, 1861.

46. George William Brown, *Baltimore and the Nineteenth of April 1861* (Baltimore, 1887), p. 45 (see his footnote about an unnamed, extremely wealthy local merchant, indicted for this, though his case never went to trial); OR, II, 16–17; Frank Towers, "'A Vociferous Army of Howling Wolves': Baltimore's Civil War Riot of April 19, 1861," *The Maryland Historian,* XXIII (1992), 8. On May 3, 1861, George Kane wrote a memo about his activities on April 19: See the Maryland Archives Web site for this document.

47. The Confederate flag-bearer: *Ibid.* But Edward Ayrault Robinson, who was there, recalled this man as Washington Goodrich, "a notorious ruffian": reprint, *Maryland Historical Magazine* (1932).

48. "somewhat swollen": *Boston Traveler,* May 3, 1861. In addition to the sources previously mentioned, see a plethora of letters from members of the Sixth, available on the Web site, *www.letterscivilwar.com*: Letter,

Albert S. Follansbee to H. H. Wilder, April 20, 1861; Letter, "J.J.D.," April 19, 1861, and, Letter, Timothy A. Crowley, *Lowell Daily Evening Advertiser,* April 25, 1861; Letter, James F. Rowe, April 20, 1861, *ibid.,* April 26, 1861; Letter, Jim Whittaker to Charles, April 20, 1861, and, Letter, Stephen Flanders, April 20, 1861, *Woburn* [Massachusetts] *Journal,* April 27, 1861; Letter, James Conroy, *Lowell Daily Courier,* April 26, 1861, and, Letter, *L,* April 25, 1861, *ibid.,* May 1, 1861; Letter, James M. Harmon to Cyrus Barker, April 20, 1861, and, Letter, C. H. Stanley to Father, *Lawrence* [Massachusetts] *Daily Journal,* April 26, 1861; Letter, Daniel S. Yeaton to H. F. Lane; Letter, F. M. Sweetser, April 20, 1861, *Woburn Journal,* April 27, 1861. Ladd's alleged deathbed phrase: *Philadelphia Press,* May 1, 1861. The fate of Mickey Clark: Letter from an eyewitness, *Washington Star,* April 22, 1861.

49. The best study of this topic is John Work Garrett: Festus P. Summers, *The Baltimore and Ohio in the Civil War* (New York, 1939), especially pp. 15–57.

50. Colonel Jones's report: OR, II, 8. Hall's testimony was printed in the *Baltimore Sun's* extensive retrospective of that period, July 24–25, 1901. See, also, Letter, "W. D. G." to the Editor, April 20, 1861, *Cambridge Chronicle,* April 27, 1861; *Baltimore Sun,* April 20, 1861; Benjamin F. Watson, "The Passage of Company K Through Baltimore, the Baltimore Riots," *Lowell Weekly,* April 24, 1886.

Chapter Eight: Malice and Compassion

51. Matthew Ellenberger, "Whigs in the Streets? Baltimore Republicanism in the Spring of 1861," *Maryland Historical Magazine,* LXXXVI (Spring 1991), 36.

52. In addition to Jones's report, OR, II, 8, see: *Baltimore Sun,* April 22, 1861, which quotes from the inquest; George William Brown, *Baltimore and the Nineteenth of April 1861* (Baltimore, 1881; reprint, Baltimore, 2001), pp. 52–53; Frederic Emory, "The Baltimore Riots," *Annals of the War* (Philadelphia, 1879), pp. 785–86.

53. George M. Gill, OR, II, 21.

54. "sudden impulse": *Ibid.*; the phrase was repeated later by Mayor Brown. Makeup of the crowd: Emory, p. 777; Frank Towers, "Secession in an Urban Context: Municipal Reform and the Coming of the Civil War in Baltimore," unpublished copy, 2001.

55. *Ibid.,* p. 10; Salmon P. Chase, *The Salmon P. Chase Papers* (Kent, Ohio, 1996), III, 55, 59–62.

56. William J. Evitts, *A Matter of Allegiances: Maryland from 1850 to 1861* (Baltimore, 1974), p. 184.

57. Telegraph lines: William R. Plum, *The Military Telegraph during the Civil War in the United States* (Chicago, 1892), I, 65.

58. Small's letter to Buchanan: OR, CXXII, 57–58; see, also, *Philadelphia Public Ledger,* April 20, 1861. *Baltimore Sun,* April 26, 1861, names one of the killed Pennsylvanians.

59. *Baltimore Sun,* April 20, 1861; the reports of Brown and others: OR, II, 9, 10, 20–21.

60. Statement, A. S. Young, *Lowell Daily Courier,* April 26, 1861; Statement, R. P. Winn; Statement, Victor Lorendo; Statement, Charles H. Colburn, *Boston Journal,* April 23, 1861; undated article, *Boston Saturday Evening Courier,* quoted in *The Rebellion Record,* edited by Frank Moore, I, 38–39.

61. Frank Towers says five: "'A Vociferous Army of Howling Wolves': Baltimore's Civil War Riot of April 19, 1861," *The Maryland Historian,* XXIII (1992), 15; others are mentioned in assorted articles in the *Philadelphia Public Ledger,* April 22, 23, 1861.

62. See Mrs. Burton Harrison [Constance Cary], *Recollections Grave and Gay* (New York 1911).

Chapter Nine: Controlling a Maelstrom

63. Drawn from various city newspapers, published just afterward: especially the *Sun,* the *Exchange,* the *American,* the *Clipper,* and the *South.*

64. See, for example, the official reports of Mayor Brown and Charles Howard, head of the Police Board: OR, II, 7–11.

65. The conversation in Hicks's room: OR, II, 12–15.

66. Burning bridges: see Baltimore newspapers of April 22, 1861, particularly the *Sun.* Hicks's reputation: *Dispatch,* April 30, 1861.

67. David Hunter Strother, "Personal Recollections of the War," *Harper's New Monthly Magazine,* XXXIII (June 1866), 16–17.

68. John C. Robinson, "Baltimore in 1861," *Magazine of American History,* XIV (1885), 257–68; Howard's report, OR, II, 11.

69. *Baltimore Sun,* April 22–24, 1861; George William Brown, *Baltimore and the Nineteenth of April 1861* (Baltimore 1887), p. 77. Huger: See, e.g., Frederick Emory, "The Baltimore Riots," The Annals of the Civil War (reprint, New York, 1994), p. 791; David Detzer, *Allegiance* (New York, 2001), pp. 60–62, 85, 86.

70. Cockeysville: OR, CVII, 365–66.

Chapter Ten: The Yard

71. The history of the navy yard: Edward Phelps Lull, *History of the United States Navy-Yard at Gosport, Virginia* (Washington, 1874). See, also, Robert Collins Suhr, "Firing the Norfolk Navy Yard," *America's Civil War* IX (November 1996), 52–57; John D. Hays, "Loss of the Norfolk Yard," *Ordnance,* VIII (September–October, 1961), 220–23; Alan B.

Flanders, "The Night They Burned the Yard," CWTI, XVIII (February, 1980), 30–39; Thomas O. Selfridge, Jr., *Memoirs of Thomas O. Selfridge, Jr.* (New York, 1924), pp. 24–35.

72. Gideon Welles, *The Diary of Gideon Welles* (New York, 1911), I, 41. See, also, John Niven, *Gideon Welles: Lincoln's Secretary of the Navy* (New York, 1973), especially pp. 339–45; Welles, "Mr. Welles in Answer to Mr. Weed: The Facts of the Abandonment of the Gosport Navy Yard," *The Galaxy*, X (July 1870), pp. 11–13.

73. The wedding of Commodore Buchanan's daughter: David D. Porter, *Naval History of the Civil War* (New York, 1886), p. 27. On Pickens's intelligence about Gosport: Letter, Francis Pickens to W. S. Pettigrew, May 18, 1864, Pickens Papers, SCL.

74. OR, II, 771; *ibid.*, CVIII, 16.

75. This note—and, unless indicated, all other internal naval messages mentioned here: ORN, IV, 272–98.

76. Welles, pp. 44–46; Alden to Welles, November 20, 1861, in *House Reports*, 37th Cong., 3d sess., pp. 103–04. For a broad view, see the "Report of the Select Committee to Inquire into the Circumstances Attending the Surrender of the Navy Yard at Pensacola and the Destruction of Property of the United States Navy Yard at Norfolk," Senate, 37th Cong., 2d sess., 1861–1862.

77. See Scott's original orders, as well as Wright's follow-up report about his assignment: OR, II, 21–23.

78. Wardrop's reaction: Letter, anonymous to editor, April 20, 1861, *Greenfield* (Massachusetts) *Democrat*, May 3, 1861.

79. For a worm's eye view of the arrival of the Third Massachusetts, see: Letters: "Kewy" to Editor, April 19; F. Hurley to Messrs. Taber, Read & Co., April 22; David W. Wardrop to unknown, April 22, 1861, *New Bedford* [Massachusetts] *Daily Evening Standard*, April 20, 27, and 30, 1861; Daniel O'Conner to Editor, April 24, *Woburn* [Massachusetts] *Weekly Budget*, May 3, 1861; "F. S. G." to Allen & Bliss, April 21, 1861, in *New Bedford* (Massachusetts) *Daily Evening Standard*, April 27, 1861. On the tension at the *Pawnee*'s appearance: Selfridge, pp. 31–32; Lull, p. 55. Selfridge was the officer at the forward gun.

Chapter Eleven: And in Washington

80. 37th Cong., 3d sess., *Report of the Joint Committee on the Conduct of the War* (Washington, 1863), II, 137.

81. Nicolay to Therena Bates, April 11, 1861, *With Lincoln in the White House*, edited by Michael Burlingame (Carbondale, Illinois, 2000), p. 33.

82. Edward Davis Townsend, *Anecdotes of the Civil War in the United States* (New York, 1884), pp. 25–26.

83. Adam Gurowski, *Diary* (Boston, 1862), I, 24. John G. Nicolay

and John Hay, *Abraham Lincoln: A History* (New York, 1904–17), IV, 106–07. "jocosely": Quoted in Edgar Langsdorf, "Jim Lane and the Frontier Guard," *Kansas Historical Quarterly*, IX (February 1940), 16ff. See, also, Edward A. Miller, Jr., *Lincoln's Abolitionist General: The Biography of David Hunter* (UNCP, 1997), pp. 55–56.

84. There are myriad valuable sources on both women. For Dix's visit to the White House, see the private diary of John Hay, *Inside Lincoln's White House*, edited by Michael Burlingame and John R. Turner Ettlinger (Carbondale, Illinois, 1997), p. 3.

85. John B. Dennis, "March of the Old 6th Massachusetts Through Baltimore, April 19, 1861," MOLLUS (Omaha, 1888); *Washington Star*, April 20, 1861; Benjamin F. Butler, *Autobiography and Reminiscences* (Boston, 1892), p. 180.

86. Nicolay, pp. 35–36.

87. William R. Plum, *The Military Telegraph during the Civil War in the United States* (Chicago, 1892), I, 64.

88. "Mark of Cain": *Lawrence (Massachusetts) Daily Journal*, April 25, 1861. See, also, letter dated April 22, 1861, "P" to Editor, *Charlestown (Massachusetts) Advertiser*, April 27, 1861.

89. For a detailed overview of the emotional spasm inside the District, the *Washington Star* from this period is excellent, especially the issues of April 22 and 23, 1861. For more individualized views, see, e.g., John H. Wheeler, Diary, LC; George Williamson Smith, "A Critical Moment in Washington," *Records of the Columbia Historical Society*, XXI (1918), 87–113; Lucius E. Chittenden, *Invisible Siege: The Journal of Lucius E. Chittenden, April 15, 1861–June 14, 1861* (San Diego, 1969), pp. 1–17; and John G. Nicolay, *The Outbreak of the Rebellion* (New York, 1881), p. 102. The suicides: Smith, p. 104. The Treasury clerk and the vault: Chittenden, p. 10.

90. "two different nights": Lyman Van Buren Furber to Louisa, April 27, 1861, Furber Papers, Maryland Historical Society. "great excitement": "W.D.G." (Alpha B. Farr) to editor, April 20, 1861, *Cambridge Chronicle*, April 27, 1861. "I hope it will come soon": "D" to editor, *Boston Post*, April 30, 1861. "Prussian Legation": Frederick W. Seward, *Seward at Washington* (New York, 1891), II, 553.

91. Seward, p. 553. The takeover of the four ships: Mary Alice Wills, *The Confederate Blockade of Washington, D.C., 1861–1862* (Parsons, West Virginia, 1975), pp. 1–17.

92. Military orders: OR, II, 585, 600, and CVII, 330.

93. Chittenden, p. 10; Wheeler, April 22, 1861; *Star*, April 22, 1861; Charles P. Stone, "Washington in March and April, 1861," *Magazine of American History*, XIV (July 1885), 8.

94. Charles P. Stone, "A Dinner with General Scott," *The Magazine of American History*, XI (June 1884), 528–32.

Chapter Twelve:
The Curious Marriage of Great Britain and Ben McCulloch

95. Alfred Hoyt Bill, *The Beleaguered City: Richmond, 1861–1865* (New York, 1946), pp. 41–42.

96. Among the many recent excellent books on this topic, the following are particularly worthwhile: Howard Jones, *Union in Peril: The Crisis over British Intervention in the Civil War* (UNCP, 1992); Martin Crawford, *The Anglo-American Crisis of the Mid-Nineteenth Century: The Times and America, 1850–1862* (Athens, Georgia, 1987); Norman Ferris, *Desperate Diplomacy: William H. Seward's Foreign Policy, 1861* (Knoxville, 1976); Mary Ellison, *Support for Secession: Lancashire and the American Civil War* (Chicago, 1972). The participants in 1861 leaned on several tomes on international law, none of which were exactly pertinent: Emmerich de Vattel, *The Law of Nations* (Philadelphia, 1817); Henry Wheaton, *The Elements of International Law* (Boston, 1836); John Austin, *The Province of Jurisprudence Determined* (London, 1832); and the assorted opinions of Hugo Grotius. On Seward's position: Frederick W. Seward, *Seward at Washington* (New York, 1891), II, 540–41, 545.

97. *New York Tribune*, April 27, 1861; *Baltimore American*, April 24, 1861; John Nicolay, *With Lincoln at the White House*, edited by Michael Burlingame (Carbondale, Illinois, 2000), p. 79; Benjamin F. Butler, *Butler's Book* (Boston, 1892), pp. 219–20.

98. Montgomery *Mail*, April 13, 1861; *Southern Recorder*, April 30, 1861; *Picayune*, April 18, 1861; *Goldsboro Tribune* and *Raleigh Standard*, April 24, 1861; *Examiner*, April 23, 1861.

99. The *Post* article was reprinted in the *Baltimore Sun*, April 12, 1861; *Vicksburg Whig*, April 20, 1861.

100. Thomas W. Cutrer, *Ben McCulloch and the Frontier Military Tradition* (UNCP, 1993); Samuel C. Reid, Jr., *Scouting Expeditions* (Philadelphia, 1847); Victor Marion Rose, *The Life and Services of Gen. Ben McCulloch* (Philadelphia, 1888); Jack W. Gunn, "Ben McCulloch: A Big Captain," *Southwestern Historical Quarterly*, LVIII (July 1954).

101. Cutrer, pp. 190–93.

Chapter Thirteen: What if...?

102. George W. Bagby, "Pawnee Sunday," Bagby Papers, VHS; Ernest B. Furgurson, *Ashes of Glory: Richmond at War* (New York: Alfred A. Knopf, 1996), pp. 39–40.

103. Seward, *Seward at Washington*, (New York, 1891), II, 560–61.

104. John G. Nicolay and John Hay, *Abraham Lincoln: A History* (1904–17), IV, 97–100; the authors include comments made later by Simon Cameron and Montgomery Blair, but it seems clear neither was

a direct witness of the discussion. Lee's letter to Reverdy Johnson: J. William Jones, *Life and Letters of Robert Edward Lee* (New York, 1906), p. 141 and *The Wartime Papers of R. E. Lee*, edited by Clifford Dowdey (New York, 1961), p. 4. Lee's conversation with Scott: Edward D. Townsend, *Anecdotes of the Civil War in the United States* (New York, 1884), pp. 31–32; Cf. Douglas Southall Freeman, *R. E. Lee: A Biography* (New York, 1934–35), I, 437–38n.

105. Lee to Scott, Lee to Anne Marshall, Lee to Sydney Smith Lee: *Wartime Papers*, pp. 8–11.

106. OR, CVIII, 18–19, 24. Stephens's speech: *Richmond Dispatch*, April 23, 1861.

107. Shooting the horse: *Dispatch*, April 24, 1861. Unclean birds: *ibid.*, June 20, 1861. VD and male prostitution: Bell Irvin Wiley, *The Life of Johnny Reb* (LSUP, 1943), pp. 53–56. Army order: May 27, 1861, OR, ser. 1, LI/2, 114. Richmond's reaction: Thomas Cooper DeLeon, *Belles, Beaux and Brains* (New York, 1909), p. 60. "Dislike": Furgurson, p. 62. Richmond's ordinances, the growing mood of suspicion, and crimes of all types, see her newspapers during these weeks: In addition to the *Dispatch*, the *Enquirer* and the *Whig* provide innumerable examples.

108. OR, CVIII, 32–33; *Wartime Papers*, p. 11. Arrival of the South Carolinians: *Richmond Enquirer*, April 25, 1861.

109. Cocke to Lee, Lee to Cocke, Lee to Ruggles: OR, II, 776–778. Lee to Letcher, April 27, 1861, Lee to Mary Lee, April 30, 1861: *Wartime Papers*, pp. 14–15.

110. OR, CVIII, 21, 39.

111. CSA, *Congressional Journal*, I, 160–69.

112. "bank of the Susquehanna": Davis to Joseph Emory Davis, June 18, 1861, JD, VII, 203. Steuart's request and responses: OR, II, 773–74, CVIII, 24, 35.

Chapter Fourteen: The Contents of a Velvet Glove

113. "miserably weak": Letter, Wadsworth to Morgan, May 23, 1861, quoted in Henry Greenleaf Pearson, *James S. Wadsworth of Geneseo* (New York, 1913), p. 61.

114. Hay's remark: George Williamson Smith, "A Critical Moment for Washington," *Records of the Columbia Historical Society*, 21 (1918), 95–96. Lincoln's words to Hay: John Hay, *Inside Lincoln's White House: The Complete Civil War Diary of John Hay*, edited by Michael Burlingame and John R. Turner Ettlinger (Carbondale, 1997), pp. 19–20.

115. "nothing in this": John Hay, *At Lincoln's Side: John Hay's War Correspondence and Selected Writings*, edited by Michael Burlingame (Carbondale, 2000), p. 126. On Fredericksburg: William O. Stoddard, *Inside*

the White House in War Times (New York, 1890), p. 179; Burlingame, p. xvi, notes there is some doubt about Lincoln's words on this occasion, but the tenor of this sentiment can be found elsewhere in Lincoln's statements, public or private.

116. Hay, *Inside*, p. 11.

117. Scott's daily reports to Lincoln: John G. Nicolay and John Hay, *Abraham Lincoln: A History* (New York, 1904–17), IV, 64–66, 95–97, 143–44. Trip to the White House's highest point and ordering Hay to the Navy Yard: *Ibid.*, pp. 5, 11. "fairly groaned": Henry Villard, *Memoirs of Henry Villard* (New York, 1904), I, 169–70. "Why don't they come?": Nicolay and Hay, IV, 153. "nervous tension": *Ibid.*, p. 151. Lincoln's story to Schurz, Carl Schurz, *The Reminiscences of Carl Schurz* (New York, 1907), II, 227–28. Alternate interpretation and "imperturbable": Smith, pp. 111–112 (since Smith does not mention Schurz's tale, one must assume he had no knowledge of it, even though it had been published eleven years earlier). "if I were Beauregard": A. K. McClure, *Abraham Lincoln and Men of War-Times* (Philadelphia, 1892), p. 61.

118. Lincoln, Scott, and the emissaries: AL, IV, 340–41; Memorandum, John G. Nicolay, *With Lincoln in the White House*, edited by Michael Burlingame (Carbondale, 2000), pp. 34–36, and notes.

119. Lincoln's first Sunday meeting with Brown: *Ibid.*, p. 37; George William Brown, *Baltimore and the Nineteenth of April 1861* (Baltimore, 1887), pp. 71–72. AL, IV, 340–41. (Nicolay's personal memorandum of these events, p. 37, suggests that Brown's reply to the president came in earlier than Brown would later recall, that Nicolay woke up Lincoln at one o'clock in the morning to give him Brown's response.) "learned man": SHSP, XXIX, 264.

120. OR, II, 583–84; Brown, p. 73. Welles's spirited action and words: drawn from an editorial footnote, Nicolay, p. 201. Lincoln to Hunter: Hay, *Inside*, p. 6.

121. I have pieced together this dialogue from two — somewhat contradictory — sources, using from each what seems like the most natural wording: AL, IV, 341–42; *Baltimore Sun*, April 23, 1861. For example, the *Sun* used the word "spunk," and the semi-official account used "manhood." Lincoln might have used either term, but in informal settings like this one it was his tendency to be earthier.

122. "Kill them": Alan D. Gaff, *If This Is War* (Dayton, Ohio, 1991), p. 41.

123. "blamed by its friends": Hiram Barney to Chase, April 23, 1861, Chase Papers (Microfilm, University Publication of America). Chase to Lincoln, April 25, 1861, *Ibid.* Both notes, Lincoln to Scott: AL, IV, 344 and 347. Among those pressing Lincoln to arrest the Maryland legislators was Ben Butler, in Annapolis, and it may have been his im-

portunities that triggered Lincoln's April 25 note to Scott: Hay, *Inside*, p. 12.

124. *Ibid.*, p. 16.

Chapter Fifteen: On the Road

125. Laura Winthrop Johnson, *The Life and Poems of Theodore Winthrop* (New York, 1884); G. W. "Theodore Winthrop," *Atlantic Monthly*, VIII (August 1861), 242–51; Elbridge Colby, *Theodore Winthrop* (New York, 1965); Eugene T. Woolf, *Theodore Winthrop: Portrait of an American Author* (Washington, 1981); Willard E. Martin, "The Life and Works of Theodore Winthrop," PhD dissertation (Duke, 1944); Ellsworth Elliot, Jr., *Theodore Winthrop* (New Haven, 1938). The best study of Winthrop remains Martin's 1944 unpublished dissertation, from which most of the quotations used here have been drawn. No direct evidence exists about Winthrop's sexual tendencies, but his novels — especially *Cecil Dreeme* — suggest his sexual ambiguity.

126. The best general histories of the Seventh are William Swinton, *History of the Seventh Regiment, National Guard* (New York, 1870) and Emmons Clark's two volume *History of the Seventh Regiment of New York, 1806–1889* (New York, 1890). A good modern account of the Seventh during these few days is William J. Roehrenbeck, *The Regiment that Saved the Capital* (New York, 1961).

127. Theodore Winthrop, "New York Seventh Regiment: Our March to Washington," *Atlantic Monthly*, VIII (June 1861), 745.

128. Decision-making in Philadelphia: In addition to the works, mentioned above, see OR, II, 582–85; Benjamin F. Butler, *Autobiography and Personal Reminiscences* (Boston, 1892), p. 181; Butler, *Private and Official Correspondence of Gen. Benjamin F. Butler during the Period of the Civil War* (Norwood, Massachusetts, 1917), pp. 17–20 (p. 20 contains his note to Andrew about his heroism); Robert Patterson, *A Narrative of the Campaign in the Valley of the Shenandoah in 1861* (Philadelphia, 1865), pp. 26–27. "earnest, grim": F. J. O'Brien, "The Seventh Regiment: How It Got from New York to Washington," in *The Rebellion Record*, edited by Frank Moore (New York, 1861), I, 150. The Annapolis option was not stumbled into, but was considered by many. Patterson had suggested it a day earlier. In New York an army officer, Samuel P. Heintzelman, jotted a note into his diary this very day, stating that he considered it the best route, given what he had just read in the morning's newspaper about Baltimore. During the afternoon he even shared this notion with several prominent New Yorkers: April 20, 1861, Heintzelman, Diary ("long version"), LC, Reel 7. (The pitiful, battered marching band of the Sixth Massachusetts stumbled into the railroad station on the trek

from Baltimore while Butler was there. He told them to go home, and they left Philadelphia by train just before he and the Eighth went southward: Charles H. Colburn, *Boston Journal*, April 23, 1861.)

129. OR, II, 586–87.

130. O'Brien, I, 151.

131. Butler, *Private*, p. 25; Butler, *Autobiography*, p. 195.

132. Winthrop, pp. 748–49.

133. Swinton, p. 75. The presence of the horsemen at the Junction: *Baltimore Sun*, April 24, 1861.

134. Butler, *Autobiography*, pp. 198–201.

135. Lefferts's note: Swinton, p. 90. The alleged confrontation the next morning: *Ibid.*, pp. 91–92.

136. OR, CVII, 1272–73.

137. Butler, *Private*, p. 32.

138. Winthrop, p. 752.

139. Theodore Winthrop, "Washington As a Camp," *Atlantic Monthly*, IX (July 1861), 114.

140. O'Brien, p. 153.

141. Charles P. Stone, "Washington in March and April, 1861," *Magazine of American History*, XIV (July 1885), 17–20.

142. OR, II, 600.

143. *Baltimore Sun*, April 26, 1861.

144. *New York Tribune*, April 25, 1861.

145. Lucius E. Chittenden, *Invisible Siege: The Journal of Lucius E. Chittenden, April 15, 1861–June 14, 1861* (San Diego, 1969), p. 14; *Washington Star*, April 25, 1861; Emmons Clark, *History of the Seventh Regiment of New York, 1806–1889* (New York, 1890), II, 5.

Chapter Sixteen: The Best Defense

146. William Swinton, *History of the Seventh Regiment, National Guard* (New York, 1870), pp. 130–32, 140.

147. Sprague: OR, CXXII, 82. See, also, Augustus Woodbury, *A Narrative of the Campaign of the First Rhode Island Regiment* (Providence, 1862), pp. 7–35.

148. Duncan's report: *Ibid.*, 33. "toes sublime": John Hay, *Inside Lincoln's White House: The Complete Civil War Diary of John Hay*, edited by Michael Burlingame and John R. Turner Ettlinger (Carbondale, Illinois, 1997), p. 19.

149. "premature": Letter, Lee to Jackson, May 10, 1861, Jackson Papers, VHS. "your line": Lee to Philip St. George Cocke, May 15, 1861, *The Wartime Papers of R. E. Lee* (New York, 1961), p. 30.

150. "severely censured": Letter, Barney to Chase, April 23, 1861, Chase Papers, microfilm University Publication of America (Frederick,

Maryland). Committee: Memorandum, May 7, 1861, John Nicolay, *With Lincoln in the White House,* edited by Michael Burlingame (Carbondale, Illinois, 2000), p. 41.

151. Scott's quotations are from the *New York Times,* July 26, 1861. Scott's concerns about Britain may have been valid: see R. J. M. Blackett, *Divided Heart: Britain and the American Civil War* (Baton Rouge: Louisiana State University Press, 2002). Lincoln on Ellsworth: AL, IV, 333.

152. Lane and Schurz: Hay, p. 13.

153. Mansfield's Report: OR, II, 618–19. Lincoln to Johnson, Letter, April 23, 1861, AL, IV, 342–43.

154. Memorandum, McDowell to Chase, May 16, 1861, Chase Papers.

155. Scott and Mansfield's planning: OR, II, 40–41; United States, Congress, Joint Committee on the Conduct of the War, 37th Cong., 3d sess., *Report of the Joint Committee on the Conduct of the War* (Washington, 1863), I, 119; Robert Garth Scott (ed.), *Forgotten Valor: The Memoirs, Journals, & Civil War Letters of Orlando B. Willcox* (Kent, Ohio: Kent State University Press, 1999), pp. 252–61. See, also, Heintzelman's "long" Diary for these weeks, LC.

156. Reports to Walker: OR, CVIII, 64–65. The information from Hutton: *Ibid.,* II, 27. Wheeler's journal entry: John H. Wheeler, Diary, May 5, 1861, Wheeler Papers, LC.

157. Cocke's proclamation was printed in the Richmond *Enquirer,* May 6, 1861. Cocke's orders to Taylor and Taylor's rationale: OR, II, 24, 26–27. *The Confederate Military History,* edited by Clement A. Evans (Atlanta, 1899), II, 92, claims that the Confederacy did put cannon on Arlington Heights on April 25. If so, these guns must have been withdrawn soon after. It is likely, however, that Evans was only using Duncan's dubious report to Montgomery, mentioned earlier.

158. Lucius E. Chittenden, *Invisible Siege: The Journal of Lucius E. Chittenden, April 15, 1861–June 14, 1861* (San Diego, 1969), pp. 53–55; unnamed enlisted man, *New York Tribune,* June 6, 1861; songs of frogs: George M. Finch, "The Boys of '61," *G. A. R. War Papers* (Cincinnati, 1891), p. 245; crossing the Chain Bridge: *Washington Evening Star,* May 24, 1861. "mild, dewy": Theodore Winthrop, "Washington as a Camp," *Atlantic Monthly,* IX (July 1861), 114. "blisters": William Swinton, *History of the Seventh Regiment, National Guard* (New York, 1870), p. 202. Seward's family: Frederick W. Seward, *Seward at Washington* (New York, 1891), II, 65.

Postscript: Luke's Question: The Beginning of an End

159. Elizabeth Lomax, *Leaves from an Old Washington Diary, 1854–1863* (New York, 1943), pp. 156–57.

160. Robert S. Holzman, *Stormy Ben Butler* (New York, 1954), p. 38.

161. The 1st Vermont and Hampton: Selden Connor, "The Boys of '61," in MOLLUS, Maine (Portland, 1898), I, 323–43; OR, series 1, II, 35–36, 648–9.

162. Both notes: OR, II, 593–94.

163. Andrew's letter and Butler's reply: Benjamin F. Butler, *Private and Official Correspondence of Gen. Benjamin F. Butler during the Period of the Civil War* (Norwood, Massachusetts, 1917), pp. 37–41.

164. John Hay, *Inside Lincoln's White House*, edited by Michael Burlingame and John R. Turner Ettlinger (Carbondale, Illinois, 1997), p. 22.

165. For information about the germination of the "contraband" theory: Edward Lille Pierce, "The Contrabands at Fortress Monroe," *Atlantic Monthly* (November, 1861), VIII, 626–40; Pierce, *Boston Traveller,* July 10, 1861; *Boston Courier,* July 9, 1861; Charles Carleton Coffin, *Drum-Beat of the Nation* (New York, 1888), p. 77; Frank Moore (ed.), *The Rebellion Record* (New York, 1861), I, 110–11; OR, Series 2, CXIV, 749–55; Louis S. Gerteis, *From Contraband to Freedman: Federal Policy Toward Southern Blacks, 1861–1865* (Westport, Connecticut, 1973), pp. 12–15; John G. Nicolay and John Hay, *Abraham Lincoln: A History* (New York 1905), IV, 387–88. See, also, Hay, *Lincoln and the Civil War in the Diaries and Letters of John Hay* (Westport, Connecticut, 1939), p. 22.

166. The matter of slaves' surnames is complicated. In some regions the practice of slaves using surnames was common, even encouraged, by the white leadership, but in most others, not. This topic has often been permeated by delicate strata of subtle racism, of all types — like so many aspects of this subject.

Index